Social Representations

Social Representations

Explorations in Social Psychology

Serge Moscovici

Edited by Gerard Duveen

Polity

The right of Serge Moscovici and Gerard Duveen to be identified as authors of
this work has been asserted in accordance with the Copyright, Designs and
Patents Act 1988.

First published in 2000 by Polity Press
in association with Blackwell Publishers Ltd

Editorial office:
Polity Press
65 Bridge Street
Cambridge CB2 1UR, UK

Marketing and production:
Blackwell Publishers Ltd
108 Cowley Road
Oxford OX4 1JF, UK

ISBN 0-7456-2225-9
ISBN 0-7456-2226-7 (pbk)

A catalogue record for this book is available from the British Library.

Typeset in 10 on 12pt Times New Roman
by Graphicraft Limited, Hong Kong
Printed in Great Britain by T.J. International Ltd, Padstow, Cornwall

This book is printed on acid-free paper.

Contents

Acknowledgements

I should like first of all to thank Serge Moscovici, whose enthusiastic co-operation has been essential for this project. I would also like to acknowledge the patient support of John Thompson, a friend and colleague at Cambridge, and the publisher at Polity Press. Ivana Marková not only provided much assistance with the preparation of the interview in chapter 7, but was also a very constructive reader of the chapters I translated. Many other friends and colleagues have provided invaluable assistance through conversations and discussions about social representations. I would particularly like to acknowledge the contribution of Rob Farr, whose research and scholarship have been of inestimable value.

Gerard Duveen

The essays are reprinted here with the permission of their publishers, whose cooperation is gratefully acknowledged. The original sources are:

Chapter 1: The Phenomenon of Social Representations. In R. Farr and S. Moscovici (eds), *Social Representations*. Cambridge: Cambridge University Press, 1984, pp. 3–69.

Chapter 2: Society and Theory in Social Psychology. In J. Israel and H. Tajfel (eds), *The Context of Social Psychology*. London: Academic Press, 1972, pp. 17–68.

Chapter 3: The History and Actuality of Social Representations. In U. Flick (ed.), *The Psychology of the Social*. Cambridge: Cambridge University Press, 1998, pp. 209–47.

Chapter 4:   The Concept of Themata (with Georges Vignaux). In C. Guimelli
             (ed.), *Structures et transformations des représentations sociales*.
             Neuchâtel: Delachaux et Niestlé, 1994, pp. 25–72.
Chapter 5:   The Dreyfus Affair, Proust, and Social Psychology. *Social Re-
             search*, 1986, 53, 23–56.
Chapter 6:   Social Consciousness and Its History. *Culture and Psychology*,
             1998, 4, 411–29.
Chapter 7:   Ideas and their Development: A Dialogue between Serge Moscovici
             and Ivana Marková. An earlier version of this interview appeared
             as 'Presenting Social Representations: A Conversation' in *Culture
             and Psychology*, 1998, 4, 349–410.
Chapters 6 and 7 are reprinted by permission of Sage Publications Ltd.

Introduction: The Power of Ideas

Gerard Duveen

1   A SOCIAL PSYCHOLOGY OF KNOWLEDGE

Imagine you are looking at an outline map of Europe, with no features marked
on it except for the city of Vienna near the centre, and to the north of it the
city of Berlin. Where would you then locate the cities of Prague and Budapest? For most people who have grown up since the end of the Second World
War both these cities belong to the eastern division of Europe, while Vienna
belongs to the West, and consequently both Prague and Budapest should be
to the east of Vienna. But now look at a map of Europe and see the actual
locations of these cities. Budapest, to be sure, lies further east, downstream
along the Danube from Vienna. But Prague lies in fact to the west of Vienna.

This small example illustrates something of the phenomena of social representations. Our image of the geography of Europe has been reconstructed in
terms of the political division of the Cold War, in which the ideological
definitions of East and West have come to be substituted for the geographical
ones. We can also observe in this example how patterns of communication in
the post-war years have influenced this process and stabilized a particular
image of Europe. Of course, in the West there has been a fear and anxiety
about the East which antedated the Second World War, and which persists
even today, a decade after the fall of the Berlin Wall and the end of the Cold
War. But where this representation of a divided Europe in the post-war years
had its most powerful influence was in the eclipse of the old image of
Mitteleuropa, of a Central Europe embracing the heartlands of the old Austro-
Hungarian Empire and stretching northwards towards Berlin. It was this
Central Europe which was dismembered by the Cold War which also ideologic-
ally repositioned Prague to the east of 'Western' Vienna. Today the idea of
Mitteleuropa is again being discussed, but perhaps the sense of the eastern
'otherness' has marked the image of Prague so clearly that it may take a long

time before these new patterns of communication reposition the city back to the west of Vienna.

As well as illustrating the role of communication and influence in the process of social representation, this example also illustrates the way in which representations become common sense. They enter into the ordinary and everyday world which we inhabit and discuss with our friends and colleagues, and they circulate in the media we read and watch. In short, representations sustained by the social influences of communication constitute the realities of our daily lives and serve as the principal means for establishing the affiliations through which we are bound to one another.

For more than four decades Serge Moscovici, together with his colleagues, has advanced and developed the study of social representations, and this collection brings together some of the central essays drawn from a much larger body of work which has appeared over these years. Some of these essays have appeared in English before, while some are translated here for the first time. Together they illustrate the ways in which Moscovici has elaborated and defended the theory of social representations, while, in the concluding interview with Ivana Marková, he provides the main elements of the history of his own intellectual itinerary. At the heart of this project has been the idea of constructing a social psychology of knowledge, and it is within the context of this wider project that his work on social representations needs to be viewed.

What, then, might a social psychology of knowledge look like? What terrain would it seek to explore, and what would be the key features of this terrain? Moscovici himself introduced this theme in the following way:

> There are numerous sciences which study the way in which people handle, distribute and represent knowledge. But the study of how and why people share knowledge and thereby constitute their common reality, of how they transform ideas into practice – in a word, the power of ideas – is the specific problem of social psychology.   (Moscovici, 1990a, p. 164)

Thus, from the perspective of social psychology, knowledge is never a simple description or a copy of a state of affairs. Rather, knowledge is always produced through interaction and communication, and its expression is always linked to the human interests which are engaged. Knowledge emerges from the world in which people meet and interact, the world in which human interests, needs and desires find expression, satisfaction or frustration. In short, knowledge arises from human passions and, as such, is never disinterested; rather, it is always the product of particular groups of people who find themselves in specific circumstances in which they are engaged in definite projects (cf. Bauer and Gaskell, 1999). A social psychology of knowledge is concerned with the processes through which knowledge is generated, transformed and projected into the social world.

2 *A LA RECHERCHE DES CONCEPTS PERDUS*

Moscovici introduced the concept of social representation in his pioneering study of the ways in which psychoanalysis had penetrated popular thought in France. However, the work in which this study is reported, *La Psychanalyse: Son image et son public*, first published in French in 1961 (with a second, much revised edition in 1976), remains untranslated into English, a state of affairs which has contributed to the problematic reception of the theory of social representations in the Anglo-Saxon world. Of course, an English version of this text would not in itself resolve all the differences between Moscovici's ideas and the dominant patterns of social-psychological thinking in Britain and the USA, but it would at least have helped to reduce the number of misunderstandings of Moscovici's work which have added a penumbra of confusion to discussions of these ideas in English. More than this, however, the lack of a translation means that a predominantly monolingual Anglo-Saxon culture has not had access to a text in which the key themes and ideas in the theory of social representations are presented and elaborated in the vital context of a specific research study. When these ideas are put to work in structuring a research project and in ordering and making intelligible the mass of empirical data which emerge, they also take on a concrete sense which is only weakly visible in more abstract theoretical or programmatic texts.

But if Moscovici's work has been obscured in the Anglo-Saxon world, the concept of social representation itself has had a problematic history within social psychology. Indeed, Moscovici entitled the opening chapter of *La Psychanalyse* 'Social representation: a lost concept', and introduces his work in these terms:

> Social representations are almost tangible entities. They circulate, intersect and crystallize continuously, through a word, a gesture, or a meeting in our daily world. They impregnate most of our established social relations, the objects we produce or consume, and the communications we exchange. We know that they correspond, on one hand, to the symbolic substance which enters into their elaboration, and on the other to the practice which produces this substance, much as science or myth corresponds to a scientific or mythical practice.
>
> But if the reality of social representations is easy to grasp, the concept is not. There are many good reasons why this is so. For the most part they are historical, which is why we must entrust historians with the task of discovering them. The non-historical reasons can all be reduced to a single one: its 'mixed' position at the crossroads between a series of sociological concepts and a series of psychological concepts. It is at this crossroads that we have to situate ourselves. The route certainly has something pedantic about it, but we can see no other way of freeing such a concept from its glorious past, of revitalizing it and understanding its specificity.   ([1961]/1976, pp. 40–1; my translation)

The primary point of departure for this intellectual journey, however, has been Moscovici's insistence on a recognition of the existence of social representations as a characteristic form of knowledge in our era, or, as he puts it, an insistence on considering 'as a *phenomenon* what was previously seen as a *concept*' (chapter 1, p. 17).

Of course, to develop a theory of social representations implies that the second step of the journey must be to begin to conceptualize this phenomenon. But before turning to this second step, I want to pause for a moment at the first step and ask what it can mean to consider as a phenomenon what was previously seen as a concept, since what might appear as a small *aperçu* in fact contains some characteristic Moscovician tropes. First of all, there is a boldness in this idea which is not inhibited from expressing a conclusive generalization, a generalization which also has the effect of radically separating Moscovici's conception of the aims and scope of social psychology from the predominant forms of the discipline. More precisely, here Moscovici is affiliating himself with a strand of social-psychological thinking which has always been a minority or marginal strand within a discipline dominated in this century first by behaviourism, and more recently by a no less reductive cognitivism, and throughout this time by a thoroughgoing individualism. Yet in its origins social psychology was formed around a different set of concerns. If Wilhelm Wundt is mostly remembered today as the founder of experimental psychology, he is also increasingly recognized for the contribution his *Völkerpsychologie* made to the establishment of social psychology (Danziger, 1990; Farr, 1996; Jahoda, 1992).

For all its faults, Wundt's theory nevertheless clearly situated social psychology at the same crossroads between sociological and psychological concepts indicated by Moscovici. Far from opening a productive line of research and theory, Wundt's work was soon eclipsed by a growing mainstream of psychological thought which rejected any association with the 'social' as compromising the scientific status of psychology. What Danziger (1979) has termed the 'positivist repudiation of Wundt' served to ensure the exclusion of the social from the theoretical purview of the emerging social psychology. At least, this was the case in what Farr (1996) has called its 'psychological' form, but, as he also notes, a 'sociological' form has persisted as well, stemming largely from Mead's work, in which Wundt's *Völkerpsychologie* was a major influence (and one should add that a concern with the social is also characteristic of Vygotsky's psychology; cf. chapters 3 and 6). Indeed, Farr has gone on to suggest that Durkheim's ([1891]/1974) radical separation of 'individual' from 'collective' representations contributed to the institutionalization of a crisis for social psychology which persists today. Throughout the last century, whenever 'social' forms of social psychology have emerged we have witnessed the same drama of exclusion which marked the reception of Wundt's work. A 'compulsion to repeat' masks a kind of ideological neurosis, which has been mobilized whenever the social has threatened to invade the psychological. Or, to shift from a Freudian to an anthropological metaphor, the social has consistently represented a polluting danger to the purity of scientific psychology.

Why has it proved so difficult to establish a social psychology which can embrace both the social and the psychological? Although in the quotation above Moscovici suggested that this was a question for historians, he himself has contributed something to clarifying this enigma, as several of the texts collected here bear witness (see chapters 1, 2, 3 and 7). In a major historical essay, *The Invention of Society*, Moscovici ([1988]/1993) offers a further set of considerations by addressing the complementary question of why psychological explanations have been seen as illegitimate in sociological theory. Durkheim formulated this idea explicitly in his aphorism that 'every time that a social phenomenon is directly explained by a psychological phenomenon, we may be sure that the explanation is false' ([1895]/1982, p. 129). But, as Moscovici shows, this prescription against psychological explanation not only runs like a connecting thread through the work of classical writers on modern social theory, it is just as surreptitiously contradicted in these very same texts. For in producing social explanations for social phenomena, these sociologists (Weber and Simmel are the examples analysed by Moscovici alongside Durkheim) also need to introduce some reference to psychological processes to provide coherence and integrity to their analyses. In short, in this work Moscovici is able to demonstrate through his own analyses of these founding texts of modern sociology that the explanatory frame required for making social phenomena intelligible must include psychological as well as sociological concepts.

Yet the question of why it has been so difficult to achieve a stable theoretical frame embracing both the psychological and the social remains obscure. To be sure, there has been just as much hostility to 'sociologism' among psychologists as there has been towards 'psychologism' among sociologists. To say that social psychology as a mixed category represents a form of pollution remains descriptive as long as we do not understand why the social and the psychological are considered to be exclusive categories. This is the heart of the historical conundrum, and it retains its distinctive power even today. While it would be naïve to pretend to offer a clear account of its origin, we can glimpse something of its history in the opposition between reason and culture which, as Gellner (1992) argues, has been so influential since Descartes's formulation of rationalism. Against the relativism of culture, Descartes proclaimed the certainty stemming from reason. The argument for the *cogito* introduced a scepticism about the influences of culture and the social which has been difficult to overcome. Indeed, if Gellner is right in seeing in this argument an opposition between culture and reason, then any science of culture will be a science of unreason. From here it is a short step to becoming an unreasonable science, which seems to be the reputation earned by every attempt to combine sociological and psychological concepts in a 'mixed' science. Yet it is just such an 'unreasonable science' which Moscovici has sought to resuscitate through a return to the concept of representation as central to a social psychology of knowledge.

3   DURKHEIM THE AMBIGUOUS ANCESTOR

In seeking to establish a 'mixed' science centred on the concept of representation, Moscovici has acknowledged an enduring debt to the work of Durkheim. However, as we saw above, Durkheim's formulation of the concept of collective representations has proved an ambiguous inheritance for social psychology. The effort to establish sociology as an autonomous science led Durkheim to argue for a radical separation between individual and collective representations, and to the suggestion that the former should be the province of psychology while the latter formed the object of sociology (interestingly, in some of his writings on this theme Durkheim toyed with the idea of calling this science 'social psychology', but preferred 'sociology' in order to eliminate any possible confusion with psychology; cf. Durkheim, [1895]/1982). It is not only Farr who has noticed the difficulties which Durkheim's formulation has carried for social psychology. In an earlier discussion of the relation between Durkheim's work and the theory of social representations, Irwin Deutscher (1984) also wrote of the complexity in taking Durkheim as an ancestor for a social-psychological theory. Moscovici himself has suggested that in preferring the term 'social' he wanted to emphasize the dynamic quality of representations as against the rather fixed or static character which they have in the Durkheimian account (cf. chapter 1, where Moscovici illustrates the way in which Durkheim used the terms 'social' and 'collective' interchangeably). In commenting on this point further in his interview with Marková in chapter 7, Moscovici refers to the impossibility of sustaining any clear distinction between the 'social' and the 'collective'. These two terms do not refer to distinct orders in the arrangement of human society, but neither is it the case that the terms 'social representation' and 'collective representation' only mark a distinction without establishing a difference. In other words, Moscovici's social psychology cannot simply be collapsed into a variant of Durkheimian sociology. How then should we understand the relation of social representations to the Durkheimian concept?

From a social-psychological perspective one might be tempted to think that the resolution of this ambiguity could be sought through a clarification of the terms 'individual' and 'collective' as they are used in Durkheim's argument. However, it is by no means clear that such an endeavour could successfully reclaim some theoretical space for a *social* psychology, particularly since, as

Farr (1998) points out, the question is rendered problematic by the recognition of individualism as a powerful collective representation in modern society.

A more productive approach can be seen through a further reflection on Durkheim's argument itself. Durkheim was not simply concerned to establish the *sui generis* character of collective representations as one element in his effort to sustain sociology as an autonomous science. His whole sociology is itself consistently oriented to what it is that holds societies together, that is, to the forces and structures which can conserve or preserve the whole against any fragmentation or disintegration. It is within this perspective that collective representations take on their sociological significance for Durkheim; their constraining power helps to integrate society and conserve it. Indeed, it is partly this capacity for sustaining and conserving the social whole which gives collective representations their sacred character in Durkheim's discussion of *The Elementary Forms of Religious Life* (1912/1995). Moscovici's social psychology, on the other hand, has been consistently oriented to questions of how things change in society, that is, to those social processes through which novelty and innovation become as much a part of social life as conservation or preservation. I have already alluded to his interest in the transformation of common sense in his study of social representations of psychoanalysis. It is in the course of such transformations that anchoring and objectification become significant processes (cf. chapter 1). A clearer statement of this focus of Moscovici's work can be found in his study of social influence (1976) which, in fact, carries the title *Social Influence and Social Change*. The point of departure for this study was his dissatisfaction with models of social influence which apprehended only conformity or compliance. If this were the only process of social influence which existed, how would any social change be possible? Such considerations led Moscovici to an interest in the process of minority influence or innovation, an interest he has pursued through a series of experimental investigations. It is this concern with innovation and social change which also led Moscovici to see that, from a social-psychological perspective, representations cannot be taken for granted, nor can they serve simply as explanatory variables. Rather, from this perspective it is the construction of these representations which is the issue to be addressed, hence his insistence both on considering 'as a phenomenon what was previously viewed as a concept' and in emphasizing the dynamic character of social representations against the static character of collective representations in Durkheim's formulation (a more extended discussion of this point by Moscovici can be found in chapter 1).

Thus, where Durkheim looks to collective representations as the stable forms of collective understanding with the power of constraint which can serve to integrate society as a whole, Moscovici has been more concerned to explore the variation and diversity of collective ideas in modern societies. This diversity itself reflects the lack of homogeneity within modern societies, in which differences reflect an unequal distribution of power and generate a heterogeneity of representations. Within any culture there are points of tension, even of fracture, and it is around these points of cleavage in the representational system of a culture that new social representations emerge. In other words, at these points of cleavage there is a lack of meaning, a point where the unfamiliar appears, and just as nature abhors a vacuum, so culture abhors an absence of meaning, setting in train some kind of representational work to familiarize the unfamiliar so as to re-establish a sense of stability (cf. Moscovici's discussion of unfamiliarity as a source of social representations in chapter 1). Cleavages in meaning can occur in many ways. It can be very dramatic, as we all saw as we watched the fall of the Berlin wall and felt the structures of meaning which had held a settled view of the world since the end of the war evaporate. Or again, the sudden appearance of new and threatening phenomena, such as HIV/AIDS, can be the occasion for representational work. More frequently social representations emerge around enduring points of conflict within the representational structures of culture itself, for example, in the tension between the formal recognition of the universality of the 'rights of man' and their denial to particular groups within society. The struggles which have ensued have also been struggles for new forms of representations.

The phenomenon of social representations is thus linked to the social processes woven around differences in society. And it is in giving an account of this linkage that Moscovici has suggested that social representations are the form of collective ideation in conditions of modernity, a formulation which implies that under other conditions of social life the form of collective ideation may also be different. In presenting his theory of social representations, Moscovici has often drawn this contrast (cf. chapter 1), and at times suggested that it is a major reason for preferring the term 'social' to Durkheim's 'collective'. There is an allusion here to a complex historical account of the emergence of social representations which Moscovici sketches in only very lightly and, without attempting to provide a more detailed or extensive account, it will be helpful in understanding something of the character of social representations to draw attention here to two related aspects of this historical transformation.

Modernity always stands in relation to some past which is considered as traditional, and while it would be mistaken (as Bartlett, 1923, saw so presciently) to consider pre-modern – or traditional – societies as effectively homogeneous, the central thread in Moscovici's argument about the transformation of the forms of collective ideation in the transition to modernity is concerned with the question of legitimation. In pre-modern societies (which in this context means feudal society in Europe, although this point may also be relevant to other forms of pre-modern society) it is the centralized institutions of Church and State, Bishop and King, which stand at the apex of the hierarchy of power and regulate the legitimation of knowledge and beliefs. Indeed, within feudal society the very inequalities between different social layers within this hierarchy were recognized as legitimate. Modernity, in contrast, is characterized by more diverse centres of power which claim authority and legitimacy, so that the regulation of knowledge and belief is no longer exercised in the same way. The phenomenon of social representations can, in this sense, be seen as the form in which collective life has adapted to decentred conditions of legitimation. Among the new forms of knowledge and belief which have emerged in the modern world, science has been an important source, but so too, as Moscovici reminds us, has common sense. Legitimacy is no longer guaranteed by divine intervention, but becomes part of a more complex and contested social dynamic in which representations of different groups in society seek to establish a hegemony.

The transition to modernity is also characterized by the central role of new forms of communication, originating with the development of the printing press and the diffusion of literacy. The emergence of new forms of mass communication (cf. Thompson, 1995) has both generated new possibilities for the circulation of ideas and also drawn wider social groups into the process of the psychosocial production of knowledge. This theme is too complex to deal with adequately here, except to say that in his analysis of the different forms of representation of psychoanalysis in the French mass media, Moscovici (1961/1976) shows how propagation, propaganda and diffusion take the forms they do because different social groups represent psychoanalysis in different ways, and seek to structure different kinds of communication about this object through these different forms. Each of these forms seeks to extend the influence of a particular representation, and each of them also claims its own legitimacy for the representation it promotes. It is the production and circulation of ideas within these diffuse forms of communication that distinguishes the modern era from the pre-modern, and helps to distinguish social representations as the form of collective ideation distinct from the autocratic and theocratic forms of feudal society. Questions of legitimation and communication serve to emphasize a sense of the heterogeneity of modern social life, a view which has helped to give research on social representations a distinct focus on the emergence of new forms of representation.

4 SOCIAL REPRESENTATIONS AND SOCIAL PSYCHOLOGY

The reception of the theory of social representations within the broader discipline of social psychology has been both fragmentary and problematic. If one looks back to the 'golden era' of social psychology, one can see a certain affinity between Moscovici's work and that of such predecessors as Kurt Lewin, Solomon Asch, Fritz Heider or, perhaps the last representative of that era, Leon Festinger – an affinity rather than a similarity, for while Moscovici's work shares with these predecessors a concern with analysing the relations between social processes and psychological forms, his work retains a distinctive quality, just as these authors differ from one another. Nevertheless, it is not hard to imagine the possibility of a productive conversation based on this affinity. But it is difficult to imagine such a productive conversation across the discipline of social psychology existing today, where the predominance of information-processing paradigms and the emergence of varieties of 'postmodernist' forms of social psychology have increased the segmentation of the field.

Moscovici (1984b) himself has suggested that contemporary social psychology continues to exhibit a kind of discontinuous development of changing and shifting paradigms, 'lonely paradigms' as he describes them. Within this flux each paradigm appears more or less disconnected from its predecessors and leaves little trace on its successors. In this context it has been the common fate of theoretical interventions in social psychology to flicker briefly before passing into a kind of shadowland at the margins of a discipline which has shifted its centre towards the next paradigm, leaving little time for ideas to be assimilated and turned to productive use. From this point of view there is something remarkable in the persistence of the theory of social representations over a period of forty years. In spite of its problematic relation to the shifting terrain of the mainstream of the discipline, the theory of social representations has survived and prospered. It has become not only one of the most enduring theoretical contributions in social psychology, but also one that is widely diffused across the world.

In his discussion of paradigms in social psychology, Moscovici goes on to argue that:

> concepts that operate at great depths seem to take over fifty years to penetrate the lowest layers of a scientific community. This is why most of us are only now beginning to sense the meaning of certain ideas that have been germinating in sociology, psychology and anthropology since the dawn of the century. (Moscovici, 1984b, p. 941)

It is this constellation of ideas that forms the focus for some of the essays in this collection (see especially chapters 3 and 6 and the interview in chapter 7), and within which the theory of social representations has taken shape.

To appreciate the distinctiveness of Moscovici's contribution it is important to recall first of all what his social-psychological innovation reacted against. The cognitive revolution in psychology initiated in the 1950s legitimated the reintroduction of mentalistic concepts which has been proscribed by the more militant forms of behaviourism which had dominated the first half of the twentieth century, and subsequently, the idea of representations has been a central element in the emergence of cognitive science in the past two decades.

But from this perspective, representation has generally been viewed in a very restricted sense as the mental construction of an external object. While this has allowed the development of an informational calculus in which representations have been central terms, the social or symbolic character of representations has rarely figured in such theories. To return for a moment to the example of the map of Europe, while contemporary forms of cognitive science might recognize the displacement of Prague in popular representations, it has no concepts through which to grasp the significance of this displacement nor the influences of the social processes which underlie it. At best, such a displacement would appear as one of the many 'biases' in ordinary thinking which have been documented in theories of social cognition. But whereas such theories in social psychology have discussed 'biases' as examples of how ordinary thought departs from the systematic logic of science, from the point of view of social representations they are seen as forms of knowledge produced and sustained by particular social groups in a given historical conjuncture (cf. Farr, 1998).

Thus, whereas the 'classical' forms of cognitive psychology (including social cognition, which has become the predominant contemporary form of social psychology) treat representation as a static element of cognitive organization, in the theory of social representation the concept of representation itself is given a more dynamic sense, referring as much to the process through which representations are elaborated as to the structures of knowledge which are established. Indeed, it is through its articulation of the relation between process and structure in the genesis and organization of representations that the theory offers a perspective in social psychology distinct from that of social cognition (cf. Jovchelovitch, 1996). For Moscovici the source of this relationship lies in the function of representations themselves. Echoing earlier formulations by McDougall and Bartlett, Moscovici argues that 'the purpose of all representations is to make something unfamiliar, or unfamiliarity itself, familiar' (cf. chapter 1, p. 37). Familiarization is always a constructive process of anchoring and objectification (cf. chapter 1) through which the unfamiliar is given a place within our familiar world. But the same operation which constructs an object in this way is also constitutive of the subject (the correlative construction of subject and object in the dialectic of knowledge was also a characteristic feature of Jean Piaget's genetic psychology and Lucien Goldmann's genetic structuralism). Social representations emerge, not merely as a way of understanding a particular object, but also as a form in which the subject (individual or group) achieves a measure of definition, an identity function which is one way in which representations express a symbolic value (something which also lends Moscovici's notion of familiarization an inflection which is distinct from McDougall or Bartlett). In the words of Moscovici's long-term colleague Denise Jodelet, representation is 'a form of practical knowledge [*savoir*] connecting a subject to an object' (Jodelet,

1989, p. 43, my translation), and she goes on to note that 'qualifying this knowledge as "practical" refers to the experience from which it is produced, to the frameworks and conditions in which it is produced, and above all to the fact that representation is used for acting in the world and on others' (Jodelet, 1989, pp. 43–4, my translation).

Representations are always the product of interaction and communication, and they take their particular shape and form at any moment as a consequence of the specific balance of these processes of social influence. There is a subtle relationship here between representations and communicative influences, which Moscovici identifies when he defines a social representation as:

> a system of values, ideas and practices with a twofold function: first, to establish an order which will enable individuals to orientate themselves in their material and social world and to master it; and secondly to enable communication to take place among the members of a community by providing them with a code for social exchange and a code for naming and classifying unambiguously the various aspects of their world and their individual and group history. (1976, p. xiii)

This relationship between representation and communication may well be the most controversial aspect of Moscovici's theory, and in his own work it is most clearly expressed in the second part of his study of *La Psychanalyse*, the analysis of representations in the French media that I described above (and this is one point where an understanding of the theory of social representations has been most seriously hampered by the lack of an English translation of this text, as Willem Doise (1993) has noted; this section of the book has rarely figured in Anglo-Saxon discussions of the theory).

In relation to cognitive psychology it is not difficult to see why this conception should be controversial, since the enduring weight of the idea of psychology as a natural science focused on processes removed from the polluting influence of the social has made the idea that our beliefs or actions may be formed out of such influences all but unthinkable. Of course, Moscovici's is not the first psychology to propose such a theme. Freudian psychoanalysis, for instance, has sought the origins of thoughts in libidinal processes, which, especially for the school of object relations, reflect the child's early experiences in the world of others (cf. Jovchelovitch, 1996). Mead too could be said to have made a similar argument in his analysis of the development of the self (cf. Moscovici, 1990b). But Moscovici's work does not address the libidinal origins of our thoughts (though Lucien Goldmann (1976) has made a suggestive parallel between the organization of psychoanalytic and social constructions), nor is he primarily concerned with the interpersonal sources of the self. His main focus has been to argue not simply that collective ideation is organized and structured in terms of representations, but that this organization and structure is both shaped by the communicative influences at work in society and at the same time serves to make communication possible. Representations may be the product of communication, but it is also the case that without representation there could be no communication. Precisely because of this interconnection representations can also change, the stability of their organization and structure is dependent on the consistency and constancy of the patterns of communication which sustain them. Changing human interests can generate new forms of communication resulting in innovation and the emergence of new representations. Representations in this sense are structures which have achieved stability through the transformation of an earlier structure.

If the perspective offered by the theory of social representations has generally been too sharply contrasted with the mainstream of the discipline for a constructive dialogue to emerge (although an interest in it is beginning to emerge in the United States; cf. Deaux and Philogene, 2000), what has been both more surprising and more disappointing has been the reception of the theory among those currents of social-psychological thought which have been its neighbours in this marginal shadowland. With some notable exceptions (e.g. Billig, 1988, 1993; Harré, 1984, 1998, which have entered into a dialogue of constructive engagement from rhetorical and discursive perspectives) most commentaries from outside the mainstream have been antagonistic or even hostile to the theory of social representations (see, for example, the catalogue of objections in the recent contribution from Potter and Edwards, 1999). There is no space here to give a systematic account of all the criticisms levelled at Moscovici's work, but a focus on some key themes will not only serve to give a flavour of the issues raised, but also to elaborate a little further some of the central characteristics of the theory itself.

In one sense, as I mentioned earlier, Moscovici's work formed part of the European perspective in social psychology which emerged in the 1960s and 1970s. However, looking back at this work now one also notices the differences within this 'European' outlook. For example, the collection edited by Israel and Tajfel (1972, a work often cited as a primary source for the European view, and for which chapter 2 of this collection was Moscovici's contribution) appears now to be characterized as much by the diversity of their views as by a common critical spirit among the contributors. Some of the strongest criticism of social representations has come from Gustav Jahoda (1988; see also Moscovici's 1988 reply), who belongs to the same generation of social psychologists as Moscovici, and who has made his own contribution to the 'European' tradition. For Jahoda, far from helping to illuminate the problems of social psychology, the theory of social representations has rather served to obscure them. In particular, he finds the theory vague in the construction of its concepts, a charge which has been an important theme in discussions of social representations, surfacing again recently in a more sympathetic commentary by Jan Smedslund (1998; see also Duveen, 1998).

Vagueness, of course, is largely a matter of a point of view. Where one writer finds a theory to be so lacking in precision as to present nothing more than a series of chimeras, for other writers the same theory can open new pathways for considering old problems. Thus Jahoda suggests that, shorn of its rhetoric, the theory of social representations contributes little which is not already contained in the traditional social psychology of attitudes. But, as Japars and Fraser (1984) have shown, while the original formulation of the concept of social attitudes in the work of Thomas and Znaniecki (1918–20) may have some important similarities with the concept of social representations, the concept of attitude has itself undergone a considerable transformation in subsequent social-psychological theories. In this transformation the idea of attitude has been stripped of its social and symbolic content and origins. In contemporary social psychology, attitudes appear as individual cognitive or motivational dispositions, so that the idea of an inherent connection between communication and representation has evaporated. If research in social representations has continued to employ some of the technology of attitude measurement, it has sought to frame these attitudes as part of a broader representational structure (see also the discussion of the relations between attitudes and representations in the interview in chapter 7).

From another perspective, the more radical strands of discourse theory in social psychology (e.g. Potter and Edwards, 1999) have objected to the idea of representation itself as being a lingering attachment to 'modernist' cognitive psychology. From this point of view all social psychological processes resolve themselves into the effects of discourse, and the fleeting achievements and reformulations of identity which it sustains. It is the activity of discourse alone which can be the object of study in this form of social psychology, and any talk of structure and organization at the cognitive level appears as a concession to the hegemony of information-processing models (and it matters little for these critics that the theory of social representations has always insisted on the symbolic character of cognition; see also Moscovici's comments in the interview in chapter 7). Here the vagueness of social representations is held to be its insufficiently radical departure from a 'mentalistic' discourse, but as Jovchelovitch (1996) has observed, the rush to evacuate the mental from the discourse of social psychology is leading to the re-creation of a form of behaviourism.

Whatever its critics might suggest, the theory of social representations has appeared sufficiently clear and precise to support and sustain a growing body of research across diverse areas of social psychology. Indeed, from a different point of view one could argue that research on social representations has contributed as much as if not more than other work in social psychology to our understanding of a wide range of social phenomena (such as the public understanding of science, popular ideas of health and illness, conceptions of madness, or the development of gender identities, to name but a few). Nevertheless, the insistence with which the charge of vagueness has been levelled against the theory deserves some further consideration. Some sense of what is intended by this characterization of the theory can be identified by considering some of the central research studies it has inspired. In addition to Moscovici's own study of representations of psychoanalysis, Denise Jodelet's ([1989]/1991; see also chapter 1) study of social representations of madness in a French village offers a second paradigmatic example of research in this field. Methodologically these two studies adopt quite different approaches (indicating the importance of what Moscovici has referred to as the significance of 'methodological polytheism'). Moscovici employed survey methods and content analysis while Jodelet's study is based on ethnography and interviews. What both studies share, however, is a similar research strategy in which the initial step is the establishment of a critical distance from the everyday world of common sense in which representations circulate. If social representations serve to familiarize the unfamiliar, then the first task of a scientific study of representations is to make the familiar unfamiliar in order that they may be grasped as phenomena and described through whatever methodological techniques may be appropriate in particular circumstances. Description, of course, is never independent of the conceptualization of phenomena, and in this sense the theory of social representations provides the interpretative framework both for making representations visible and for rendering them intelligible as forms of social practice.

The question of vagueness can be seen to be largely a methodological issue, since it refers primarily to what different social-psychological perspectives render visible and intelligible. In this respect different perspectives in social psychology operate with different criteria and conditions. Armed with the conceptual apparatus of traditional social psychology, one will struggle to see anything other than attitudes, just as the discursive perspective will uncover only the effects of discourse in social-psychological processes. Each of these approaches operates within a more or less hermetically sealed theoretical universe. Within each perspective there is a conceptual order which brings clarity and stability to the communication within it (each perspective, we could say, 'establishes its own code for social exchange'). What lies outside a particular perspective appears vague, and the harbinger of disorder. This, of course, is no more than an expression of the enduring crisis in the discipline of social psychology, which continues to exist as a set of 'lonely paradigms'. Recognizing this state of affairs by itself confers no special or privileged status on the theory of social representations. What gives Moscovici's work its particular interest, and the reason why it continues to command attention, is that his work on social representations forms part of a broader enterprise to establish (or re-establish) the foundations for a discipline which is both social and psychological.

5 TOWARDS A GENETIC SOCIAL PSYCHOLOGY

From this point of view it is important to situate Moscovici's studies of social representations within the context of his work as a whole, since it is as part of a wider contribution to social psychology that this work remains of capital significance. I have already alluded to the sense in which his work has expressed a critical and innovative spirit in relation to the discipline, and in this sense it also contributed to a wider critical reappraisal of the dominant forms of social psychology, which began in the 1960s and was for a time associated with a distinctively European perspective on the discipline (something of this critical spirit is evident in many of the chapters in this collection, but particularly in chapter 2 and the interview in chapter 7). What has marked Moscovici's contribution as innovative is that it has not been limited to a negative critique of the weaknesses and shortcomings of the predominant forms of social psychology, but has always rather sought to elaborate a positive alternative. In this respect, it is also important to recognize that while the theory of social representations has been one centre of this theoretical endeavour, Moscovici's work has ranged more widely across social psychology, encompassing studies of crowd psychology, conspiracy and collective decisions, as well as the work on social influence. In all of these contributions one finds the same inspiration at work, a particular form of what we might describe as the 'social-psychological imagination'. If Moscovici's work can be seen as offering a distinct perspective on social psychology, it is a perspective which is broader than what is connoted simply by the term social representations, although this term has often been taken as emblematic of this perspective.

Moscovici himself has only rarely ventured into efforts at articulating the interconnections between these different areas of work (though the interview in chapter 7 offers some significant thoughts). In part this reflects the fact that each of these areas of work has been articulated through different methodological procedures. His studies of social influence and group processes, for instance, have been rigorously experimental, while his study of the crowd drew on a critical analysis of earlier conceptualizations of mass psychology. In part it may also reflect the sense that these studies focus on different levels of analysis, from face-to-face interaction through to mass communication and the circulation of collective ideas. Yet all these studies seem to be 'pregnant' with the ideas which have been articulated around the concept of social representations so that a focus on this concept can indicate something of his underlying perspective. In this respect the essay on Proust in chapter 5 offers an illuminating study of the intricacies of the relations between influence and representation. Another example is his critical analysis of Weber's discussion of the Protestant ethic in *The Invention of Society* (Moscovici ([1988]/1993). What is apparent in both of these essays is that influence is always directed at sustaining or changing representations, while conversely, specific representations become stabilized through a balance achieved in a particular pattern of influence processes. Here, as in the studies of decision-making in groups, it is the relationship between communication and representation which is central.

In his book on social influence, Moscovici (1976) identified the perspective he described as a 'genetic social psychology' to emphasize the sense that influence processes emerged in the communicative exchanges between people. The use of this term 'genetic' echoes the sense it was given by both Jean Piaget and Lucien Goldmann. In all of these instances, particular structures can only be understood as the transformations of earlier structures (cf. the essay on themata in chapter 4). In Moscovici's social psychology, it is through communicative exchanges that social representations are structured and transformed. It is this dialectical relationship between communication and representation which is at the core of Moscovici's 'social-psychological imagination', and is the reason for describing this perspective as a genetic social psychology (cf. Duveen and Lloyd, 1990). In all communicative exchanges there is an effort to grasp the world through particular ideas and to project those ideas so as to influence others, to establish a certain way of making sense so that things are seen in *this* way rather than *that* way. Whenever knowledge is expressed it is for some purpose; it is never disinterested. When Prague is located to the east of Vienna a certain sense of the world and a particular set of human interests is being projected. The pursuit of knowledge returns us to the hurly-burly of human life and human society; it is here that knowledge takes shape and form through communication, and at the same time contributes to the shaping and forming of communicative exchanges. Through communication we are able to affiliate with or distance ourselves from others. This is the power of ideas, and Moscovici's theory of social representations has sought both to recognize a specific social phenomenon and to provide the means for making it intelligible as a social-psychological process.

1

The Phenomenon of
Social Representations*

I THINKING CONSIDERED AS ENVIRONMENT

(1) Primitive thought, science,
and everyday understanding

The belief on which primitive thought – if such a term is still acceptable – is based is a belief in the 'mind's unlimited power' to *shape* reality, to penetrate and activate it and to determine the course of events. The belief on which modern scientific thought is based is the exact opposite, that is, a belief in the 'limitless power of objects' to *shape* thought, to wholly determine its evolution and to be interiorized in and by the mind. In the first case, thought is seen as acting on reality; in the second, as reaction to reality; in the one, the object emerges as a replica of thought; in the other, thought is a replica of the object; and if, for the former, our wishes become reality – or wishful thinking – then, for the latter, to think amounts to turning reality into our wishes, to depersonalizing them. But since the two attitudes are symmetrical, they can only have the same cause, and one with which we have long been familiar: man's instinctive dread of powers he cannot subdue and his endeavour to compensate for this impotence imaginatively. The one difference being that, whereas the primitive mind dreads the forces of nature, the scientific mind dreads the power of thought. In so far as the first has enabled us to survive for millions of years, and the second to achieve so much in a few centuries, we must assume that each, in its way, represents a true aspect of the relation between our inner and outer worlds; an aspect, moreover, which is well worth investigating.

* Translated by Sacha Rabinovitch.

Social psychology is obviously a manifestation of scientific thought and, therefore, when studying the cognitive system it postulates that:

(i)   normal individuals react to phenomena, people or events in the same way as scientists or statisticians do and
(ii) understanding consists in information processing.

In other words, we perceive the world, such as it is, and all our perceptions, ideas and attributions are responses to stimuli from the physical or quasi-physical environment in which we live. What distinguishes us is the need to assess beings and objects correctly, to grasp reality fully; and what distinguishes the environment is its autonomy, its independence of us or even, one might say, its indifference to us and to our needs and desires. What are known as cognitive biases, subjective distortions, affective tendencies obviously do exist, as we are all aware, but they are precisely biases, distortions and tendencies in relation to a model, to rules, seen as the norm.

Yet it seems to me that some ordinary facts contradict these two postulates:

(*a*)   *First*, the familiar observation that we are unaware of some of the most obvious things, that we fail to see what is before our very eyes. It is as though our sight or our perception were dimmed, so that a given class of persons, either because of their age – e.g. the old for the young and the young for the old – or because of their race – e.g. blacks for some whites, etc. – become invisible when, in fact, they are 'staring us in the face'. This is how a gifted black writer describes such a phenomenon:

> I am an invisible man. No, I am not a spook like those who haunted Edgar Allan Poe; nor am I one of your Hollywood-movie ectoplasms. I am a man of substance, of flesh and bones, fibre and liquids – and I might even be said to possess a mind. I am invisible, understand, simply because people refuse to see me. Like the 'bodiless' head you see sometimes in circus sideshows, it is as though I have been surrounded by mirrors of hard, distorting glass. When they approach me they see only my surroundings, themselves, or figments of their imagination – indeed anything except me.   (Ellison, 1965, p. 7)

This invisibility is not due to any lack of information conveyed to the eyeball, but to a pre-established fragmentation of reality, a classification of the people and things which comprise it, which makes some of them visible and the rest invisible.

(*b*)   *Secondly*, we often notice that some facts we had taken for granted, that were basic to our understanding and behaviour, suddenly turn out to be mere illusions. For thousands of years men were convinced that the sun circled round a stationary earth. Since Copernicus we bear in our minds the image of a planetary system where the sun remains stationary while the earth circles around it; yet we still see what our forefathers saw. Thus we distinguish the appearance from the reality of things, but we distinguish them precisely because we can switch from appearance to reality by means of some notion or image.

(c)   *Thirdly*, our reactions to events, our responses to stimuli, are related to a given definition, common to all the members of the community to which we belong. If, while driving along a road, we see an overturned car, a wounded person and a policeman making a report, we assume that there has been an accident. We read daily about collisions and crashes in the papers under such a heading. Yet these are only 'accidents' because we define as such any involuntary interruption in the progress of a motor car which has more or less tragic consequences. In all other respects there is nothing accidental about a motor-car accident. Since statistical calculations enable us to assess the number of victims, according to the day of the week and the locality, motor-car accidents are no more due to chance than the disintegration of atoms in an accelerator at high pressure; they are directly related to a given society's degree of urbanization, the speed and number of its private vehicles and the inadequacy of its public transport.

In each of these cases we note the intervention of representations which either direct us towards that which is visible and to which we have to respond; or which relate appearance and reality; or again which define this reality. I do not wish to imply that such representations don't correspond to something we call the outside world. I simply note that, where reality is concerned, these representations are all we have, that to which our perceptual, as well as our cognitive, systems are adjusted. Bower writes:

> We usually use our perceptual system to interpret representations of worlds we can never see. In the man-made world we live in, the perception of representations is as important as the perception of real objects. By a representation I mean a man-made stimulus array intended to serve as a substitute for a sight or sound that could occur naturally. Some representations are meant to be stimulus surrogates; to produce the same experience as the natural world would have done. (Bower, 1977, p. 58)

In fact, we only experience and perceive a world in which, at one extreme, we are acquainted with man-made things representing other man-made things and, at the other extreme, with substitutes for stimuli of which we shall never see the originals, their natural equivalents, such as elementary particles or genes. So that we find ourselves, at times, in a predicament where we require some sign or other which will help us to distinguish one representation from another or a representation from that which it represents, that is, a sign that will tell us: 'This is a representation,' or: 'This is not a representation.' The painter René Magritte has illustrated such a predicament to perfection in a painting where a picture of a pipe is contained in a picture that also represents a pipe. On this picture within a picture we can read the message: 'This is not a pipe' which indicates the difference between the two pipes. We then turn to the 'real' pipe floating in the air and notice that it is real while the other is only a representation.[1] However, such an interpretation is incorrect since both are painted on the same canvas in front of our eyes. The idea that one of them is a picture which is itself within a picture, and thus a little 'less real' than the other, is totally illusory. Once you have agreed to 'enter the frame' you are already caught: you accept the image as reality. There remains none the less the reality of a painting which, hung in a museum and defined as an art object, provides food for thought, provokes an aesthetic reaction and adds to our understanding of painting.

As ordinary people, without the benefit of scientific instruments, we tend to consider and analyse the world in a very similar way; especially as the world with which we deal is social through and through, which means that we are never provided with any information which has not been distorted by representations 'superimposed' on objects and on persons which give them a certain vagueness and make them partially inaccessible. When we contemplate these individuals and objects, our inherited genetic predisposition, the images and habits we have learnt, the memories of them which we have preserved and our cultural categories all combine to make them such as we see them. So, in the last analysis, they are only one element in a chain-reaction of perceptions, opinions, notions and even lives, organized in a given sequence. It is essential to recall such commonplaces when approaching the domain of mental life in social psychology. My aim is to re-introduce them here in a manner which, I hope, will be fruitful.

(2)   The conventional and prescriptive nature of representations

In what way can thought be considered as an environment? Impressionistically, each of us is obviously surrounded, both individually and collectively, by words, ideas and images which penetrate his eyes, his ears and his mind, whether he likes it or not, and which solicit him without his knowing it, just as the thousands of messages conveyed by electro-magnetic waves circulate in the air without our seeing them and are turned into words in a telephone receiver or into images on a television screen. However, such a metaphor is not really adequate. Let's see if we can find a better way of describing how representations intervene in our cognitive activity and to what extent they are independent of it or can be said to determine it. If we accept that there is always a certain amount of both autonomy and constraint in every environ-ment, whether natural or social – and in the present case it is both – let us say that representations have precisely two roles.

(*a*)   First they *conventionalize* the objects, persons and events we encounter. They give them a definite form, locate them in a given category and gradually establish them as a model of a certain type, distinct and shared by a group of people. All new elements adhere to this model and merge into it. Thus we assert that the earth is round, we associate communism with the colour red, inflation with the decreasing value of money. Even when a person or an object doesn't conform precisely to the model, we constrain it to assume a given form, to enter a given category, in fact to become identical to the others, at the risk of its being neither understood nor decoded.

Bartlett concludes from his studies of perception that:

> When a common and already conventional form of representation is in use before the sign is introduced, there is a strong tendency for peculiar character-istics to disappear, and for the whole sign to be assimilated to the more familiar form. Thus 'lightning flash' practically always fell into a common, regular zig-zag form, and 'chin' lost its very sharp angle, becoming much more like ordinary conventional representations of this feature.   (Bartlett, 1932, p. 106)

These conventions enable us to know what stands for what: a change of direction or of colour indicates motion or temperature, a given symptom does or does not derive from a disease; they help us to solve the general problem of knowing when to interpret a message as significant in relation to others and when to see it as a fortuitous or chance event. And this meaning in relation to others further depends on a number of preliminary conventions, by means of which we can distinguish whether an arm is raised to attract atten-tion, to hail a friend or to convey impatience. Sometimes it is sufficient simply to transfer an object, or person, from one context to another, in order for us to see it or him in a new light and for us to wonder whether or not they are, indeed, the same. The most striking instance has been provided by Marcel Duchamp who, from 1912 on, restricted his artistic output to signing ready-made objects and who, by this single gesture, has promoted factory-produced objects to the status of art objects. A no less striking example is that of war criminals who are responsible for atrocities that will not easily be forgotten. Yet those who knew them, and were familiar with them both during and after the war, have praised their humanity and their kindness, as well as their routine efficiency, as being comparable to that of thousands of individuals peacefully employed in office jobs.

These examples show how each experience is added to a reality predeter-mined by conventions, which clearly define its frontiers, distinguish signific-ant from non-significant messages and which link each part with the whole, and assign each individual to a distinct category. Nobody's mind is free from the effects of the prior conditioning which is imposed by his representations, language and culture. We think, by means of a language; we organize our thoughts, in accordance with a system which is conditioned, both by our representations and by our culture. We see only that which underlying conventions allow us to see, and we remain unaware of these conventions. In this respect, our position is very similar to that of the ethnic African tribe, of which Evans-Pritchard wrote:

> In this web of belief every strand depends upon every other strand, and a Zande cannot get out of its meshes because it is the only world he knows. The web is not an external structure in which he is enclosed. It is the texture of his thought and he cannot think that his thought is wrong. (Evans-Pritchard, 1937, p. 194)

We may, with an effort, become aware of the conventional aspect of reality, and thus evade some of the constraints which it imposes on our perceptions and thoughts. But we should not imagine that we could ever be free of all convention, or could eliminate every prejudice. Rather than seeking to avoid all convention, a better strategy would be to discover and make explicit a single representation. Thus, instead of denying conventions and prejudices, this strategy would enable us to recognize that representations constitute, for us, a type of reality. We should seek to isolate which representations are inherent in the persons and objects we encounter and exactly what it is they represent. Among these are the cities we inhabit, the gadgets we use, the passers-by in the street and even the pure, unpolluted nature which we seek out in the country or enclose in our gardens.

I know that some account is taken of representations in actual research practice so as to describe more clearly the context within which the individual is called upon to react to a particular stimulus and to explain, more accurately, his subsequent responses. After all, the laboratory is one such reality which represents another, just like Magritte's picture within a picture. It is a reality in which it is necessary to indicate 'this is a stimulus' and not simply a colour or a sound, and 'this is a subject' and not a left- or right-wing student who wants to earn some money to pay for his studies. But we must take account of this in our theory. Hence, we must introduce to centre stage that which we had sought to keep in the wings. This might well be what Lewin had in mind when he wrote: 'Reality for the individual is, to a high degree, determined by what is socially accepted as reality' (Lewin, 1948, p. 57).

(*b*) Secondly, representations are *prescriptive*, that is, they impose themselves upon us with an irresistible force. This force is a combination of a structure which is present before we have even begun to think, and of a tradition which decrees *what* we should think. A child born today in any

Western country will encounter that of psychoanalysis, for example, in his mother's or the doctor's gestures, in the affection with which he is surrounded to help him through the trials and tribulations of the Oedipal conflict, in the comics he reads and later, in schoolbooks, conversations with classmates or even in a psychoanalytic cure, should he have recourse to one if social or educational problems arise. This is to say nothing of the papers he will read, the political speeches he will hear, the films he will see, etc. He will find a ready-made answer, in psychoanalytic jargon, to all his questions, and to each of his abortive or successful actions an explanation will be available which relates back to his earliest childhood or to his sexual desires. We have mentioned psychoanalysis as a representation. We could as easily have mentioned mechanistic psychology, or man-as-machine or the scientific paradigm of a particular community.

Whilst these representations, which are shared by many, enter into and influence the mind of each they are not thought by them; rather, to be more precise, they are re-thought, re-cited and re-presented.

If someone exclaims: 'He's a fool!', stops, and then corrects himself, saying: 'No, I mean he's a genius,' we immediately conclude that he has made a Freudian slip. But this conclusion isn't the result of reasoning, neither does it prove that we have a capacity for abstract reasoning, since we have simply recalled, without thinking, and whilst thinking of something else, the representation or definition of what a Freudian slip is. We might, indeed, have such a capacity, and ask ourselves why the speaker in question used one word in place of another, without arriving at any answer. Thus, it is easy to see why the representation which we have of something is not directly related to our manner of thinking but, conversely, why our manner of thinking, and what we think, depend on such representations, that is, on the fact that we have, or have not, a given representation. I mean that they are forced upon us, transmitted, and are the product of a whole sequence of elaborations and of changes which occur in the course of time and are the achievement of successive generations. All the systems of classification, all the images and all the descriptions which circulate within a society, even the scientific ones, imply a link with previous systems and images, a stratification in the collective memory and a reproduction in the language, which invariably reflects past knowledge, and which breaks the bounds of current information.

Social and intellectual activity is, after all, a rehearsal or recital, yet most socio-psychologists mistakenly treat it as if it were amnesic. Our past experiences and ideas are not dead experiences or dead ideas, but continue to be active, to change and to infiltrate our present experience and ideas. In many respects, the past is more real than the present. The peculiar power and clarity of representations – that is, of social representations – derives from the success with which they control the reality of today through that of yesterday and the continuity which this presupposes. Indeed, Jahoda himself has recognized them as autonomous properties which are 'not necessarily identifiable in the thinking of particular individuals' (Jahoda, 1970, p. 42); a remark to which his compatriot McDougall subscribed, half a century earlier, in the terminology of his day: 'Thinking, by aid of the collective representations, is said to have its own laws quite distinct from the laws of logic' (McDougall, 1920, p. 74). Laws which, obviously, modify those of logic, both in practice and outcome. In the light of history, and of anthropology, we can affirm that these representations are social entities, with a life of their own, communicating between themselves, opposing each other and changing in harmony with the course of life; vanishing, only to re-emerge under new guises. Generally, in civilizations as divided and mobile as our own, they coexist and circulate through various spheres of activity, where one of them will take precedence in response to our need for a certain coherence in accounting for persons and things. However, should a change occur in their hierarchy, or a given idea–image be threatened with extinction, our whole universe will be upset. A recent event, and the comment to which it gave rise, may serve to illustrate this point.

The American Psychiatric Association recently announced its intention to discard the terms 'neurosis' and 'neurotic' to define specific disorders. A journalist's comments on the decision, in an article entitled 'Goodbye Neurosis' (*International Herald Tribune*, 11 September 1978), are highly significant:

If the dictionary of mental disorders will no longer accept 'neurotics', we laymen can only do the same.

But consider the cultural loss: whenever someone is called 'neurotic' or 'a neurotic', it involves an implicit act of forgiveness and understanding; 'Oh, So-and-So is just neurotic' means 'Oh, So-and-So is excessively nervous. He didn't really want to toss the china at your head. It's just his way.' Or 'So-and-So is just neurotic' – meaning 'He can't help himself. He doesn't mean it every time he tosses china at your head.'

By calling someone neurotic we place the burden of adjustment not on the someone, but rather on ourselves. It's sort of a call to kindness, to a sense of social generosity.

Would the same be true if the 'disordered' were tossing the china? We do not think so. To excuse So-and-So by citing his disorder – the specific category of his disorder to boot – is like excusing a car for faulty brake-lining – it damn well ought to be repaired and quick. The burden of adjustment would sit squarely on the discorderee. No compassion would be asked of society at large, and naturally none would be forthcoming.

Think too of the self-esteem of the neurotic himself, who has long been comforted by the knowledge that he is 'just a neurotic' – quite a few pegs safely below a psychotic, but quite a few above the common run of men. A neurotic is an eccentric touched by Freud. Society gives him an honorable, often a lovable, place. Would the same niche be given the sufferers of 'somatoform disorders' or 'major depressive disorders' or 'dissociative disorders'? Not bloody likely.

Such cultural gains and losses are obviously related to fragments of social representations. A word, and the dictionary's definition of this word, contain a means of classifying individuals, as well as implicit theories concerning their constitution, or the reasons for their behaving in one way rather than another – an almost physical image of each individual, which corresponds to such theories. Once this content has diffused, and become accepted, it constitutes an integral part of ourselves, of our intercourse with others, of our way of judging them, and of interacting with them; it even defines our place in the social hierarchy, and our values. If the word 'neurosis' were to disappear, and to be replaced by the word 'disorder', such an event would have consequences far beyond its mere significance in a sentence, or in psychiatry. It is our inter-relations, and our collective thought, which are involved and transformed.

I hope that I have amply demonstrated how, by setting a conventional sign on reality on the one hand, and, on the other, by prescribing, through tradition and age-old structures, *what* we perceive and imagine, these creatures of thought, which are representations, end up by constituting an actual environment. Through their autonomy, and the constraints they exert (even though we are perfectly aware that they are 'nothing but ideas') it is, in fact, as unquestionable realities that we are led to envisage them. The weight of their history, custom and cumulative content confronts us with all the resistance of a material object. Perhaps it is an even greater resistanc since what is invisible is inevitably harder to overcome than what is visible.

(3)   The era of representation

All human interactions, whether they arise between two individuals, or between two groups, presuppose such representations. Indeed this is what characterizes them. 'The paramount fact about human interactions,' wrote Asch, 'is that they are happenings, that they are psychologically *represented* in each of the participants!' (Asch, 1952, p. 142). Once this fact is overlooked, all that remain are exchanges, that is, actions and reactions, which are non-specific and, moreover, impoverished into the bargain. Always, and everywhere, when we encounter persons or things, and become acquainted with them, such representations are involved. The information we receive, and to which we try to give a meaning, is under their control and has no other significance for us than what they give it.

To enlarge the framework a little, we could maintain that what is important is the nature of change, whereby social representations become capable of influencing the behaviour of the individual participant in a collectivity. This is how they are created inwardly, for it is in this form that the collective process itself penetrates, as the determining factor, into individual thought. Such representations, thus, appear to us almost as material objects, in so far as they are the product of our actions and communications. They are, in fact, the product of a professional activity: I am referring to those pedagogues, ideologues, popularizers of science or priests, that is, the representatives of science, cultures and religions, whose task it is to create and transmit them, often, alas, without either knowing or wishing it. In the general evolution of society, these professions are destined to multiply, and their work will become more systematic and more explicit. Partly for that reason, and in view of all that this entails, this era will become known as the era of representation, in every sense of that term.

This does not undermine the autonomy of representations, in relation either to the consciousness of the individual, or even to that of the group. Individuals and groups create representations in the course of communication and cooperation. Representations, obviously, are not created by individuals in isolation. Once created, however, they lead a life of their own, circulate, merge, attract and repel each other, and give birth to new representations, while old ones die out. As a consequence, in order to understand and to explain a representation, it is necessary to start with that, or those, from which it was born. It is not enough to start directly from such-and-such an aspect, either of behaviour or of the social structure. Far from reflecting either behaviour or social structure, a representation often conditions and even responds to them. This is so, not because it has a collective origin or because it refers to a collective object, but because, as such, being shared by all and strengthened by tradition, it constitutes a social reality *sui generis*. The more its origin is forgotten, and its conventional nature ignored, the more *fossilized* it becomes. That which is ideal gradually becomes materialized. It ceases to be ephemeral, changing and mortal and becomes instead lasting, permanent, almost immortal. In creating representations we are like the artist, who bows down before the statue he has sculpted and worships it as a god.

In my opinion, the main task of social psychology is to study such representations, their properties, their origins and their impact. No other discipline is dedicated to this task, and none is better equipped for it. It was, indeed, to social psychology that Durkheim entrusted the task:

As for the laws of the collective formation of ideas, these are even more completely unknown. Social psychology, whose task it should be to determine them is hardly more than a term which covers all kinds of general questions, various and imprecise, without any defined object. What should be done is to investigate, by comparing mythical themes, legends and popular traditions, and languages, how social representations are attracted to or exclude each other, amlgamate with or are distinguishable from each other, etc. (Durkheim, [1895]/ 1982, pp. 41–2)

Despite numerous further studies, fragmentary ideas and experiments, we are now no more advanced than we were nearly a century ago. Our knowledge is like a mayonnaise which has curdled. But one thing is certain: the principal forms of our physical and social environment are fixed in representations of this kind and we ourselves are fashioned in relation to them. I would even go so far as to say that, the less we think about them, and the less we are aware of them, then the greater their influence becomes. This is so much the case that the collective mind transforms everything it touches. Therein lies the truth of the primitive belief which has dominated our mentality for millions of years.

II What is a Thinking Society?

'We think through our mouths.' Tristan Tzara

(1) Behaviourism and the study of social representations

We live in a behaviourist world, practise a behaviourist science and use behaviourist metaphors. I say this without pride or shame. For I am not going to embark on a critique of what must, perforce, be called *one* view of contemporary man, since its defence or refutation is not, as far as I can see, the concern of science, but rather of culture. One neither defends nor refutes a culture. This said, it is obvious that the study of social representations must go beyond such a view, and must do so for a specific reason. It considers man in so far as he tries to know and to understand the things that surround him, and tries to solve the commonplace enigmas of his own birth, his bodily existence, his humiliations, of the sky above him, of the states of mind of his neighbours and of the powers that dominate him: enigmas that occupy and preoccupy him from the cradle, and of which he never ceases to speak. For him, thoughts and words are real – they are not mere epiphenomena of behaviour. He concurs with Frege who wrote:

> The influence of one person on another is brought about for the most part by thought. One communicates a thought. How does it happen? One brings about changes in the common outside world which, perceived by another person, are supposed to induce him to apprehend a thought and take it to be true. Could the great events of world history have come about without the communication of thought? And yet, we are inclined to regard thoughts as unreal because they appear to be without influence on events, while thinking, judging, stating, understanding are facts of human life. How much more real a hammer appears compared with a thought. How different the process of handing over a hammer is from communication of a thought.   (Frege, 1977, p. 38)

This is what books and articles are always hammering into our heads: hammers are more real than thoughts; attend to hammers rather than to thoughts. Everything, in the last analysis, is behaviour, a matter of driving stimuli into the walls of our organism, like nails. When we study social representations we study man, in so far as he asks questions and seeks answers or thinks, and not in so far as he processes information or behaves. More precisely, in so far as his aim is not to behave, but to understand.

What is a 'thinking' society? That is our question, and that is what we would like to observe and to understand, by studying (*a*) the circumstances in which groups communicate, make decisions and seek either to reveal or to conceal something, and (*b*) their achievements and their beliefs, that is, their ideologies, sciences and social representations. It could not be otherwise; the mystery is profound, yet understanding is the most common human faculty. It was at one time believed that this faculty was stimulated, first and foremost, by contact with the external world. But we have come increasingly to realize that it actually arises from social communication. Recent studies of very young children have shown that the origins and development of meaning and thought depend on social intercourse; it is as though a baby came into the world primarily equipped for a relationship with others, with its mother, its father and with all who await it and care for it. The world of objects constitutes but a backdrop for persons and their social interactions.

When asking the question: what is a thinking society? we refute at the same time the conception which, I believe, prevails in the human sciences, that is, that a society does not think, or, if it does, that this is not an essential attribute. The denial that society 'thinks' can assume two different forms: (*a*) by declaring that our minds are little black boxes, contained within a vast black box, which simply receives information, words and thoughts which are conditioned from the outside in order to turn them into gestures, judgements, opinions and so forth. In fact, we know perfectly well that our minds are not black boxes but, at best, are black holes, possessing a life and activity of their own, even when this is not obvious, and when individuals exchange neither energy nor information with the outside world. Madness, that black hole in rationality, irrefutably proves that this is how things are. The second form is (*b*) by maintaining that groups and individuals are always and completely under the sway of a dominant ideology which is produced and imposed by their social class, the State, the Church or the school, and that what they think and say only reflects such an ideology. In other words, it is maintained that they don't as a rule think, or produce anything original, on their own: they reproduce and, in turn, are reproduced. Despite its progressive nature, this conception is essentially in accordance with that of Le Bon, who asserts that the masses neither think nor create; but that it is only individuals, the organised elite, who do so. Here we discover, whether we like it or not, the metaphor of the black box, except that now it is invested with ready-made ideas, and no longer with objects. Such may be the case, but we cannot tell, for even if ideologies and their impact have been widely discussed, they have not been extensively researched. That much has been acknowledged by Marx and Wood: 'Yet in comparison with other areas, the study of ideology has been relatively neglected by sociologists, who generally feel more comfortable studying social structure and behaviour than studying belief and symbols' (Marx and Wood, 1975, p. 382).

So what we are suggesting is that individuals and groups, far from being passive receptors, think for themselves, produce and ceaselessly communicate their own specific representations and solutions to the questions they set themselves. In the streets, in cafés, offices, hospitals, laboratories, etc., people analyse, comment, concoct spontaneous, unofficial 'philosophies' which have a decisive impact on their social relations, their choices, the way they bring up their children, plan ahead and so forth. Events, sciences and ideologies simply provide them with 'food for thought'.

(2) Social representations

It is obvious that the concept of social representations has come to us from Durkheim. But we have a different view of it – or, at any rate, social psychology must consider it from a different angle – than does sociology. Sociology sees or, rather, has seen social representations as explanatory devices, irreducible by any further analysis. Their theoretical function was similar to that of the atom in traditional mechanics, or of the gene in traditional genetics, that is, atoms and genes were known to exist, but nobody bothered about what they did or what they were like. Similarly, one knew that social representations occurred in societies, but nobody worried about their structure or about their inner dynamics. Social psychology, on the other hand, is and must be preoccupied solely with both the structure and the dynamics of representations. For us, it is summed up in the difficulty of penetrating the interior to discover the inner mechanisms and vitality of social representations in the greatest possible detail; that is, in 'splitting representations', just as atoms and genes have been split. The first step in this direction was taken by Piaget when he studied the child's representation of the world, and his enquiry remains, to this day, exemplary. So what I propose to do is to consider as a *phenomenon* what was previously seen as a *concept*.

Moreover, from Durkheim's point of view, collective representations described a whole range of intellectual forms which included science, religion, myth, modalities of time and space, etc. Indeed, any kind of idea, emotion or belief which occurred within a community was included. This presents a serious problem for, by attempting to include too much, one grasps little: grasp all, lose all. Intuition, as well as experience, suggests that it is impossible to cover such a wide range of knowledge and beliefs. They are too hetero-geneous in the first place and, moreover, they cannot be defined by a few general characteristics. As a consequence, we are obliged to add two signific-ant qualifications:

(*a*)   *Social representations should be seen as a specific way of understand-ing, and communicating, what we know already.* They occupy in effect a curious position, somewhere between concepts, which have as their goal abstracting meaning from the world and introducing order into it, and per-cepts, which reproduce the world in a meaningful way. They always have two facets, which are as interdependent as the two faces of a sheet of paper: the iconic and the symbolic facets. We know that: Representation = image/meaning; in other words, that it equates every image to an idea and every idea to an image. Thus, in our society, a 'neurotic' is an idea associated with psychoanalysis, with Freud, with the Oedipus Complex and, at the same time, we see the neurotic as an egocentric, pathological individual, whose parental conflicts have not yet been resolved. So, on the one hand, the word evokes a science, even the name of a classical hero, and a concept and, on the other, it evokes a definite type, characterized by certain features, and a readily imagined biography. The mental mechanisms set in motion in this instance, and which carve out this figure in our universe and give it a significance, an interpretation, obviously differ from those whose function it is to isolate a precise perception of a person or of a thing, and to conceive a system of concepts that explains them. Language itself, when it conveys representa-tions, is located halfway between what is called the language of observation and the language of logic; the first, expressing pure facts – if such things exist – and the second, abstract symbols. This is, perhaps, one of the most remark-able phenomena of our time – this welding of language and of representation. Let me explain.

Until the dawn of the century, ordinary verbal language was a means both of communication and of knowledge; of collective ideas and of abstract research, since it was common to both common sense and science. Nowadays, non-verbal language – mathematics and logic – which has appropriated the sphere of science, has substituted signs for words, and equations for proposi-tions. The world of our experience and of our reality has split in two, and the laws which govern our everyday world now have no obvious relation to those which govern the world of science. If we are much interested today in lin-guistic phenomena, this is partly because language is on the decline, just as we worry about plants, and nature and animals because they are threatened with extinction. Language, excluded from the sphere of material reality, re-emerges in that of historical and conventional reality; and, if it has lost its relation to theory, it maintains its relation to representation, which is all that it has left. Thus, if the study of language is increasingly the concern of social psychology, this is not because the latter wants to imitate what has been happening in other disciplines, or wishes to add a social dimension to its individual abstractions, or for any other philanthropic motives. It is simply connected with the change which we have just mentioned and which links it so exclusively to our common, everyday method of understanding and of exchanging our ways of seeing things.

(*b*)   *Durkheim – true to the Aristotelian and Kantian tradition – has a rather static conception of these representations – somewhat akin to that of the Stoics.* As a consequence, representations, in his theory, are like a thickening of the fog, or else they act as stabilizers for many words or ideas – like layers of stagnant air in a society's atmosphere, of which it is said that one could cut them with a knife. Whilst this is not entirely false, what is most striking to the contemporary observer is their mobile and circulating character; in short, their plasticity. We see them more as dynamic structures, operating on an assembly of relations and of behaviours which appear and disappear together with the representations, just as the disappearance from our dictionaries of the word 'neurotic' would also banish some feelings, a certain type of relationship towards a particular person, a way of judging him and, consequently, of judging ourselves.

I stress these differences for a purpose. The social representations with which I am concerned are neither those of primitive societies, nor are they survivals, in the subsoil of our culture, from prehistoric times. They are those of our current society, of our political, scientific, human soil, which have not always had enough time to allow the proper sedimentation to become immutable traditions. And their importance continues to increase, in direct proportion to the heterogeneity and the fluctuation of the unifying systems – official sciences, religions, ideologies – and to the changes which these must undergo in order to penetrate everyday life and become part of common reality. The mass media have accelerated this tendency, multiplied such changes and increased the need of a link between, on the one hand, our purely abstract sciences and beliefs in general and, on the other, our concrete activities as social individuals. In other words, there is a continual need to reconstitute 'common sense' or the form of understanding that creates the substratum of images and meanings, without which no collectivity can operate. Similarly, our collectivities could not function today if social representations were not formed that are based on the stock of theories and ideologies which they transform into shared realities, relating to the interactions between people which thus constitute a separate category of phenomena. And the specific feature of these representations is precisely that they 'embody ideas' in collective experiences and interactions in behaviour which can, more profitably, be compared to works of art than to mechanical reactions. The biblical writer was already aware of this when he asserted that the word became flesh; and

Marxism confirms it when it states that ideas, once released amongst the masses, are, and behave like, material forces.

We know almost nothing of this alchemy which transmutes the base metal of our ideas into the gold of our reality. How to change concepts into objects, or into people, is the enigma which has preoccupied us for centuries and which is the true purpose of our science as distinct from other sciences which, in fact, enquire into the reverse process. I am well aware that an almost insuperable distance separates the problem from its solution, a distance very few are prepared to bridge. But neither shall I cease to repeat that if social psychology does not try to bridge this gap, it fails in its task and thus will not only fail to progress but will even cease to exist.

To sum up: if, in the classic sense, collective representations are an explanatory device, and refer to a general class of ideas and beliefs (science, myth, religion, etc.), for us they are phenomena which need to be described and to be explained. They are specific phenomena which are related to a particular mode of understanding and of communicating – a mode which creates both reality and common sense. It is in order to stress such a distinction that I use the term 'social' instead of 'collective'.

(3) Sacred and profane sciences; consensual and reified universes

The place which representations occupy in a thinking society is what concerns us here. Formerly, this place would have been – and up to a point was – determined by the distinction between a sacred sphere – worthy of respect and veneration and so kept quite apart from all purposeful, human activities – and a profane sphere in which trivial, utilitarian activities were performed. These separate and opposed worlds which, in varying degrees, determine within each culture and each individual the spheres of their own and foreign forces; that which we can alter and that which alters us; the *opus proprium* and *opus alienum*. All knowledge presupposed such a division of reality, and a discipline which was concerned with one of the spheres was totally different from a discipline which was concerned with the other, sacred sciences having nothing whatever in common with profane sciences. Doubtless it was possible to switch from the one to the other, but this only occurred when the contents were blurred.

This distinction has now been abandoned. It has been replaced by another, more basic distinction between consensual and reified universes. In the consensual universe, society is a visible, continuous creation, permeated with meaning and purpose, possessing a human voice, in accord with human existence and both acting and reacting like a human being. In other words, man is here the measure of all things. In the reified universe, society is transformed into a system of solid, basic, unvarying entities, which are indifferent to individuality and lack identity. This society ignores itself and its creations, which it sees only as isolated objects, such as persons, ideas, environments and activities. The various sciences which are concerned with such objects can, as it were, impose their authority on the thought and experience of each individual and decide, in each particular case, what is true and what is not. All things, whatever the circumstances, are here the measure of man.

Even our use of the pronouns 'we' and 'they' can express this contrast, where 'we' stands for the group of individuals to whom we relate and 'they' – the French, scholars, State systems, etc. – to a different group, to which we do not, but may be forced to, belong. The distance between the first and the third person plural expresses the distance which separates a social place where we feel included from a given, indeterminate or, at any rate, impersonal place. This lack of identity, which is at the root of modern man's psychic distress, is a symptom of this necessity to see oneself in terms of 'we' and 'they'; to oppose 'we' to 'they'; and thus of one's inability to connect the one with the other. Groups and individuals try to overcome this necessity either by identifying with 'we', and thus enclosing themselves in a world apart, or by identifying with 'they', and becoming the robots of bureaucracy and the administration.

Such categories as consensual and reified universes are unique to our culture. In a *consensual universe* society is seen as a group of individuals who are equal and free, each entitled to speak in the name of the group and under its aegis. Thus, no one member is assumed to possess an exclusive competence, but each can acquire any competence which may be required by the circumstances. In this respect, everybody acts as a responsible 'amateur' or 'curious observer', in the catch phrase of the last century. In most public meeting-places these amateur politicians, doctors, educators, sociologists, astronomers, etc. can be found expressing their opinions, airing their views and laying down the law. Such a state of affairs requires a certain complicity, that is, linguistic conventions, questions that must not be asked, topics that can or cannot be ignored. These worlds are institutionalized in the clubs, associations and cafés of today as they were in the 'salons' and academies of the past. The waning art of conversation is what they thrive on. This is what keeps them going and encourages social relations which otherwise would dwindle. In the long run, conversation creates nodes of stability and recurrence, a communality of significance between its practitioners. The rules of this art maintain a whole complex of ambiguities and conventions without which social life could not exist. They enable individuals to share an implicit stock of images and of ideas which are taken for granted and mutually accepted. Thinking is done out loud. It becomes a noisy, public activity which satisfies the need for communication and thus maintains and consolidates the group whilst conveying the character each member requires of it. If we think before speaking and speak to help ourselves think, we also speak to provide a sonorous reality to the inner pressure of those conversations through which, and in which, we bind ourselves to others. Beckett has summed up the situation in *Endgame*:

Clov: What is there to keep me here?
Hamm: Conversation.

And the motive is profound. Whoever keeps his ears pinned back in those places where people converse, whoever reads interviews with some attention, will realize that most conversations are about highly 'metaphysical' problems – birth, death, injustice, etc. – and about society's ethical laws. Thus they provide a permanent commentary on major national, scientific or urban events and features, and are therefore the modern equivalent of the Greek chorus which, though no longer on the historical stage, remains in the wings.

In a reified universe society is seen as a system of different roles and classes whose members are unequal. Only acquired competence determines their degree of participation according to merit, their right to function 'as physician', 'as psychologist', 'as trade unionist' or to abstain, in so far as 'they have no competence in the matter.' Permutations of roles, the ability to take somebody else's place, are so many ways of acquiring competence or of isolating oneself, of being different. Thus we confront each other, within the system, as pre-established organizations, each with its rules and regulations, whence the compulsions we experience and the feeling that we cannot alter them at will. There is a proper behaviour for every circumstance, a linguistic formula for every confrontation and, needless to say, the appropriate information for a given context. We are bound by that which binds the organization and which corresponds to a sort of general acceptance and not to any reciprocal understanding, to a sequence of prescriptions and not to a sequence of agreements. History, nature, all those things which are responsible for the system are equally responsible for the hierarchy of roles and classes, for their solidarity. Every situation contains a potential ambiguity, a vagueness, two possible interpretations, but their connotations are negative, they are obstacles we must overcome before everything becomes clear, precise, totally unambiguous. This is achieved by processing information, by the processors' lack of involvement and the existence of appropriate channels. The computer serves as the model for the type of relations which are thus established, and its rationality, we can only hope, is the rationality of that which is computed.

The contrast between the two universes has a psychological impact. The boundary between them splits collective and, indeed, physical reality in two. It is readily apparent that the sciences are the means by which we understand the reified universe, while social representations deal with the consensual. The purpose of the first is to establish a chart of the forces, objects and events which are independent of our desires and outside our awareness and to which we must react impartially and submissively. By concealing values and advantages they aim at encouraging intellectual precision and empirical evidence. Representations, on the other hand, restore collective awareness and give it shape, explaining objects and events so that they become accessible to everyone and coincide with our immediate interests. They are, according to William James, concerned with: 'practical reality, reality for ourselves; and to have that, an object must not only appear, but it must appear both *interesting* and *important*. The world whose objects are neither interesting nor important we treat simply negatively, we brand them as unreal' (W. James, [1890]/1980, p. 295).

The use of a language of images and of words that have become common property through the diffusion of reported ideas enlivens and fertilizes those aspects of society and nature with which we are here concerned. Doubtless – and this is what I set out to demonstrate – the specific nature of such representations expresses the specific nature of the consensual universe of which they are the product and to which they pertain exclusively. It thus ensues that social psychology is the science of such universes. At the same time, we see more clearly the true nature of ideologies, which is to facilitate the transition from the one world to the other, that is, to cast consensual into reified categories and to subordinate the former to the latter. Hence they have no specific structure and can be perceived either as representations or as sciences. This is how they come to concern both sociology and history.

III   THE FAMILIAR AND THE UNFAMILIAR

To understand the phenomenon of social representations, however, we must begin at the beginning and advance step by step. Up to this point, I have done no more than suggest certain reforms and tried to vindicate them. I couldn't avoid stressing specific ideas if I wanted to defend the point of view I was upholding. But, in so doing, I have demonstrated the fact that:

(a) social representations must be seen as an 'environment' in relation to the individual or the group; and
(b) they are, in certain respects, specific to our society.

Why do we create these representations? What, in our motives for creating them, explains their cognitive properties? These are the questions we shall tackle first. We could respond by recourse to three traditional hypotheses: (i) the hypothesis of desirability, that is, an individual or a group seeks to create images, to make up sentences that will either express or conceal his or their intentions, these images and sentences being subjective distortions of an objective reality; (ii) the hypothesis of imbalance, that is, all ideologies, all concepts of the world, are means of solving psychic or emotional tensions due to a failure or a lack of social integration. Thus they are imaginary compensations which are aimed at restoring a degree of inner stability; and (iii) the hypothesis of control, that is, groups create representations so as to filter information derived from the environment and thus to control individual behaviour. They function, therefore, as a kind of manipulation of thought and of the structure of reality, similar to those methods of 'behavioural' control and of propaganda that exert a compulsive coercion on all those to whom they are directed.

Such hypotheses are not entirely devoid of truth. Social representations may indeed answer a given need; respond to a state of imbalance; and further the unpopular but ineradicable domination of one section of society over another. But these hypotheses have, none the less, the common failing of being too general; they do not explain why such functions should be fulfilled by this method of understanding and communicating rather than by some other, such as science or religion, for instance. Thus we must seek a different hypothesis, less general and more in keeping with what researchers in the field have observed. Moreover, for want of space, I can neither elaborate my reservations nor justify my theory any further. I shall have to expose, without more ado, an intuition and a fact I believe to be true, that is, that *the purpose of all representations is to make something unfamiliar, or unfamiliarity itself, familiar.*

What I mean is that consensual universes are places where everybody wants to feel at home, secure from any risk of friction or strife. All that is said and done there only confirms acquired beliefs and interpretations, corroborates rather than contradicts tradition. The same situations, gestures, ideas are always expected to recur, over and over again. Change as such is only perceived and accepted in so far as it provides a kind of liveliness and avoids the stifling of dialogue under the weight of repetition. On the whole, the dynamic of relationships is a dynamic of familiarization, where objects, individuals and events are perceived and understood in relation to previous encounters or paradigms. As a result, memory prevails over deduction, the past over the present, response over stimuli and images over 'reality'. To accept and understand what is familiar, to grow accustomed to it and make a habit of it, is one thing; but it is quite another to prefer it as the standard of reference and to measure all that happens, and is perceived, against it. For, in this case, we don't simply register what typifies a Parisian, a 'respectable' person, a mother, an Oedipus Complex, etc., but this awareness is also used as a criterion to evaluate what is unusual, abnormal and so on, or, in other words, what is unfamiliar.

In fact, for our friend the 'man in the street' (now threatened with extinction, along with strolls in the streets, and soon to be replaced by the man in front of the TV set), most of the opinions derived from science, art and economics which relate to reified universes differ, in many ways, from the familiar, handy, opinions he has constructed out of bits and pieces of scientific, artistic and economic traditions and from personal experience and hearsay. Because they differ, he tends to think of them as invisible, unreal – for the world's reality, like realism in painting, is largely a matter of limitations and/or convention. Thus he may experience this sense of non-familiarity when frontiers and/or conventions disappear; when distinctions between the abstract and the concrete become blurred; or when an object, which he had always thought of as abstract, suddenly emerges in all its concreteness, etc. This may occur when he is presented with a picture of the physical reconstruction of such purely notional entities as atoms or robots or, indeed, with any atypical behaviour, person or relation which might prevent him from reacting as he would before the usual type. He doesn't find what he expected to find, and is left with a sense of incompleteness and randomness. It is in this way that the mentally handicapped, or people belonging to other cultures, are disturbing, because they are like us and yet not like us; so we say they are 'uncultured', 'barbarian', 'irrational' and so on. In fact, all banned or remote things, topics or persons, those which have been exiled to the very frontiers of our universe, are always endowed with imaginary characteristics; and they preoccupy and disturb precisely because they are there without being there; perceived without being perceived; their unreality becomes apparent when we are in their presence; when their reality is forced upon us – it is like coming face to face with a ghost or with a fictional character in real life; or like the first occasion when we see a computer playing chess. Then, something we had thought of as a fancy becomes reality before our very eyes; we can see and touch something we were precluded from seeing and touching.

The actuality of something absent, the 'not quite rightness' of an object, are what characterize unfamiliarity. Something seems to be visible without being so; similar, while being different; accessible, yet inaccessible. The unfamiliar attracts and intrigues individuals and communities while, at the same time, it alarms them, compels them to make explicit the implicit assumptions that are basic to consensus. This 'not quite rightness' worries and threatens, as when a robot that behaves exactly like a living creature, although it lacks life itself, suddenly becomes the Frankenstein monster, something both fascinating and terrifying. The fear of what is strange (and of strangers) is deep-rooted. It has been observed in young children during the third quarter of their first year, and a number of children's games are really a means of overcoming this fear, of controlling its object. Phenomena of mass panic frequently stem from the same cause and are expressed in the same dramatic movements of flight and distress. This is because the dread of losing customary landmarks, of losing touch with what provides a sense of continuity, of mutual understanding, is an unbearable dread. And when otherness is thrust upon us in the form of something 'not quite' as it should be, we instinctively reject it, because it threatens the established order.

The act of re-presentation is a means of transferring what disturbs us, what threatens our universe, from the outside to the inside, from far off to near by. The transfer is effected by separating normally linked concepts and perceptions and setting them in a context where the unusual becomes usual, where the unknown can be included in an acknowledged category. Thus when trying to define and make more accessible the psychoanalyst's dealings with his patient – that 'medical treatment without medicine' which seems eminently paradoxical to our culture – some people will compare it to a 'confession'. The concept is thus detached from its analytical context and transposed to one of priests and penitents, of father confessors and contrite sinners. Then the method of free association is likened to the rules of confession. In this way, what had first seemed offensive and paradoxical becomes an ordinary, normal process. Psychoanalysis is no more than a form of confession. And later, when psychoanalysis has been accepted and is a social representation in its own right, confession is seen, more or less, as a form of psychoanalysis. Once the method of free association has been separated from its theoretical context and given religious connotations it ceases to be surprising and disturbing and assumes instead a very ordinary character. And this is not, as we might be tempted to believe, a simple matter of analogy but an actual, socially significant merging, a shifting of values and feelings.

In this case, as well as in others we observed, the images, ideas and language shared by a given group always seem to dictate the initial direction and expedient by which the group tries to come to terms with the unfamiliar. Social thinking owes more to convention and memory than to reason; to traditional structures rather than to current intellectual or perceptive structures. Denise Jodelet ([1989a]/1991) has analysed the reactions of the inhabitants of various villages to the mentally handicapped people who were placed in their midst. These patients, because of their almost normal appearance, and notwithstanding the instructions the villagers had received, continued to be seen as alien, despite the fact that their presence had been accepted for many, many years and that they shared the villagers' daily life and even their homes. Thus it became apparent that the representations to which they gave rise derived from traditional views and notions and that it was these that determined the villagers' relations with them.

However, though we are able to perceive such a discrepancy, no one can do away with it. The basic tension between the familiar and the unfamiliar is always settled, in our consensual universes, in favour of the former. In social thinking, the conclusion has priority over the premise, and in social relations, according to Nelly Stephane's apt formula, the verdict has priority over the trial. Before seeing and hearing a person we have already judged him, classified him and created an image of him, so that all the enquiries we make and our efforts to obtain information only serve to confirm this image. Moreover, laboratory experiments corroborate this observation:

> The common errors which subjects make suggest that there is a general factor governing the order in which such checks are carried out. Subjects seem to be biased toward attempts to *verify* a conclusion, whether it is their own initial answer, or they are given them by the experimenter to evaluate. They seek to determine whether the premises could be combined in such a way as to render the conclusion true. Of course, this merely shows that conclusion and premises are consistent, not that the conclusion follows from the premises. (Wason and Johnson-Laird, 1972, p. 157)

When all is said and done, the representations we fabricate – of a scientific theory, a nation, an artefact, etc. – are always the result of a constant effort to make usual and actual something which is unfamiliar or which gives us a feeling of unfamiliarity. And through them we overcome it and integrate it into our mental and physical world which is thus enriched and transformed. After a series of adjustments, that which was far away seems close at hand; that which seemed abstract becomes concrete and almost normal. However, while creating them we are always more or less aware of our intentions, since the images and ideas by means of which we grasp the unusual only bring us back to what we already knew and had long been familiar with and which, therefore, gives a reassuring impression of *déjà vu* and *déjà connu*. Bartlett writes: 'As has been pointed out before, whenever material visually presented purports to be representative of some common object, but contains certain features which are unfamiliar in the community to which the material is introduced, these features invariably suffer transformation in the direction of the familiar' (Bartlett, 1932, p. 178).

It is as though, whenever a breach or split occurred in what is usually perceived as normal, our minds healed up the wound and refashioned from within that which had been without. Such a process reassures and comforts us, restores a sense of continuity in the group or individual threatened with discontinuity and meaninglessness. That is why, when studying a representation, we should always try to discover the unfamiliar feature which motivated it and which it has absorbed. But it is particularly important that the development of such a feature be observed from the very moment it emerges in the social sphere.

The contrast with science is striking. Science proceeds in the opposite way, from premise to conclusion, especially in the field of logic, just as the aim of the law is to ensure the trial's priority over the verdict. But it has to rely on a complete system of logic and proof in order to proceed in a manner that is quite foreign to the natural process and function of thought in an ordinary consensual universe. It must, furthermore, lay down certain laws – uninvolvement, repetition of experiments, distance from the object, independence from author-ity and tradition – which are never fully applied. To make the permutation of both terms of the argument possible, it creates a wholly artificial milieu by resorting to what is known as the rational reconstruction of facts and ideas. Then, to overcome our tendency to confirm what is familiar, to prove what is already known – a tendency which hampers research and the avoidance of error – the scientist is required to falsify, to try to invalidate his own theories and to confront evidence with counter-evidence. But that is not the whole story. Since it has become modern and has broken off with common sense, science is successfully occupied in constantly demolishing most of our cur-rent perceptions and opinions, in proving that impossible results are possible and in giving the lie to the bulk of our customary ideas and experiences. In other words, its object is to *make the familiar unfamiliar* in its mathematical equations as well as in its laboratories. And in this way it proves, by contrast, that the purpose of social representations is precisely that which I have already indicated.

IV ANCHORING AND OBJECTIFYING, OR THE TWO PROCESSES THAT GENERATE SOCIAL REPRESENTATIONS

(1) Science, common sense and social representations

Science and social representations are so different from each other and yet so complementary that we have to think and speak in both registers. The French philosopher Gaston Bachelard observed that the world in which we live and the world of thought are not one and the same world. Yet we cannot help yearning for a single, identical world and striving to achieve it. Contrary to what was believed in the nineteenth century, far from being the antidote to representations and ideologies, the sciences now actually generate such rep-resentations. Our reified worlds increase with the proliferation of the sciences. As theories, information and events multiply, they have to be duplicated and reproduced at a more immediate and accessible level by acquiring a form and energy of their own. In other words, they are transferred to a consensual universe, circumscribed and re-presented. Science was formerly based on common sense and made common sense less common; but now common sense is science made common. Unquestionably, every fact, every common-place conceals within its very platitude a world of knowledge, a digest of culture and a mystery that make it both compulsive and fascinating. 'Can anything be more appealing,' asked Baudelaire, 'more fruitful and more posit-ively *exciting* than a commonplace?' And, we might add, more collectively effective? It isn't easy to make unfamiliar words, ideas or beings usual, close and actual. To give them a familiar face, it is necessary to set in motion the two mechanisms of a thought process based on memory and foregone conclusions.

The first mechanism strives to *anchor* strange ideas, to reduce them to ordinary categories and images, to set them in a familiar context. Thus, for instance, a religious person tries to relate a new theory or the behaviour of a stranger to a religious scale of values. The purpose of the second mechanism is to *objectify* them, that is, to turn something abstract into something almost concrete, to transfer what is in the mind to something existing in the physical world. The things the mind's eye perceives seem to be before our physical eyes and an imagined being begins to assume the reality of something seen, something tangible. These mechanisms make the unfamiliar familiar, the first by transferring it to our own particular sphere where we are able to compare and interpret it, the second by reproducing it among the things we can see and touch and thus control. Since representations are created by these two mechanisms it is essential that we understand how they function.

Anchoring.   This is a process which draws something foreign and disturbing that intrigues us into our particular system of categories and compares it to the paradigm of a category which we think to be suitable. It is rather like anchoring a stray boat to one of the buoys in our social space. Thus, for the villagers in Denise Jodelet's study, the mental patients placed in their midst by the medical association were immediately judged by conventional standards and compared to idiots, tramps, spastics or to what in the local dialect were known as 'loonies' ('*bredins*'). In so far as a given object or idea is compared to the paradigm of a category it acquires characteristics of that category and is readjusted to fit within it. If the classification thus obtained is generally accepted, then any opinion that refers to the category will also refer to the object or idea. For instance, the aforementioned villagers' opinion of idiots, tramps and spastics is transferred, unmodified, to the mental patients. Even when we are aware of a certain discrepancy, of the approximation of our assessment, we cling to it, if only to preserve a minimum of coherence between the unknown and the known.

To anchor is thus to classify and to name something. Things that are unclassified and unnamed are alien, non-existent and at the same time threatening. We experience a resistance, a distancing when we are unable to evaluate something, to describe it to ourselves or to other people. The first step towards overcoming such resistance, towards conciliating an object or person, is taken when we are able to place it or him in a given category, to label it or him with a familiar name. Once we can speak about something, assess it and thus communicate it – even vaguely, as when we say of someone that he is 'inhibited' – then we can represent the unusual in our usual world, reproduce it as the replica of a familiar model. By classifying what is unclassifiable, naming what is unnameable, we are able to imagine it, to represent it. Indeed, representation is, basically, a system of classification and denotation, of allotting categories and names. Neutrality is forbidden by the very logic of the system, where each object and being must have a positive or a negative value and assume a given place in a clearly graded hierarchy. When we classify a person among the neurotics, the Jews or the poor, we are obviously not simply stating a fact but assessing and labelling him. And, in so doing, we reveal our 'theory' of society and of human nature.

In my opinion, this is a vital factor in social psychology which has not received all the attention it deserves; indeed, existing studies of the phenomena of evaluation, classification, categorization (Eiser and Stroebe, 1972) and so forth fail to take into account the substrata of such phenomena or to realize that they presuppose a representation of beings, objects and events. Yet the process of representation involves the coding of even physical stimuli into a specific category, as an enquiry into the perception of colours in various cultures has revealed. Thus scholars admit that individuals, when shown different colours, perceive them in relation to a paradigm – though such a paradigm may be totally unknown to them – and classify them by means of a mental image (Rosch, 1977). In fact, one of the lessons contemporary epistemology has taught us is that any system of categories presupposes a theory which defines and specifies it and specifies its use. When such a system disappears, we are entitled to assume that the theory too has disappeared.

However, let us proceed systematically. To classify something means that we confine it to a set of behaviours and of rules stipulating what is, and is not, permissible in relation to all the individuals included in this class. When we classify a person as a Marxist, an angler or a reader of *The Times*, we confine him to a set of linguistic, spatial and behavioural constraints and to certain habits. If we then go so far as to let him know what we have done, we will bring our influence to bear on him by formulating specific demands related to our expectations. The main virtue of a class, that which makes it so easy to handle, is that it provides a suitable model or prototype to represent the class and a sort of photo-kit of all the individuals supposed to belong to it. This photo-kit represents a sort of test case that sums up the features common to a number of related cases, that is, it is, on the one hand, an idealized conflation of salient points and, on the other, an iconic matrix of readily identifiable points. Thus most of us, as our visual representation of a Frenchman, have an image of an undersized person wearing a beret and carrying a long loaf of French bread.

To categorize someone or something amounts to choosing a paradigm from those stored in our memory and establishing a positive or a negative relation with it. When we switch on the radio in the middle of a programme without knowing what it is, we assume it is a 'play' if it is sufficiently similar to P, when P stands for the paradigm of a play, that is, dialogue, plot, etc. Experience shows that it is much easier to agree on what constitutes a paradigm than on the degree of an individual's resemblance to it. From Denise Jodelet's enquiry it emerges that, although the villagers were of one mind as to the general classification of the mental patients living with them, they were much less united in their opinion as to each patient's resemblance to the generally accepted 'test case'. When any attempt was made to define this test case, innumerable discrepancies came to light which were not usually obvious, thanks to the complicity of all concerned.

By and large, however, it can be said that classifications are made by comparing individuals to a prototype generally considered to represent a class, and that the former is defined by his approximation to, or coincidence with, the latter. Thus we say of certain personalities – de Gaulle, Maurice Chevalier, Churchill, Einstein, etc. – that they are representative of a nation, of politicians or of scientists, and we classify other politicians or scientists in relation to them. If it is true that we classify and judge people and things by comparing them to a prototype, then we will inevitably tend to notice and select those features which are most representative of this prototype, just as Denise Jodelet's villagers were more clearly aware of the mental patients' speech and behavioural 'oddities', during the ten or twenty years of their stay, than of the general pleasantness, diligence and humanity of these unfortunate people.

Indeed, anyone who has been a journalist, a sociologist or a clinical psychologist knows how the representation of such and such a gesture, occurrence or word can clinch a news item or a diagnosis. The ascendency of the test case is due, I believe, to its concreteness, to a kind of vividness which leaves such a deep imprint in our memory that we are able to use it thereafter as a 'model' against which we measure individual cases and any image that even remotely resembles it. Thus every test case, and every typical image, contains the abstract in the concrete, which further enables them to achieve society's main purpose: to create classes from individuals. Thus we can never say that we know an individual, nor that we try to understand him, but only that we try to recognize him, that is, to find out what sort of person he is, to what category he belongs and so forth, which really means that anchoring too involves the priority of the verdict over the trial and of the predicate over the subject. The prototype is the quintessence of such priority, since it fosters ready-made opinions and usually leads to over-hasty decisions.

Such decisions are generally reached in one of two ways: by generalizing or by particularizing. At times a ready-made opinion comes to mind straight away and we try to find the information or 'particular' that fits it; at others, we have a given particular in mind and try to get a precise image of it. By generalizing, we reduce distances. We select a feature at random and use it as a category: Jew, mental patient, play, aggressive nation, etc. The feature becomes, as it were, coextensive with all the members of this category. When it is positive, we register our acceptance, when negative, our rejection. By particularizing, we maintain the distance and consider the object under scrutiny as a divergence from the prototype. At the same time, we try to detect what feature, motivation or attitude makes it distinct. While studying the social representations of psychoanalysis, I was able to observe how the basic image of the psychoanalyst could, by the exaggeration of a specific feature – wealth, status, relentlessness – be modified and particularized to produce that of 'the American psychoanalyst', and that sometimes all these features were stressed at the same time. In fact, the tendency to classify either by generalization or by particularization is not, by any means, a purely intellectual choice, but reflects a given attitude towards the object, a desire to define it as normal or aberrant. That is what is mainly at stake in all classifications of unfamiliar things – the need to define them as conforming to, or diverging from, the norm. Besides, when we talk about similarity or dissimilarity, identity or difference, we are really saying precisely that, but in a detached form which is devoid of social consequences.

There is a tendency, among social psychologists, to see classification as an analytic operation involving a sort of catalogue of separate features – colour of skin, texture of hair, shape of skull and nose and so on, if it is a question of race – to which the individual is compared and then included in the category with which he has most features in common. In other words, we would adjudicate his specificity or non-specificity, his similarity or difference according to one feature or another. And little wonder that such an analytic operation should have been envisaged, since only laboratory examples have been considered to date, and systems of classification which bear no relation to the substratum of social representations, for example, the collective view of what is thus classified. It is because of this tendency that I feel I should say something more about my own observations concerning social representations which have revealed that when we classify we always compare to a prototype, always ask ourselves whether the object compared is normal or abnormal in relation to it and try to answer the question: 'Is it as it should be or not?'

This discrepancy has practical consequences. For, if my observations are correct, then all our 'prejudices', whether national, racial, generational or what have you, can only be overcome by altering our social representations of culture, of 'human nature' and so on. If, on the other hand, it is the prevailing view that is correct, then all we need do is persuade antagonistic groups or individuals that they have a great many features in common, that they are, in fact, amazingly similar, and we will have done away with hard and fast classifications and mutual stereotypes. However, the very limited success of this project to date might suggest that the other is worth trying.

On the other hand, it is impossible to classify without, at the same time, naming. Yet these are two distinct activities. In our society, to name, to bestow a name on something or someone, has a very special, almost a solemn significance. In so naming something, we extricate it from a disturbing anonymity to endow it with a genealogy and to include it in a complex of specific words, to locate it, in fact, in the *identity matrix* of our culture.

Indeed, that which is anonymous, unnameable, cannot become a communicable image or be readily linked to other images. It is relegated to the world of confusion, uncertainty and inarticulateness, even when we are able to classify it approximately as normal or abnormal. Claudine Herzlich (1973), in a study on the social representations of health and illness, has admirably analysed this elusive aspect of symptoms, the often abortive attempts we all make to contain them in speech, and the way they evade our grasp as a fish slips through the wide meshes of a net. To name, to say that something is this or that – if need be, to invent words for the purpose – enables us to fabricate a mesh that will be fine enough to keep the fish from escaping, and thus enables us to represent this thing. The result is always somewhat arbitrary but, in so far as a consensus is established, the word's association with the thing becomes customary and necessary.

By and large, my observations prove that to name a person or thing is to precipitate it (as a chemical solution is precipitated) and that the consequences of this are threefold: (*a*) once named, the person or thing can be described and acquires certain characteristics, tendencies, etc.; (*b*) he or it becomes distinct from other persons or things through these characteristics and tendencies; and (*c*) he or it becomes the object of a convention between those who adopt and share the same convention. Claudine Herzlich's (1973) study reveals that the conventional label 'fatigue' relates a complex of vague symptoms to certain social and individual patterns, distinguishes them from those of illness and health and makes them seem acceptable, almost justifiable to our society. It is thus permissible to talk about our fatigue, to say we are suffering from fatigue and to claim certain rights which normally, in a society based on labour and welfare, would be forbidden. In other words, something which was formerly denied is now admitted.

I was able to make a very similar observation myself. I noticed that psychoanalytical terms such as 'neurosis' or 'complex' give consistency, and even reality, to states of tension, maladjustment, indeed of alienation which used to be seen as halfway between 'madness' and 'sanity' but were never taken very seriously. It was obvious that once they had been given a name they ceased to be disturbing. Psychoanalysis is also responsible for the proliferation of terms derived from a single model, so that we see a psychic symptom labelled 'timidity complex', 'sibling complex', 'power complex', 'Sardanapalus complex', which, of course, are not psychoanalytic terms but words coined to imitate them. Simultaneously the psychoanalytic vocabulary becomes anchored in the vocabulary of everyday life and thus becomes socialized. All that had been disturbing and enigmatic about these theories is related to symptoms or to persons who had seemed disturbed and disturbing, to constitute stable images in an organized context that has nothing in the least disturbing about it.

In the end, that which was unidentified is given a social identity – the scientific concept becomes part of common speech, and individuals or symptoms are no more than familiar technical and scientific terms. A meaning is given to that which previously had none in the consensual world. We might almost say that this duplication and proliferation of names corresponds to a *nominalistic* tendency, a need to identify beings and things by fitting them into a prevalent social representation. We noted earlier the multiplication of 'complexes' that accompanied the popularization of psychoanalysis and took the place of current expressions, such as 'shyness', 'authority', 'brothers', etc. By this means, those who speak and those who are spoken of are forced into an identity matrix they have not chosen and over which they have no control.

We might even go so far as to suggest that this is how all normal and deviant manifestations of social existence are labelled – individuals and groups are stigmatized, either psychologically or politically. For instance, when we call a person whose opinions do not conform to the current ideology an 'enemy of the people', this term, which according to that ideology evokes a definite image, excludes that person from the society to which he belongs. Thus it is obvious that naming is not a purely intellectual operation aiming at clarity or logical coherence. It is an operation related to a social attitude. Such an observation is dictated by common sense and should never be ignored, for it is valid in every case and not simply in the exceptional cases I have given as examples.

In short, classifying and naming are two aspects of this anchoring of representations. Categories and names partake of what the art historian Ernst Gombrich (1972) has called a 'society of concepts', and not simply in their content but also in their relations. I do not in any way deny the fact that they are naturally logical and tend towards stability and consistency, as Heider and others maintain, nor that such order is probably compelling. However, I can't help observing that these relations of stability and consistency are highly rarefied and rigorous abstractions that partake neither directly nor operationally in the creation of representations. On the other hand, different relations can be seen at work which are induced by social patterns and produce a kaleidoscope of images or emotions. Friendship seems to play an important part in Fritz Heider's (1958) psychology when he analyses personal relationships. Doubtless he calls it by the general name of stability, but it must be obvious to all that, among every conceivable example of stability, he has chosen this one as the prototype for all the others.

The family is another very popular image for relationships in general. Thus intellectuals or workers are described as brothers; complexes as fathers; and neurotics as sons ('the complex is the neurotic's father' as someone recently stated in an interview); and so on and so forth. Conflict stands for another type of relationship and is always implicit in any description of contrasting pairs: what the term 'normal' implies and what it excludes; the conscious and the unconscious part of an individual; what we call health and what we call illness. Hostility is also in the background whenever we compare races, nations or classes. And relations of strength and weakness frequently define preferences where hierarchy enters the various categories of names. I quote at random, but it would be worthwhile to explore in detail the ways in which the logic of language expresses the relation between the elements of a system of classification and the process of naming. More suggestive patterns might emerge than those with which we are acquainted at the moment. Our present patterns are, anyhow, too artificial from a psychological point of view, and socially devoid of meaning. The fact is that if we visualize stability as a kind of friendship or conflict as outright hostility, it is simply because they are more accessible and concrete in such forms and can be correlated with our thoughts and emotions; we are thus better able to express them or to include them in a description which will be readily intelligible to anyone. This is the result of routinization – a process which enables us to pronounce, read or write down a familiar word or notion in the place of, or in preference to, a less familiar word or notion.

At this point, the theory of representations entails two consequences. *First of all*, it excludes the idea of thought or perception which is without anchor. This excludes the idea of so-called biases in thought or perception. Every system of classifications and of the relations between systems presupposes a specific position, a point of view based on consensus. It's impossible to have a general, unbiased system any more than there exists a primary meaning for any particular object. The biases that are often described do not express, as they say, a social or cognitive deficit or limitation on the part of the individual but a normal difference in perspective between heterogeneous individuals or groups within a society. And they cannot be expressed for the simple reason that their opposite – the absence of a deficit or of a social or cognitive limitation – does not make sense. This is equivalent to admitting the impossibility of a social psychology from the point of view of Sirius, as those of yesteryear wanted it to be who pretended, at one and the same time, both to be in society and to observe it from the outside; who affirmed that *one* of the positions within society was normal and all the others deviations from it. This is a totally untenable position.

Secondly, systems of classification and naming are not simply means of grading and labelling persons or objects considered as discrete entities. Their main object is to facilitate the interpretation of characteristics, the understanding of intentions and motives behind people's actions, in fact, to form opinions. Indeed, this is a major preoccupation and groups, as well as individuals, are prone, under certain conditions, such as over-excitement or bewilderment, to what we might call interpretation mania. For we must not forget that to interpret an unfamiliar idea or being always requires categories, names, references in order that it may be integrated into Gombrich's 'society of concepts'. We fabricate them for this purpose as meanings emerge, make them tangible and visible and similar to the ideas and beings we have already integrated and with which we are familiar. In this way, pre-existing representations are somewhat modified and those things about to be represented are modified even more, so that they acquire a new existence.

Objectifying.   The English physicist James Clerk Maxwell once said that what seemed abstract to one generation becomes concrete to the next. Amazing, incredible theories which nobody takes seriously turn out to be normal, credible and brimful of reality at a later date. How such an improbable fact as a physical body producing a reaction at a distance, in a place where it is not actually present, could become, in less than a century, a common, unquestionable fact, is at least as mysterious as its discovery – and of far greater practical consequence. We might indeed improve on Maxwell's statement by adding that what is unfamiliar and unperceived in one generation becomes familiar and obvious in the next. This is not simply due to the passage of time or to habit, though both are probably necessary. This domestication is the result of objectification, which is a far more active process than anchoring, and one which we will now discuss.

Objectification saturates the idea of unfamiliarity with reality, turns it into the very essence of reality. Perceived at first in a purely intellectual, remote universe, it then appears before our eyes, physical and accessible. In this respect we are justified in asserting, with Kurt Lewin, that every representation realizes – in the proper sense of the term – a different level of reality. These levels are created and maintained by a collectivity and vanish with it, having no reality of their own; for instance, the supernatural level, which was once all-pervasive and is now practically non-existent. Between total illusion and total reality there is an infinity of gradations which must be taken into account, for we created them, but illusion and reality are achieved in exactly the same way. The materialization of an abstraction is one of the most mysterious features of thought and speech. Political and intellectual authorities, of every kind, exploit it to subdue the masses. In other words, such authority is based on the art of turning a representation into the reality of a representation, the word for a thing into a thing for the word.

To begin with, to objectify is to discover the iconic quality of an imprecise idea or being, to reproduce a concept in an image. To compare is already to picture, to fill what is naturally empty with substance. We have only to compare God to a father and what was invisible instantly becomes visible in our minds as a person to whom we can respond as such. A tremendous stock of words is in circulation in every society referring to specific objects, and we are under constant compulsion to provide their equivalent concrete meanings. Since we assume that words do not speak about 'nothing', we are compelled to link them to something, to find non-verbal equivalents for them. Just as most rumours are believed by virtue of the saying: 'There is no smoke without fire,' so a collection of images is created by virtue of the saying: 'Nobody speaks about nothing.'

Yet not all the words that constitute this stock can be linked to images, either because there are not enough images readily available, or because those they call to mind are taboo. Those which, owing to their ability to be represented, have been selected, merge with, or rather are integrated into, what I have called a pattern of *figurative nucleus*, a complex of images that visibly reproduces a complex of ideas. For example, the popular pattern of the psyche inherited from psychoanalysis is divided in two, the unconscious and the conscious – reminiscent of more common dualities such as involuntary–voluntary, soul–mind, inner–outer – located in space one above the other. It so happens that the higher brings pressure to bear on the lower and this 'repression' is what gives rise to the complexes. It is also noteworthy that the terms represented are those that are best known and most commonly employed. Yet the absence of sexuality or *libido* is perhaps surprising since it plays such a significant part in the theory and is liable to be heavily charged with imagery. However, being the object of a taboo, it remains abstract. I have indeed been able to establish that not all psychoanalytic concepts undergo a similar transformation, not all are equally favoured. Thus it seems that a society makes a selection of those to which it concedes figurative powers, according to its beliefs and to the pre-existing stock of images. Thus I noted some time ago: 'Though a paradigm is accepted because it has a strong framework, its acceptance is also due to its affinity with more current paradigms. The concreteness of the elements of this "psychic system" derives from their ability to translate ordinary situations' (Moscovici, [1961]/1976).

This does not, by any means, imply that changes do not occur subsequently. But such changes take place during the transmission of familiar outlines that gradually respond to the recent intake, just as a river bed is gradually modified by the waters flowing between its banks.

Once a society has adopted such a paradigm or figurative nucleus it finds it easier to talk about whatever the paradigm stands for, and because of this facility the words referring to it are used more often. Then formulae and clichés emerge that sum it up and join together images that were formerly distinct. It is not simply talked about but exploited in various social situations as a means of understanding others and oneself, of choosing and deciding. I showed (Moscovici, [1961]/1976) how psychoanalysis, once popularized, became a key that opened all the locks of private, public and political existence. Its figurative paradigm was detached from its original milieu by continuous use and acquired a sort of independence, just as a well-worn saying is gradually detached from the person who first said it and becomes an unmediated fact. Thus, when the image linked to a word or idea becomes detached and is let loose in a society it is accepted as a reality, a conventional one, of course, but none the less a reality.

Although we all know that a 'complex' is a notion whose objective equivalent is highly vague, we still think and behave as though it were something that really existed when we assess a person and relate to him. It doesn't simply symbolize his personality or his way of behaving, but actually represents him, *is* his 'complexed' personality and way of behaving. Indeed, it can be said unequivocally that in all cases, once the transfiguration has been achieved, then collective idolatry is a possibility. All images can be endowed with reality and efficiency to start with and end up by being worshipped. In our day, the psychoanalyst's couch or 'progress' are ready examples of this fact. This occurs to the extent that the distinction between image and reality is obliterated. The image of the concept ceases to be a sign and becomes a replica of reality, a simulacrum in the true sense of the word. Then the notion or entity from which it had proceeded loses its abstract, arbitrary character and acquires an almost physical, independent existence. It has the authority of a natural phenomenon for those who use it. Such is precisely the complex, to which as much reality is generally conceded as to an atom or a wave of the hand. This is an example of the word creating the means.

The second stage, in which the image is wholly assimilated and what is *perceived* replaces what is *conceived*, is the logical outcome of this state of affairs. If images exist, if they are essential for social communication and understanding, this is because they are not (and cannot remain) without reality any more than there can be smoke without a fire. Since they *must* have a reality we *find* one for them, no matter what. Thus, by a sort of logical imperative, images become elements of reality rather than elements of thought. The gap between the representation and what it represents is bridged, the peculiarities of the replica of the concept become peculiarities of the phenomena or of the environment to which they refer, become the actual referent of the concept. Thus everyone, nowadays, can perceive and distinguish a person's 'repressions' or his 'complexes' as if they were his physical features.

Our environment is largely composed of such images, and we are forever adding to it and modifying it by discarding some images and adopting others. Mead writes: 'We have just seen that imagery which goes into the structure of objects, and which represents the adjustment of the organism to environments which are not there, may serve toward the reconstruction of the objective field' (Mead, 1934, p. 374).

When this takes place, images no longer occupy that peculiar position somewhere between words which are supposed to have a significance and real objects to which only we can give a significance, but they exist as objects, they are what is signified.

Culture – though not science – incites us nowadays to make reality out of generally significant ideas. There are obvious reasons for this, of which the most obvious, from society's point of view, is to appropriate and make common property of what originally pertained to a specific field or sphere. Philosophers have spent a lot of time trying to understand the process of transfer from one sphere to another. Without representations, without the metamorphosis of words into objects, there can clearly be no transfer at all. What I said about psychoanalysis is confirmed by painstaking research:

> By objectifying the scientific content of psychoanalysis society no longer confronts psychoanalysis or the psychoanalyst, but a set of phenomena which it is free to treat as it pleases. The evidence of particular men has become the evidence of our own senses, an unknown universe is now familiar territory. The individual, in direct contact with this universe without the mediation of experts or their science, has progressed from a secondary to a primary relationship with the object, and this indirect assumption of power is a culturally fruitful action.   (Moscovici, [1961]/1976, p. 109)

Indeed, we thus find incorporated, in an anonymous manner, in our speech, our senses and our environment elements that are preserved and established as ordinary everyday material, the origins of which are obscure or forgotten. Their reality is a blank in our memory – but isn't all reality one? Don't we objectify precisely so as to forget that a creation, a material construct is the product of our own activity, that something is also someone? As I said: 'In the last analysis, psychoanalysis could be dead and buried, yet still, like Aristotle's physics, it would permeate our view of the world and its jargon would be used to describe psychological behaviour' (Moscovici, [1961]/1976, p. 109).

The model for all learning in our society is the science of mathematical physics or the science of quantifiable, measurable objects. In so far as the scientific content, even of a science of man or of life, presupposes this sort of reality, all the beings to which it refers are conceived according to such a model. Since science refers to physical organs and since psychoanalysis is a science, then the unconscious, for example, or a complex will be seen as organs of the psychic system. Therefore a complex can be amputated, grafted and perceived. As you can see, the living is assimilated to the inert, the subjective to the objective and the psychological to the biological. Every culture has its basic device for turning its representations into reality. Sometimes people and sometimes animals have served this purpose. Since the beginning of the mechanical age, objects have taken over and we are obsessed with a *reverse animism* that peoples the world with machines instead of living creatures. Thus we could say that where complexes, atoms or genes are concerned we don't so much imagine *an* object as create an image with *the help of the* object in general, with which we identify them.

However, no culture has a single, exclusive device. Because ours is partial to objects, it encourages us to objectify everything we come across. We personify indiscriminately feelings, social classes, the great powers, and when we write we personify culture, since it is language itself that enables us to do so. Gombrich writes:

> It so happens that Indo-European languages tend to this particular figure which we call personification, because so many of them endowed nouns with a gender which makes them indistinguishable from names for living species. Abstract nouns in Greek, in Latin, almost regularly take on the feminine gender and so the way is open for the world of ideas being peopled by personified abstractions such as *Victoria, Fortuna* or *Justitia.* (Gombrich, 1972, p. 125)

But chance alone cannot account for the extensive use we make of the peculiarities of grammar, nor can it explain their efficiency.

This can best be done by trying to objectify grammar itself, which is achieved very simply by putting substantives – which, by definition, refer to substances, to beings – in the place of adjectives, adverbs, etc. Thus attributes or relationships are turned into things. In fact, there is no such thing as *a* repression, since it refers to an action (to repress a memory), or *an* unconscious, since this is an attribute *of* something else (the thoughts and desires of a person). When we say that someone is dominated by his unconscious or suffers from repression as if he had a goitre or a sore throat, what we really mean is that he is not conscious of what he does and thinks; likewise when we say that he suffers from anxiety we mean that he is anxious or behaves anxiously.

However, once we have chosen to use a noun to describe a person's state, to say that he is dominated by his unconscious or suffers from anxiety rather than that his behaviour betrays a given particularity (that he is unconscious or anxious), we add to the number of beings by adding to the number of nouns. Thus a tendency to turn verbs into nouns, or a partiality for these among grammatical categories of words with similar meanings, is a sure sign that grammar is being objectified, that words don't merely represent things but create them and invest them with their own properties. In these circumstances language is like a mirror that can separate appearance from reality, separate what is seen from what is and represent it immediately in the form of an object's or a person's visible appearance, while enabling us to assess this object or person as if they were not distinct from reality, as if they were real – and particularly one's own self, to which one has no other way of relating. Thus the nouns we invent and create to give an abstract form to complex substances or phenomena *become* the substance or the phenomenon, and that is what we never cease to do. Every self-evident truth, every taxonomy, every reference in the world represents a crystallized set of significances and tacitly acknowledged names; their tacitness is precisely what ensures their chief representative function: to express first the image and then the concept as reality.

To have a clearer understanding of the consequences of our tendency to objectify, we might consider such dissimilar social phenomena as hero-worship, the personification of nations, races and classes, etc. Each case involves a social representation that transmutes words into flesh, ideas into natural powers, nations or human languages into a language of things. Recent events have shown that the outcome of such transmutations can be sinister and disheartening in the extreme for those of us who would like all the world's tragedies to have a happy ending and to see right prevail. The defeat of rationality and the fact that history is so sparing with its happy endings should not deter us from examining these significant phenomena and especially from the conviction that the principles involved are simple and not dissimilar to those we have considered above.

Thus our representations make the unfamiliar familiar, which is another way of saying that they depend on memory. Memory's density prevents them from undergoing sudden modifications on the one hand and, on the other, allows them a certain amount of independence from present events – just as accumulated wealth protects us from a hand-to-mouth existence. It is from this padding of common experiences and memories that we draw the images, language and gestures required to overcome the unfamiliar with its attendant anxieties. Experiences and memories are neither inert nor dead. They are dynamic and immortal. Anchoring and objectifying are therefore ways of handling memory. The former keeps it in motion; since it is inner-directed it is always putting in and taking out objects, persons and events which it classifies according to type and labels with a name. The second, being more or less other-directed, draws concepts and images from it to mingle and reproduce them with the outside world, to make things-to-be-known out of what is already known. It would be appropriate to quote Mead again here: 'The peculiar intelligence of the human form lies in this elaborate control gained through the past' (Mead, 1934, p. 116).

V   RIGHT-WING CAUSALITIES AND LEFT-WING CAUSALITIES

(1)   Attributions and social representations

Farr (1977) has rightly pointed out that there is a relation between the way we picture a thing to ourselves and the way we describe it to others. Let us therefore accept this relation while noting that the problem of causality has always been crucial for those concerned with social representations, such as Fauconnet, Piaget and, more modestly, myself. However, we consider the problem from a very different angle to that of our American colleagues –

American being used here in a purely geographical sense. The transatlantic social psychologist bases his enquiries on the theory of attribution and is mainly concerned with how we attribute causes to the people and things that surround us. It would hardly be an overstatement to say that his theories are based on a single principle – man thinks like a statistician – and that there is only one rule to his method – to establish the coherence of the information we receive from the environment. In these circumstances a lot of ideas and images – indeed, all those society provides – either do not tally with statistical thinking and so are seen as negligible since they cannot be fitted in, or else *blur* our perception of reality such as it is. They are, therefore, purely and simply ignored.

The theory of social representations, on the other hand, takes as its point of departure the diversity of individuals, attitudes and phenomena, in all their strangeness and unpredictability. Its aim is to discover how individuals and groups can construct a stable, predictable world out of such diversity. The scientist who studies the universe is convinced that there exists a hidden order under the apparent chaos, and the child who never stops asking 'Why?' is no less sure of it. This is a fact: if, then, we seek an answer to the eternal 'Why?' it isn't on the strength of the information we have received, but because we are convinced that every being and every object in the world is other than it seems. The ultimate aim of science is to eliminate this 'Why?', whereas social representations can hardly do without it.

Representations are based on the saying: 'No smoke without fire.' When we hear or see something we instinctively assume it is not fortuitious but that it must have a cause and an effect. When we see smoke we know that a fire has been lit somewhere and, to find out where the smoke comes from, we go in search of this fire. Thus the saying is not a mere image but expresses a thought process, an imperative – the need to decode all the signs that occur in our social environment and which we cannot leave alone so long as their significance, the 'hidden fire', has not been located. Thus, social thought makes extensive use of suspicions which set us on the track of causality.

I could give any number of examples. The most notable are those trials where the accused are presented as culprits, wrongdoers and criminals, and the proceedings only serve to confirm a pre-established verdict. The German or Russian citizens who saw their Jewish or subversive compatriots sent to concentration camps or shipped to the Gulag islands certainly didn't think they were innocent. They had to be guilty since they were imprisoned. Good reasons for putting them in prison were attributed (the word is apt) to them because it was impossible to believe that they were accused, ill-treated and tortured for no reason at all.

Such examples of manipulation, not to say of the distortion of causality, prove that the smokescreen is not always intended cunningly to conceal repressive measures, but may indeed even draw our attention to them so that onlookers will be led to assume that there were undoubtedly very good reasons for lighting the fire. Tyrants are usually masters of psychology and know that people will automatically proceed from the punishment to the criminal and the crime so as to make these strange and horrible occurrences tally with their idea of trial and justice.

(2) Bi-causal and mono-causal explanations

The theory of social representations makes the assumption, based on innumerable observations, that we generally act on *two* different sets of motivations, in other words, that thought is *bi-causal* rather than *mono-causal* and establishes simultaneously a relation of cause to effect and a relation of ends to means. This is where the theory differs from attribution theory and where, in this duality, social representations differ from science.

When a phenomenon recurs we establish a correlation between ourselves and it and then find some meaningful explanation that suggests the existence of a rule or law yet to be discovered. In this case the transition from correlation to explanation is not stimulated by our perception of the correlation or by the recurrence of the events, but by our awareness of a discrepancy between this correlation and some others, between the phenomenon we perceived and the one we had anticipated, between a specific case and a prototype, between the exception and the rule; in fact, to use the terms I have previously employed, between the familiar and the unfamiliar. This is indeed the decisive factor. To quote MacIver: 'It is the exception, the deviation, the interference, the abnormality that stimulates our curiosity and seems to call for an explanation. And we often attribute to some one "cause" all the happening that characterizes the new or unanticipated or altered situation' (MacIver, 1942, p. 172).

We see a person or a thing that does not tally with our representations, does not coincide with its prototype (a woman prime minister), or a void, an absence (a city with no hoardings), or we find a Muslim in a Catholic community, a physician without physic (a psychoanalyst), etc. In each case we feel challenged to find an explanation. On the one hand, there is a lack of recognition, on the other a lack of cognition; on the one hand, a lack of identity, on the other, a statement of non-identity. In these circumstances we are always obliged to stop and think and finally to admit that we don't understand why this person behaves as he does or that object has such-and-such an effect.

How can we answer this challenge? This *primary causality* to which we spontaneously turn depends on finalities. Since most of our relationships are with live human beings, we are confronted with the intentions and purposes of others which, for practical reasons, we cannot understand. Even when our car breaks down or the apparatus we are using in the laboratory doesn't work, we can't help thinking that the car 'refuses' to go, the hostile apparatus 'refuses to collaborate' and so prevents us from pursuing our experiment. Everything people do or say, every natural disturbance, seems to have a hidden significance, intention or purpose which we try to discover. Likewise, we tend to interpret intellectual polemics or controversies as personal conflicts and to wonder what reason there can be for the protagonists' animosity, what private motives are at the bottom of such antagonisms.

Instead of saying: 'For what reason does he behave like that?' we say: 'For what purpose does he behave like that?' and the quest for a cause becomes a quest for motives and intentions. In other words we interpret, look for hidden animosities and obscure motives such as hatred, envy or ambition. We are always convinced that people don't act by chance, that everything they do corresponds to a plan, whence the general tendency to personify motives and incentives, to represent a cause imagistically as when we say of a political dissident that he is a 'traitor', an 'enemy of the people', or when we use the term 'Oedipus Complex' to describe a certain type of behaviour, etc. The notion becomes an almost physical 'agent', a performer who, in certain circumstances, carries out a precise intention. And this notion comes to embody the thing itself rather than being seen as a representation of our particular perception of this thing.

Secondary causality, which is not spontaneous, is an efficient causality. It is dictated by our education, our language, our scientific view of the world, all of which tend to make us divest the actions, conversations and phenomena of the outside world of their share of intention and responsibility and to see them only as experimental data to be studied impartially. Therefore we tend to gather all the information we can about them so as to classify them in a given category and thus identify their cause, explain them. Such is the historian's attitude, the psychologist's or indeed any scientist's. For instance, we infer from a person's behaviour that he is middle-class or lower-class, schizophrenic or paranoid; thus we explain his present behaviour. Proceeding from effect to cause, on the basis of information we have gleaned, we relate one to the other, ascribe effects to specific causes. Heider had already shown, long ago, that a person's behaviour derives from two different sets of motivations, inner and outer, and that the latter derive not from the person but from his environment, his social status and from the compulsions other people exert over him. Thus the person who votes for a political party does so by personal conviction; but in some countries such a vote may be compulsory and to vote for a different party or to abstain from voting entails expulsion or imprisonment.

So, to sum up the way in which the process of attribution operates, we might say that, first and foremost, there exists a prototype which serves as a measuring-rod for events or behaviours that are considered as effects. If the effect conforms to the prototype it is assumed that it has an exterior cause; if not, if the effect does not conform, the cause is assumed to be specific and inner. A man wearing a beret and carrying a long loaf of French bread under his arm is a Frenchman, since such is our representation of the type. But if the person turns out to be an American he no longer conforms to this model and we assume that his behaviour is singular or even aberrant since it is not true to type.

Obviously all this is grossly oversimplified; what actually takes place in the mind is not so easily inferred. But I wanted to make the following fact clear: in social representations the two causalities act in concert, they merge to produce specific characteristics and we constantly switch from one to the other. On the one hand, by seeking a subjective order behind apparently objective phenomena, the result will be an inference; on the other, by seeking an objective order behind apparently subjective phenomena, the result will be an attribution. On the one hand, we reconstruct hidden intentions to account for a person's behaviour: this is a first-person causality. On the other hand, we seek invisible factors to account for visible behaviour: this is a third-person causality.

The contrast between these two kinds of causality should be stressed, since the circumstances of social existence are often manipulated for the purpose of showing up either the one or the other, for example, to pass off an end as an effect. Thus, when the Nazis set fire to the Reichstag they did so to make their persecutions look, not like the execution of a plan, but like a result whose cause was the fire supposedly lit by their opponents and whose smoke concealed a very different 'fire'. Nor is it uncommon for a person to provoke, on a minor scale, a fire of this kind to obtain promotion, for instance, or even a divorce. Moreover, these examples enable us to see that attributions always involve a relation between ends, or intentions, and means. As MacIver says: 'The why of the motivation lies, often obscurely, behind the why of objective' (MacIver, 1942, p. 17).

The biological and social sciences try to reverse the psychological order of the two questions and to present motivations as causes. When they examine a phenomenon they ask to what purpose does it correspond? What function does it fulfil? Once the purpose or function has been established they present the former as an impersonal cause and the latter as the mechanism it triggers off. Such was Darwin's procedure when he discovered natural selection. The term *causalization* would be apt in this case, suggesting, as it does, that ends are disguised as causes, means as effects and intentions as results. Relations between individuals, as well as those between political parties or groups of any kind, make extensive use of this procedure whenever the behaviour of other people has to be interpreted, whenever, in fact, the question 'Why?' has to be answered. And the answer given often suffices to set minds at rest, to preserve a representation, or to convince an audience that was only too ready to be convinced.

(3) Social causality

To sum up, a theory of social causality is a theory of the attributions and inferences individuals make and also of the transition from the one to the other. Clearly, such a transition is inseparable from a scientific theory that deals with this phenomenon. However, psychologists are in the habit of studying either attributions or inferences and of ignoring the transition between them. Thus they ascribe causes to an environment or to an individual each seen independently, which is just as ridiculous as studying the relation of an effect to its cause without first formulating a theory or defining a paradigm to account for this relation. This very peculiar attitude has its limitations, as I hope to prove with the following example.

Attribution theory gives a number of reasons to account for why an individual attributes certain behaviours to another person and other behaviours to the environment – to the fact that Peter is good at games or else that he lives in the suburbs, for example. But, as we noted earlier, these are based on a single principle: man is a statistician and his brain works like an infallible computer.[2] Psychoanalysis, on the other hand, would see such behaviours as the simple rationalization of hostile or kindred feelings since, for the psychoanalyst, all our assessments are based on emotions. This trivial example clearly illustrates the fact that any explanation depends primarily on the idea we have of reality. It is this idea that governs our perceptions and the inferences we draw from them. And it governs our social relations as well. Thus we can assert that when we answer the question 'Why?' we start from a social representation or from the general context in which we have been led to give this specific answer.

Here is a concrete example: unemployment at the moment is widespread and each of us has at least one unemployed man or woman among his personal acquaintances. Why doesn't this man or woman have a job? The answer to this question will vary according to the speaker. For some, the unemployed just don't bother to find a job, are too choosy or, at best, unlucky. For others they are the victims of an economic recession, of unjustified redundancies or, more commonly, of the inherent injustice of a capitalist economy. Thus the former ascribe the cause of unemployment to the individual, to his social attitude, while the latter ascribe it to the economic and political situation, to his social status, to an environment that makes such a situation inevitable. The two explanations are utterly opposed to each other and obviously stem from distinct social representations. The first representation stresses the individual's responsibility and personal energy – social problems can only be solved by each individual. The second representation stresses social responsibility, denounces social injustice and advocates collective solutions for individual problems. Shaver has noted such reactions even in the United States:

> Personal attributions about the reason for welfare lead to speeches about 'welfare chiselers', appeals for a return to simpler days or the Protestant ethic, and laws designed to make needed financial assistance more difficult to obtain. Situational attributions, on the other hand, are likely to suggest that expanded government-supported employment, better job training, and increased educational opportunity for all will provide more lasting reductions in public assistance. (Shaver, 1975, p. 133)

However, I do not entirely agree with my American colleague. I myself would reverse the order of the factors involved, stressing the primacy of representations and saying that it is these, in each case, that dictate the attribution either to the individual or to the society. By so doing, I obviously do not deny the idea of rationality and a correct manipulation of received information, but simply maintain that what is taken into account, the experiences we have, that is, the causes we select, are dictated, in each case, by a system of social representations.

Thus I come to the following proposition: in the societies we inhabit today, personal causality is a right-wing explanation and situational causality is a left-wing explanation. Social psychology can't ignore the fact that the world is structured and organized according to such a division and that there is a permanent one. Indeed, each of us is necessarily compelled to adopt one of these two kinds of causality together with the view of the other which it entails. The consequences which derive from such a proposition could not be more precise: the motives for our actions are dictated by, and related to, social reality, a reality whose contrasting categories divide human thought as neatly as do dualities like high and low, male and female, etc. It had seemed that motivation could be ascribed to a simple thought-process and now it turns out to be determined by environmental influences, social status, one person's relation to other people, his preconceived opinions, all of which play their part. This is highly significant and, once it has been accepted, it precludes the existence of supposedly neutral categories of personal and situational attribution and replaces them by definitely right- or left-wing categories of motivation. Even if the substitution does not hold in all cases it is generally observable.

Experiments carried out by certain psychologists (Hewstone and Jaspars, 1982) confirm the notion of such a substitution. Here, for instance, is a typical example: the American psychologist M. J. Lerner has suggested that we explain someone's behaviour on the premise that 'People only get what they deserve.' This has come to be known as 'the just world hypothesis'. He sees this as an almost innate way of thinking. The Canadian psychologists

Guimond and Simard tried to substantiate this theory, and were not surprised to find that such an attitude was mainly that of people belonging to a majority or a ruling class. On the other hand, there was no trace of it among those who belonged to minorities or underprivileged classes. To be precise, they were able to establish that English-speaking Canadians tended to see the French Canadians as responsible for their status and provided individualistic explanations. French Canadians, however, held the English Canadians responsible and their explanations involved the structure of society itself.

If a laboratory experiment can be taken as an example of what occurs in society we might improve somewhat on these findings. Dominating and dominated classes do not have a similar representation of the world they share but see it with different eyes, judge it according to specific criteria, and each does so according to their own categories. For the former, it is the individual who is responsible for all that befalls him and especially his failures. For the latter, failures are always due to the circumstances which society creates for the individual. It is in this precise sense that the expression right-wing/left-wing causality (an expression which is as objective and scientific as the dualities high/low, person/environment, etc.) can be applied to concrete cases.

(4) Conclusions

By restricting itself to an individual and an inductive frame of reference, attribution theory has proved less fruitful than it might otherwise have been. This state of affairs could be remedied by: (*a*) switching from the individual to the collective sphere; (*b*) abandoning the idea of man as statistician and of a mechanistic relation between man and the world; (*c*) reinstating social representations as necessary mediators.

Suggestions have already been made to improve the theory (Hewstone and Jaspars, 1982). However, we must bear in mind that causality does not exist on its own, but only within a representation that vindicates it. Nor should we forget that when we consider two causalities we have also to consider the relation between them. In other words, we should always seek those super-causes that have a dual action, both as agents and as efficient causes, which constitute this relation. Each of our beliefs, thought-processes and conceptions of the world has a cause of this kind to which we have recourse as a last resort. It is in this we put our trust and it is this we invoke in all circumstances. What I have in mind are words such as 'God', 'Progress', 'Justice', 'History': they refer to an entity or a being gifted with social status and acting both as cause and as end. They are notable in that they account for all that happens in every possible sphere of reality. There is no difficulty in identifying them, but I think we would be hard put to explain the part they play and their extraordinary power.

I am convinced that, sooner or later, we shall achieve a clearer idea of causality. And I shall consider our present enquiries concluded, even if their final aim is not achieved, when psychologists have at their command a common language which will enable them to establish a concordance between the forms of thought of individuals and the social content of those thoughts.

VI   A SURVEY OF EARLY RESEARCH ON SOCIAL REPRESENTATIONS

(1)   Some common methodological themes and links with other social sciences

The body of research on which these theories are based and from which they evolved is somewhat restricted. But it is all we have to date [i.e. in 1984]. Whatever the specific objective of these enquiries has been they have, however, always shared the following four methodological principles:

(*a*)   *To obtain material from samples of conversations normally exchanged in a society.* Some of these exchanges deal with important topics, whilst others concern topics that may be foreign to the group – some action, event or personality, about which or whom they wonder 'What's it all about?', 'Why did it happen?', 'Why did he do it?', 'What was the purpose of that action?' – but all tending towards mutual agreement. Tarde (1910) was the first to maintain that opinions and representations are created in the course of conversations as elementary ways of relating and of communicating. He demonstrated how they emerge in specially reserved places (such as salons, cafés, etc.); how they are determined by the physical and psychological dimensions of those encounters between individuals (Moscovici, 1967) and how they change with the passage of time. He even elaborated a plan for a social science of the future which would be a comparative study of conversations. Indeed, the interactions that naturally occur in the course of conversations enable individuals and groups to become more familiar with incongruous objects or ideas and thus to master them (Moscovici, [1961]/1976). Such infra-communications and thought, based on rumour, constitute a kind of intermediate layer between private and public life and facilitate the passage from the one to the other. In other words, conversation is at the hub of our consensual universes because it shapes and animates social representations and thus gives them a life of their own.

(*b*)   *To consider social representations as a means of re-creating reality.* Through communication individuals and groups give a physical reality to ideas and images, to systems of classification and naming. The phenomena and people with whom we deal in everyday life are not usually raw data but are the products or embodiments of a collectivity, an institution, etc. All reality is the reality of someone or is reality *for* someone else, even if it be that of the laboratories where we carry out our experiments. It would not be logical to think of them otherwise by taking them out of context. Most of the problems we face in the course of our social and intellectual pursuits are not derived from the difficulty of representing things or people, but from the fact that they are representations, that is, substitutes for other things or other people. Thus before embarking on a specific study we must enquire into the origins of the object, and consider it as a work of art and not as raw material. Though, to be precise, it is something re-made, re-constructed rather than something constructed anew since, on the one hand, the only reality available is that which has been structured by past generations or by another group, and on the other, we re-produce it in the outside world and thus cannot avoid distorting our inner images and models. What we create, in fact, is a referent, an entity to which we refer which is distinct from any other and corresponds to our representation of it. And its recurrence – either during a conversation or in the environment (for instance a 'complex', a symptom, etc.) – ensures its autonomy, rather as a saying becomes independent from the person who first said it when it has been repeated often enough. The most remarkable result of this re-construction of abstractions as realities is that they become detached from the group's subjectivity, from the vicissitudes of its interactions and therefore from time, and thus they acquire permanence and stability. Isolated from the flow of communications that produced them, they become as independent from these as a building is independent from the architect's plan or the scaffolding employed in its construction.

It might be opportune to point out a few distinctions that should be taken into account. Some representations concern facts and others ideas. The first displace their object from an abstract to a concrete cognitive level; the second, through a change of perspective, either compose or decompose their object – they may, for instance, present billiard balls as an illustration of the atom, or consider a person psychoanalytically as divided into a conscious and an unconscious. Yet both create pre-established and immediate frames of reference for opinions and perceptions within which objective reconstructions of both persons and situations occur automatically and which underlie individual experience and thought. It is not so much the fact that such reconstructions are social and influence everybody that is surprising and has to be explained, but rather that sociability requires them, expresses in them its tendency to pose as non-sociability and as part of the natural world.

(*c*) *That the character of social representations is revealed especially in times of crisis and upheaval*, when a group or its images are undergoing a change. People are then more willing to talk, images and expressions are livelier, collective memories are stirred and behaviour becomes more spontaneous. Individuals are motivated by their desire to understand an increasingly unfamiliar and perturbed world. Social reconstructions appear unadorned, since the divisions and barriers between private and public worlds have become blurred. But the worst crisis occurs when tensions between reified and consensual universes create a rift between the language of concepts and that of representations, between scientific and ordinary knowledge. It is as though society itself were split and there is no longer a means of bridging the gap between the two universes. Such tensions can be the result of new discoveries, new conceptions, their popularization in everyday speech and in the collective awareness – for instance, the acceptance by traditional medicine of modern theories such as psychoanalysis and natural selection. These can be followed by actual revolutions of common sense which are no less significant than scientific revolutions. The way in which they occur and reconnect one universe with the other casts some light on the process of social representations and gives exceptional significance to our enquiries.

(*d*)   *That the people who elaborate such representations be seen as something akin to amateur 'scientists' and the groups they form as modern-day equivalents to those societies of amateur scholars that existed about a century ago.* Such is the nature of most unofficial gatherings, discussions in cafés and clubs or political reunions where the modes of thought and expression reflect the curiosities that are voiced and the social links that are established at the time. On the other hand, many representations derive from professional works that are addressed to this 'amateur' public; I am thinking of those pedagogues, popularizers of science and journalists of a certain kind (Moscovici, [1961]/1976) whose writings make it possible for anyone to see himself as a sociologist, economist, physicist, doctor or psychologist. I myself have been in the situation of Agatha Christie's doctor who observes: 'Psychology's all right if it's left to the psychologist. The trouble is, everyone is an amateur psychologist nowadays. My patients tell *me* exactly what complexes and neuroses they're suffering from, without giving me a chance to tell them.'

Perhaps, after all, this volume is appearing too late in the day. Indeed, a number of my theories concur with those of various schools of sociology and of the sociology of knowledge in English-speaking countries. Farr (1978, 1981) refers, in a couple of articles, to the relation between the theories outlined above and theories of attribution, the social construction of reality, ethnomethodology, etc. However, from another point of view this volume seems to be appearing at just the right time for a reassessment of the field of social psychology in relation to related disciplines.

It cannot be denied that the programme for a sociology of knowledge, though often discussed, has not even begun to be realized. Indeed, works such as that of Berger and Luckmann (1966) refer to a theory of the origins of common sense and of the structure of reality, but I believe that this theory, unlike my own, has not been tested. As to ethnomethodology, it originated from the distinction between the 'rationality' of science and the 'rationality' of common sense as applied to everyday life. It has examined this distinction by deliberately splitting the social fabric and then, in the light of attempts to restore the tissue's unity, exposing the social norms and conventions that constituted its continuity and texture. Once again, the result is a structure of reality stemming from a generally shared choice of rules and conventions.

I myself, on the other hand, have found it more rewarding to take advantage of the breaks which occur naturally and which reveal the propensity of both individuals and groups to intervene in the normal sequence of events and to modify their development, and how they achieve their aim. In this way, it is not only the rules and conventions that come to light, but also the 'theories' on which they are based and the languages that express them. In my opinion, this is essential – social regularities and harmonies figure in a common representation and cannot be understood independently. Besides, the work of construction in which the sociologists are interested consists mainly, in our societies, in a process of transformation from a reified to a consensual universe, to which everything else is subordinated.

I have chosen these two examples to underline the affinities, but a number of others could be added. What they all have in common is their concern for social representations, and investigators would do well to recall Durkheim's advice: 'Since observation reveals the existence of a type of phenomenon known as representation with specific features that distinguish it from other natural phenomena, it is impractical to behave as if it didn't exist' (Durkheim, [1895]/1982).

Today a high proportion of the sociological imagination is preoccupied with consensual universes even to the extent of being more or less restricted to them. Such an attitude may be justified in that it fills a gap left by social psychology. But it would be better if there was a regrouping of disciplines around this 'type of phenomenon known as representation' clarifying the task of sociology and giving to our own discipline the breadth of scope it so badly needs.

(2) A brief review of some of the major field studies

In a recent publication I had the pleasure of noting that, at last, American psychologists are prepared to acknowledge, though without actually naming them, the importance of social representations: 'Such tacit, global theories, as well as many more specific theories, including theories about specific individuals or classes of individuals, govern our understanding of behaviours, our casual explanation of past behaviour and our predictions of future behaviours' (Nisbett and Ross, 1980).

Or, we might add, serve to conceal, ignore and replace behaviour. And since *Gedankenexperiments* or *Gedankenbehaviours* are at least as important in everyday life as they are in science, it would be a mistake to ignore them simply because they explain and predict nothing. But a lack of interest in anything written in languages other than English or in experiments carried out in another country – a lack of interest which, a generation ago, would have disqualified any scholar, whether in the United States or elsewhere – leads them to assert with total confidence:

> There has been surprisingly little research on those beliefs and theories shared by the mass of people in our cultures. Heider (1958) was perhaps the first to emphasize their importance, and Abelson (1968) was the first (and nearly only) investigator to attempt to study them empirically. What little research has been done on people's theories has focused on individual differences in belief and theories.   (Nisbett and Ross, 1980)

Now it so happens that, at these precise dates, research on 'people's theories' was thriving and producing widely acclaimed results. I do not suggest that such research was superior to that mentioned, or even excellent in itself, but simply that it occurred and was not restricted to the study of 'individual differences'. If investigators in our field continue to see the whole of science represented by that of their own country, there will always be a Joe Bloggs or a Jacques Dupont to invent everything, like Ivan Popoff before them, which is something we can very well do without.

As we said, it is during the process of transformation that phenomena are more easily perceived. Therefore we concentrated on the emergence of social representations: either starting from *scientific theories* – so as to follow the metamorphosis of the latter within a society and the manner in which they renewed common sense – or from *current events*, experiences and 'objective' knowledge which a group had to face in order to constitute and control its own world.

Both starting-points are equally valid since, in one case, it is a question of observing the effect of a change from one intellectual and social level to another and, in the second, of observing the organization of a complex of quasi-material objects and environmental occurrences that an implicit representation normally encapsulates. The mechanisms involved are, anyhow, identical.

Common sense is continually being created in our societies, especially where scientific and technical knowledge is popularized. Its content, the symbolic images derived from science on which it is based and which, rooted in the mind's eye, shape common speech and behaviour, are constantly being touched up. In the process the store of social representations, without which a society cannot communicate or relate to and define reality, is replenished. Moreover, these representations acquire an ever greater authority as we receive more and more material through their mediation – analogies, implicit descriptions and explanations of phenomena, personalities, the economy, etc., together with the categories required to account for the behaviour of a child, for instance, or of a friend. That which, in the long run, acquires the validity of something our senses or our understanding perceive directly always turns out to be the secondary, modified product of scientific research. In other words, common sense no longer circulates from below to on high, but from on high to below; it is no longer the point of departure but the point of arrival. The continuity which philosophers stipulate between common sense and science is still there but it is not what it used to be.

The spread of psychoanalysis in France provided a practical example on which to start our investigations into the genesis of common sense. How did psychoanalysis penetrate the various layers of our society and influence our outlook and behaviour? What modifications did it undergo in order to do so? We investigated methodically the means by which its theories were anchored and objectified, a system of classification and of the naming of persons and behaviours was elaborated, a 'new' language stemming from psychoanalytic terms was created and the part played by bi-causality in normal thinking. Apart from this, we explained how a theory shifts from one cognitive level to another by becoming a social representation. We naturally took political and religious backgrounds into account and stressed their role in such transitions. Finally, our enquiry enabled us to specify the way in which a representation shapes the reality we inhabit, creates new social types – the psychoanalyst, the neurotic, etc. – and modifies behaviour in relation to this reality.

Simultaneously we studied the problem of mass communications and their role in establishing common sense. In this case, common sense could be elevated to the rank of a major ideology, for such is the status of psychoanalysis in present-day France – comparable, in every way, to that of an official creed. It became clear that, as far as evolution is concerned, the presence of a social representation constitutes the necessary preliminary to the acquisition of status. Moreover, we can state quite definitely the order of the three phases of this evolution: (*a*) *the scientific phase* of its elaboration from a theory by a scientific discipline (economics, biology, etc.); (*b*) *the 'representative' phase* in which it diffuses within a society and its images, concepts and vocabulary are recast and adapted; (*c*) *the ideological phase* in which the representation is appropriated by a party, a school of thought or an organ of state and is logically reconstructed so that a product, created by the society as a whole, can be enforced in the name of science. Thus every ideology has these two elements: a content, derived from below, and a form from above that gives common sense a scientific aura. Other investigations were concerned with more scientific theories (Ackermann and Zygouris, 1974; Barbichon and Moscovici, 1965), and our findings contributed to the formulation of a more general theory of the popularization of scientific knowledge (Roqueplo, 1974).

In a second series of studies we examined more specifically the dynamics of technical and theoretical changes. To put it briefly, during the years 1950 to 1960, a vast diffusion of medical techniques and theories occurred in France as a result of an increase in medical consumption. Together with a new doctor–patient relationship, a whole new attitude to health and the body was rapidly transforming long-standing images and theories. One of the first to study the situation was Claudine Herzlich in her work on the representations of health and illness. Her purpose was to highlight the emergence of a system of classification and interpretation of symptoms in response to what must some day be acknowledged as a cultural revolution in our views of health, illness and death (Herzlich, 1973). If one is nostalgic to see the disappearance of death from our awareness and from our rituals, this dates from the time when confidence in the scientific powers of medicine was established.

A further study dealt with the social representation of the body. This revealed that our perceptions and conceptions of the body were no longer suited to the reality that was taking shape, and that a major upheaval was inevitable. We therefore analysed these representations; and in due course, under the influence of youth movements, the women's liberation movement and the spread of biodynamics, etc., ways of seeing and experiencing the body were radically changed. By taking up our enquiry again after this profound change of representations had occurred, we were able to take advantage of something akin to a natural experiment. Indeed, a significant cultural revolution having taken place, we were in a position to observe its effects, step by step, and to compare what we had previously observed to what was now the case. In other words, we began to grapple with the problem of modification in social representations and of their evolution. This constitutes the bulk of Denise Jodelet's work (1984) at the moment. But she was well prepared for such an investigation as a result of her study of mental patients farmed out among the inhabitants of various French villages. By observing this fostering over a period of some two years, she was able to describe, in great detail, the development of the relationships between villagers and patients and how, by its very nature, it gave rise to discriminations aimed at 'situating', in a familiar world, the mental patients whose presence was eminently disturbing. These discriminations, moreover, were based on a vocabulary and on social representations which had been delicately elaborated by the small communities. These communities felt somehow threatened by the harmless beings who had been placed in their midst by personal misfortune and institutional routine.

Finally, a wholly original study by René Kaës (1976) on group psycho-therapy shows, on the one hand, how such groups produce certain types of representation concerned with what constitutes a group and how it functions and, on the other, how such representations reflect the group's evolution. There is no doubt that they have a cultural, not to say a scientific significance and it is somewhat surprising to see them surface in such circumstances. None the less, the fact remains that such representations canalize the flow of emotions and of fluctuating interpersonal relationships.

Denise Jodelet's collaboration with Stanley Milgram (Jodelet and Milgram, 1977; Milgram, 1984) on the social images of Paris proves that urban space, or the raw material of everyday life, is utterly determined by representations and is by no means as factitious as we tend to believe. Moreover, it admirably confirms our contention that thinking is an environment, since nothing could be more pregnant with ideas than a city. The theories expressed in the first four sections of this essay have been corroborated by this first generation of investigations. Others bearing on culture (Kaës, 1968), intergroup relations (Quaglino, 1979), educational methods (Gorin, 1980), etc. elaborated certain aspects we had overlooked, while studies of the representations of the child stressed the heuristic importance of the subject as a whole (Chombart de Lauwe, 1971).

VII THE STATUS OF REPRESENTATIONS: STIMULUS OR MEDIATOR?

(1) Social representations as independent variables

J. A. Fodor writes:

> It has been a main argument of this book that if you want to know what response a given stimulus is going to elicit you must find out what internal representation the organism assigns to the stimulus. Patently, the character of such assignments must in turn depend upon what kind of representational system is available for mediating the cognitive processes of the organism.   (Fodor, 1975)

A healthy concern with both the theory and the fact of representations can now be observed more or less everywhere. Thus what takes place within a society has become a major preoccupation rather than simply how it creates and transforms the environment. But although such concern exists it is, none the less, essential to guard against traditional half-measures like those comprising the injection of a minimum of subjectivity and thought into the 'black box' of our brains or simply adding a surplus of soul to our dehumanized, mechanized world.

Indeed, if Fodor's text – which sums up a wide assortment of writings – is read with some attention, the use of two words cannot fail to astonish: 'internal' and 'mediating'. These terms imply that representations relay the flow of information coming to us from the outside world: that they are mediating links between the real cause (stimulus) and the concrete effect (response). Thus they are mediating, or chance causes. This reconditioned behaviourism, to which we always resort at difficult times, is a clever piece of tinkering, but it is *ad hoc*, by definition, and not very convincing.

Here, we must stress the firm stand the theory of representations has taken in this respect: *as far as social psychology is concerned* social representations are independent variables, explanatory stimuli. This does not mean that, for instance, where sociology or history is concerned, what for us is explanatory does not itself require explaining.[3] It is readily obvious why this should be so. Each stimulus is selected from a vast variety of possible stimuli and can produce an infinite variety of reactions. It is the pre-established images and paradigms that both determine the choice and restrict the range of reactions. When a child sees its mother smile it perceives a number of different signs – wide-open eyes, distended lips, movements of the head – which incite it to sit up, scream, etc. Such images and paradigms portend what will appear to the actor or the spectator as stimulus or response: the child's arms stretched towards the mother's smiling face or the mother's smiling face lowered towards the child's outstretched arms.

Emotional reactions, perceptions and rationalizations are not responses to an exterior stimulus as such, but to the category in which we classify such images, to the names we give them. We react to a stimulus in so far as we have objectified it and re-created it, at least partially, at the moment of its inception. The object to which we respond can assume a number of aspects and the specific aspect it does assume depends on the response we associate with it before defining it. The mother sees the child's arms stretched out to *her* and not to someone else when she is already preparing to smile and is aware that her smile is indispensable to the child's stability.

In other words, social representations determine both the character of the stimulus and the response it elicits, just as in a particular situation they determine which is which. To know them and explain what they are and what they signify is the first step in every analysis of a situation or a social encounter, and constitutes a means of predicting the evolution of a group's interactions, for instance. In most of our experiments and systematic observations we in fact manipulate representations when we think we are manipulating motivations, inferences and perceptions, and it is only because we do not take them into account that we are convinced to the contrary. The laboratory itself, where a person comes in order to be the object of an experiment, represents both for him and for us the prototype of a reified universe (see Farr, 1984). The presence of apparatus, the way the space is organized, the instructions he

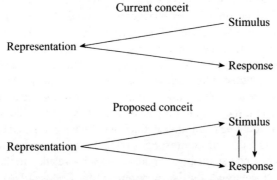

Figure 1.1. Models of representation

is given, the very nature of the undertaking, the artificial relationship between experimenter and subject, and the fact that all this occurs within the context of an institution and under the aegis of science, reproduce many essential features of a reified universe. It is quite clear that the situation determines both the questions we will ask and the answers these will elicit.

(2)   Social representations in laboratory settings

Some investigations have sought to restore meanings and representations to laboratory settings and to corroborate, as far as possible, the theoretical postulate of their autonomy, without which both experiment and theory must forgo much of their significance. In 1968 Claude Faucheux and I tried to prove that representations shape our behaviour in the context of a competitive game. We based our experiments on familiar card games. The one variant we introduced was that some of the subjects were told they were playing against 'nature', while others were told their opponent was 'chance'. The first term evokes a more reassuring, comprehensible and controllable image of the world, while the idea of chance, underscored here by the presence of a pack of cards, recalls adversity and irrevocability. As we expected, the subjects' choice, and especially their behaviour, differed according to their representation of their opponent. Thus most of the subjects confronted with 'nature' spent some time studying the rules and working out some kind of strategy, whereas those subjects who faced 'chance' concentrated all their attention on the pack of cards, trying to guess what card would be dealt, and didn't worry about the rules of the game. The figures speak for themselves: 38 out of 40 of those playing against 'nature' were able to rationalize the rules, while only 12 out of 40 of the others were able to do so (Faucheux and Moscovici, 1968).

Thus our inner representations, which we have either inherited from society or fabricated ourselves, can change our attitude to something outside ourselves. Together with Abric and Plon (Abric et al., 1967) we carried out another variant of this experiment. Here one group was told they would play against a computer, that the choices they would make would be programmed and that the computer, like themselves, would have to try to accumulate a maximum of points. The other group's aim was identical but in their case they were told they would play against *another* student like themselves, whose choices would be communicated to them by telephone. Once again, we observed different, or even contrasting, strategies and rationalizations according to the group. Understandably, a more cooperative relation to the *other* than to the computer emerged. Further experiments by Codol (1974), concerned with the anchoring process of various representations of the self, of the group and of the task to be accomplished, cast a peculiar light on their variety and impact in a competitive situation. Abric (1976), in a very ambitious and systematic experiment, dissected each of these representations and showed why they behaved as they did. An account of the wide range of results obtained was published in 1984.

In another series of equally convincing and straightforward experiments, Flament, in collaboration with Codol and Rossignol (Codol and Flament, 1971; Rossignol and Flament, 1975; Rossignol and Houel, 1976) considered the same problem at another, more significant level. Indeed, social psychology is largely concerned with the discovery of so-called universal mechanisms which, written in our brains or in our glands, are supposed to determine our every action and thought. They occur in society without being social. They are, furthermore, formal mechanisms quite unrelated to an individual or a collective content of any kind or to the history responsible for such a content. One of these supposedly unique and universal mechanisms is that of coherence and stability. This suggests that individuals try to organize their beliefs into internally coherent structures. Consequently, we prefer stable to unstable structures. The implied postulate can be stated thus: positive and negative interpersonal relations are determined by the principle of stability. The two propositions that sum it up – 'My friends' friends are my friends' and 'My enemies' enemies are my friends' – serve as immutable laws, unrelated to any implicit meaning and independent of any particular circumstance. In other words, the two axiomatized sayings form the basis of a syntax of relations between people and determine their own semantics or pragmatics.

Doubtless it was already obvious, before Flament, that such propositions apply only to 'objects' having a common frame of reference or those situated along a cognitive dimension (Jaspars, 1965). But Flament's use of the theory of social representations enabled him to go both further and deeper. To begin with, he showed that each individual, who has to assess the relation between a number of other individuals, possesses a range of representations of the group to which they belong and of the kind of links that exist between them. These may be conventional or even somewhat mythical (e.g. the fraternal or Rousseauist group, etc.). The principle of stability will characterize such relations only if a person already has the notion of a basic, egalitarian, friendly group in mind. Then he will try to form a coherent opinion of the members that constitute it. In other words, it is only in a social context of this kind that 'my friends' friends' must necessarily be 'my friends'. In such cases, Heider's principle of cognition and affectivity expresses only the particular group's collective norm and internal links, but not a general tendency. Indeed, Flament appositely shows that it is the representation of such a principle that gives particular prominence to the friendliness and egalitarianism of its members, and not the reverse. In representations of a different kind of group, friendliness and egalitarianism are not necessarily linked and do not have the same significance. Finally, it seems that the function of the stability principle consists in creating a social paradigm of positive and negative interpersonal relationships and that its significance depends on this paradigm, which simply means that the principle of equilibrium, far from determining, is itself determined by how the context of interpersonal relations is represented. And it is not really surprising that this had not emerged earlier.

Many contemporary studies in social psychology take as their paradigm such a group of like-minded people tending to have similar opinions and tastes and anxious both to avoid conflicts and to accept the *status quo*. But what they overlook is the fact that such a group is an objectification of the traditional, mythical notion of an ideal community. In this case, the tendency towards stability and coherence can well be seen as a determining factor of interpersonal relationships. But, if we then compare this social representation of the group to others, we will soon realize that such 'general' tendencies are really peculiar to it, that we have mistaken the effect for the cause. The enquiries carried out by Flament and his Aix-en-Provence team have made it possible for us to reinterpret Heider's theories through a reassessment that takes into account the social and historical dimension of our perceptions and opinions of others.

We have referred only to a restricted number of experiments. Yet each of them proves, in its specific field (competition, awareness of others, etc.) that our postulate has a wide significance. Rather than motivations, aspirations, cognitive principles and the other factors that are usually put forward, it is our representations which, in the last resort, determine our reactions, and their significance is thus that of an actual cause. Through them society behaves somewhat in the manner of Marcel Duchamp; like this painter with his ready-made objects, it sets its signature on society-made processes and thus modifies their character. We hope to have demonstrated that, indeed, all the elements of the psychic field are reversed once the social signature has been set on them.

The lesson to be drawn from the above is that the present manner of proceeding – which we owe to Muzafer Sherif and which consists in showing how psychic mechanisms are turned into social processes – should be reversed. For such is the process of evolution itself and, by following it, we shall be better able to understand it. It is only logical to consider that social and public processes were the first to occur and that they were gradually interiorized to become psychic processes. Thus, when we analyse *psycho*-social processes we discover that they are psycho-*social*. It is as though our psychology contained our sociology in a condensed form. And one of the most urgent tasks of social psychology is to discover the one in the other and to understand this process of condensation.

FINAL OBSERVATIONS

I cannot conclude this exposition without mentioning some of the more general implications of the theory of social representations. First of all, the study of these representations should not be restricted to a mere shift from the emotional to the intellectual level and they should not be seen as solely pre- or anti-behavioural. If this were the case, there would be no point in dwelling on them. No, what is required is that we examine the symbolic aspect of our relationships and of the consensual universes we inhabit. For all 'cognition', all 'motivation' and all 'behaviour' only exist and have repercussions in so far as they signify something, and signifying implies, by definition, at least two people sharing a common language, common values and common memories. This is what distinguishes the social from the individual, the cultural from the physical and the historical from the static. By saying that representations are social we are mainly saying that they are symbolic and possess as many perceptual as so-called cognitive elements. And that is why we consider their *content* to be so important and why we refuse to distinguish them from psychological mechanisms as such.

In other words, we noticed, on various occasions, that social psychology tends to single out a simple mechanism, take it out of its context, and then to ascribe a general value to it – just as instincts were once singled out for a similar purpose. Some of these are pseudo-mechanisms, such as 'stability' or 'coherence', which appear to explain what they actually define. Since thought naturally tends to substitute order for disorder, simplicity for diversity, etc., to assert that thought tends towards coherence amounts to little more than saying that thought tends towards thought. Other mechanisms, such as 'dissonance', 'attribution', 'reactance', etc., are seen as universal and are applied to all possible social fields, categories or contents. They are supposed to process certain information and to produce different information, no matter what. When assessing the majority of studies carried out on this basis, Herbert

Simon concluded: 'When the processes underlying these social phenomena are identified, as they are in the chapters of this book, particularly those of the second and third parts, they turn out to be the very same information processes we encounter in non-social cognitions' (Carroll and Paine, 1976).

This is a disturbing coincidence, for *either* the social has an existence and meaning which must produce certain effects, *or* the study of these information processes, as isolated mechanisms, is a mistake that creates the illusion of a possible and easy contact with the essence of reality.

Social representations, like scientific theories, religions or mythologies, are the representations of something or of someone. They have a specific content – specific implying, moreover, that it differs from one sphere or one society to another. However, these processes are significant only in so far as they reveal the birth of such a content and its variations. After all, how we think is not distinct from what we think. Thus we cannot make a clear distinction between the regularities in representations and those in the processes that create them. Indeed, if we follow in the footsteps of psychoanalysis and anthropology we should find it much easier to understand what it is that representations and mechanisms have in common.

The second implication – and one which could have been foreseen – can be expressed in a few words: the study of social representations requires that we revert to methods of observation. I have no intention of criticizing experimental methods as such. Their value is indisputable when studying simple phenomena that can be taken out of context. But this is not the case for social representations which are stored in our language and which were created in a complex human milieu. I am well aware that a number of my colleagues despise observations which they see as a cowardly abdication of scientific rigour, a sign of prolixity, laziness and fuzziness. I believe that they are over-pessimistic. Social psychology is no longer what it was half a century ago. Since then, we have come to appreciate the requirements of theory, of the accurate analysis of phenomena; but we have also come to appreciate the reverse, that is, the limitations of theories that explain only what can be experimented upon and of the experiment as something to which reality is made to adjust. And what we require of observation is that it will preserve some of the qualities of experiment while freeing us from its limitations. It has succeeded in doing so for ethnology, anthropology and child psychology, and we see no reason why it should not have similar results in social psychology.

But clearly, something more is at stake than the comparative merits of one method or another. And this has to be said unambiguously; quite apart from its technical merits, experiment has come to stand for the exclusive association of social psychology with general psychology and for its departure from sociology and the social sciences. Doubtless such was not the intention of its founders, but that is the way in which it has evolved. Furthermore, its syllabi of research and teaching turn out psychological experts who are sociological ignoramuses. A return to observation would involve reverting to the human sciences. During the last decade these have made significant advances and have demonstrated that discoveries can be achieved without obsessive rituals, so that there might be worse fates than to take our place amongst them.

The third implication, which is a natural consequence of the second, concerns description. During a certain period we were preoccupied only with the explanatory mechanisms for attitude change, influence, attribution, etc. without giving much thought to collecting data. Such collecting is seen as a minor activity, a proof of intellectual sloth and even as downright useless. To devise hypotheses and to verify them in the laboratory seems to be the word of command to which we rally. But, contrary to appearances, this word of command has nothing to do with science. Most sciences – from linguistics to economics, from astronomy to chemistry, from ethnology to anthropology – describe phenomena and try to discover regularities on which to base a general theory. Their comprehensiveness consists mainly in the store of data at their disposal and the significance of the regularities revealed, which successive theories interpret. I have no wish to analyse here the reasons for this word of command nor its negative consequence for our discipline. Whatever the reasons, the fact remains that only a careful description of social representations, of their structure and their evolution in various fields, will enable us to understand them, and that a valid explanation can only be derived from a comparative study of such descriptions. This does not imply that we should discard theory for a mindless accumulation of data, but that what we want is a theory based on adequate observations that will be as accurate as possible.

Finally, the fourth implication concerns the time factor. Social representations are historical in their essence and influence individual development from early childhood, from the day a mother, with all her images and concepts, begins to become preoccupied with her baby. These images and concepts are derived from her own schooldays, from radio programmes, from conversations with other mothers and with the father and from personal experiences, and they determine her relationship with her child, the significance she will give to his cries, his behaviour, and how she will organize the environment in which he will grow up. The parents' understanding of their child fashions his personality and paves the way for his socialization. That is why we assume: 'that it is the transmission of understanding to the infant rather than his behaviour or his discriminative abilities which ought to be a matter of central concern to developmental psychologists' (Nelson, 1974; see also Palmonari and Ricci Bitti, 1978).

Our representations of our bodies, of our relations with other people, of justice, of the world, etc. evolve from childhood to maturity. A detailed study of their development might be envisaged, which would explore the way a society is conceived and experienced simultaneously by different groups and generations. There would be no reason to see the civilized young adult as the prototype of the human race and thus to ignore all genetic phenomena. And this leads us to the more general concept of a link between the psychology of growing up and social psychology, the former being a social psychology of the child and the latter a psychology of the growing up of adults. In both, the phenomenon of social representations plays a central part, and this is what they have in common. If we added to these certain aspects of a sociology of everyday life – which has not, moreover, been adequately formulated – we might reconstruct a general science which would encapsulate a whole galaxy of related investigations. I see it as a concrete realization of Vygotsky's remark: 'The problem of human thought and language thus extends beyond the limits of natural science and becomes the focal point of historical human psychology, i.e., of social psychology' (Vygotsky, 1986, p. 95).

This would be a science of consensual universes in evolution, a cosmogony of physical human existence. I do not ignore the difficulties of such an undertaking, nor the fact that it may be unrealizable, any more than I ignore the gap between such a project and the modest achievements that are our own to date. But I can't see this as a sufficient reason for not considering it and setting it forth as clearly as possible in the hope that others will share my faith in it.

Notes

1 Editor's note: Moscovici is referring to a painting by Magritte which may be less familiar to English-speaking readers. The better-known picture dates from 1926 and shows a simple image of a pipe with the legend 'Ceci n'est pas une pipe' written below it. In 1966 he produced another painting called 'Les Deux Mystères' ('The Two Mysteries') in which the 1926 painting is shown on an easel in a plain room with a second image of a pipe floating in the air above it. Questions of representation related to both these pictures are discussed extensively by Michel Foucault (1983).

2 Experiments by Tversky and Kahneman (1974) have happily succeeded in proving that this assumption is unfounded and owes its popularity to a misunderstanding that stems from artificial tenets.

3 We discuss social representations again after we have outlined the criticisms levelled at the concept of attitude which is, by definition, a mediating cause. In this way we hope to demonstrate the autonomy of social psychology and to include in the collective context a theory (i.e. that of attitudes) that has become too individualistic. The work of Jaspars and Fraser (1984) lends much weight to this point of view.

2

Society and Theory in
Social Psychology*

1   THE DAY OF THE FIRST JUDGEMENT

We are, as European social psychologists, in a quandary; for most of us our science has just begun; but at the same time we belong to societies and cultures which have a long past behind them. This is why an intimate journal of European social psychology tends to be written as an autobiography inserted in an ancient civilization, while our American colleagues enjoy a conjunction of events which is an exact reversal of our own case.

What is at stake when questions are asked about what social psychology is or should be? First of all, there is no doubt that the answers which are sought are a reflection of the circumstances in which the questions are asked. This is why it seems advisable to begin by making these circumstances explicit rather than leaving them in the background. Two of them appear to be of major importance.

The first is the attempt to create in Europe a social psychology and the drawing together of a group of people who are trying – with varying success – to achieve this aim. Many of us had to use autodidactic methods; we began by learning or reinventing procedures while consulting the only literature available to us, of which we knew neither the function nor the roots in its own society and in its own cultural tradition. Before us, ahead of us and around us there was – and still is – American social psychology. It is unnecessary to dwell on the role played in its development by people like Lewin, Festinger, Heider, Deutsch, Asch, Schachter, Sherif, Kelley, Thibaut, Lazarsfeld, Bavelas, Berkowitz and many others. But despite the respect we have for their work – and despite, in some cases, a network of personal

---

* Translated from the French by Henri Tajfel.

friendships – it is no secret that acceptance is becoming increasingly difficult. As we read them and try to understand and assimilate the principles that guide them we must often conclude that they are strangers to us, that our experience does not tally with theirs, that our views of man, of reality and of history are different. Before my first visit to the United States there was little, save a few publications by Lewin, Festinger and Sherif, which did not leave me with the impression of strangeness.

Consider as an example the book on small groups by Thibaut and Kelley (1959) to which I shall return later. When I tried to read it for the first time several years ago, I could neither understand it nor find much of interest in it. As is well known, the book analyses all social relations in terms of trans-actions. These are based on an individual's rational calculation of how other people are likely to bring him most satisfaction, i.e. a maximum of rewards and a minimum of penalties. But as I read the book I thought of innumerable examples of social interaction which have nothing to do with an equation of supply and demand, such as the role of reciprocity and of values, or the reality of social conflict and of social identity. These gaps were disturbing, and I never managed to finish the book; yet I knew that it was considered to be an important book, though I could not understand why it should be. I encountered similar difficulties with some of the maxims implicit in a good deal of current research: 'We like those who support us'; 'The leader is a person who understands the needs of the members of his group'; 'We help those who help us'; 'Understanding the point of view of another person pro-motes cooperation.'

This 'social psychology of the nice person' was to me then – as it still is today – offensive in many ways; it had little relevance to what I knew or had experienced. Its implicit moral stance reminded me of another maxim (which is perhaps not as uncontroversial as it appears): 'It is better to be healthy and rich than to be ill and poor.' I knew from my social experience that we seek out those who differ from us and that we can identify with them; that we can love someone who is contemptuous of us; that leaders may impose themselves on others through violence or through following unremittingly their own ideals – and that often, in doing this, they are not only admired but also loved; and that, after all, is it not an opponent who often comes to know us best?

It was only after I had been to the United States and discussed these matters with American social psychologists that I began to understand their point of view and to see its background. I was then able to read the book by Thibaut and Kelley and gain some insight into its formulations and its maxims. But I also concluded that, in Europe, we must turn towards our own reality, towards our own maxims from which we must derive our own 'scientific' consequences. The fact that social psychology is at present almost exclusively American constitutes a double handicap. From the point of view

of American social psychologists, this cannot fail to set limits on the relevance of their results and to create uncertainty and doubt about the validity of
the ideas and laws that they propose. For social psychologists elsewhere, this
casts a doubt on the validity of their scientific attitude: they have the choice
between building a social psychology appropriate to their society and culture
or to rest content with the application to their teaching and research of a
model from elsewhere which is highly restricted.

It must not be forgotten that the real advance made by American social
psychology was not so much in its empirical methods or in its theory construction as in the fact that it took for its theme of research and for the
contents of its theories the issues of *its own* society. Its merit was as much
in its techniques as in translating the problems of American society into
sociopsychological terms and in making them an object of scientific enquiry.
Thus, if all that we do is to assimilate the literature which is transmitted to
us – be it only for comparative purposes – we do no more than adopt the
preoccupations and traditions of another society; we work in the abstract, to
solve the problems of American society. And thus we must resign ourselves
to be a small part of a science which is made elsewhere and to be isolated in
a society – our own – in which we have shown no interest. We can achieve in
this way scientific recognition as methodologists or experimenters – but never
as social psychologists. It is true that we have many inducements for imitation. But we must try to work in a spirit of contradiction, to become partners
in a stimulating dialogue; the differences between the 'big brother' and the
'little brother' should become less marked with age; their persistence only
shows that on both sides real maturity has not been attained.

This point of view is shared by others whose experience has been similar
to mine; but despite our common background we have not succeeded in
creating a language, a model and a definition of problems which would genuinely correspond to our social reality. It is not just this social reality that is
shared; for many of us the ideas of, for example, Marx, Freud, Piaget or
Durkheim are of direct relevance because they are familiar and because the
questions that they were trying to answer are also our own questions. Thus
the social class structure, the phenomenon of language, the influence of ideas
about society, all appear critically important and claim priority in the analysis
of 'collective' conduct, though they hardly make an appearance in contemporary social psychology.

Confronted with this situation, some seek refuge in methodology and in the
respectability that it offers, though they know full well that this is not a
solution. The fact that there are so few of us is also important: it is difficult
simply to continue writing for each other, to become isolated within our
discipline and to be the only judges of what we do, while neglecting what
happens elsewhere. Anthropology, linguistics, sociology, psychoanalysis and
philosophy claim our attention; their practitioners demand that we communicate

with them. It is impossible to ignore their questions and also those of the students who insist on getting answers. Social psychology as it is today is not of much help in confronting these pressures. It is an inward-looking pursuit and its development has been characterized by a neglect of the questions from which these pressures arise; or rather, it has developed in reaction to other pressures of which economics, behaviourism and industry are the most important.

The second major problem relates to what is now often called the 'student revolution'. There are many different opinions about the 'revolutionary' character of the student movement and about how we should act towards it or react to it. My own view is that it has had a positive balance because it has helped us to confront problems which we have tended to forget. There is nothing healthier than to be brought face to face with one's own contradictions. We have been asserting for many years that science seeks truth, that its role is to promote civilized values, to extend the reign of reason, and to create human beings capable of objective judgement who would help to enact the ideals of democracy, equality and freedom. But the ideals dominated our discourse while reality judged us on our actions. Max Weber taught us that legitimate violence is the mainstay of the body politic, but we concerned ourselves with legitimacy while forgetting violence. The students took us at face value, for they took seriously what we taught them. Thus, for them, ideals are there to be implemented, and not just to be talked about. They are often blamed for their use of violence; but we must not forget the failure of another generation which aspired to be the counsellors of princes and became instead their servants. And, after all, who gave first the example of violence? Dictatorships, tortures, concentration camps were not born with the present generation of students. Phraseology alone becomes, sooner or later, empty of meaning, particularly when it distorts reality in attempting to convince the prisoner that he is free, the poor and the exploited that they live in an affluent society, the man who works fifty hours a week without any holiday that he is a member of a leisured society. No one ignores all this, but everyone helps in sweeping it under the carpet. Any visitor to a museum knows what is hidden under the fig-leaves and that their function has nothing to do with art. Why then attach a useless appendage to the human body? David's penis on the Piazza della Signoria in Florence is incomparably more beautiful. In their search for truth and sincerity the students turned against the sciences, particularly the social sciences, the institutions that shelter them and the men who practise them. Our disciplines do not appear to the younger generation as disinterested and objective as we claim them to be. They have taken it upon themselves to remind us of the ideological implications of what we do and its role in the preservation of the established order, as well as of the absence of social criticism in our work. They blame us for finding refuge in methodology under the pretext that using adequate methods is equivalent to scientific investigation. We assert that our interest is in the problems of society. They answer that we calmly ignore social inequalities, political violence, wars, under-development or racial conflict. As far as they are concerned, we are safely ensconced in the 'establishment'.

Sometimes all this leads to the extreme view that social science is 'use-less'. But a political movement which pursues long-term objectives cannot afford the luxury of withdrawing its support from science or of neglecting the contributions that science can make. No doubt many of us would have preferred to see the development of a science of 'movement' rather than that of a science of 'order' – to use an expression current in France. As Martin Deutsch (1969) wrote in his paper on the organizational and conceptual barriers to social change: 'Indeed, many of the implicit assumptions of the social sciences buttress the barriers to change – or constitute major obstacles themselves' (p. 9). It is, however, unfortunate that neither Marxism nor the socialist countries have contributed to such a new social science of 'movement'. It is indeed a remarkable phenomenon, of which an explanation will have to be sought one day, that most of the social sciences, such as linguistics, anthropology, economics or social psychology, were founded or developed in the twentieth century without a significant influence or contribution from Marxism or the Marxists; this does not, of course, apply to Marx himself, whose ideas have had a profound impact. But the fact that such a science of movement does not exist today does not mean that its future development is not possible. And, as there is no *tabula rasa* in history, I would suppose that when it finally comes into being it will have to borrow a good deal from its predecessors. But this cannot be done if criticism remains unproductive. It is not enough to reinterpret – as is often done in France nowadays – a whole domain of research by showing that the social sciences, and social psychology in particular, depend upon implicit assumptions about society and upon an ideology which social psychologists have not been able to relinquish. This reinterpretation, which in the light of Marxist and Freudian ideas can be referred to as hermeneutic, led to the development in post-war Germany of a Freudian–Marxist ontology, while elsewhere in Europe (particularly in France) it resulted in a Freudian–Marxist epistemology.

The positivistic dream of a science without metaphysics – which today is often translated into a demand for a science without ideology – is not likely to become a reality. To my knowledge, no one has ever been able to show that as sciences were born, they succeeded in pulling out their roots in social values and philosophies. If a change was created it was precisely in the transforma-tion of these values and philosophies so as to forge links of a different nature. The notion of a complete independence of social science from pre-scientific conceptions is a fairy tale that the scientists like to tell each other.

The conference on which *The Context of Social Psychology* is based was organized in response to specific pressures. We gave ourselves the task of considering a science which for some should not exist at all, and for others does not exist as yet. As I have already written, the social psychology that we ought to create must have an origin in our own reality, or at least in its relevant aspects. But this has not been, until now, the principal focus of attention. In addition – whether this is welcome or not – the role of ideology in science and the political relevance of science have become more salient than ever before. Some problems used to be considered by many as 'extra-scientific', and science itself had the privilege of extraterritoriality. The time has now come to revise these notions. Science is a social institution and, as such, it is an object of analysis like any other, in the same sense as experimenters and their subjects are engaged in social interaction like everybody else. But even beyond this, the real question is simple enough, though fundamental: we must ask what is the aim of the scientific community. Is it to support or to criticize the social order? Is it to consolidate it or to transform it? We are requested from all sides to state our position on this issue. There is little doubt that academic peace will not be restored for some time to come and that ivory towers will continue to crumble, one after another. It is therefore better to accept this as a fact of life than to regret a past which, after all, was not quite untarnished.

In the pages that follow, I wish to present a few ideas about the changes and transformations which appear to me necessary. I can foresee some of the objections that will be raised. It is my view, however, that some of the criticisms which originate from various political, philosophical or even scientific quarters can safely be ignored. They represent a solution which is both easy and facile, as they derive from a lack of familiarity with the contents of the social sciences. My reference here is to some of the texts published by the Frankfurt School, which are also discussed by Ragnar Rommetveit (1972). A similar movement exists in France: Kant, Hegel and Marx are taken up *ad nauseam*, compared and confronted; in turn, the authors confront their own 'proper' image of the social sciences with that found in the 'dominant' conceptions. Their victory on paper is assured and gives them the feeling of having helped in the advancement of social science. It would be an interesting experience to see them at work and to have them demonstrate how they would achieve what they propose. In science, as in other pursuits, it is not enough to point to a defect or to throw a stone at the sinner. It is foreseeable that if concomitant work of proof and validation is not done at some time or another, all those texts written in fervour will soon be forgotten.

In much of the European writing there is a tendency to attribute to the Americans most of the responsibility for our failings and to confuse the criticism of social science with a criticism of the United States. This is easy for us: it is they who took all the risks. If we are 'pure' it is because we have done very little and because we have not, as they have done, exploited the pre-war heritage of psychology, social psychology and sociology. I am convinced that if social psychology subsists as a discipline, the contribution to it of American social psychology will remain and last. In the sections that follow, I shall be critical of many American writers; the reason is that it is they who have done most of the work. In America, as in Europe, many social psychologists – particularly those of the younger generation – share a pre-occupation with the same problems.

2   WHO SETS THE PROBLEMS AND WHO PROVIDES THE ANSWERS?

It is quite evident that the development of social psychology was directly influenced by concrete social events. For example, fascism and World War II led Kurt Lewin to his work on group decisions and on the democratic, authoritarian and *laissez-faire* types of groups. No great insight is required to understand that the needs of the market and of the manufacturing and service industries provide the background for much of the research that is done today. Nevertheless it remains important to analyse the manner in which research reflects these needs. It is here that we are made aware of one of the crucial requirements for a radical change. At present 'society' (i.e. industrial and political groups, etc.) puts the questions and also suggests what kind of answers should be given. I shall illustrate this with examples from a few areas of research.

Let us begin with group dynamics. The central themes of research in this area are work efficiency and the functioning of a group in a given social environment. The real issue is the increase of productivity and the achievement of an optimal organization of industrial and military units. This is why all that was shown not to be directly linked to productivity, such as satisfaction in work, has been largely neglected. As Collins and Guetzkow (1964) wrote: 'Since early studies failed to reveal a positive correlation between satisfaction and productivity, satisfaction appears to have lost its place as one of the central variables in social psychology' (p. 11). The ideal which is aimed at is that of a good worker, a good foreman or a good officer; its content is determined by the management. Thus the networks of communication as well as the structuring of decisions and motivations are conceived within the framework of a system geared towards lowering costs and increasing profits.

The studies of change obey the same imperatives, as was clearly shown in the well-known experiment of Coch and French (1953) on the resistance to change. The aim was set in advance: it was the reconversion of an industrial firm. The management had difficulties with the workers and in order to achieve its aims it wished to reduce their resistance. In the Coch and French study, all that pertained to the attitudes of the workers was conceived as 'resistance' while the intentions of the management were seen as fostering 'change', and thus progress. In reality there was no question at all of a change in the overall functioning of the system; the aim was to achieve control of the transformation by the management, which at the same time required that the workers should share its aims and its conception of the social processes which were involved.

What is the situation in the studies of conflicts and game theory? The problems are set in advance in a perspective which is fully and specifically political: the antagonisms are based on a conflict of interests. It is the conflict between the United States and the Soviet Union which looms in the background. This is not a conflict in which representatives of two social classes or two social systems or different ideologies confront one another: it is a conflict of interest between two national states. The same kind of reasoning is applied to Vietnam. It is based on the idea that as soon as each of the opponents can achieve insight about the interests and the strategy of the other, the conflict becomes soluble. No doubt there are many disagreements amongst social psychologists about the mode of resolution to be adopted. In an excellent article Michel Plon (1970) analysed the debate on this subject between Morton Deutsch and Harold Kelley. The former has shown experimentally that reduction of threat and increase in communication during conflict can promote cooperation. The latter questioned this thesis in his own experiments and insisted that, in some measure, a show of force is needed to facilitate conflict resolution. But both 'social-psychological' hypotheses and the recipes that they imply are, in reality, a reflection of the two dominant political options: on the one hand, the liberal tendency, represented by Deutsch, with its stress on dialogue and the development of trust; on the other, Kelley's option of *realpolitik*, that is, a strategy of negotiation supported by the realities of power. For the one and for the other the options existed before they initiated their research work in this area of social psychology.

My last example is provided by the marginalist school which is dominant at present in political economy. This school has worked out a refined model of market processes in which partners to an exchange have each their ordered scales of abilities or of preferences and, through a series of transactions, manage to establish a balance of prices, to distribute the goods and to satisfy their needs. I am not concerned here with the mathematical analysis used in this model or with its logical coherence. The real problem is that the model is based on a series of psychological presuppositions which are responsible for a vision of social reality that is profoundly individualistic. In fact, the book by Thibaut and Kelley (1959) which I have already mentioned elaborates the psychological counterpart of this theory; it accepts *en gros* its premises and combines them with a behaviourist model of conduct. As is well known, Thibaut and Kelley assume that each individual has at his disposal a sort of internal 'clock' or scale which determines the comparison level (C.L.) which

indicates the profit that he might obtain if he engaged in a relationship alternative to the one in which he is engaged at present. If this profit is greater,
he abandons the current relationship; if not, he stays with it. Thus, all social
relations are capable of being translated in terms of supply and demand. The
possibility that a demand which reflects the needs of an individual, or which
he feels is his due, can be satisfied elsewhere on better terms defines the
limits of the power that an offer may have. It is from this nucleus of ideas that
Thibaut and Kelley proceed to the definitions of norms of work in groups, of
power, etc. What appears to me significant is the attempt to construct a theory
of collective processes on the basis of an individualistic theory; and this seems
to be done through the assimilation of these processes into the functioning of
a market economy. The market is a special social institution characteristic of
a certain historical period; nevertheless, a general sociopsychological theory
is founded on the principles of its functioning.

My concern is not at present with the logical basis of this trend of research
or with the theoretical and experimental validity of its results. It is rather with
what it excludes when it allows itself to be confined to the context just
described. Thus, it is striking that in the field of group dynamics questions
have never been asked about the manner in which the group is a product of its
own activity. Groups do not just adapt to their environments; in some ways
they create this environment and in others they treat it as a resource rather
than as something that exists predeterminately. In other words, we are confronted with a study of group dynamics which, paradoxically, shows no interest in the genesis of groups (cf. G. de Montmollin, 1959, 1960). If we consider
what happened around us historically we can see – and this is constantly
being confirmed through ethological studies – that men always created the
collective institutions and organizations which they needed. Productivity is,
in reality, only a by-product: the first task of a group is not to function better
but to function. Bavelas's networks – ingenious as they are – provide an
example of this lack of interest in human creative activity, as it is expressed
in society and in groups that create themselves. Some of the work done by
Claude Faucheux and myself (1960) was concerned with the study of creating
a system of social relations in an environment. Claude Flament (1965) has
also tried to bridge the gap between the 'genetic' and the 'productivist' perspectives. More recently, Jean-Claude Abric (1984) was able to show that the
manner in which individuals conceive of a task leads them to create a form of
social organization which is adapted to it.

Similar comments can be made about the study by Coch and French (1953).
Social change cannot be envisaged solely in terms of techniques and of
environmental constraints. There are always two factors in it, exemplified
by those who initiate change and those who are at the receiving end of it.
Together they constitute a system of intergroup relations with its special characteristics. This is a system of dynamic interactions in which each of the parts

acts upon the other. In addition, resistance to change is a necessary ingredient of all change: it is not an abstract or a causal factor and it must be considered as a consequence of the social situation. As the process of change develops, resistance to it affects both its 'receiver' and its 'initiator'. The fact that the management called in social psychologists in the case of the Coch and French study is proof in itself of some form of a modification of perspective in the initiator, which was due to the pressure exerted by the other part of the social system.

It is indeed remarkable that the authors almost completely neglected the interactional aspects of the situation: they asked themselves no questions about the conduct of the management, its motivation or its intentions, nor did they investigate the history of the relations between the management and the workers. In this way, all the issues pertaining to the analysis of the total social system as such are by-passed and an *inter*group situation is transformed into one of *intra*group relations. All the issues are reduced to problems of motivation. The general perspective remains that of the management, since the stages of the process of change are defined as 'resistance', i.e. as obstacles to the effective implementation of what *must* come. The issue of *who* wishes the changes to be introduced and *whose* interests they would serve is not even touched upon; nor is anything said about the possibility that resistance might be legitimate, that its roots may be in the objective situation and that perhaps it is a real necessity for those who resist. It must be stressed once again that the authors' reasoning implies that change could take place without anyone resisting it, or rather that it is the resisting group which is exclusively at the origin of the difficulties while it could take the option of simply accepting what is being proposed. Anyone who has had an opportunity of studying situations of this kind knows that the initiators of change, be they managers or administrators, are very often opposed to any change by which they themselves would be affected; if they request changes from others it is in order to maintain themselves even more securely in their own positions (Moscovici, 1961a).

To summarize: Coch and French adopted a partial definition of the situation which enabled them to consider social change as a means of ensuring social control; this in turn enabled them to consider resistance as a negative and accidental variable instead of recognizing that it is an aspect of the situation which is positive and necessary. Finally, they envisaged intergroup relations from an intragroup point of view. They were aware, however, of the intergroup nature of the problem as is shown in the following passage:

In this conflict between the power field of management and the power field of the group, the group attempted to reduce the strength of the hostile power field relative to the strength of their own power field. This change was accomplished in three ways: (a) The group increased its own power by developing a more cohesive and well-disciplined group. (b) They secured 'allies' by getting the backing of the union in filing a formal grievance about the new piece rate. (c) They attacked the hostile power field directly in the form of aggression against the supervisor, the time-study engineer, and the higher management. Thus the aggression was derived not only from individual frustration, but also from the conflict between two groups.

But the authors have no interest in this conflict.

It cannot be said that the study of conflict in social psychology has been an example of an adequate scientific analysis of a problem. It has suffered from a narrow dependence upon game theory, which itself contributed to the view that wars are a normal way of solving differences between nations and that they can be stopped through the use of an appropriate strategy – that is, a rational strategy. It is surprising that, at a time when social and political ideologies play such an important role in human affairs, so little interest is being shown in their effects on social conduct and in the definition of the nature of conflicts. Individuals or groups often have different conceptions of reality, and as soon as an appropriate analysis is made of the nature of these differences the conflicts of interests or of motives become secondary. It is then discovered that the opponents do not share a common framework, that they do not focus on the same aspects of the environment and that their weighing up of gains and losses is by no means identical. Because of all this, they do not have a common language or the will to communicate; if and when a dialogue does begin the conflict is already almost resolved. What then is the meaning of proposing a solution which consists of suggesting that attempts should be made to 'understand' the other so that cooperation can replace competition? The implication is that the opponents were never strangers to one another and that the more they fight the more interest they have in becoming closely acquainted. It is only too well known that peace was never achieved in this way.

The same considerations apply to the relations between individuals and between small groups. I shall go even further: the alternative of competition–cooperation is unrealistic, or at least it is only one amongst several possible alternatives. Division of labour, definition of boundaries and the exercise of influence and of power all represent other modes of conflict solution which can be observed again and again in history as well as in everyday life. They deserve to be taken into account, analysed and assessed – at least in their theory if not in the design of experiments.

This brings me back to the economic conception which we have so easily and spontaneously accepted in developing the kind of social psychology imagined by the exchange theory and in our modes of thinking about decisions and conflict. Here also we are dealing with an individualistic conception in the sense that it considers all that happens in society in terms of individual

choices and decisions. It confines the field of economic behaviour to processes of utilization of means that are considered as given in advance for the
purpose of achieving aims which are also pre-established. This applies to the
means that an individual has at his disposal and to his anticipations, as well as
to the technical and social procedures which can be employed for reaching, in
the long run, social aims and objectives. Thus the aim of economic theory
becomes the planning of distribution for the sake of an optimal satisfaction of
pre-established aims and needs through the employment of pre-established
means. One could say that, at the limit, the human individual becomes unnecessary. It was enough for Pareto to have a 'photography of his tastes';
after that he could disappear. There is no room in this system for the agent
of economic conduct nor for socio-economic processes; there are only scarce
resources and supernumerary needs which have to be coordinated. And even
when the fact that a market economy has its uncertainties draws attention
to the existence of people acting within it, no account is taken of the uncertainties that they may have about the resources available to them and about
their reciprocal goals.

It is in this way that some economists have projected the attitudes and the
norms of a capitalist society on the processes of exchange. Their 'psychological' reconstructions belong in this context: human action is conceived as
determined by the imperatives of a cash economy and of profit. But there is
more to it than that: all that is social is simply excluded from this kind of
economics. Collective investments, expenditure which is not channelled
through the market or so-called external economics are not within its purview. In consequence, decisions which are truly collective, norms which
determine the mode of utilization of resources and political interactions –
which are very different phenomena from simple administrative deliberations
leading to choices or to decisions that are of secondary interest – are also
outside its competence; nor are the processes through which means of action
become available and goals become defined within its province, because in
an individualistic perspective they are considered as 'givens' in Man's nature.
As a result of all this, this version of economics conceives of an immense
area of human conduct as *irrational since within its practice all that goes
beyond individualism and all that diverges a little from a capitalist model
enters by definition the domain of irrationality.*

What is the background of this conception? First, it is a rationality which is
purely Cartesian and mechanical: thus, conduct is rational in so far as it
conforms to principles of conservation (the means are provided once and for
all, and they are immutable) and of maximization (the search for optimal
satisfaction). Second, the calculations are purely individual because they are
limited to relationships between two individuals. But if psychologists adopt
such hypotheses, which they have a perfect right to do, they must also realize
that their intellectual universe comes to be confined within a very specific

sector of the society and that they are only interested in a small and specific fraction of mankind. Reading a few anthropological studies or an acquaintance with other cultures would be instructive on this point. The gift, the reciprocity, the bonds of consanguinity and of religion are all there to indicate the limits of the law of supply and demand, and also of social-psychological theories. In fact, the manner in which the processes of choice and of its evolution are envisaged in the theory of cognitive dissonance are not compatible with the premises of market economy. The remarkable experimental studies on needs carried out by Zimbardo (1969) prove that needs cannot be considered in advance as a 'given'. Mark Mulder's research on power (1959) also contradicts in many respects a conception of this issue based on utilitarian principles.

But I should remind the reader that it is not my aim to criticize these theories and the research arising from them. I wish rather to demonstrate how much they are tied to the questions asked and the answers provided in a specific context. Our chances of progress and of renewal depend upon our ability to remain open to the problems of our collective reality. We have not been sufficiently receptive to them in Europe. Indeed, something important and precious can be learned from the openness and receptivity of our American colleagues. Society changes and invents, and its demands are an important source of stimulation. But it is for us to give the answers, or at least to attempt to find them. Because of our background, our functions and our traditions we are, or should be, in a position to analyse, examine and place the questions in a wider framework.

If the studies of conflict and of means to resolve it were placed in the perspective of all possible situations – that is, of those enacted in history – and beyond the limited horizon of political interaction, they would lead to the formulation of answers which would differ from those that were until now envisaged. The same applies to change, to group dynamics or even to the very definition of what is social in human conduct. In fact, it is probable that, through a process of feedback, the questions themselves would be transformed. As of now – and this is what I wish to stress again – social psychologists have done no more than operationalize questions and answers which were imagined elsewhere. And thus the work in which they are engaged – in which we are all engaged – is not the work of scientific analysis but of *engineering*, with all the weight of methodology that this implies. The confusion between science and engineering is very marked in the social sciences, and particularly in social psychology. This is why it seems to me that if we must allow society to ask the questions – since this is implied in the nature of our activities – it is, in contrast, our duty to elaborate and redefine these questions ourselves. This is a necessary condition for establishing a real dialogue in which we can rediscover the freedom to analyse objectively all the aspects of a problem and to consider the various points of view emanating from the society in which we live.

3   THE PLACE OF THEORY IN A WORLD OF FACTS

3.1   The tacit compromise

It must be admitted that social psychology is not truly a science. We wish to give it an appearance of science by using mathematical reasoning and the refinements of experimental method; but the fact is that social psychology cannot be described as a discipline with a unitary field of interest, a systematic framework of criteria and requirements, a coherent body of knowledge or even a set of common perspectives shared by those who practise it. It would be nearer to the truth to say that it consists of a movement of research and methodology which periodically attracts a collection of diverse interests that sometimes succeed in enriching it in new and unexpected ways; but a solid foundation for the future has not been laid.

This movement is not one which proceeds steadily in a certain direction. From time to time the interests of the researchers are mobilized by themes or areas which appear new and important at the moment; but sooner or later these prove to be sterile or exhausted and they are abandoned. Thus, research spreads here and there in a haphazard fashion rather than accumulating and ascending to new levels. It oscillates between two poles. One consists of a collection of separate and unrelated topics, so that, for example, anyone interested in doing research on small groups or on networks of communication or on comparisons between individual and group performance will identify himself as a social psychologist. At the opposite pole there is an illusion of coherence since research is organized around general themes, such as the processes of social influence or of attitude change, but these themes remain eclectic and unstructured. The domain of the subject is split into 'topics', 'clans', 'schools' and 'establishments' which each have their own methods of asking questions, their own language and their own interests; what is more, each develops out of its peculiarities its own criteria of truth and excellence. Thus social psychology is at the same time a field which is fenced in and a mosaic; our appearance of cohesion is due to external pressures, but our dependence upon diverse interests, techniques and sciences continues to separate us from one another.

It seems to me that the *creation of a system of theoretical activities* is essential for a coherent development of the subject. It is the absence of such a system that is the main obstacle in providing answers which would be relevant to the questions set for us by society. It is only a commonly shared framework of criteria and principles that can enable scientists to free themselves from external pressures, to take account of the relevant aspects of reality and to be critical both about their own activities and about the activities of those who are their patrons. Theories determine not only what is 'interesting' but also what is 'possible'. But they do not originate *ex nihilo*; they are the result of a collective endeavour and of the collective inspirations of those who are the practitioners of a discipline. The point I wish to insist upon is that our entire 'scientific ideology' – to take up a term used by Henri Tajfel – is an obstacle to this kind of development in social psychology. Three aspects of this ideology are, in my view, particularly important.

The first is the predominance of a positivistic epistemology. Its main tenets are that facts are 'given' in the environmental reality, that they can be inductively isolated through a description of regularities, and that experimentation is the hallmark of science. In this perspective, theory is a language and a tool which is both subordinate to the empirical method and subsequent to it chronologically. We are not very clear about our identity; and therefore, in order to become 'scientists', we try to follow as closely as possible the prevailing norms, from which we derive our emphasis on experimental and statistical techniques and the ritualism that goes with them. Many of us work away peacefully in our own corners, guided by the idea that it is essential for the moment to accumulate facts which will serve one day to build a conceptual structure.

In the second place, the neglect of theoretical activity results in a sort of *tacit compromise* whereby we avoid facing questions about the nature of laws with which our discipline is concerned and about their mode of validation. This is reflected in conflicts between observation and experimentation, and between the role of the 'psychological' and the role of the 'social'. The dividing line between observation and experimentation is not due in our subject to a distribution of tasks or to a specialization of techniques of research; rather, it is due to a differentiation of research strategies determined by the nature of the problems which are being studied. It is a genuine split which divides the scientific community so deeply that one is entitled to ask if we are not dealing with two distinct kinds of scientists or two separate disciplines. To opt for one or the other of these methodologies is like becoming a member of a club which one can join on condition one adopts a credo that needs no justification or explanation. The game is all played out between these two clubs and mutual criticism eliminates all possibility of a *rapprochement*, though attempts are still being made here and there to create it. The criticisms that each side makes of the other are well known. Experimental social psychologists are blamed for the artificiality of the situations which they use in studying social phenomena and thus for the fact that their scientific method is inadequate to take hold of social reality. Non-experimentalists are told that the complexity of social processes cannot be grasped in their 'natural' context and that their simple collection of data is not a procedure capable of providing a rigorous verification of the hypotheses which may be suggested by observation. The argument against them hinges on the incompatibility of their vision of social reality with a properly scientific mode of procedure.

The real issue at stake in this debate is the definition of sociopsychological theory and its validation. To the experimentalists, the *post hoc* interpretations of observed facts – however coherent they may be – cannot result in truly scientific conceptualizations and cannot therefore provide the foundations of a science. The non-experimentalists find little interest in the hypotheses which form the background of experiments; efficient prediction is achieved, according to them, at the cost of neglecting most of the parameters and missing altogether the specificity of what is being studied. A common articulation of the two approaches becomes even more difficult in view of the fact that theories which lead to experimentation have a structure which differs from those which originate in systematic observation. And thus it is far more comfortable not to raise these problems too often, not to face choices or stimulate passions, and to leave the choice of future directions to the passage of time and to 'natural selection'.

But if a choice really had to be made, would our conceptual generalizations tend in a 'psychological' or in a 'social' direction? The acceptance of a psychological perspective essentially means that social psychology would become a specialized branch of general psychology whose function would be to deepen our knowledge of very general processes, such as perception, judgement or memory, which remain unchanged throughout their modes and conditions of operation and production. The data of social psychology would thus enable us to do no more than specify in more detail certain variables in human or animal behaviour which, in the last analysis, are reducible to laws of 'animal' or 'individual' psychology, of psychophysics or psychophysiology. Thus, for example, social perception should be studied in the same way as auditory or visual perception; sociopsychological phenomena, such as processes of influence, of attitude change or of problem solution in groups, should be no more than special instances of conditioning or motivational principles to which the general laws of learning should be applied. The work of Zajonc (1966) is an excellent example of this tendency.

This kind of extension pres- poses an implicit acceptance of three postulates. The first is that the diffe ice between social and elementary non-social processes is only one of degi and that a hierarchy of phenomena can be established in which they are ordered from simpler to more complex, and from individual to collective. The second postulate is that social processes do not imply the existence of social phenomena governed by their own laws, but rather that they are accounted for by psychological laws which can at the same time be based on hypothetical laws of physiology. The final postulate is that there is no difference in kind between social and non-social behaviour: other people intervene only as a part of the general environment. The early doctrine of F. H. Allport (1924) remains the credo of many social psychologists: 'The significance of social behaviour is the same as that of non-social, namely, the connection of an individual's biological maladjustment to his environment. In and through others, many of our most urgent wants are fulfilled; and our behaviour towards them is based on the same fundamental needs as our reactions towards all objects, social or non-social' (pp. 3–4).

Opposed to this tendency, though still timidly, is another trend of thought which tends to conceive sociopsychological processes from a sociological point of view. Examples of it are provided by research on the structures of small groups, on the hierarchy of roles and statuses through which are defined an individual's identity and his social position, on mass communications, on frames of reference and on intergroup relations. Social psychology becomes here a way of studying – if possible in the laboratory and with methods that have proved their usefulness – the social processes which exist on a wider scale in the society at large. The study of cultures is another example – though more marginal to social psychology – of a similar approach; it subordinates sociopsychological mechanisms to the cultural and social context of behaviour, to the social framework of the fundamental aspects of psychological functioning or to the cultural aspects of the processes of learning and socialization. By contrast – as Claude Faucheux (1970) has clearly shown – the cross-cultural studies in social psychology have completely neglected the properly cultural or social dimensions of comparison.

Amongst social psychologists it was undoubtedly Sherif who pursued most steadily the attempt to generalize from the laboratory to the society at large. The least that can be said is that, as a result, he has certainly not achieved much popularity. The proof needs to be sought no further than in the book by Deutsch and Krauss (1965) on theory in social psychology, in which no reference is made either to his research or to his theoretical position. This lapse is obviously the result of a tacit consensus. If the problem of generalization had been taken more seriously, it would have been impossible to neglect this kind of orientation and to avoid an attempt to clarify the issues that it raises. These issues are confronted directly by Israel, Rommetveit and Tajfel, who each approach them from their own points of view; in doing so, they force us to face difficulties that many would prefer to forget and some might think of as being 'old hat'. Nevertheless, the problems are there and they remain permanently at the background of all our work. They need not perhaps be solved before we can run the next experiment; but we must find a solution to them if we wish to engage in building a theory.

Last, but not least, the avoidance of theory and of theoretical debate also has its emotional aspects. The social sciences, including social psychology, developed in confrontation with philosophy. As a result of this, there exists a kind of reactive fear of indulging in 'philosophical' speculation. Manipulation of ideas is therefore acceptable on condition that it leads more or less directly to experimentation or, alternatively, if it is capable of a mathematical formalization which, however weak or dubious, offers at least an appearance of 'respectability'. Because of the prevailing insecurity, the milieu of the social sciences has become so repressive that it has made science completely uninteresting; the fundamental problems of Man and society are lost in a cloud of fragmentary 'fields' and techniques which succeed in turning away genuine talent and in freezing all enthusiasm. Experiments play a negative role, as a barrier and a signal, only enabling us to prove to the world that we are doing science and not philosophy. If we lose this mark of identity, we will lose all our assurance and will not know whether our theoretical constructions can be recognized as 'scientific'. But all this is no more than a trap; neither methods nor formal languages have ever guaranteed the 'scientific' character of anything. At any rate, why should we despair before we have even started. Not everything in science is 'scientific': biological theories of the origins of life or cosmological theories about the structure of the universe have not yet reached this level.

3.2   Some consequences for research and theory

The weight of positivism, the tensions between observational and experimental methods, and the fear of speculation are the causes of the slow development of theory in social psychology. One of the consequences is the respect of good common sense, of the psychology of well-tried aphorisms. I shall not insist on this delicate theme; as is well known, it contributes greatly to the accusations of banality that are often thrown at us. I should like, however, to insert a few comments on the subject.

Common sense is reputed to be shared out more equitably than almost anything else in the world. It does not, however, necessarily reflect a stable and immutable set of data corresponding to the existence of a firmly validated version of reality. On the contrary, it is a product of culture which, in our society, is meshed in with scientific theories. In a study of the public image of psychoanalysis (Moscovici, [1961]/1976), I described the extent to which psychoanalytic theory has penetrated common sense in everyday judgements, discussions and interpretations of people's actions. Claudine Herzlich (1969) analysed similar phenomena in our conceptions of health and illness. In the same way, Marxist vocabulary is part and parcel of our heritage and of, as it were, the spontaneous philosophy of millions of people. The same is true of behaviourism, of functional sociology, of economic models or of evaluation of actions in historical or in probabilistic terms. Thus, to respect common sense is to respect theories that we have implicitly accepted. But we must also learn to distrust the 'wisdom of the people'. The fact that it accords with our intuitions proves nothing but the existence of a consensus. The German socialist Auguste Babel used to say that he was always worried when he was in agreement with his opponents or when they agreed with him. I think that the social psychologist should have the same attitude when he observes or discovers that his results do no more than confirm something that is known to everybody.

This does not mean that we should strive to be original at all costs. And yet, in science it is only true discovery that is astonishing and original. This is why we must try to accept things for what they are in our discipline. In its beginnings, social psychology had the task of verifying certain hypotheses and interpretations even if they were not very different from what everyone would accept without difficulty. The time has now come to recognize that we must leave this first stage behind and go further. To multiply experiments in order to rediscover what is obvious can only lead to a paradoxical situation. In fact, the principal *raison d'être* of experimental method is to invent and validate *new* consequences of a theory or to produce *unexpected* effects. If we conduct experiments which do not have these characteristics and which do no more than confine to the laboratory what is already diffused in the culture, we proceed in a fully non-experimental fashion. Our experiments then become a kind of systematic survey aimed at inscribing in numbers and transcribing in books the beliefs which are transmitted by oral tradition. Thus most of the experiments on social influence, on the effects of a majority, on leadership or on threat are no more than a long interview which we conduct with society about its social theory.

However, the reign of common sense is only one of the consequences of the absence of theoretical effort; the mortality and sterility of findings in some of the areas of research is another. Studies on group dynamics and on Bavelas's networks provide a clear example of this. I would not be far wrong in estimating that there must exist about 5000 articles on these topics; this figure is probably an underestimate. Most of these studies are no more than validations of industrial folklore and miniaturizations of real situations; they contain practically no valuable scientific information. The books that were written about these studies and the autopsies that were conducted on them revealed that, in most cases, they were completely devoid of any preoccupation with conceptual problems. As McGrath and Altman (1966) wrote: 'The research production has kept mounting at an enormous rate. Theory was minimal throughout most of the 1950s and has continued to be so till the present' (p. 9). For these reasons, the authors of the various reviews of the field were reduced to compiling bibliographies or, at best, presentations of classified lists of results; indeed, it cannot be said that what remains is a set of confirmed propositions or of properly defined variables. I have the suspicion that the same is true of the study of conflict.

The third consequence of the absence of interest in theory is the isolation of various areas of research, or rather the fact that no consistent efforts have been made to arrive at theoretical generalizations. With regard, for example, to the work on conflict, one may ask whether its main preoccupation was with processes of conflict – which are central to all psychological and social phenomena – or rather with particular actions said to be 'conflictual'. As is well known, the latter is true; no effort has been made to analyse the relations between this particular area of behaviour and the central processes of conflict or to see how they manifest themselves in various kinds of real situations. As I am not very familiar with this field of work, I shall not discuss it further; instead, I shall take the example of a subject which is nearer to my own interests and on which a great deal of work has been done in recent years: this is the phenomenon of 'risky shift'.

Let us first describe briefly the well-known paradigm used in these studies. The subjects are generally confronted with choices between various alternatives, involving a change in the situation, in the relations with peers, etc. of a person. Each of the choices represents various degrees of risk for the person who makes them. Working alone, each subject makes ten or twelve such choices. Then the subjects are brought together in groups of various sizes and requested to select for each problem a level of risk unanimously acceptable to all the members of the group. Once the group discussion is completed, the subjects are again separated and asked again to indicate their personal preferences for the solution of each problem. Groups are generally found to favour riskier solutions than individuals.

This finding was arrived at by chance. In science and in technology chance findings of this kind have always been fully exploited. A good deal of attention has been drawn to risky shift because, from the time of the early experiments by F. H. Allport and by Sherif, it has been maintained that, in social situations, individual opinions and judgements tend to converge towards the mean and to shift away from extreme positions. Allport attributed this tendency to the rational nature of collective decisions, which stand in contrast to the spontaneous behaviour of crowds characterized by extreme judgements and irrational actions. Thus the results of the experiments on risk, which have been replicated many times, constitute an exception to a type of conduct which was thought to be universal. This brought in its wake two questions: the first concerned the conditions in which it was possible to produce a 'conservative shift', and the second was the question of why groups took more risks than individuals.

Conservative shift was rarely obtained in experiments; when it did happen, it was through making more salient the ethical dimensions of risk. On the whole, it was disappointingly difficult to produce this phenomenon.

Diverse explanations of risky shift have been proposed. Wallach, Kogan and Bem (1964) offered the hypothesis of diffusion of responsibility in a group: as each individual in a group feels less responsible than he does when making decisions on his own, he dares to take more risks. Brown (1965) started from the idea that in individual situations people are in a state of 'pluralistic ignorance' which causes them to keep on the side of caution. When they find themselves in a social situation they abandon caution and take more extreme positions, particularly as risk has a positive value connotation in our society. Finally, Kelley and Thibaut (1969) took the position that there exists a 'rhetoric of risk', i.e. that arguments in favour of taking a risk are made more convincing and are elaborated more than those preaching conservatism. In addition, some authors tried to show that risk-taking depends upon personality characteristics, and hence relates to the influence exerted on a group by its most extreme members.

My own view is that if all these theories have some truth in them, then one thing is certain: risky shift presents no interest as an object of study and does not deserve the efforts of experimental and theoretical analysis expended on it. Indeed, if it all comes down to a combination of questions of influence, of rhetoric, of personality and of conformity to norms, then risky shift is no more than a secondary phenomenon and it would be more useful to study influence or conformity directly. Judgements concerning risk could thus be seen as not differing in any way from judgements that are made about love, aggression or drugs. And if these show the kind of displacement found in the case of risk, the logic implied in the theories just mentioned could lead us to propose a theory of love-shift, aggression-shift or drug-shift. One could then multiply the examples indefinitely and finally arrive at a specific 'theory' for each of these aspects of social conduct. To complete the picture, one could proceed to one of these 'syntheses' or 'comparisons', learning perhaps that the risky shift of the Germans is greater than that of the French, that there is no distinction between a 'love-shift' and a 'cuisine-shift', and finally that altogether more risks are taken in groups. Then, in a manner which is purely inductive and *post hoc*, we could reproduce *ad infinitum* a phenomenon which was first discovered by chance. All research would then be concentrated on risk without any new light being thrown on cognitive or on social phenomena.

But a very different situation arises if a strange phenomenon – strange in the sense that it contradicts generally accepted principles – leads to questions about the general implications that it might have. For example, when physicists learned about Roentgen's discovery they did not spend much time in questioning its validity or in searching for its various manifestations; they enquired immediately about its bearing on the theory of matter. When Kogan worked for a time in my laboratory we discussed his experiments; I adopted an attitude which seemed to me guided by the same concern for generalization and tried to go beyond the explanations specific to the phenomenon of risky shift and to keep at the level of its basic significance, which is that it constitutes an exception to the apparently 'universal' law about the influence of the group on an individual. This leads to the first question: Is this shift due to semantic content or to another property of this content? A brief analysis led to the formulation of a fairly straightforward hypothesis: the majority of studies which have shown the convergence of opinions in a group used stimuli which presented no significant meaning to the subjects and did not provoke any deep commitment.

It then became important to see if the same effect could be obtained by using judgement or attitude scales containing this feature of 'significance' and of 'commitment' which the previous scales had lacked. The next point was concerned with the difference between 'risky' and 'conservative' shifts: the only interest that it might have originates from a consideration of the semantic content; it is only through this that the direction of judgement becomes important and that we confront two distinct phenomena. In contrast, from the psychological or even from the social point of view, the main question is whether we are dealing here with one and the same phenomenon which is mistakenly being given two different explanations. This would amount to proceeding according to an Aristotelian type of epistemology which distinguishes between an upward and a downward movement, between circular movement and movement in a straight line, and which offers a separate theory to account for each. The Galilean treatment of the same problem abandons the descriptions of diversity and attempts to separate the unity and the common nature of the forces involved. Whether a body goes up or down, it is always subject to gravity and it is gravity that must be studied.

In the same way, whether the judgement of a group is more conservative or more risky than that of its individual members, it reflects the same phenomenon, namely a departure from the mean or a polarization of attitudes. Experiments on familiarization have, at a certain point of time, given the impression that individuals could show extremization in their judgements without any intervention of social interaction. This phenomenon was not confirmed in subsequent experiments. But in the experiment by Kogan and Wallach (1964), the validity of which has not been questioned by anyone, it was shown that individuals took greater risks after discussing the questionnaire of choice dilemmas and without having reached consensus. Therefore, all that can be said is that individuals reach more extreme opinions after social interaction; it cannot be claimed that groups take greater risks than individuals. Thus, the various theories mentioned above were so many attempts to answer a question that does not exist. But another question which has not been raised does exist and should have been answered since it motivated the initial interest in risky shift. Why, for example, does a group decision tend towards either a compromise (the mean) or polarization? In other words, why should either an effect of group averaging or one of group polarization be observed?

In relation to this question two points should be made, which are of significance to the general modes of procedure in social psychology. First, the question I have just formulated on a theoretical level has always been asked purely in technical terms. For example, the statistical analysis of risky shift is usually conducted as follows: first, the mean is calculated, i.e. the numerical value that would express consensus if individuals behaved according to the law of convergence; then, the difference between this 'theoretical' consensus and the consensus that has really taken place is used as the measure of 'shift'. Consequently, the relation between group averaging and group polarization is considered in purely statistical terms.

The second point concerns obstacles to generalization. The restriction of interest to semantic content bars all progress towards more fundamental phenomena. Thus, if we focus entirely on risk we deal with an exception to a general law which can be distorted and turned about before we reach the point of analysing what is exceptional about it and why. The possibility of its serving to question a model or a theoretical concept cannot be exploited until we cease to concentrate on this particular aspect. In this way, the concrete imprisons the abstract. The experiments by Moscovici and Zavalloni (1969), by Doise (1969) and by Fraser et al. (1971) have shown that the polarization effect must be considered in a more general framework than the risky shift, which is only a special case of another phenomenon. Other experiments have enabled us to study the conditions in which either group averaging or group polarization could be obtained with the items first used to demonstrate risky shift. But this was possible only because the issues raised at the beginning were modified to integrate the initial discovery into a wider context. It then became obvious that the modified phenomenon is of direct relevance to social decision. It is also relevant to processes of judgement and of attitude change, to the averaging and summation of social categories, and to intragroup – and even intergroup – relations in the formation of prejudice. The studies by Anderson (1968), Sherif et al. (1965), Tajfel and Wilkes (1964) and Fishbein and Raven (1962) confirm these views. Hence the present task is to find an explanation for the totality of these results, and the study of risky shift in isolation loses all its interest.

3.3   Towards a phlogiston theory

The respect of common sense, the proliferation of experimental studies lacking theoretical preoccupations, and the isolation of various areas of research in social psychology combine to explain the accumulation of facts and notions which do not amount to real progress, since they are not conceptually integrated and since no theory is, in any real sense, disconfirmed or replaced by another. The concepts employed have their origin in other fields; theoretical models exist side by side in a relationship which constitutes neither real dialogue nor fertile contradiction. It is therefore not surprising that the empirically established facts are nothing but a heterogeneous collection, as are the theories on which they are supposed to depend. The experiments and empirical studies are not really capable of confrontation in a common framework; the contradictory results published about the same phenomenon rarely lead to a conceptual analysis which could provide a decision and transform our knowledge.

This situation is reflected in the textbooks. The most useful among them adopt a vague outline of structure enabling them, at best, to classify a few empirical results which are usually presented outside their theoretical context – assuming that such a context exists. Contradictory examples are rarely taken into consideration, and when they are it is in an abstract and remote manner. As a result, the student gains the impression of a well-ordered and fruitful discipline – for the very reason that difficult or contradictory points are ignored.

What happens when a theory does emerge? How is it presented, criticized or understood? The theory of cognitive dissonance is a case in point (Festinger, 1957, 1964). It is true thas this is not truly a sociopsychological theory; but there is no doubt of its importance as an intellectual discovery, its ability to stimulate research or its originality of perspective. In a properly constituted science, a theory of this kind would immediately become a point of departure for new concepts which would integrate it in a sociopsychological context and translate it into truly social terms. Its fate was radically different. With the exception of Bem (1965), interest was focused entirely on details of methodology. In a notorious article Chapanis and Chapanis (1962) devoted all their attention to the mode of selection of subjects and to points of statistics. Others reproached Festinger because he failed to provide a measure of dissonance and was therefore unable to make predictions. And it all stopped there. Many social psychologists continued to work on social reinforcement or on exchange theory as if the theory of cognitive dissonance did not exist and did not contradict the very principles of behaviour they took for granted. If they had really taken these principles seriously, a controversy created by dissonance theory should have been a centre of intellectual activity. Could one imagine the chemists calmly continuing research in their own little corners while some believed in phlogiston and others in oxygen? It is obvious to anyone familiar with the history of ideas that real progress emerges from theoretical confrontation, and facts and methods play a role which is relatively less important. Even if Festinger and his pupils did not fully conform to the experimental ritual, the facts which they demonstrated retain their interest and importance. The facts established by Piaget on the basis of a solid and coherent theory also failed to conform to all the rules of the game – and yet they survived the passage of time and the attacks of the critics.

Festinger and his pupils were often reproached for their tendency to seek results which were not obvious, and which were at variance with common sense. This is an objection which is astonishing but significant: it shows how distant is our conception of experimentation from truly scientific thought. I wrote earlier that experimentation should always aim at invention and at creating new effects. The natural sciences are sciences of effects; as distinct from them, the social sciences – and particularly social psychology – remain sciences of phenomena and of appearances. The belief that everything or nearly everything about human conduct is already known from direct observation prevents our discipline from generating true discovery and from contributing data that would modify pre-scientific knowledge. And thus our knowledge takes the form of a refinement of pre-knowledge, and the banality of our results is concealed behind the refinement of techniques and methods.

It is not my intention to defend here the theory of cognitive dissonance, for it needs no defence. But it is important to stress that when a theory of this quality appears in social psychology no serious attempts are made either to develop further its relevance to collective processes or to invalidate it. Even when attempts at disconfirmation are made they can hardly be described as scientific. Instead, theories of cognitive consistency are given uniform treatment as if they all had the same potential scientific impact; the recipe for this eclectic cuisine can be found, for example, in the recent book edited by Abelson et al. (1968).

It would not be very useful to discuss this situation in social psychology without attempting to outline how we might remedy the deficiencies. Practically all sciences have their theoreticians and their experimentalists, and also their theoretical and experimental journals. Why should we not accept the same kind of division and specialization? We could then let the theorists define their aim, their 'culture' and the structure of their problems. At any rate, theory and experiment have never fully interlocked; the advance of knowledge is a result of contradictions between them and of the attempts to communicate made on both sides. In a study of the history of mechanics (Moscovici, 1968), I was able to show that the essential feature of its evolution was not the predominance of theory or of experimentation but the tension that developed between the two. There is no reason why attempts should be made to avoid these tensions and the fruitful contradictions that go with them. Experiment and theory do not stand in a transparent relation to one another; it is the role of the theory to make experimentation unnecessary, and the role of experimentation to render the theory impossible. The dialectic relationship that exists between these two propositions needs to be properly used if knowledge is to advance.

But in order to achieve this, decisions must be taken about the kind of theories which should provide the frame of reference and about the intellectual tradition that should form their background. It is my opinion that more independence is needed from the predictive function of theory. As things stand today, whenever a concept or a model is proposed, it is evaluated exclusively in terms of its utility, of the phenomena which it is able to predict and of the experiments which it suggests. This results in the creation of restricted models, which are more like reflections about certain aspects of a phenomenon than a genuine theory of it. Models of this kind are useful in stimulating a few interesting experiments, but their application is limited, since very soon a point is reached when nothing new is contributed by further experiments. In addition, it is often difficult to decide experimentally about the validity of the different models because they concentrate on different categories of variables pertaining to the same phenomenon; this is, for example, the case with models of group dynamics. This situation is reflected in a juxtaposition of experiments which are as numerous as they are inefficient; and it illustrates that an atheoretical science has no memory and is incapable of achieving integration of its restricted models. The usual progression of events can be described as follows: someone obtains data or proposes a hypothesis about, for example, 'risky shift' or 'social categorization'. Once the findings are firmly established and the hypothesis confirmed, attempts are immediately made at further reproduction through varying such factors as age, personality, or cognitive style. The phenomenon is thus reduced to the context of individual or inter-individual psychology. In this way, the framework of social psychology is progressively abandoned. Instead of proceeding in depth, one proceeds by extension; instead of establishing links between sociopsychological phenomena, one makes them disappear through their absorption in processes which are not sociopsychological.

It seems therefore more useful to turn towards theories which are explanatory or which offer a systematization of a set of propositions. Should these theories start from fact and experiments? The answer could be 'yes' and 'no' at the same time. It would have to be negative if they were theories of a 'Baconian' type consisting of a 'critical review', a 'synthesis' or a 'clarification and definition of concepts'. This is so for two reasons: first, there is not enough coherence in what we consider to be established knowledge in social psychology; second, it is Utopian to hope that a theory might emerge from a simple integration of parts which themselves do not bear the mark of a theory. The book by Collins and Guetzkow (1964), which summarized the experiments on small groups, showed the impossibility of such an attempt at integration.

But the answer could be positive if a theory offers a fresh perspective in which experiments or surveys are considered as no more than temporary expedients in sketching a new image of reality. Despite the criticisms I made earlier of the book by Thibaut and Kelley (1959), it seems to me that it offers an example of a theoretical tradition that is worth preserving. The essential requirement is to have new ideas which can be outlined and developed. There is no need to search immediately and at all cost for empirical validation or to wait until one is guided by experimental data. As Novalis wrote: 'If theory had to wait on experiment, it would never come into being.'

To clarify my view, I should perhaps simply state my preference for *any* theory to absence of theory. As things are today in social psychology, we have – with a few exceptions – nothing but proto-scientific conceptualizations. It would be better to have at our disposal even something like the phlogiston theory than to continue with the lack of communication, dispersion and anomie which is evident at present. The phlogiston theory was useful in chemistry because it defined the central processes of the scientific undertaking, served as a guide for research, forced the scientists to confront each other and provided them with a common language. Social psychology could well use a similar intellectual discipline, and one might perhaps venture the suggestion that it is time to halt the collection of data. Henri Poincaré wrote: 'An accumulation of facts is no more a science than a heap of stones is a house.' We do have the stones, but we have not built the house. If we decided to abandon for a while the collection of new data, we could view them in perspective and reflect on what has been achieved; we might then be able to define better the nature of the questions we have been asking, the purpose of our search and the meaning of our findings. In exhorting our students to produce new data we reflect the pressures of academic and economic institutions whereas our efforts should instead be directed towards helping them to educate themselves. A basis for this education could be found in a return to Lewin and to the classical writers of anthropology and sociology; in taking into account recent developments in ethnology, linguistics and genetic epistemology; and in re-examining the approaches represented by the theories of exchange and of dissonance, with the object of transcending their individual and inter-individual context in order to place them resolutely in a wider social framework.

The suggestion that we should aim towards, or at least not reject, theories which are proto-scientific may be found offensive in some quarters. But the idea is not as scandalous as it may seem. Whether we like it or not, the ideas of Heider, the postulate of balance, and the notions of attribution are all pre-scientific. If we have to pay for our scientism by the absence of theory, then it is preferable not to be 'scientific' when developing new theoretical ideas.

4   IN SEARCH OF A SOCIAL PSYCHOLOGY

'The determining cause of a social fact must be sought in social facts and not in the effects of individual consciousness.' Durkheim.

4.1   Are there one, two or three social psychologies?

No theoretical study can be fruitful unless its objectives are clearly defined. Chemistry or linguistics, physics or economics became sciences only when their practitioners began to seek reasons for the occurrence of the phenomena they observed. Certainly the aims of science are not immutable and theoretical advance depends upon an awareness of their progressive changing context; but there can be no further progress without a common definition of these aims.

There are many who think that general agreement about such a definition is no longer a problem in social psychology. In their view, social psychology is a science of behaviour – the science of social behaviour; hence they feel that the object of the discipline is identical with that of psychology in general, even if it is envisaged in a special context. It is this conception of the discipline which needs to be carefully and critically examined.

It is often forgotten that initially a strong impetus was given to the development of social psychology by the hope that it would contribute to our understanding of the conditions which underlie the functioning of a society and the constitution of a culture. The purpose of social theory was to explain social and cultural phenomena; the practical aim was to use the principles which it was hoped would be discovered in order to engage in a critique of the social organization. Thus the domain of social psychology was seen to include the study of everyday life and relationships between individuals and between groups, as well as of ideologies and of intellectual creativity in both its individual and collective forms.

Seen in this perspective, social psychology offered the promise of becoming a truly social and political science. Such ideas were soon forgotten, however, when our science became a 'science of behaviour'. This new orientation shifted the basis of the argument from society to individual and inter-individual phenomena which were theoretically envisaged from a quasi-physical rather than a symbolic point of view. The field of research was drastically narrowed in its horizons as well as in its potential impact. It is perhaps worth recalling that, as James Miller once confessed, this change of emphasis to 'behavioural science' was also meant to provide some reassurance in the quarters responsible for disbursing research funds, because the idea of 'social sciences' tended to create distrust and confusion. The label of a 'behavioural science' appeared more acceptable.

But this change of terminology reflected a corresponding change in values and in interests. Indeed, workers in the new social sciences restricted their ambitions to searching for palliatives for the dysfunctions of society without questioning either its institutions or its psychological adequacy in the face of human needs. This narrowing of horizons is closely related to the restriction of the subject to the 'study of behaviour'. The close association with general psychology that this restriction represents conceals its social and political implications; it prevents us from viewing in their true perspectives the phenomena we are supposed to be studying, and it even provides some justification for the opinion that we contribute to the alienation and to the bureaucratization of our social life.

Independently of all this, the notion of 'social behaviour', however useful it may be in helping to define empirical indices, remains much too vague. Far from helping us to unify the subject, it has resulted in our having today not one but two or even three social psychologies.

The first of these is taxonomic; its aim is to determine the nature of the variables which might account for the behaviour of an individual confronted with a stimulus. This psychology ignores the nature of the subject and it defines 'social' as a property of *objects* which are divided into *social* and *non-social*. Thus, the general scheme of the Ego–Object relation can be represented as follows:

Subject		*Object*	
Undifferentiated	Undefined	Differentiated into	
		Social	Non-social

In this scheme, the aim of the study is the discovery of how social stimuli affect the processes of judgement, perception or the formation of attitudes; the fact that socially determined changes are themselves one of the basic aspects of these processes is not taken into account. For example, research in social perception has been mainly concerned with the classification of independent variables as perceived objects which are either 'persons' ('human beings' – as in the experiments on person perception) or elements of a class of physical objects endowed with social value (as in the studies on the judgement of magnitudes of coins as a function of their value). Muzafer Sherif's (1936) studies on the autokinetic effect also belong to this taxonomic perspective: modes of response are related in them to the structure of the stimuli. The same is true of the work of the Yale group (e.g. Hovland et al., 1953), which aimed at accounting for persuasive communications in terms of the social characteristics of the source (such as its prestige, credibility, etc.). This kind of social psychology is 'taxonomic' in the sense that it limits itself to a psychological description of various types of stimuli and to a classification of the differences between them. It uses a definition of 'social' and 'non-social' in which phenomena that are inherently products of social activity are conceived as being, from their inception, a part of 'nature'. As its exclusive concern is with the enumeration of various kinds of reaction to the environment, it is bound to exclude from its range of interest the nature of the relationship between Man and his environment.

The second social psychology is 'differential'. Its principle is to reverse the terms of the relationship between Ego and Object and to seek in the characteristics of the individual the origin of the behaviour that is observed. On this basis, the nature of the stimulation is of little importance; the main preoccupation is to classify individuals by criteria of differentiation which often vary according to the school of thought to which the researcher belongs or the nature of the problem he is studying. Thus, subjects may be classified in terms of their cognitive styles (e.g. abstract–concrete, field dependent–field independent), their affective characteristics (e.g. anxious–not anxious, high or low self-esteem), their motivations (e.g. achievement motivation or approval needs) or their attitudes (e.g. ethnocentric or dogmatic) etc. The relationship between the subject and his environment can be represented as follows:

Subject	*Object*
Differentiated by his personality	Undifferentiated
characteristics	

Whatever kind of typology is adopted in this perspective, the aim is always the same: to find out how different categories of individuals behave when they are confronted with a problem or with another person. Ultimately, this tends towards the establishment of a differential psychology of responses and – at the limit – towards a description of the psychological composition of social groups from which their properties can be inferred. One example of this approach is a symptomatological analysis of subjects who are easily influenced, followed by a demonstration that the same individuals are highly suggestible when confronted with any kind of message. In the same way the social phenomena of leadership, risky shift or competition are perceived at the level of psychological traits of the individuals involved; what is completely ignored is that some of these traits may be no more than a reflection at the individual level of a phenomenon which is inherent in a network of social relations or in a specific culture. Thus, it is evident that achievement motivation (McClelland et al., 1953) is related to the imperatives of Protestantism and of economic rationalism, as was shown by Max Weber. But to transform this ideal Weberian type into an individual characteristic is to transplant it as a criterion for the differentiation of a particular psychological structure, which is then immediately assumed, without any justification, to have some kind of universality. Very often these personality descriptions are redundant and tautologous.

Like differential psychology, which measures individual differences in intelligence or in manual dexterity, this kind of social psychology aims to measure personality dimensions or aspects of affectivity which have only a tenuous relationship to social phenomena. It is because of its attempts to explain what happens in a society in terms of the characteristics of individuals that the interest of this social psychology in the 'social' is more apparent than real.

Finally, there exists a third kind of social psychology which can be described as 'systematic'. Its interest is focused on the global phenomena which result from the interdependence of several subjects in their relation to a common environment, physical or social. Here the relationship between Ego and Object is mediated through the intervention of another subject; this relationship becomes a complex triangular one in which each of the terms is fully determined by the other two. The situation can be represented in the following schema:

Subject

Object

Subject

It is, however, important to stress that this relationship between object and subject in a common environment has been conceived in two different ways, one static and one dynamic. In the former, the main objects of study have been the modifications in the behaviour of individuals participating in inter-action; in the latter, the interest was focused more directly on the specific effects that these relationships produce because they engage the total indi-vidual, the interactions between individuals, and also their orientation in the environment. From this distinction, two separate trends of theoretical and experimental work can be identified. One is concerned with the processes of facilitation or of exchange and with an analysis, at the level of observable performance, of the sequential progress of a relationship. It analyses the modifications occurring in responses in terms of the mere presence of another individual, or of the relationships of dependence and independence between two individuals; and it views these modifications as a function of the stimula-tion or the reward brought into the situation by the presence, the intervention or the response of another individual, or by the control that two individuals may exert upon one another. The work of Zajonc on social facilitation pro-vides a good example of this tendency. The second approach considers a social relationship as providing the basis for the emergence of processes which create a sociopsychological field in which the observed psychological phenomena find their place and their origin. Examples here would be work on small groups of the Lewinian school, the work of Festinger on pres-sure towards uniformity and on social comparison, and Sherif's work on the development of intergroup relations.

The three social psychologies – taxonomic, differential and systematic – today coexist peacefully in the textbooks. Perhaps this precarious equilibrium is understandable when one thinks of the requirements presented by teach-ing and of the absence of strong constraints which might upset the balance in one direction or another. Nevertheless the mixture remains arbitrary and its ingredients are incompatible. Indeed, how can it be possible to outline and articulate the findings of differential social psychology together with those of systematic social psychology when, by definition, the former stands in contradiction to the latter? For example, if it is considered that individual differences in readiness to be influenced provide a sufficient basis for the understanding of the effects of a message, nothing more needs to be done than to study the distribution of these differences in the population; there are no further requirements for a theoretical analysis of the mechanisms of social communication. In the same way, if one postulates that it is the presence of competitive subjects that makes a conflict situation competitive, then the study of conflict must be replaced by the study of the functioning of a certain personality type. If, on the other hand, one is genuinely interested in the nature of conflict or of communication, it is as useless to study personality factors as it would be to base the study of the laws of the pendulum on data about its humidity or the quality of its fibres. There is no doubt that these factors intervene as *parameters*; but to consider them as *variables* is to deny to sociopsychological phenomena the autonomy of functioning within their own specific system.

Some may think that I am flogging dead horses and that all these problems have long been familiar; this kind of argument is invoked each time someone questions the legitimacy of a consensus which, with the passage of time, has become second nature. My own view is that these problems are crucial and that, until they are resolved in one way or another, we shall not be able to guide our research in directions which would enable it to become the foundation of a sociopsychological science.

4.2 What is 'social' in social psychology?

It would be difficult to outline here in detail the reasons for my view that it is only systematic social psychology which is really worth pursuing and that other approaches, which interpret social phenomena in terms of the properties of stimuli or of personality, do not have much to contribute. At any rate, this view has been brilliantly developed by now 'classical' authors in social psychology and there is no need to repeat their arguments. I do wish, however, to push a little further the analysis of the manner in which our discipline nowadays attempts to define 'the social' as an interaction between two subjects and an object; an examination of this issue will help us to clarify our views about what has implicitly always been, and still is today, the true object of our discipline.

The triangle Ego–Alter–Object is crucial to this discussion since it is the only scheme capable of explaining and systematizing the processes of interaction. However, the manner in which it has been used has not always contributed to the definition of social conduct or of the system within which this conduct is inserted. Two indices have often been implicitly accepted as reflecting the influence of social context on an individual's behaviour: the presence of another in his social field; and 'numerosity'. Thus, for many researchers, the behaviour of an organism becomes 'social' only when it is affected by the behaviour of other organisms. Such a definition is equally valid for Man and for other species and it enables one to use a series of analogies in order to extrapolate across species.

Acceptance of these views led to the neglect of some fundamental aspects of social phenomena. Society has its own structure, which is not definable in terms of the characteristics of individuals; this structure is determined by the processes of production and consumption, by rituals, symbols, institutions, norms and values. It is an organization which has a history and its own laws and dynamics that cannot be derived from the laws of other systems. When the 'social' is studied in terms of the presence of other individuals or of 'numerosity', it is not really the fundamental characteristics of the system that are explored but rather one of its subsystems – the subsystem of inter-individual relationships. The kind of social psychology that emerges from this approach is a 'private' social psychology which does not include within its scope the distinctiveness of most of the genuine collective phenomena. It can therefore be argued that, for reasons which are partly cultural and partly methodological, the systematic perspective in social psychology has not been truly concerned either with social behaviour as a product of society or with behaviour *in* society. This is not to say that there have been no attempts to analyse phenomena such as power, authority or conflict; however, the perspective of this analysis has always been inter-individual and consequently these phenomena have been removed from the context to which they properly belong.

For these reasons, it is ambiguous to maintain that social behaviour is currently the real object of our science. From one point of view this assertion is justified, since our preoccupation has been with one category of social acts and with one specific segment of social life; on the other hand, it has never been properly recognized that the 'social' exists primarily in the intrinsic properties of human society.

This is why systematic social psychology must be renewed and redeveloped so as to become a real science of those social phenomena which are the basis of the functioning of a society and the essential processes operating in it. But – as it is obvious that not *all* such phenomena are within the purview of social psychology – it is important to select those that should be its main focus. The central and exclusive object of social psychology should be the study of all that pertains to *ideology* and to *communication* from the point of view of their structure, their genesis and their function. The proper domain of our discipline is the study of cultural processes which are responsible for the organization of knowledge in a society, for the establishment of inter-individual relationships in the context of social and physical environment, for the formation of social movements (groups, parties, institutions) through which men act and interact, for the codification of inter-individual and intergroup conduct which creates a common social reality with its norms and values, the origin of which is to be sought again in the social context. In parallel, more attention should be paid to language, which has not until now been thought of as an area of study closely related to social psychology. Present texts on psycholinguistics devote their attention entirely to clear and scholarly expositions of linguistic phenomena as they relate to learning and memory or to phonetic and lexical structures. They contain very little about the exchange functions of language and about the social origin of its characteristics. It is taken for granted that language is an essential feature of communication; but this is not used as a basis for theoretical studies. In this way, the social nature of language remains at the periphery of approaches to psycholinguistic problems; the implication is that sociopsychological questions about language do not differ from those asked in psycholinguistics. Rommetveit (1972) discusses some of the general consequences for psycholinguistics of this reductionist perspective.

The notion of ideology does have its place in contemporary social psychology. Many phenomena which are at present being studied are either inherent parts of ideology or theoretical substitutes for it. This is true of habits, prejudices, stereotypes, belief systems, psycho-logic, etc. But this accumulation does not cover the full range of the major theoretical theme, which still remains segmented. There are, however, some signs that the study of the phenomenon of ideology may well be developed further; the promise of it is contained in the systematic analysis of social thinking and in some of the work on cognitive dissonance, on the unity of cognitive and non-cognitive processes, and on social motivation.

Research in the social psychology of communication has not advanced very far, despite the fact that, as a discipline, social psychology is well suited for this undertaking; it should be able to look at the basic aspects of communication from the point of view of the genesis of social relationships and social products, and also it should be able to consider Man as a product of his own activity – as, for example, in education and in socialization. But in order to achieve this aim, we must go beyond superficial explorations. To ask questions about the effects of mass media, about the influence exerted by an authoritative or a non-authoritative source, about the effectiveness of a message announced at the beginning or at the end of a speech, is to confine our discipline to purely pragmatic boundaries traced by the requirements of the owners or the manipulators of mass media. The real problems are much wider. They reside in questions about why we communicate and according to what kind of rhetoric, and about the manner in which our motivation to communicate is reflected in our modes of communication. The mass media, whose object is to persuade, are a negligible part of the total network of communications. There is no reason why they should be given a privileged status as compared with the processes of the exchange of information which takes place in social, scientific, political or religious communities, in the worlds of theatre, cinema, literature or leisure. Culture is created by and through communication; and the organizing principles of communication reflect the social relations which are implied in them. This is why we must envisage communication in a new and wider perspective. Until the present, it has mainly been considered as a *technique*, as a means towards realizing ends which are external to it. The study of communication can become a proper object of science if we change this perspective and conceive of communication as an autonomous process which exists at all levels of social life.

Social life is the common basis of communication and of ideology. The task of social psychology in the study of these phenomena is one for which the discipline is well equipped; it concerns the relationships between the individual and society. These relationships are a focus of tensions and contradictions, and they represent the meeting-point of Man's need for freedom and of his tendencies towards alienation; they are also the chosen battlefield of many political movements. Though it is true that social psychologists are aware of the problems involved, they do no more than eliminate their real interest and relevance when they reduce them to processes of socialization.

The views which stress the overriding importance of socialization can be summarized as follows: the child learns and internalizes a set of values, a language, and social attitudes; he models his behaviour on the behaviour of adults and of his peers. Finally, when he himself becomes an adult, he integrates into the group which prepared him so thoroughly for membership. When this stage is achieved, difficulties of adjustment arise only if the individual has not succeeded in the appropriate assimilation or the adequate application of the principles which he has been taught.

The development of this conception depends, in fact, on the acceptance of several postulates. The first is that the individual is a biological unit which must be transformed into a social unit; the second, that society is an immutable 'given' encountered by the individual as a ready-made environment in the structure of concentric circles consisting of the family, the peer groups, and the wider groups and institutions in which he moves and to which he must adapt. The third postulate is that the individual is inescapably absorbed by his social surroundings: he ceases to be an individual from the moment he becomes affiliated, submits to social pressures and becomes a role-player. Finally, it is assumed that society plays an equilibrating part in the individual's life, since it reduces his tensions and his uncertainties. In fact, these postulates imply a conception of the individual which is fully organic, together with a conception of society which limits its role to that of a mediator for the needs of the individual organisms. In this conception society is not seen as a product of individuals, nor are they seen as products of the society. The sociopsychological laws that emerge are not concerned with transformations that take place within the scope of the 'social', but with transformations from the biological to the social. The primary interests of social psychology, which mainly focuses on the processes of learning, of socialization and of conformity, can be traced directly to these postulates and to their application.

And yet, the problem of the relations between Man and society intrinsically concerns both terms of the *rapport*; they jointly intervene in the economic, political and social processes. It must not be forgotten that the individual is not a 'given' but a product of society, because it is society that forces him to become an individual and to stress his individuality in his behaviour. For example, our market economy forces us all to become buyers and sellers of goods and services; our electoral democracy is based on the principle that each man represents a vote. But these are not universal principles; their boundaries are cultural. The antagonisms that capitalist societies created in bringing individualism to its highest peak are – in reality – a result of the close interdependence of all sectors of everyday life that is the mark of these societies. The system that has emerged combines the anonymity of urban life with physical, psychological and social interdependence; it also introduces a sharp cleavage between private and public life. The individual created by this society has very little in common with a purely biological organism. The jurists have been more successful than the psychologists in establishing a distinction between the moral person and the physical person. It is inherent in our society that individuals are primarily moral persons and as such they behave as parties to social encounters and as actors in their diverse milieux. For all these reasons, the notion of an 'individual' is entirely relative: trade unions or political parties can be considered collectively as individuals who behave as such towards one another and in their relations with the society at large. Society produces individuals according to its own principles; thus it can be compared to a 'machine' which socializes and individualizes at the same time. Its mode of action consists not only – as is too often believed – of establishing uniformities, but also of maintaining and accentuating differences. Consequently, as the individual becomes social, so also does society acquire individuality; this is why there exist not one but many societies which differ from each other both in their origins and in the characteristics of social actors who compose and produce them.

This perspective enables us to understand the contrast between individualism and the tendency of the social actor to minimize his differences for the sake of pursuing his goals and interests and conforming to his notion of what is 'good' and 'true'. The main question that social psychologists have been asking is: Who socializes the individual? They have neglected the second aspect of the problem contained in the question: Who socializes society? A new approach to the relationship between the individual and society will have to recognize two basic phenomena. The first is that the individual is not a biological datum but a social product; and the second is that society is not an environment geared to training the individual and reducing his uncertainties but a system of relationships between 'collective individuals'. This view of social dynamics has direct scientific implications as well as psychological and political significance; it forces us to envisage social control and social change in a common perspective rather than treating them separately, as has been the case in the past. There is no reason at all why priority should be given to those aspects of socialization which tend towards the transmission of existing traditions and the stability of the *status quo*; the opposite tendencies, which engender reforms and revolutions, are just as important.

Our exclusive interest has been in the formation of 'social objects'; and this is reflected in the conception we have of the individual organism as the passive party to a relationship that reaches its maturity in conforming to an immutable and pre-established model. The time has now come to insist on the formation of 'social subjects' (Moscovici and Plon, 1968) – be they groups or individuals – who acquire their identity through their relationships with others. This change of perspective can already be seen in the work of Brehm (1966) on 'psychological reactance', of Rotter (1966) on internal and external control and of Zimbardo (1969) on cognitive control. We must also recognize the essential role played in the formation of 'social subjects' by 'social solidarity' (i.e. social comparison and social recognition), decision processes (both social and individual), social organization and social influence. We already have a fund of theoretical notions and of experimental studies relevant to each of these phenomena. In order to reach a new level of understanding of the relations between Man and society, we must relate this knowledge to processes of communication and the influence exerted by ideologies. In this sense, control and change constitute two lines of development which must be analysed simultaneously in order to enable us to understand as well as to criticize the important aspects of social life. If we adopt this approach as a guide for research, we shall cease to consider our environment as an immutable 'external' milieu and see it instead as the humanized background to the relationships in which men engage and a tool for these relationships (Moscovici, [1968]/1977). This environment is not inherently ambiguous or structured, and neither is it purely physical or social; it is determined by our knowledge and methods of approach. Environment explains nothing; on the contrary, it itself stands in need of explanation, since it is both constructed and limited by our techniques, our science, our myths, our systems of classification and our categories. In most of the theories concerned with exchange or with influence, these processes are conceived as responses determined by resources present in the environment or by its organization. In consequence, questions concerning the genesis of social objects do not even arise. But progress in ethology, some recent studies on social influence (Moscovici and Faucheux, 1969; Moscovici et al., 1969; Alexander et al., 1970) and historical evidence about the transformation of the environment provide indications that the emphasis is changing: from a conception stressing the inertia of the material world we are turning towards the study of its significance.

In sum, the field of social psychology consists of social subjects, that is, groups and individuals who create their social reality (which is, in fact, their only reality), control each other and create their bonds of solidarity as well as their differences. Ideologies are their products, communication is their means of exchange and consumption, and language is their currency. This parallel with economic activities is, of course, no more than an analogy; but it enables us to define better those elements of social life that are most worthy of theoretical and empirical study; and it also underlines the need to introduce more direction and coherence into the definition of our potential field of investigation.

Where does 'behaviour' stand in relation to all this? It also needs to be envisaged in a new perspective: instead of locating 'social' in behaviour, we must locate behaviour in 'social'. In textbooks and other publications social behaviour is usually considered in the same way as any other kind of behaviour, the only difference being that social behaviour is supposed to include superimposed social characteristics. It is considered as being determined by the same psychological causes as other kinds of behaviour, and by the same systems of physical stimulation. From the point of view of the present discussion, social behaviour must be looked upon as a problem in its own right: its essential feature is that it is symbolic. The stimuli which elicit social behaviour and the responses engendered are links in a chain of symbols; the behaviour thus expresses a code and a system of values which are a form of language; or it could be said perhaps that it is social behaviour itself which constitutes a language. It is essentially social and it is created by social relations; indeed, there could be no symbolism confined to one individual or to one individual confronted by material objects alone.

Symbolic behaviour has often been confused with the general psychological processes referred to as 'cognitive'. Thus, theories which introduced the concept of consistency into the study of social influence or of motivation were classed as 'cognitive' theories. The reason for this was that these theories were concerned with a symbolic mode of organization of actions, and 'symbolic' has been subsumed under 'cognitive'. The difficulty of this view is not only due to the illegitimacy of assimilating the symbolic to the cognitive; it is also in the fact that, in doing this, one masks the distinction between the two terms. When the terms 'affective', 'motor' or 'motivational' are replaced by the term 'cognitive', the underlying assumption is that one has done no more than move from one level to another. The focus of analysis still remains on the individual as a unit within the classical scheme of stimulus–response. But the fundamental aspects of symbolic behaviour consist of its verbal and non-verbal manifestations, which are understood and become 'visible' only in relation to the common meanings they acquire for those who receive the messages and those who emit them. Symbolic behaviour is supported and made possible by social norms and rules and by a common history reflecting the system of implicit connotations and reference points that inescapably develops in every social environment.

Social psychology is a science of behaviour only if this is understood to mean that its interest is in a very specific mode of that behaviour – the symbolic mode. It is this which distinguishes sharply its field of interest from that of general psychology. All that has been said in the present section is concerned solely with the development of this fundamental proposition.

5   A SOCIOPSYCHOLOGICAL PROBLEM: THE ABSENCE OF DANGEROUS TRUTHS

If the study of symbolic processes became our main object, we would be forced to explore the domain and boundaries of the social reality in which we live. Indeed, if we wish to grasp real social facts rather than individual facts in a social context, if we wish to abandon a vision of society in which individuals enclosed in the cells of their 'primary' groups move as if at random, if we wish to destroy the illusion that we can one day achieve an empty universality of laws through getting to know general and abstract mechanisms without reference to their contents, then we must clearly admit that we have, until the present time, tended to ignore concrete social processes and their collective forms.

Despite its technical achievements, social psychology has become an isolated and secondary science (cf. Jaspars and Ackermann, 1966–7). This judgement is certainly true for Europe, but I believe that it also applies elsewhere. This is probably the result of an intense desire to achieve professional recognition and academic respectability. Nevertheless, it is true that we have succeeded in conducting scientific experiments, in having our research programmes accepted by universities, in producing – though for a very limited market – students who know their literature, can employ statistical methods, manipulate apparatus and produce good dissertations. On the other hand, the gap that has been created between our discipline and other social sciences (such as anthropology, sociology, linguistics or economics) has led us into a situation of ignorant expertise. The questions we ask are most often very restricted; and if it happens that important problems are taken up, we manage to transform them again into minor questions.

But all this does not seem to disturb anyone, since it appears that we have achieved our principal aims of applying correctly the rules of the art of experimentation and of receiving for this success the approval of our own group. And yet, there is ample evidence that our control and minutiae have little significance for the really important aspects of the problems we are studying. For example, in their studies of primates the ethologists have never been able to use methods as refined as those we use in our studies of interaction. Despite this, they have courageously attacked crucial problems which are of direct interest both in the study of the social organization of animal species and of Man; they have produced a harvest of knowledge which appears richer and nearer to our present preoccupations than social psychology has ever been able to accumulate. By contrast, social psychology has become a psychology of private life, and at the same time it has managed to transform its practitioners into members of a private club. Even in the field of methodology, in which until recently we were well ahead, we have now been outpaced by other disciplines. It certainly cannot be said that there is a dearth of important problems: war, profound social change, race and international relations, individual alienation, struggles for political freedom, and violence. One might add the problems created by science, technology and the change of scale in the evolution of our world – and yet there is no trace of any of this in our journals and our textbooks; it is as if the very existence of all these problems was being denied.

It is not enough, however, to recognize that these issues are 'relevant' in order to make them proper objects of investigation. They must also be approached in a manner which is 'relevant'; that is, in a manner which would enable us to understand simultaneously how they concern Man and society, and how their study would contribute to a genuine advance of knowledge. A greater lucidity and a stronger intellectual commitment are indispensable for this task. For example, it will not be sufficient to discern in the social field only the work of forces that conserve, because forces that push towards gradual change or revolution are at least as important. History is not only made of societies that survive; it is also made of societies that die. We must learn to face these realities; an exclusive search for a science which would be only an art of compromise would, in the end, compromise science itself. It has become evident that social equilibrium and peaceful individual satisfaction are not the supreme achievements towards which men strive. Values are not only Utopias or useless appendages; the ideals of justice, truth, freedom and dignity have made people live and die, people who recognized in them their desire not to accept just any kind of life or death. It is difficult to see why we should forget, together with today's social psychologists, that the processes of revolution, of innovation, of the irreducibility of conflict are an inherent part of the evolution of human groups.

The second point I wish to stress is that social psychology must now come out of the academic ghetto or, perhaps one should say, out of the American ghetto that the European offshoots of this discipline have entered (Back, 1964). Meditation in a vicious circle has never expanded any horizon. One would have to be more than human to escape completely the influence of one's immediate surroundings and not to be affected by the perspectives in which questions in one's milieu are being asked. It is well known that the inhabitants of a ghetto share a common vision and do not resist strongly what is familiar to them. At present many of the arguments, judgements and research topics in social psychology reflect the values of the middle class from which most social psychologists have not yet become disengaged. Thus they remain prisoners of a pragmatic culture which has for its main preoccupation the avoidance of what is called 'metaphysics' or, in other words, of all the sombre and non-immediate realities of existence.

Most of the experiments conducted in England, in France or in the United States on social influence, on group polarization (risky shift) or on conflict employed students as subjects. No work has been done on the various regions of a country, on different social classes, on ideological or on national, religious or racial groups. At the same time, few of us have been concerned with a careful study and an adequate formulation of the problems and preoccupations of these groups. Consequently, social psychologists find it difficult to see in proper perspective their own environment and values, and thus they cannot enrich and diversify their discipline. It is necessary and unavoidable that a science should sooner or later become an academic pursuit, but this does not mean that it should start by isolating itself either in the university or within the boundaries of a nation, a class, an age-group or a political movement.

Our discipline must now turn towards realities of which in the past it was unaware, and it must participate in social experiments and in the establishment of new social relationships. Social psychology cannot afford to remain a 'science of appearance'; it must not only begin to discover the deeper aspects of social reality but also to participate in the general dynamics of knowledge through which certain concepts are destroyed and new ones created. The aim should be not only to systematize existing knowledge but to postulate entirely new concepts. It is now fully recognized that the exact sciences create new aspects of nature; social sciences must create new aspects of society. It is only the exploration of new realities that will enable social psychology to progress and take it out of the restricted framework of commercial and industrial activities within which it is confined at present. Until now its practitioners have preferred to concern themselves with the view of the world current in some academic circles and to neglect what they could be taught by artists and writers about human psychology and the mechanics of a society. They have not taken as their guide the epistemological principles which lead to an analysis of what is rare and about which little is known; it is this kind of analysis that helps to throw new light on well-established and familiar phenomena. As Durkheim once wrote: 'If a science of societies is to exist, we must expect that it will not consist of a simple paraphrase of traditional prejudices but rather that it will lead us to see things in ways diverging from views currently accepted.'

The history of science shows that this principle is at the heart of all discovery. The great intellectual innovations due to Descartes or to Galileo were possible because of their serious interest in optical instruments, which were familiar only to very few people at the time; the majority of philosophers continued to practise a science based on everyday observations which had also been the basis of Aristotle's universe. This is only one example amongst many; perhaps its importance is to show that new and unexpected ideas in a science are not due only to the inspiration and the genius of an individual but also to his readiness to upset the conceptions which are current in his time. But this creation of new departures also depends upon the susceptibility of a science to new ideas and its capacity to remain open to conceptions which have previously been considered to lie outside its field of interest. The classical writers in social psychology were outstanding in their ability and willingness to receive a wide range of ideas. If we turn back to them, we shall perhaps be able to achieve a better grasp of wider perspectives and to dedicate ourselves to the pursuit of significant ideas rather than to the pursuit of data. At present we respect the maxim that methodology makes a science, instead of remembering that science should choose its methods.

It is only if we hold on to the belief that there *is* a royal road, and try to find it, that we shall be able to transcend the present limitations of social psychology and make it more than a secondary science. It is the destiny of all truth to be critical, and therefore we shall have to be critical. The present conjunction of events is favourable for such a mutation. In order that our discipline may become truly scientific its field of interest must remain free and its gates must be wide open to other sciences and to the demands of society. The aims of science are knowledge through action together with action through knowledge. It is unimportant whether these aims are reached through mathematics, experimentation, observation or philosophical and scientific reflection. But for the present, the terms 'science' and 'scientific' are still imbued with fetishism, the abandonment of which is the *sine qua non* of knowledge. Social psychology will be unable to formulate dangerous truths while it adheres to this fetishism. This is its principal handicap, and this is what forces it to focus on minor problems and to remain a minor pursuit. All really successful sciences managed to produce dangerous truths for which they fought and of which they envisaged the consequences. This is why social psychology cannot attain the true idea of a science unless it also becomes dangerous.

3

The History and Actuality of
Social Representations*

1 THE SCANDAL OF SOCIAL THOUGHT

One often hears that good science should begin by proposing clear and carefully defined concepts. Actually no science, not even the most exact, proceeds
in this way. It begins by assembling, ordering and distinguishing phenomena
which surprise everyone, because they are disturbing or exotic, or they create
a scandal. Now, for people living in a culture such as ours which proclaims
science and reason, there are few things as scandalous as the spectacle of
beliefs, superstitions or prejudices which are shared by millions of people;
or again the scandal of ideologies, those assemblies, according to Marx, of
'chimeras, dogmas, imaginary beings' which obscure the real determinants
of the human situation and the authentic motivations of human action. Certainly we have become more tolerant today towards religious beliefs which
suppose the immortality of the soul, the reincarnation of individuals, the
efficacy of prayer, or many other things which our knowledge of humanity
and nature excludes. It is enough to glance at popular publications to be
surprised by the number of people in our society who read their horoscopes,
consult faith healers, or consume miraculous remedies. Likewise one can
observe the intensity with which magic is practised in our milieux, in our
cities and even our universities. Those who have recourse to these things are
not the socially maladapted of the uneducated layers in society, as some
would have us believe, but the educated, engineers and even doctors. Think
of those 'high-tech' enterprises which recruit their personnel by using grapho-
logical or astrological tests. Far from wanting to hide such activities, most of

* Translated from the French by Gerard Duveen, who is grateful to Marie-Claude Gervais
for her advice, and to Alex Schlömmer for her help in tracing quotations in German texts.

the practitioners of this magic show themselves off on television, and publish books which have a wider readership than any scholarly text.

These things, which seem strange and even troubling to us, also have something to teach us about the way in which people think and what they think about. Take, for example, that strange and unknown disease, AIDS. Conversations and media were quick to take possession of it, and immediately catalogued it as the punitive illness of a permissive society. The press represented it as a condemnation of 'degenerate behaviours', the punishment of 'irresponsible sexuality'. A conference of Brazilian bishops spoke out against the campaign for condoms, describing AIDS as the 'consequence of moral decadence', the 'punishment of God' and the 'retribution of nature'. There was also a series of publications arguing that the virus was manufactured by the CIA for the extermination of undesirable populations, and so on. This example shows (as others could just as well have done) the frequency with which incredible and alarming ideas or images circulate, which neither good sense nor logic can stop. Needless to say, a type of mental functioning which clearly confirms this irrationality has generated much research. And this brings us to the heart of the matter.

One can summarize the results of such research by saying that, to our not very great surprise, they show that most individuals prefer popular ideas to scientific ideas, making illusory correlations which objective facts are incapable of correcting. In general they take no account of the statistics which play such a large role in our decisions and everyday discussions. They distort the information available to them. Moreover, as has repeatedly been said without being contradicted, people accept above all those facts or perceive those behaviours which confirm their habitual beliefs. And they do this even when their experience tells them 'it's wrong' and reason tells them 'it's absurd.' Should we take all of this lightly, arguing that people are the victims of prejudice, deceived by some ideology or constrained by some power? No, the facts are too widespread for us to be content with such explanations, and to pretend that we do not feel some uneasiness at seeing how far *Homo sapiens*, the only animal gifted with reason, has proved to be unreasonable.

It is possible to understand these facts, I repeat, but without ceasing to think that they have consequences for the relations between individuals, for political choices, for attitudes towards other groups, and for everyday experience. I could continue by evoking racism, ethnic wars, mass communication, and so on. But the most glaring question is this: Why do people think in non-logical and non-rational ways? A worrying, a very worrying question. Without any doubt, it is a question which belongs to social psychology, and I need to explain briefly why it does.

From the perspective of the individual, it has been agreed, since Descartes I think, that people have the capacity to think correctly about the evidence presented to them by the external world. On the one hand, they are in a position to distinguish the information available, and on the other, from the ensemble of premises concerning it, they know how to draw a certain conclusion. It should, one supposes, be a matter of following logical rules, of which the most important is that of non-contradiction. In so far as such reasoning and the conclusion seem correct, one can also consider that the way in which the rules and logical procedures were applied provides the best explanation of persistent beliefs and knowledge. But from the moment that one sees that the reasoning is flawed and the conclusion is wrong, one must look for other causes for the bad application of the rules, non-logical causes which can explain why individuals make mistakes. Among these causes there are, first, affective problems, but, above all, social influences which would submit the psychic apparatus to external pressures. Social influences would incite individuals to yield before habits, or to turn themselves away from the external world so that they succumb to illusions or to the satisfaction of a need to invent.

Thus we uncover a duality which is at the bottom of most explanations in this domain. It can be described in a few words: our individual faculties of perception and observation of the external world are capable of producing true knowledge, whereas social factors provoke distortions and deviations in our beliefs and our knowledge of the world. Let us not pause for the moment over the indetermination of this duality, but examine the three ways in which it is expressed. First, by the idea that one touches the true processes of knowledge when these are considered within the individual, independently of their culture, and actually, of every culture. In this sense, as Gellner writes, 'culture, a shared set of ideas, held to be valid simply because they constitute the joint conceptual banks of customs of an ongoing community, is spurned. It is spurned *because* it is culture. Its social and customary origin is the *fatal taint*' (1992, p. 18).

Then there is the conviction, expressed particularly in mass psychology, that individuals gathered in a group can be seen to change their psychic qualities, losing some and acquiring others. Or again, more precisely, it is agreed that individuals who behave morally and rationally when isolated become immoral and irrational when acting in a group (Moscovici, 1985). Last, and most recently, in the light of the research I mentioned earlier, the ordinary person, the 'novice', has a tendency to neglect the information given, to think in a stereotyped way, failing to take account of the errors this induces. In other words, the ordinary person is, as they say, a *cognitive miser*.

Here is a very unflattering image of the way in which people think and act when they are brought together in the society to which they belong. I do not believe in a kind of mental infirmity which is invoked and recognized through what appears as an array of habitual beliefs, of deviations or distortions of our knowledge of the world which surprises or scandalizes. But the fact is that it appears as the symptoms of a psychopathology of social origin. I should add that here this is not a metaphor, recalling that social psychology has for a long time been assimilated through this motif to pathological psychology. This is expressed in the very title of a famous American review: the *Journal of Abnormal and Social Psychology*.

This association also comes, perhaps above all, from the fact that psychologists such as Freud, Jung and Janet, who all contributed so much to psychopathology, also dedicated important books and articles to collective psychology. Evidently for them, as for so many others, the normal thought of groups has its counterpart in the mental anomalies of individuals. And this holds for the civilized masses, the so-called primitive societies, or exotic religions. Although we speak about it less openly or are less conscious of it, this relation between collective thought and pathological thought is also inscribed in our theories and methods of observation. It signifies that finally reason and society or culture are antithetical. As a consequence the total self-sufficiency of the individual becomes represented as the reference situation and the norm, whereas the association of individuals in the social unity becomes a derived situation, one of dependence in relation to an environment which modifies this norm in a positive or negative sense.

In the course of this discussion, however, something could not help but strike us, which forces me to make a supplementary remark. We not only accept that it goes without saying that there is a duality between the forms of non-social thought and the forms of common thought and belief. We also presuppose that the concepts and laws of the former serve as the reference for the latter. As Wyer and Srull (1984) observe, 'This argument is that the processes involved in dealing cognitively with non-social events are simpler and conceptually more fundamental than the processes involved with social events. The study of cognitive processing in the context of non-social stimuli provides a foundation on which the more complex social cognitive principles can be built' (p. 25). This presupposition, the most limiting and also unfounded, is what we need to try and liberate ourselves from. In any case, it is only in the context of a *different* psychology that we can elucidate the meaning of these forms of common thought and belief.

It is also right to indicate that things are changing. The pre-eminence of the social is more and more recognized in the fields of epistemology, language and social psychology. Personally I am convinced that this is a tendency which will deepen. Meanwhile, I would not have written this chapter if I was not also convinced that it is not sufficient to recognize the pre-eminence of the social by paying lip-service to it, even in the sense of a general consensus. Above all, we need to recover a theoretical perspective which can illuminate these surprising phenomena as a normal part of our culture and our life in society. All things considered, it is a question of reformulating the polarity of the individual and society in clearer and more sharply defined terms.

2   AN ANTI-CARTESIAN NOTION:
COLLECTIVE REPRESENTATIONS

Nothing in what I have said so far, it seems to me, takes me further away from what is known today as the psychology of the social. The problem is not to choose between the pre-eminence of the individual or of society, it is something more concrete. It has to do with the explication of the phenomena of belief, religion or magic, of ordinary and popular knowledge, of the ideological forms of collective thought and action. To begin with, why does society create such beliefs and ideas, whether or not they are correct? Then, why are they accepted and transmitted from one generation to the next? Even if the social nature of our thought, language and so on were recognized in psychology, which is not the case today, the problem would be posed in the same terms, and those who discuss it and would continue to discuss it would somehow have to resolve it. It is not possible to seek refuge in the trivialities of intersubjectivity or linguistic constructions. And it is because it has not confronted this problem that I think that social cognition is bound to remain less than convincing.

I am therefore led today to acknowledge this simple and evident fact, although it is not without meaning. Leaving aside psychoanalysis, which has related collective psychology and individual psychology through the unconscious, only the line of thought which has developed towards a theory of social representations is seriously dedicated to the solution of this problem. And this is nearly a century after the appearance of its first notions required the autonomy of our psychology for the solution itself. You see that, in an era in which labels change so quickly and where everyone can break as radically as possible with the past, I hesitate to appeal to a line of thought which began with the human sciences themselves and which forms, as it were, a part of their genetic code. But one can also think that the fact that it persists, that one can return to this line of thought without being limited by any tradition of a school, means that it touches something fundamental and precious in the way people live.

The theory of social representations is unique, it seems to me, in that it tends more and more to being a general theory of social phenomena and a special theory of psychic phenomena. This paradox, as we shall see, owes nothing to chance; on the contrary, it comes from the deep nature of things. It is a general theory to the extent that, as far as it is concerned, society could not be defined by the simple presence of a collective which brought individuals together through a hierarchy of power, for example, or exchanges based on mutual interests. Certainly power and interests exist, but to be recognized as such in society there must be representations or values which give them meaning, and above all, to make the efforts of individuals converge and to unite them through beliefs which ensure their existence in common. This is guided by opinions, symbols and rituals, by beliefs, that is, and not simply by knowledge or technique. They are of a different order: beliefs about life in common, about what it should be, about what should be done; beliefs about the just, the true and the beautiful; and still others which all have an impact on ways of behaving, of feeling or of transmitting and exchanging goods.

It is when knowledge and technique are changed into beliefs that they bring people together and become a force which can transform individuals from passive members into active members, who participate in collective actions and in everything that brings existence in common alive. Societies break apart if there is only power and diverse interests to unite people, if there is not the sum of ideas and values in which they believe to bind them to a common passion which is transmitted from one generation to the next (Moscovici, 1993a). In other words, what societies think of their ways of living, the meanings they attach to their institutions and the images they share are a necessary part of their reality, and not simply a reflection of it. As the Polish philosopher Leszek Kolakowski has observed, 'the reality of a society depends in part on what is in its representation of itself' (1978, p. 94).

Before continuing we need to take account of an important but embarrassing fact: there are psychic phenomena which, although they vary in complexity, have in common a social origin and are indispensable for life in common. But as soon as one looks at society from this point of view an enigma surfaces. Indeed, one no longer understands how societies are able to survive while maintaining religious or magical beliefs, and allowing themselves to be guided by illusions, ideologies and the biases attributed to them. Further, one wonders why people create this hotch-potch of irrationality through which they fool themselves. In speaking of religious beliefs, which interested him above all, Durkheim wrote:

> It is unthinkable that systems of ideas like religions, which have held such a large place in history – the well to which peoples in all the ages have come to draw the energy they had to have in order to live – could be mere fabrics of illusion. Today we agree to recognise that law, morals, and scientific thought itself were born in religion, were long confounded with it, and have remained imbued with its spirit. How could a hollow phantasmagoria have been able to mold human consciousness so powerfully and so lastingly? . . . But if the people themselves created those systems of mistaken ideas, and at the same time were duped by them, how could this amazing dupery have perpetuated itself through the whole course of history?   ([1912]/1995, p. 66)

I suspect that, rightly, it is this abasement of shared beliefs, this contempt for popular ideas and knowledge, for other cultures in general which offended Durkheim. How to conceive a society where confidence and solidarity would not be only an illusion? Must we admit that culture has the secular function of furnishing humanity with phantasmagoria and errors? What is the content of the collective consciousness of a society which endeavours to fool itself about its ideas and values? We need to retain the deep sense of these interrogations about things we manage to slide over so easily, even today in psychology and even in sociology. Whatever they may be, we need to pay less attention to their abnormal character, from the point of view of the individual and their beliefs and knowledge, and more to their social character, to the mental and psychic life which they express. In order first to describe them and then to explain them as the common being of a group of individuals, we need to take account of three things.

1   We suppose that individuals essentially know both the natural world and the social world (Heider, 1958) by means of sensory perceptions of information which is waiting to be observed and explained by adequate concepts. They are like Adam on the day of his creation, opening his eyes on animals and other things, deprived of tradition, lacking shared concepts with which to coordinate his sensory impressions. This image cannot really be applied to individuals living in society, who have a common way of life which indicates how beings or objects should be classified, how to judge them according to their value, what information is worthy of belief, and so on. One could say of each of us what the English philosopher Cornford said of the philosophers and the scholarly:

> Wherever and whenever a professed man of science upholds such an opinion, we may be certain that he is not formulating a description of observed facts, but turning his knowledge to the defence of a belief which he has learnt, not direct from Nature, but at his mother's knee; in other words a collective representation. And this particular representation is not the outcome of long accumulated results of science and philosophy. On the contrary, the further back we trace it the more firmly planted it appears, and the daily contradictions of all experience have not yet uprooted it from the popular mind.   (1912, p. 43)

This means that the attempt to understand the complex knowledge and beliefs of a society on the basis of elementary laws of individual knowledge, which are, in the last analysis, based on sensory givens or sensory experience, is always hopeless, not because any conclusions which might be drawn from it have no value, but because the premises from which it begins are artificial and lack depth.

2   We have no reason to exclude totally individual experience and perceptions. But, in all justice, we must remember that nearly everything a person knows they have learnt from another, either through their accounts, or through the language which is acquired, or the objects which are used. These are, in general, the knowledge connected with the most ancient kind, whose roots

are submerged in the way of life and collective practices in which everyone participates and which need to be renewed every instant. People have always learnt from one another, and have always had knowledge that they do so. This is not exactly a discovery. The importance of this proposition for our theory is that significant knowledge and beliefs have their origin in a mutual interaction, and are not formed in any other way.

3   The ideas and beliefs which enable people to live are incarnated in specific structures (clans, churches, social movements, families, clubs, etc.) and adopted by the individuals who are a part of them. The meaning they communicate and the obligations they recognize are profoundly incorporated in their actions and exercise a constraint which extends to all the members of a community. It is probably this constraint which obliges us, according to Weber, not to ignore the causal role of collective forms of thought in the orientation of our ordinary activities and those we expect. Thus he writes:

> These concepts of collective entities which are found both in common sense and in juristic and other technical forms of thought, have a meaning in the minds of individual persons, partly as something actually existing, partly as something with normative authority. This is true not only of judges but of ordinary private individuals as well. Actors thus in part orient their action to them, and in this role such ideas have a powerful, often a decisive, causal influence on the course of action of real individuals.   (Weber, [1968]/1972, p. 14)

If Weber is right, then forms of collective thought are strongly incorporated in the motivations and expectations of individuals, which depend for their efficacy on their action in general. This is precisely what he attempted to show in his study of the spirit of capitalism: rational economic practices were born in the beliefs of puritan sects and the teachings of the Bible, as in the premeditated hope of their own salvation.

These three things – the primacy of representations or beliefs, the social origin of perceptions and beliefs, and the causal, and sometimes constraining, role of these representations and beliefs – are the background on which the theory of social representations was developed. I think I have traced their outline sufficiently clearly to justify a remark, which is that this background contributes to the solution of the problem evoked earlier. One can see an outline of it in the work in which Durkheim focused on this problem, *The Elementary Forms of the Religious Life* ([1912]/1995). The descriptive parts of the book give a lot of space to the religious beliefs of the indigenous Australians, whereas the explicative parts, in the middle and at the end of the work, are devoted to the creation and the meaning of these beliefs as the cement of society in general. The book exposes in great detail the peculiarities of human thought, the strange illusions and practices shared by a community, or its ideas, which may be very curious but only weakly scientific.

Thus Durkheim gives a detailed examination of what seems to be the general aspect of the adoration of animals and plants, knuckle-bones or wood, as well as the hazy outline of ideas, such as the famous mana, and the formulas which accompany each ritual. Nothing more is hidden from us, either the delirious frenzy of the collective dance around the totem in the course of which each individual psyche becomes suggestible, or the licentious character of the ritual ecstasy which suspends the conscious relation with reality. It is in this state of effervescence that beliefs are created and given life in common, inculcated in each of the participants. The morning after the ritual ceremony, the 'savages' awake full of sadness, but they part from one another having made these shared perceptions and values their own. One also sees elsewhere, through prayers and magical manipulations for the propitiation of the spirits, how beliefs bring success to hunting or fishing, or provide a remedy for some illness.

The thing which is interesting here is that, through these fantastic and even bizarre elements, a universe of sacred, and hence impersonal, things is constituted in these Australian societies, a universe which figures animals as totems, then the objects associated with these totems, and finally even the individuals themselves. Nothing would be easier than to trace the analogy with the religious or political universes of our societies and to show – an opportunity which hasn't been missed – how far their beliefs are founded on symbolic thought, on the displacement of observations, extreme rituals and intense emotions.

Durkheim acknowledges that such things must appear chimerical or irrational to those who judge them on the basis of their relation to physical reality. But if the reader will excuse me for returning to things I have discussed elsewhere (Moscovici, [1988]/1993), in effect, one arrives at the opposite conclusion as soon as one assumes that behind these illusions, rituals or emotions there are collective representations which are shared and transmitted from one generation to the next without changing. The impression is confirmed and strengthened when one realizes that, through totems and rituals, society celebrates its own cult by interposed divinities. Their diffuse and impersonal authority over individuals is that of the society itself to which they belong.

It is true that each person, in worshipping a plant or an animal, seems to be the victim of an illusion. But if everyone together recognizes their group in this way, then we are dealing with a social reality. Then they represent not only beings or things, but the symbols of beings and things. It is about them that they think, it is face to face with them that they conduct themselves, as we do when faced with the flag or the flame in the Arc de Triomphe. In the same way, ritual behaviours have, as their real aim, not so much to make it rain or to mourn a death as to maintain the community, to reinvigorate the sense of belonging to a group, to inflame belief and faith. I am far from wanting to suggest that this explanation of the religious life is the best, or that it has resisted the criticism of time. But it is enough for me to illustrate the sense in which latent representations are expressed through mental contents and symbolic behaviours. It would be legitimate to ask whether this approach would have yielded what was expected of it, and thereby helped to solve our concrete problem, had the hypothesis been allowed to reach fruition, that is to say, the hypothesis that collective representations are rational, not in spite of being collective, but because they are collective, and even that this is the only way in which we become rational. In fact, according to Durkheim, on the basis of their varied sensations, individuals could neither arrive at general notions nor establish any regularities. One can no longer see what it is that makes them do so. Criticizing David Hume, the sociologist affirms that it is not possible to understand how or why, in our solitude, we could discover an order through our association of ideas or fleeting sensations. And even supposing that an individual were able to do so, it is impossible to grasp how this order could remain stable and impose itself on everyone. On the other hand, one can understand that a representation, which is collective because it is the work of everyone, can become stable through reproduction and transmission from one generation to another. It also becomes impersonal to the extent that it becomes detached from everyone and is shared through the means of the concepts of a common language. 'To think conceptually is not merely to isolate and group the features common to a certain number of objects. It is also to subsume the variable under the permanent and the individual under the social' (Durkheim, [1912]/1995, p. 440).

Moreover, the principal categories of representation are social in origin and are brought into play exactly where everyone seems to oppose them. Thus a mimetic rite, where shouts and movements imitate those of the animal one wishes to see reproduced, brings into play a causal process to the letter. Or again, the magic formula, 'like attracts like,' connects different things and makes some appear as the function of others. But in this way, an implicit causal power is attributed to one thing to produce its like, and this is what is essential. It is in these ways that a real category of an active causality is formed, as much in the practice of culture as in the practice of magic. Or again, to the extent that each society, as primitive as it may be, divides and classifies its members, it also necessarily tends to classify animate or inanimate beings according to the same criteria. A logic of classifications is thereby instituted, which may be crude but is no less rigorous for that. Besides, elementary religions have sketched the essentials of the concepts which, according to Durkheim, have made science and philosophy possible.

> Religion made a way for them. It is because religion is a social thing that it could play this role. To make men take control of sense impressions and

replace them with a new way of imagining[1] the real, a new kind of thought had to be created: collective thought. If collective thought alone had the power to achieve this, here is the reason: Creating a whole world of ideals, through which the world of sensed realities seemed transfigured, would require a hyperexcitation of intellectual forces that is possible only in and through society. (Durkheim, [1912]/1995, p. 239)

Whatever the circumstances, it is clear that the psychic energy created through the participation of individuals in the life of the group, and the mental categories which they crystallize, allows collective representations to become detached, forming a complex of ideas and inferences which must be called rational. Clearly I cannot stop at the concept without discussing its justification. It seems to me that Durkheim wished to designate by this term an intellectual content, resembling in some ways Thomas Kuhn's paradigms, and in other ways Cassirer's symbolic forms, which underlie religious beliefs, the opinions of a society, and science. Representation has a clearly marked intellectual character, even though the cognitive aspects were not specified by the sociologist (Ansart, 1988).

Durkheim states: 'A man who did not think with concepts would not be a man, for he would not be a social being. Limited to individual perceptions alone, he would not be distinct from an animal' ([1912]/1995, p. 440). These are strong words. One could not complain that they lack clarity. They trace a clear frontier between individual psychology and social psychology, connecting each to its own reality and to its distinct forms of thought. In these circumstances, and without falling into the banal, one concludes that, according to the sociologist, it is incumbent upon the latter, that is, our science, to attain a deeper understanding of public and cultural representations. According to Durkheim, our science needs to study, through comparisons of mythical themes, legends, popular traditions and languages, how social representations are connected or mutually exclusive, how they merge into one another or differentiate themselves, and so on (cf. Durkheim, [1895]/1982).

Durkheim's arguments on this point, the vision he expressed of the collective genesis of our beliefs, our knowledge and what makes us reasonable beings more generally, might be thought to be disputable, or even out of date. The same might be said about the influence of latent collective representations on our individual representations. But the fact remains that it is the only sketch of a coherent vision which continues to exist. Such is also the opinion given recently by the anthropologist Ernest Gellner of the solution to the problem with which we are concerned: 'No better theory is available to answer it. No other theory highlights the problem so well' (1992, p. 37). Besides, the general line of argument matters more than the arguments invoked by Durkheim's critics. And in following the line which is marked out for us, at least we know where we are going.

3   COLLECTIVE REPRESENTATIONS AND
CULTURAL DEVELOPMENT

From all sides we are denied the right to think of a psychology of common representations and to work scientifically on the basis of this hypothesis. And yet it is necessary, since the data of individual psychology are elementary and concern only extremely limited phenomena. As much in the child as in the adult one often sees psychic acts whose explanation implies other acts which do not depend on individual representations. These acts are not only the perceptions of others or attitudes towards ethnic groups. In our least constrained everyday conversations we find ourselves confronted with linguistic images or influences which come to mind without our being the origin of them, and with deductions whose formation cannot be attributed to any of our interlocutors, as is the case with rumours. All of these acts remain incoherent if we claim to deduce them from individual reasoning or expressions, but they can be arranged in a whole whose coherence can be discovered by taking account of the inferred social representations. We find in this better understanding a sufficient motive for going beyond the immediate experience of each person. And if, in another connection, we can show that the psychology of collective representations, contrary to what some people believe, clarifies the mental and linguistic operations of individuals, then our hypothesis will have received a supplementary justification.

In fact, things are like this: above all, Durkheim drew the contours of a research programme by defining a position of principle and the collective background of our mental life. He set forth, as we shall see, the idea of collective representations as the underlying, one could even say unconscious, matrix of our beliefs, our knowledge and our language. Thus, although one could disapprove of this way of speaking, there is no such thing, strictly speaking, as individual rationality, which is the downfall of one of the most widespread beliefs. As Hocart has written: 'Men of all races and generations are equally convinced that they individually draw their knowledge from reality' (1987, p. 42). By arguing that they draw their categories from the thought of society, Durkheim initiated a radical change in sociology and anthropology. But this is also the reason why this idea is still contested today, or ignored to the point where, even in the clearest biographies of the French sociologist, only a passing allusion is made to it (Giddens, 1985).

Nevertheless, we also need to recognize that, preoccupied with the opposition between the collective and the individual, and with showing the continuity between religion and science, Durkheim gave this idea a sense which is too intellectual and abstract. To approach this issue in the most concrete way, one needs to pay greater attention to the differences than to the similarities among collective representations, to connect them to different societies in order to be able to compare them in a sustained way. In this sense, it seems that it was Lévy-Bruhl who transformed this general idea into a true concept and proceeded, even if only in a fragmentary way, to make the comparison. This is incontestable from the point of view which concerns us, since, at the same time, he sketched their autonomous social psychology, the significance of which I shall return to later. We know that the premises of his work and of this psychology were, and continue to be, scandalous (Lloyd, 1990). But here I am not concerned with this scandal, or with the confused reasons which led to the rejection of Lévy-Bruhl, since there are too many books and writings on the famous 'prelogical mentality'. One can find a succinct and fair discussion of these disputed questions in a wonderful book by Gustav Jahoda (1982).

One can try to grasp the concept quickly by saying that, given the collective background, Lévy-Bruhl insisted on four aspects of these representations.

1   They have a character which today we would describe as *holistic*, which is to say that one should not attribute an isolated belief or category to an individual or a group. Thus every idea or belief assumes a large number of others with which it forms a whole representation. For example, the idea 'This man is German' assumes that the idea of 'man' is available, as well as the idea of 'German', and consequently that of 'kind', 'French', and so on. Thus the belief that 'This man is German' assumes beliefs about nations, and implies a belief that 'This man is not a Turk,' etc. The holism of a representation means that the semantic content of each idea and each belief depends on its connections with the other beliefs or ideas. Thus, contrary to what is accepted in social cognition, the error or truth of one of the ideas or beliefs does not entail that the representation shared by the collective has an erroneous or truthful character, or that their way of thinking is erroneous or truthful. Evans-Pritchard understood the importance of this aspect when he wrote that Lévy-Bruhl 'was one of the first, if not the first, to emphasize that primitive ideas, which seem so strange to us, and sometimes idiotic, when considered as isolated facts, are meaningful when seen as parts of patterns of ideas and behaviours, each part having an intelligible relationship to others' (1965, p. 86). Now it is the representation which binds the ideas and behaviour of a collective together, representations which are formed in the course of time and to which people adhere in a public way.

2   We can put an end to all the misunderstandings surrounding the nature of representations if, from now on, in the description of different sorts of beliefs we leave to one side the question of whether, to classify them, we need to know if they are intellectual or cognitive, and join them together only according to their connection and their adherence to a specific society or culture. For various reasons, this is even more true, according to Lévy-Bruhl, for so-called primitive cultures, since 'what is really "representation" to us is found

blended with other elements of an emotional or motor character, coloured and imbued by them, and therefore implying a different attitude with respect to the objects represented' ([1925]/1926, p. 36). All the symbols retained and living in a society obey a logic of the intellect as much as a logic of the emotions, even though they might be founded on a different principle. I maintain that this holds for every culture, and not only the so-called primitive ones. We should not hesitate, therefore, to treat representations as intellectual constructions of thought, while relating them to the collective emotions which accompany them or which they arouse. When you discriminate against a group you express not only your prejudices about this category, but also the aversion or contempt to which they are indissolubly linked.

3   A German proverb has it that 'the devil is in the detail,' and so it is also with collective representations. Evidently they comprise ideas and beliefs which are general, and relate them to practices or realities which are not. Moreover, it is perhaps legitimate to conceive of them and to present them as a science or a religion. But nevertheless it is advisable to search for these representations through the most trivial aspects of language or behaviour, to linger over the most obscure interpretations or the most fleeting metaphors, in order to discover their efficacy and their meaning. If one then examines them as a whole, representations must appear as continuous and internal to both society and reality, and not as their double or their reflection. In this sense, a representation is at once both an image and a texture of the thing imagined, which manifests not only the sense of things which coexist but also fills the gaps – what is invisible or absent from these things.

Reading the books of Lévy-Bruhl, one is struck by the talent with which he explored religious contents or described rituals, and even more by the minute examination of their ramifications in linguistic expressions, the use of numbers, behaviour towards the sick or attitudes towards death. In this way an understanding of so-called primitive representations increases progressively as one sees them take root in the concrete life of people. Among contemporary researchers in this domain only Denise Jodelet (1989/1991, 1991a) shows a similar care.

This, however, does not concern the method but the concept itself, which takes on a different sense. It is this that Husserl saw clearly when he wrote in a letter to Lévy-Bruhl on 11 March 1935 (the date is important here):

Of course we have long known that each human being has their 'representation of the world', that each nation, each supra-national cultural sphere lives so to speak in another world than that which surrounds them, and we also know that it is the same for each historical epoch. But faced with this empty generality, your work and its excellent theme made us see something so surprising because of its novelty; it is, in effect, possible, and absolutely crucial, to take as a task to 'feel from within' a closed humanity living in an animated and generative sociality, to understand it in so far as it contains a world in its uniformalized social life, and on this basis, that it takes this world not simply as a 'representation of the world', but as the existing world itself. In this way we come to apprehend, identify and think their customs, and hence their logic as much as their ontology, and those of the surrounding world through their corresponding categories.

This is a difficult text, because it goes beyond psychology or anthropology as they existed at the distressing moment when the great German philosopher wrote it. But its author perfectly recognized that a social representation which was only a representation of something, of a common environment or object, would be an 'empty generality'. It has often been thought of in this way, in spite of the precision I have tried to give it. It happens when one does not take sufficient account of its specificity and its 'novelty', which is to be at one and same time the representation of someone, of a collectivity which in this way creates a world for itself.

4   Lastly, one must bear in mind that all collective representations have the same coherence and value. Each has its originality and its own relevance, such that none of them has a privileged relation to the others and could not be their criterion of truth or rationality. Otherwise, as soon as such recognition is given, for example, to a scientific or modern representation, then by inference others appear inferior, incomplete or irrational. If I insist on this point, it is because it is not altogether foreign to contemporary social and cognitive psychology. Everyone can grasp the accuracy of this critique by reading the excellent book by Stephen Stich, *The Fragmentation of Reason* (1990), which draws up a balance of the research undertaken in this psychology and shows how it has suffered from this mistaken recognition.

One can think of these four aspects as specifying the concept of knowledge with which we are concerned, and which retains its value even today. But it is, above all, the fourth aspect which was the source of Lévy-Bruhl's scandalous affirmation, that is to say, that it is impossible to propose an absolute criterion of rationality which could be independent of the content of collective representations and their entrenchment in a particular society. Thus he disputed the fundamental proposition maintaining that 'primitive thought' is concerned with the same problems or the same type of problems as advanced thought. Such a view would make the former a rudimentary, even childish, form of the latter. For Lévy-Bruhl there is a discontinuity, hence a profound difference, between primitive mentality and modern or scientific mentality. It is not that people in traditional cultures have a simpler or more archaic mentality than our own. On the contrary, each is equally complex and developed, and we have no reason for despising one and glorifying the other. Each has its own categories and rules of reasoning which correspond to different collective representations.

We cannot, then, as Durkheim wished, account for the psychology of both 'primitive' and 'civilized' people in terms of the same processes of thought. If one should not reduce the psychology of the group to that of the individual, neither should one reduce the psychology of different groups to a single uniform and undifferentiated entity. As Lévy-Bruhl writes: 'we must then reject beforehand any idea of reducing mental operations to a single type, whatever the peoples we are considering, and accounting for all collective representations by a psychological and mental functioning which is always the same' ([1925]/1926, p. 28). It is a wise counsel which authorizes us, in Husserl's phrase, to 'feel from within' how mentality is fashioned and how, in its turn, it fashions, not society in general, but this Melanesian society, or this Indian one, or this European one. This could be shown in detail, but this is not the occasion to do so. Meanwhile, one can grasp the full meaning of the distinction between the two modes of thinking and representing by paying attention to the social psychology which emerges from them, in particular that of the so-called primitive cultures, which is founded on three principal ideas.

First, the idea that the non-scientific representations of these cultures are steeped in an emotional ambiance which sensitizes people to the existence of invisible, supernatural, in a word 'mystical', entities. These 'mystical' entities colour all their ways of thinking, suggesting earlier liaisons among the things represented. They also render individuals impermeable to the data of immediate experience. Secondly, there is the idea that memory plays a more important role in these cultures than in ours. This means that the world of mediated and interior perceptions dominates the world of direct and exterior perceptions. Lastly, the third idea is that the people who create these representations and put them into practice are not constrained, as we are, by 'avoiding contradiction' (Lévy-Bruhl, [1925]/1926, p. 78). On the contrary, they are enjoined to follow the logic regulated by a law of participation, which allows them to think what is forbidden to us, namely that a person or a thing can at the same time be both itself and someone or something else.

For example, an animal can participate in a person; or else individuals partake of their names, so they do not disclose them, since an enemy can surprise them and have the owner of the name at their mercy. Further, a man participates in his child, so that if the child is ill it is the man who takes the medicine instead of the child. Do we also ever apply the law of participation? Do we not think that man is what he eats, suggesting that the qualities of the animal or plant with which he feeds himself end by colouring his qualities? We can see the reason why Lévy-Bruhl qualified the primitives as 'prelogical', not because they are illogical or incapable of thinking like the more civilized, but because they follow another law of thinking governed by what is called mystical collective representations.

You are probably struck, as I was, by the resemblance between the psychology of these representations and that of the unconscious set out by Freud in the same epoch. But while for Lévy-Bruhl this psychology expresses an alternative rationality, for Freud it expresses irrationality itself. To illustrate concretely how the French thinker conceived the difference for which he was so often criticized, one might dream of two fictional cultures. The first would establish, by decree or by vote, psychoanalysis as its public representation, the second cognitive psychology. In the first one may suppose that individuals will think in terms of invisible entities: 'Oedipus complex', 'cathexes', 'superego', and that they will be able freely to associate ideas without worrying about contradictions between them. Meanwhile, in the second, they will not take account of anything except measurable information about the frequency of events or perceived behaviours, and they will be constrained to obey the principle of non-contradiction, or any other principle which regulates the calculations of a computer.

Now, this is not to say that individuals in the first culture would be incapable of thinking which respected non-contradiction, nor that those in the second culture could not manage free association, but simply that the collective representations of our two imaginary cultures differ, and impose one or the other principle on their members. Further, the inhabitants of the cognitive culture will say, and elsewhere, you can be sure, they have said so (Moscovici, 1993a), that the inhabitants of the psychoanalytic culture are 'pre-logical'. But they would be wrong to think, as they do, that this means illogical, since it is only a matter of a different logic. This imaginary example makes us see that it is the content of a representation and the nature of the corresponding group which sets forth the principle of rationality, and not the inverse. To make use of contemporary terms: the criterion of rationality appears as a norm inscribed in the language, institutions and representations of a specific culture.

A great deal of ink has been spilt over this difference between a 'primitive mentality' and a 'civilized' or 'scientific' mentality. In fact it seems to me to refer to the difference between belief and knowledge, so important but so little understood, as can be established by reading Wittgenstein's (1953) late reflections on belief. In my opinion a great many misunderstandings would be dispelled if the following suggestion were to be accepted. The difference with which we are concerned takes on a new meaning when we pay attention to the distinction between:

(a)   common representations whose kernel consists of beliefs, which are generally more homogeneous, affective, impermeable to experience or contradiction, and leave little scope for individual variations; and

(b)   common representations founded on knowledge, which are more fluid, pragmatic, amenable to the proof of success or failure, and leave a certain latitude for language, experience, and even to the critical faculties of individuals.

Let us sum up. Indifference to contradiction, mobility in the frontiers between inner reality and outer reality, homogeneity of content, these would be the characteristics of the psychology associated with the first culture; abstention from contradiction, distinction between inner reality and outer reality, permeability to experience, these would be the characteristics of the psychology associated with the second culture. But, of course, each culture combines them according to their own aims and history, imposing rules on the relations between them. Whatever the fate of this suggestion might be, I have put it forward in order to generalize and throw into relief the psychical sense of the distinction established by the French writer. In return I hope to expose, if only briefly, what its influence was and how Lévy-Bruhl's concept of collective representations became a model which has been absorbed in contemporary psychology. In fact, almost the whole of the psychology of individual or cultural development is a product of it.

4 PIAGET, VYGOTSKY AND SOCIAL REPRESENTATIONS

In the 1920s it was still possible to think in terms of evolution, and more particularly, of an evolution of 'primitive' representations being modified and transformed into 'civilized' representations. Until Lucien Lévy-Bruhl it was believed that such an evolution could be pursued by virtue of the famous 'psychic unity of mankind'. But after him it became possible to think that this evolution might consist of a discontinuous change which occurred with the passage from one culture to another. This question might seem abstruse, but we need to recall it if we wish to have a precise idea of the two major influences it exercised, one on Jean Piaget, the other on Lev Vygotsky.

Piaget was, if not the disciple, at least very close to the thought of Lévy-Bruhl, in his method as much as in his psychology. Without exaggerating one can say that the psychology of 'primitive' representations established by the French thinker is repeated in the psychology of children's representations (for example, in childhood animism, intellectual realism, etc.) which we owe to the Swiss psychologist. In other words, what one discovered in the public representations of 'exotic' societies, the other rediscovered, in a transposed way, in the supposedly private representations of Swiss children. However, Piaget distanced himself from Lévy-Bruhl (and brought himself closer to Durkheim and Freud) when he envisaged a continuous evolution stretching from these 'pre-logical' representations of the young child to the more logical and individual representations of the adolescent.

What we do know is that Vygotsky, Alexander Luria and their school turned towards the same intellectual source. Evidently their own political inclination and, above all, the socialist revolution forced them to conceive a psychology which recognized the rightful place of society and culture, that is, a profoundly Marxist psychology which is not content to pay lip-service to the primacy of society, as happens in both East and West with the accumulation of declarations and citations while continuing to pursue an individual psychology. Like many Russians of his time, Vygotsky believed in the truth of Marxism, in the coming of a new and better society whose success it was necessary to secure. He and his colleagues did not treat these questions with any ironic detachment; they were committed thinkers.

It was precisely because they took these problems seriously that they went on to a deeper examination of them. They concluded that, aside from the general frame, there was little hope of finding a fundamental concept in Marxism, or a fruitful vision for psychology. They should not be reproached for this; in fact, in the eyes of its founders and the contemporary thinkers of the revolution Marxism was not the 'science of everything' it has since become. Through a feverish analysis of psychology in the course of these years of creativity and revolution, Vygotsky and Luria discovered the path which allowed them to introduce social phenomena into psychology and to found it upon them. But above all, the introduction of the historical and cultural dimension into psychology was made by default. As one could guess, since I have been speaking about it, it is the path of collective representations and the affirmation that the higher mental processes have their origin in the collective life of people. In particular, the path which led to the concept of these representations was the psychology of Lévy-Bruhl, whose value Piaget and Werner had begun to demonstrate.

You will have no objection if, to confirm this assertion, I appeal to an erudite expert in Soviet psychology who writes:

> Taking into account an overall social orientation of Marxism one might assume that it was Marxist theory that provided an intellectual guideline for Vygotsky. This assumption holds no water, however; as Vygotsky showed in his *Crisis*, Marxist theory in the 1920s failed to develop any concepts required for a psychological study of human behaviour and cognition. The only sufficiently developed theory of human cognition as socially determined was offered by the French sociological school of Emile Durkheim, and was discussed in the related work of Lucien Lévy-Bruhl, Charles Blondel and Maurice Halbwachs. (Kozulin, 1990, p. 122)

Even if this author overestimates the convergence between these different thinkers, he summarizes in precise terms the way in which this connection was established and why it was imposed with such force. It is true that one finds in Vygotsky numerous passages which echo this connection and which could be misconstrued if the inspiration behind them is ignored. In any case, as early as these crucial years, the notion of collective representations began to fashion his vision of mental life, its linguistic mediation and its social content. Vygotsky's encounter with the categories of Lévy-Bruhl gave him a concrete sense and allowed him to set forth a theory of human cultural development. This original theory bears the imprint of Vygotsky, even if personally I am not inclined to give him as much scientific value as others do. Still, this theory proposes, in opposition to that of Piaget, a discontinuous evolution of collective representations.

Be that as it may, once the connection had been established, Vygotsky and Luria were the first to attempt an experimental proof on a true scale, which no one had previously done. As Luria recounts in his memoirs: 'The data relied upon by Lévy-Bruhl as well as by his anthropological and sociological critics – in fact the only data available to anyone at that time – were anecdotes collected by explorers and missionaries who had come in contact with exotic people in the course of their travels' (1979, p. 59). Thus the idea came to them of conceiving the first field study on a relatively large scale into the representations of the Uzbeks in Central Asia at the beginning of the 1930s: 'Although we could have conducted our studies in remote Russian villages, we chose for our research sites the hamlets and nomad camps of Uzbekistan and Khirgizia in Central Asia where great discrepancies between cultural forms promised to maximise the possibility of detecting shifts in the basic forms, as well as in the context of people's thinking' (Luria, 1979, p. 60).

One can see that this vast project sought to explore at the collective level among the nomads what Piaget explored at the individual level among children. They meant to grasp the psychological transformations occurring in a population attached to its religion and living in a traditional way but which had undergone a profound metamorphosis on a social and cultural level as a consequence of the revolution. The old frameworks of life had disintegrated, the hierarchy had disappeared, schools had been opened in numerous villages at the same time as various technological products had made their appearance, upsetting the traditional economy.

This study, which was only published many years later (Luria, 1976), in my view confirmed Lévy-Bruhl's conjecture and therefore gave a solid foundation to Vygotsky's theory of cultural and historical development. But, at a deeper level, Vygotsky and Luria remained more faithful than did Piaget to the canons of individual psychology in the face of the concept of collective representations, and made a less creative use of the psychological analyses of the French thinker. There is here an inversion: Piaget's concept of development is further away from Lévy-Bruhl, although the content of his psychology is closer to him, while with Vygotsky it is the opposite way around. Like rival brothers, they shared the same scientific background while being wholly opposed to each other. I hope that one day epistemologists with more time than I have might take up this interesting relationship.

What seems to me important here is that during the years in which his own health declined, as well as the health of the socialist revolution, Vygotsky was attacked because his theory of historical and cultural development, hence his psychology, owed so much to collective representations, and to the writings of Durkheim and Lévy-Bruhl which referred to them. In a recent article the Russian psychologist Brushlinsky (1989) reviewed again these critiques of an approximate value, and defended Rubinstein who had been among those who had made such critiques, since he in his turn had become their victim. But something more surprising is the silence, if not the lightness, with which the best specialist students of the great Russian psychologist (Wertsch, 1985) pass over his works as if it were a question of an anecdote, and not an essential moment in the history of contemporary psychology, to such a point that Vygotsky's ideas and research on historical and cultural development, even on language, appear to have arisen in his mind in the same way as the goddess Athene arose from the brain of Zeus, through a miraculous filiation. A few allusions to Mead or Marx do not render this apparition any less miraculous; rather they serve to obscure its real genesis. I suspect that this blindness towards the effective historical connection is due to something rather deeper than simple neglect of the truth.

Such blindness is the result – even in those who are convinced that psychological phenomena should not be reduced to organic or individual phenomena, and those who demonstrate a sympathy for the social – of nevertheless seeing the latter in relation to the individual, or at best as a form of intersubjectivity. Hence they can see clearly neither the limits of Marxism in psychological matters, nor in what sense the opening of a Durkheim or a Lévy-Bruhl was a unique opportunity for the Russian thinkers confronted with an extraordinary historical situation in which they were fully aware of the risks they were taking and for which they paid the consequences. This is still only a partial aspect of the representation (*Darstellung*) which concerns us. What really matters is that as they became a precise concept, social representations inspired a psychology of 'primitives' which was new and non-individualist (Davy, 1931). And this in its turn opened the way for Piaget's psychology of the child and Vygotsky's psychology of the higher psychological functions. One cannot then maintain that there was not here a truly specific notion of the social capable of giving the psychology of representation its rightful content. Is this not fundamentally the spirit which should predominate in the human sciences, and in social psychology in particular? Perhaps it is not right to go on and on about positions which have long been overtaken, in order to go further. For obvious reasons, I have not evoked the development of which one recognizes the traces in modern epistemology. But, reading Fleck's ([1935]/1979) book, one picks up these traces, mentioned by the author himself. Once again they lead to Lévy-Bruhl, in a significant if not exclusive way. In particular, the concept of collective representation is expressed through the notion of the style of thought of a collective used by Fleck. And we know that Fleck's book found an echo in the theory of Thomas Kuhn and in his epistemology of science.

5 FROM COLLECTIVE REPRESENTATIONS TO SOCIAL REPRESENTATIONS

The general subject of this chapter is the genesis and fecundity of the idea of social representation. It has served to characterize what is reckoned to be decisive in the processes of thought or the set of beliefs shared by groups or whole societies. It has also served to explain the changes or metamorphoses which these processes and these sets of beliefs have apparently undergone. If we turn towards the contemporary epoch, it is clear that the underlying problem is that of modern rationality. As we know, it implies that the forms of mental and social life conserved by tradition should be replaced by those of science and technology. Our scientific thought elevated to the rank of the norm of all thought, our logic taken as the unique viable logic stigmatize without examining them all different thoughts and beliefs, relegating them to an inferior rank. In this way the diffusion of modern thought supposes *ipso facto* the regression without exception of all others. Of course, one must pay the price: at the limit, if scientific thought imposes its rules and operations on the mind, it serves notice to other forms of thought and dooms them to disappearance.

This is the direction in which our processes of thought or sets of belief are changed and transformed. There is therefore nothing surprising if a large part of the work devoted to cultural and individual development strives to elucidate the stages through which societies or individuals reach this point in a necessary way. Today, for all that, our critical conscience is less certain of this evolution. But nevertheless, the postulate of the reducibility of all forms of thought and belief to a unity holds the high ground everywhere, as much in psychology, economics or sociology as in public discourse.

All of this may strike you as the rehearsal and description of things already well known, and hence without great interest. This would be the case if there were not, however, two consequences which deserve attention:

1 The first consequence is expressed by the fact that a tacit distinction is made between societies without science and those with science. And consequently, collective representations are studied only in the former, as if they were unrelated to the latter, in such a way that the characteristics, beginning with the beliefs instituted in these traditional or 'exotic' societies, are distinguished as if it were a question of a mental form peculiar to them alone. Further, at a deeper level, these representations are taken as models of 'total' or 'closed' societies in which the symbolic and practical constituents of social relations are perfectly integrated. In such societies every type of behaviour and cognition seems to be fashioned by the mythical and ritual nucleus of the tradition of a people. In this way the greater part of the knowledge

brought into play in the subsistence activities, the arts and everything which is exchanged in the transactions of ordinary life are put to one side. This explains, at least in part, why every representation appears to coincide with the collectivity in its entirety, and to take on a character both uniform and static.

With this framework in mind, it is striking to see a so-called primitive representation compared and contrasted with science, not only as scientists practise it, or as it is diffused in modern societies, but as it is described by the logic of science described in the works of philosophers. For example, the Melanesian rain-maker whose rites are observed and whose magical beliefs are recorded is compared with no more and no less a figure than Einstein. But this discussion would take us too far. For now I prefer simply to state my disagreement with the idea that collective representations should have a meaning in distant societies or in former times, but not in our own, with its deification of scientific beliefs. There is a good reason for that.

2   The second consequence of the postulate of reducibility is what Laudan (1977) called the *arationality assumption*. This is that the social explanations of our intellectual studies fall within sociology only when these studies fail to meet the generally recognized criteria of rationality. Even Mannheim, who in this was faithful to Marxism, invoked this hypothesis when he exempted mathematics and the natural sciences from the domain of the sociology of knowledge. But this can also be applied to ideology, because it deviates from these criteria, either by being confounded with religion, or because it is a counterfeit of science. It should nevertheless be noted that both Durkheim and Lévy-Bruhl adhered implicitly to this hypothesis. Without doubt they see the universal features of cognition – cause, time, class or number – as being founded on the features shared by all societies. This does not prevent them from explaining the passage from religious or magical beliefs to modern science as an effect of the passage from the pre-eminence of the collectivity to the pre-eminence of the individual who becomes conscious of himself and 'explicitly differentiates himself from the group of which he feels himself a member' (Lévy-Bruhl, [1925]/1926, p. 365).

When we establish a connection between these different aspects, we understand better why, following a period of extraordinary interest in collective representations, there has been a period of reserve, even abandon. They appeared as explanatory notions only with respect to societies whose beliefs, materialized in institutions, language and morals, are constraining and centred on the human universe, or, to borrow a term from Piaget, sociocentric. They could not therefore, as Bergson clearly saw, have validity beyond closed or total societies, such as a nation or a tribe. Further, in the positivist conception which then predominated, the science and rational techniques of modern societies, although derived from religious thought, had an objective and individual character.

It was here that Fleck rightly saw an incongruity, or for that matter a contradiction, in so far as objective properties depend on the particular conditions of a society, just as much as on its models of thinking. And he was not the only one, since Piaget wrote in relation to Durkheim, who sustained at the same time both the sociocentric character of collective representations and the individual character of science:

> If he was able to maintain two such incompatible positions, it is obviously because, instead of proceeding to the analysis of different types of social interactions, he constantly reverted to the global language of 'totality'. Hence, in order to demonstrate the collective nature of reason, he alternated between two sorts of argument, very different in fact, but used simultaneously under the cover of this undifferentiated notion of the social totality exercising constraint over the individual.   (Piaget, [1965]/1995, p. 72)

One cannot, then, deny that psychologists and sociologists have had some reasons for distancing themselves from a concept which seemed cut to the measure of a traditional or exotic society and marked by its positivist origins, or at the most to refer to it in a historical way (Farr, 1993). But this is unacceptable when one does not wish to resign oneself to a social psychology both individualistic and deprived of any common framework with the other human sciences, and consequently destined to become fragmented into a multitude of research fields without any links between them and without any historical continuity. Perhaps this can help us to understand why, when one turns toward the collective background of mental life and action, there is no other serious alternative than attempting to give a fresh chance to this line of thought. After all, often in the history of ideas or science a much debated notion proved useful in a new context, as was the case, for example, with the atom in the nineteenth century.

Be that as it may, through a choice whose motives have little importance here, it seems to me legitimate to suppose that all forms of belief, ideologies, knowledge, including even science, are, in one way or another, *social representations*.[2] It seemed then (Moscovici, [1961]/1976) and it seems all the more so today, that neither the opposition of the social to the individual, nor the evolution from the traditional to the modern, had, in this regard, the importance which is given to them.

But it seemed right to distinguish those forms according to the way they order their content and represent men, events, things, in a particular universe which society recognizes either as a *consensual* universe or as a *reified* universe. Social representations are marked through and through by the division into these two universes, the former characterized by a relation of trusting appropriation, even implication, and the latter by distancing, authority, detachment even – or what in German is called *Zugehörigkeit* (affiliation) and *Entfremdung* (alienation). They also correspond to the relations instituted by individuals in society and to the modes of interaction specific to each of them. Without repeating the reasons and descriptions I have given elsewhere (Moscovici, 1984a), I will just recall that this distinction puts popular knowledge, ways of thinking and acting in everyday life, common sense if you like, on one side, and science and ideology on the other. Ideology being, as Ricoeur has described it, 'simplifying and schematic. It is a grid or code for giving an overall view, not only of a group, but also of history and, ultimately, of the world' (1981, p. 226).

One might perhaps try to classify the forms of belief and knowledge according to the place assigned to them in a hierarchy, the reified forms being readily considered as higher in value and power then the consensual forms. Nothing in this would justify placing them where they might be exempt from dependence upon the social. To repeat myself, it is clear that they include some social representation. Consequently, the postulate of reducibility, that is to say, the postulate of an elimination of beliefs and common knowledge by science as a *telos* of individual and cultural development, must be renounced. In this sense, in a social sense, science and common sense – beliefs in general – are irreducible to one another in so far as they are ways of understanding the world and relating to it. Although common sense changes its content and ways of reasoning, it is not replaced by scientific theories and logic. It continues to describe the ordinary relations between individuals, it explains their activities and normal behaviour, it shapes their transactions in everyday life. And it resists every attempt at reification which would turn the concepts and images rooted in language into rules and explicit procedures (Farr, 1993).

I believe I was among the first to argue for the irreducibility of common sense to science, which has today become a philosophical position, marking one part of cognitive science. But whereas the reasons invoked by Fodor, Dennett, Putnam and others are of a logical order, I continue to think that the real reason is a psychosocial one. In any case, one can say that renouncing the myth of total rationalization, that is, of the assimilation of all social representations to scientific representations, of the consensual universe to the reified universe, implies abandoning another idea shared by many of the human sciences, psychology in particular. I mean the idea that one sees an *upgrading* of thought, from perception to reason, from the concrete to the abstract, from the 'primitive' to the 'civilized', from the child to the adult, etc., as our knowledge and our language progressively become more decontextualized. On the contrary, what we see is a *downgrading* of thought, that is, a movement in the opposite direction, as our knowledge and language circulate and become contextualized in society. This is completely normal since, as Maxwell said, the abstract of one century becomes the concrete of another. The changes and transformations take place constantly in both directions, the representations communicate among themselves, they combine and they separate, introducing a quantity of new terms and new practices into everyday and 'spontaneous' usage. In fact, scientific representations daily and 'spontaneously' become common sense, while the representations of common sense change into scientific and autonomous representations. An example of the first kind of transformation is the diffusion of biological ideas and explanations in relation to ecology or to AIDS (Herzlich, 1973; Marková and Wilkie, 1987), and of the second kind in theories of personality, or chaos, and so on.

Let us leave on one side this distinction between the *upgrading* and *downgrading* of social representations, and recognize that the popular knowledge of common sense always furnishes the knowledge which people have at their disposal; science and technology themselves do not hesitate to borrow from it when they need an idea, an image, a construction. There is nothing surprising, then, if common knowledge remains at the base of all cognitive processes, which poses a theoretical and empirical problem from the point of knowledge. If a psychologist speaks of an extrovert personality or a prototype, if a biologist evokes information and selection, or again if an economist reasons in terms of the market and competition, each of them, within their own speciality, makes an appeal to concepts drawn from their heritage, from the sources of common knowledge from which it has never been detached. We understand that even the way of naming and communicating these elements of science presupposes and conserves a link with the knowledge of common sense (Moscovici, [1961]/1976; Herzlich, 1973; Fleck, [1935]/1979; Flick, 1998).

Can one avoid commenting on the profound interest which this phenomenon holds for social psychology? And isn't this precisely the difficulty about collective representations, that they are grasped in practice indirectly through systems of belief and knowledge codified by institutions, morals and specialized languages? This comes back in some way to isolating them from the flux of social exchanges and to cutting psychic operations without being able to observe how they are articulated in real life. In such conditions it is not surprising that these representations should appear so 'closed', so 'total', and so difficult to apply to our own society. Now the point that I am going to make has led me to a clear decision. Common sense, popular knowledge – what the English call *folk science* – offers us *direct* access to social representations. It *is*, up to a certain point, social representations which combine our capacity to perceive, infer, understand, which come to our mind to give a sense to things, or to explain the situation of someone. They are so 'natural' and demand so little effort that it is almost impossible to suppress them. Imagine looking at an athletics competition without having the least idea of what the athletes are doing, or seeing two people kiss each other in the street without having the least idea that they are in love with each other. These interpretations are so evident that we normally expect everybody to agree to the truth of what passes in front of their eyes.

We have learnt to regard the representations of *folk physics*, *folk biology* or *folk economics* with some scepticism. But who does not have a representation which allows them to understand why liquids rise in a container, why sugar dissolves, why plants need to be watered, or why the government raises taxes? Thanks to this popular physics we avoid collisions on the roads, thanks to this popular biology we cultivate our gardens, and this popular economics helps us to look for a way of paying less tax. The categories of folk science are so widespread and irresistible that they seem to be 'innate'. We make use of such knowledge and know-how all the time. We exchange them among ourselves, we renew them through study or experience in order to explain behaviours confidently – and without being conscious of them – and we pass a good part of our waking life talking about the world, inventing our future and the future of our children as a function of these representations.

What is the value of *folk science*? This is a philosophical question which I don't propose to consider here, but, as the philosopher Daniel Dennett remarked about it, anyone who ventures on the motorway should judge this science reliable. The vast field of common sense, of popular sciences, allows us to grasp social representations *in vivo*, to grasp how they are generated, communicated and put to work in everyday life. To make a comparison, we can say that these fields offer prototypical material for exploring the nature of these representations, just as dreams offer an exemplary field to anyone wishing to understand the unconscious. Social representations thus lose the derived and abstract character associated with collective representations to become, in some way, a concrete and observable phenomenon. In spite of a number of critiques (Fraser and Gaskell, 1990), it was and remains my conviction that social psychology is more than ever the science of social representations and can find in them a unifying theme.

In any case, one can see why common sense and popular knowledge offer us this privileged field of exploration.

1   What I have called post-scientific common sense is, like all knowledge shared by society as a whole, interwoven with our language, constitutive of our relations and our skills. It is a structured collection of descriptions and explanations, more or less connected to each other, of personality, illness, feelings or natural phenomena, which everyone possesses, even if they are not aware of it, and which they use for organizing their experience, taking part in a conversation, or doing business with other people. It is *Umgangsdenken* (everyday thought) associated with the *Umgangssprache* (colloquial language) without which everyday life is inconceivable. Even young children easily grasp – as Freud showed in relation to the sexual theories of children – popular knowledge at an age when they have a limited

experience of human activities allowing them to deduce such knowledge (Jodelet, 1989b).

One cannot help being struck by the following contrast: on the one hand we are familiar with a good number of popular sciences, we understand them, use them, renew them easily through conversation, reading newspapers or watching television. On the other, we master hardly a small part of the scientific or technical knowledge which we use for our profession, livelihood and the practice of our whole life. In brief, as Chomsky has written, 'Grammar and common sense are acquired by virtually everyone, effortlessly, rapidly, in uniform manner, merely by living in a community under minimal conditions of interaction, exposure and care. There need be no explicit teaching or training and when the latter takes place, it has only marginal effects on the final state achieved' (1975, p. 144). Individual variations are very limited and, in a given community, everyone acquires a vast and rich store of knowledge, comparable to that of others. Bergson was right when he said that common sense is 'social sense' ([1932]/1935, p. 110).

2   Contrary to scientific and ideological representations, constructed following the demands of formal logic on the basis of fundamental terms all perfectly defined, distinct even, the representations of common sense are, in one way or another, 'cross-bred'. That is to say that the ideas, linguistic expressions, explanations of different origins are aggregated, combined and regularized more or less like several sciences in a single hybrid science, like several idioms in a creole language. People who share a common knowledge in the course of their ordinary life do not 'reason' about it, and could not place it in front of them like an 'object', or analyse its contents by placing it at a distance to 'observe' it, without themselves being implicated in it. To appropriate it they have to do exactly the opposite, they have to dive into the flux of diverse contents, participate in their concrete implementation, and strive to make them accessible to others. In this way their knowledge thus cross-bred and their disparate vocabularies have a semantic potential which is not exhausted by any particular usage, but must constantly be refined and determined with the help of the context.

It should be clear to us that these arrangements lead to two results which do not coincide in any way. Common knowledge does not only comprise scientific or religious beliefs. It also transposes them into familiar images, as if the possibility of representing abstract notions dominated the process. Further, social representations of different origins are condensed in common knowledge, in such a way that, according to needs, some can be substituted for others. If we return to the example of AIDS suggested earlier, it can be established that religious representations concerning sexual freedom combine with medical representations about the causes of the illness, or political representations about the fabrication of the virus by the CIA in order to eliminate certain populations. This gives an impression of a cognitive and social patch-work. But it is a false impression, since just as our habitual language rests upon the polysemic value of words and a creole language is as rigorous as any other, so popular representations have their own coherence and rigour. It seems to me that Billig's (1987) work has recently elaborated these aspects and clarified what I thought I had observed and which had been for me only a conjecture.

3   Common sense continues to be conceived predominantly as an archaic stage of understanding, including a mass of knowledge which has not changed for millennia and which was born in our direct perception of people and things. It thus suits the aims of our everyday life, with extraordinary success. About the time when I have suggested that social psychologists become interested in common sense, the psychologist Fritz Heider (1958) began to argue that, since relations between human beings are a function of their 'naïve psychology', we had better study the origin of this naïve psychology which gives meaning to our experience. Now, as you know, this has been done starting from the *perception* which individuals have of one another, without taking account of their beliefs, language or the meanings embedded in this language. It is curious that Fritz Heider has been taken as supporting this conception, since his analyses begin from literary and philosophical texts, and not from laboratory analyses. However that may be, this dominant con-ception is acultural and ahistorical. It would be incompatible with my presup-position. Meanwhile, considering it as a form of social representation one recognizes not only that it has cultural traits but also a historical character. In the first study I made in this field (Moscovici, [1961]/1976), I attempted to show that *folk science* is not the same for everyone and for always. It is modified at the same time that the structures or problems of society with which individuals are confronted themselves change. Further, ideas of revolutionary scope in the sciences, such as those of Freud or Marx, or artistic movements which sweep away everything in their path, are assimilated by a great many people, leaving a durable impression on their way of thinking, of speaking, of understanding themselves or of understanding the world in which they live. They can be venerated with impunity, since, used by everyone and incorporated into the very structures of language, the categories and reasoning of popular science are affected by those who have discovered psychoanalysis, physics, etc. They communicate little by little and finally everyone considers them as being independent and forming part of 'reality'.

We ourselves see social representations forming so to speak before our eyes, in the media, in public places, through this process of communication which never happens without some transformation. Whether the change affects the sense, the concepts, the images, or the intensity and association of beliefs, in the bosom of a community, change is always expressed in representations (de Rosa, 1987). Anyone neglecting this fact will never construct a psychosocial theory of thought and action. The French anthropologist Dan Sperber (1990) has formulated an interesting theory of the communication of representations. He sees them as being generated through a process of the epidemiological diffusion of individual representations. This conjecture is hard to admit, given the rule-bound and organized character of such diffusion. On different occasions we have been able to experience the advantage for our science of choosing common knowledge as a field of research and undertaking a serious comparison of one form with another. This assumes that we consider such common knowledge as the kernel of our consensual universe and recognize in it a historical, cultural and rhetorical character, failing which such knowledge is reduced to impoverished traits, to schemas and stereotypes without meaning. It seems to me important to emphasize the line between popular science, common sense and social representations (see also Flick, 1998), since it justifies at the same time both why I have returned to the tradition of this concept and the way in which it acquires the importance that it has in our society. And it is because representations are a continuous creation, because we can compare them *in statu nascenti* and grasp them directly that we can propose to offer a theory of them, that is to say, not only to articulate a concept of them, but to describe or explain these representations in so far as they are a social phenomenon.

6   REPRESENTATION, COMMUNICATION AND THE SHARING OF REALITY

I must admit that my original intention was not to introduce a concept derived from Durkheim and Lévy-Bruhl into social psychology, nor then to try and distinguish it in order to adapt it to the *Zeitgeist*. On the contrary, it was the problem of the transformation of science in the course of its diffusion and the birth of a post-scientific common sense, hence that of our social psychology, which led me to the concept. To put this clearly, if developmental psychology is concerned with the transformation in the course of children's lives of their 'spontaneous' representations into scientific and rational representations, it seems to me that social psychology must confront the inverse process, that is, to study how scientific representations are changed into ordinary representations. And like others before me, I discovered that the only line of thought which has known how to articulate beliefs and knowledge with social reality is theirs. For the rest, they must advance with their own means, since the problem of these French thinkers is not the same as ours, and the same holds true for the future. One can add, in another connection, the well-known fact that since the Second World War it has no longer been possible, as had been the case before, to found society on work or belief, but rather on communication or the production of knowledge (Moscovici, 1982). But this is precisely an aspect which most frequently escapes social psychologists, in so far as they limit their interests to interpersonal relations.

Be that as it may, the aspiration of the theory of social representations is clear. By taking as its centre communication and representations, it hopes to elucidate the links which unite human psychology with contemporary social and cultural questions. On this point we can ask ourselves what is the function of shared representations and what they are, from the moment when they are no longer considered indirectly through religion, myths, and so on. In response to this question I have suggested that the reason for forming these representations is the desire to familiarize ourselves with the unfamiliar. Every violation of existing rules, an extraordinary phenomenon or idea such as those produced by science or technology, unusual events which unsettle what appears to be the normal and stable course of things, all of this fascinates us at the same time as it alarms us. Every deviation from the familiar, every rupture of ordinary experience, everything for which the explanation is not obvious creates a supplementary meaning and sets in motion a search for the meaning and explanation of what strikes us as strange and troubling.

It is, then, not a search for an agreement between our ideas and the reality of an order introduced into the chaos of phenomena or, to simplify, a complex world which is the motivation for elaborating social representations, but the attempt to build a bridge between the strange and the familiar; and this in so far as the strange presupposes a lack of communication within the group in relation to the world which short-circuits the current of exchanges and displaces the references of language. One has the feeling that it no longer fits the matrix of life in common, that it no longer agrees with our relations with others. To master a strange idea or perception one begins by anchoring it (Doise, 1992) in existing social representations, and it is in the course of this anchoring that it becomes modified (Moscovici, 1988a). This observation is corroborated by Bartlett, who writes: 'As has been pointed out, whenever material visually presented purports to be representative of some common object but contains certain features which are unfamiliar in the community to which the material is introduced, these features invariably suffer transformations in the direction of the familiar' (1932, p. 178). The familiar cannot not change in the course of this process and find a certain social and affective satisfaction in rediscovering it, sometimes in an effective and sometimes in an illusory way.

To push our explanation of the formation of these representations further we need to clarify some difficulties. Searching for the familiar in the strange means that these representations tend towards conservatism, towards the confirmation of their significant content. Well, this would then be a pure and simple consequence of their sociocentrism, of the sociomorphic character of their cognitive and linguistic operations. This means that there is a certain distance in relation to the reality not represented by the group. But is this a question of a characteristic peculiar to non-scientific and non-rational representations, as some people maintain? Observation has shown us that scientific representations are also centred, although in a different way, on the scientific community and the society of which it forms a part. I could add that the paradigms of a normal science equally demonstrate a tendency to conservatism in the face of anomalies, up to the point that their resistance becomes impossible (Kuhn, 1962). Thus, I conclude that all representations are sociocentric and that in the familiarization of the strange, society is represented in a more implicit way (Mugny and Carugati, [1985]/1989).

I have written about these things in more detail elsewhere. Here, I simply want to specify that if we form representations in order to familiarize ourselves with the strange, then we also form them in order to reduce the margin of non-communication. This margin is acknowledged through the ambiguities of ideas, the fluidity of meanings, the incomprehension of the images and beliefs of the other, in short, through what the American philosopher C. S. Peirce spoke of as the 'vague'. What makes relations problematic, and also exchanges between individuals and groups, is the circulation of representations which nevertheless coexist in the same public space. Existence in common proves to be impossible if this margin of uncertainty persists and becomes important. In that case the members of a group risk remaining as strange in familiar conversations as if they belonged to different groups.

I maintain, therefore, that social representations are first and foremost intended to make communication in a group relatively *non-problematic* and to reduce the 'vague' through a degree of consensus among its members. In so far as this is the case, representations cannot be acquired through the study of some explicit belief or knowledge, nor established through some specific deliberation. Rather, they are formed through reciprocal influences, through implicit negotiations in the course of conversations in which people are oriented towards particular symbolic models, images and shared values. In doing so they acquire a common repertoire of interpretations and explanations, rules and procedures which they can apply to everyday life, just as linguistic expressions are accessible to everyone (Moscovici, 1984a).

I have often been asked what I mean by the sharing of a representation or shared representations. What gives it this character is not the fact that it is *autonomous* or that it is common, but rather the fact that its elements have been fashioned through communication and are related through communication. The constraints which this exercises, its rules of interaction and influence, determine the particular structure of knowledge and language which results. To simplify, we could say that any lone individual could not represent for themselves the result of the communication of thought (Freyd, 1983), of verbal and iconic messages. This is what gives these cognitive and linguistic structures the form they have, since they must be shared with others in order to be communicated. I speak therefore of shared representations to indicate that the forms of our thought and our language are made compatible with the forms of communication and the constraints which this imposes. I have shown before that there are three forms of public communication which inflect three corresponding forms of thought and public language (Moscovici, [1961]/1976).

It seems to me that the notion of sharing expresses the process through which social or public representations appropriate individual or private representations. It seems more apposite than the idea of constraint introduced by Durkheim and Lévy-Bruhl to describe the process through which collective representations fashion the mental life of individuals. For these thinkers, however, representations are formed in relation to reality and not in relation to communication with others, something which they judged to be secondary but which is essential for us.

A DEFINITION OF SOCIAL REPRESENTATIONS

Now that this point is highlighted, we can ask ourselves what defines a social representation. If this meaning should be pregnant, it must be that it corresponds to a certain recurrent and comprehensive model of images, beliefs and symbolic behaviours. Envisaged in this way, *statically*, representations appear similar to *theories* which order around a theme (mental illnesses are contagious, people are what they eat, etc.) a series of propositions which enable things or persons to be classified, their characters described, their feelings and actions to be explained, and so on. Further, the 'theory' contains a series of examples which illustrate concretely the values which introduce a hierarchy and their corresponding models of action. Here as everywhere, formulas and clichés are associated in order to recall this 'theory', to distinguish it by its origin and to distinguish it from others (Duveen and Lloyd, 1990; Palmonari, 1980).

For example, doctors' surgeries overflow with people talking about their cholesterol level, their diet, their blood-pressure, explaining that their illness is innate or acquired, and so on, referring to some medical theory. Or again, journalists devote articles to computer viruses, or the ethnic virus, and so on, making allusion to the genetic model. Nothing is more difficult than to eradicate the false idea that the deductions or explanations we draw from common sense are archaic, schematic and stereotyped. Certainly it cannot be denied that there are a great number of rigidified 'theories'. But, contrary to what is implied, this has nothing to do with their collective nature or the fact that they are shared by a mass of people. Rather, it comes from the flexibility of the group and the speed of communication of knowledge and beliefs at the heart of society.

In fact, from the dynamic point of view social representations appear as a 'network' of ideas, metaphors and images, more or less loosely tied together, and therefore more mobile and fluid than theories. It seems that we cannot get rid of the impression that we have an 'encyclopaedia' of such ideas, metaphors and images which are connected one to another according to the necessity of the kernels, the *core beliefs* (Abric, 1988; Flament, 1989; Emler and Dickinson, 1985) stored separately in our collective memory and around which these networks form. I suppose that social representations in movement more closely resemble money than language. Like money, they have an existence to the extent that they are useful, circulate, take different forms in memory, perception, works of art, and so on, while nevertheless always being recognized as identical, in the same way that 100 francs can be represented as a banknote, a traveller's cheque, or a figure in a bank statement. And their distinctive value varies according to relations of contiguity, as David Hume remarked. If I meet a colleague in the course of a trip to Germany, I represent him to myself as a compatriot, and say to myself 'Well, a Frenchman.' If I bump into him on a street in Tokyo, I make of him the image of a European. And if, in some extraordinary way, we were to meet each other on Mars I would think 'Here is a human.'

Like money, in other respects, representations are social, in so far as they are a psychological fact, in three ways: they have an impersonal aspect, in the sense of belonging to everyone; they are the representation of others, belonging to other people or to another group; and they are a personal representation, felt affectively to belong to the ego. Further, we should not forget that representations, like money, are formed with the double aim of acting and evaluating. They would not, then, belong to a separate domain of knowledge, and for this reason are subject to the same rules as other kinds of actions and social evaluations. Contrary to experts, ordinary people do not see themselves separately as a citizen, as someone who goes to church, and so on. Thus social rules are at the same time rules of inference which have a logical sense. For Max Weber's Protestants, 'honesty is the best policy' is not only a religious maxim. It is a rule which they apply when they reason, make judgements about people, and so on. In the opposite way, certain logical rules function as social rules. For example, do not contradict yourself, calculate the probabilities, and many others. This is why mental *contents* are stronger imperatives than cognitive *forms*. Briefly, we can say that *what* people think determines *how* they think.

Let us go further. All things considered, as communication in our society accelerates, the scale of the media (visual, written, audio) in the social space grows ceaselessly. Two things which deserve attention can then be observed. On the one hand, the differences between social representations are blurred, the boundaries between their iconic aspect and their conceptual aspect are obliterated. The disappearance of the differences and boundaries changes them more and more into representations of representations, makes them become more and more symbolic. And this is at the expense of the direct reference of each. In this way the question of knowing how to connect representations to realities is no longer a philosophical question but a psychosocial one.

On the other hand, the categories and meanings through which we 'choose' to confer a quality on people or properties on objects become modified. For examples, we 'choose' to describe a food by its taste or by its protein value, according to the culture to which we belong or the use we wish to make of it. To require that all these qualities be reduced to a single 'true' quality is an impossibility. It assumes that there is a once and for all ready-made, given reality for this food, which is imposed on us independently of the representation which we share.

As I argued in the first sketch of our theory, in relation to psychoanalysis ([1961]/1976), it is no longer appropriate to consider representations as a replica of the world or a reflection of it, not only because this positivist conception is the source of numerous difficulties, but also because representations also evoke what is absent from this world, they form it rather more than they simulate it. When we are asked 'what objects is our world made of?' we must in our turn ask 'within what representation?' before answering. That is to say that shared representations, their language, penetrate so profoundly into all the interstices of what we call reality that we can say that they *constitute* it. They thus constitute identity, the self (Markus and Nurius, 1986; Oyserman and Markus, 1998), the market, the characteristics of a person or a group, etc. (Mugny and Carugati, [1985]/1989). It is incontestable that they have a socially creative or constructive effect which would have been surprising not long ago but which is commonly recognized today. I have the idea that the majority of the research on discourse by Billig (1987), Potter and Litton (1985) does not contradict the theory of social representations. On the contrary they complement it, and deepen this aspect of it. To ask then, whether language or representation is the better model can have no more psychological meaning than asking the question: 'Does a man walk with the help of his left leg or his right leg?' But to realize just how true and deep this contribution is, and to accept it, one would need to begin with a much greater coherence in psychology itself. While waiting for this, I have no hesitation therefore in treating what we have learnt about rhetoric, about linguistic accounts, as being very closely related to social representations.

7 CONCLUSION

To finish, there is one consequence of this perspective about social representations which deserves to be better elaborated, but which I should nevertheless put into words. Each of us accepts without doubt the idea that the contents and meanings represented vary within the same society, the same culture, as do their means of linguistic expression. But we are obliged to assume that these differences in meaning and content should be judged according to differences in the way of thinking and understanding, in short, according to the principles of distinct rationalities. As we have seen, the specificities of the consensual universe and the reified universe, the contexts of the communication in which these representations are elaborated, are responsible for these differences. The contrasts between them are socially marked and reinforced in such a way as to distinguish each form of rationality.

If this is the case, then we must consider that *in* each society, each culture, there exist at least two types of rationality, two styles of thinking equivalent to the two extreme forms of representing and communicating. It would be impossible to reduce them to a superordinate rationality which would, in this case, be supra-social, or, in any case, normative, which could not fail to lead to vicious circles. *Mutatis mutandis*, one must assume that individuals share the same capacity to possess many ways of thinking and representing. Here there is what I have earlier called a cognitive polyphasia, which is as inherent to mental life as polysemy is to the life of language. Further, let us not forget that it is of great practical importance for communicating and for adapting to changing social necessities. The whole of our intersubjective relations to social reality depends on this capacity.

The history which leads to a theory is itself a part of that theory. The theory of social representations has developed on this background (Doise and Palmonari, 1990), and on an ever greater number of research studies which contribute to it and deepen it. These are what, justly, allow us to appreciate better retrospectively the choice of precursors and the meaning of their work. It is at least the experience which I came to have in writing this *historische Darstellung* (historical representation), which I hope will be useful for others. A great narrative, writes Frank Kermode, is the fusion of the scandalous with the miraculous. My representation began with scandal. If it contains some miracle, I would see it in the longevity and vitality of the theory of social representations.

Notes

1   In her new translation, Karen Fields renders Durkheim's *représenter* here as *imagining* (translator's note).
2   In speaking of *social* representations in place of *collective* representations, I wanted to break with the associations which the term collective had inherited from the past, but also with the sociological and psychological interpretations which in the classic way determined its nature.

4

The Concept of Themata*

THE STUDY OF SOCIAL REPRESENTATIONS: A NEW EPISTEME?

In the last thirty years a whole series of approaches have been established in the field of social psychology to try to clarify the phenomena of social representations. It is clearly a case of phenomena of which we know the salient aspects and whose elaboration we can perceive through their circulation in discourse, which constitutes their principal vector. Let us take the example of the development of representations related to AIDS (Jodelet, 1991b). The 'theories' elaborated by opinion ten years ago, before the intervention of scientific research, are no longer the same today. At first it was considered as a punitive illness striking at a sexual liberty which had become exaggerated within the context of an overly permissive society (Marková and Wilkie, 1987), and this moral representation of the phenomenon, which became a social stigma, was relayed by religious authorities. Later the idea of a conspiracy emerged among some people, notably North American minorities, with the image of a 'genocide' perpetrated by the dominant white Protestant governing class. The question of the means of propagation of this conspiracy was then established; from there came the emergence of popular theories about its transmission: if this was effected by blood and sperm, then why not also through the means of other bodily liquids such as saliva or sweat? Thus we are led back to ancient beliefs about 'humours' (Corbin, 1977). What is interesting here is the conjunction between discourses of fear and racist discourses, giving rise in this way to the permanence, if not the invariance, of a particular type of social representation in the face of adversity embracing at the same time both the moral and the biological (Delacampagne, 1983; Jodelet, [1989]/1991).

* Written with Georges Vignaux; translated by Gerard Duveen.

This means that social representations are always complex, and necessarily inscribed within the 'framework of pre-existing thought', hence always dependent on systems of belief anchored in values, traditions and images of the world and of existence. They are above all the object of a permanent social work, in and through discourse, so that every new phenomenon can always be reincorporated within explanatory or justificatory models which are familiar and therefore acceptable. This process of the exchange and composition of ideas is all the more necessary since it responds to the twofold demands of individuals and collectives: on the one hand to construct systems of thought and understanding, and on the other to adopt consensual visions of action which allow them to maintain a social bond, even a continuity of communication of the idea.

Representations therefore always play a triple role of illumination (giving sense to realities), integration (incorporating new ideas or facts into familiar frameworks) and partition (ensuring the common sense through which a given collectivity is recognized). Systems for the interpretation of the world and of events, they are in this way the essential vectors of opinions, judgements and beliefs, directed at ensuring the relevance and regularity of our bonds and of our conduct as a community.

To represent means at one and the same time both to make absent things present and to present things in such a way as to satisfy the conditions for argumentative coherence, rationality and the normative integrity of the group. That this is communicative and diffusive is all the more important, since there are no other means except discourse and the meanings it carries through which individuals and groups are able to orient and adapt themselves to it. Consequently, the status of the phenomena of social representation is that of the symbolic: establishing a bond, making an image, evoking, saying and causing to be said, sharing a meaning in some transmissible propositions, and in the best of cases summarizing in a cliché which becomes an emblem. At the limit it is a question of phenomena affecting all those symbolic relations a society engenders and maintains and which share whatever produces effects in matters of economy or power. It is not ideology, of which there is little in the form in which it has been conceived, but all those interactions which from the depths to the heights, from brute givens right up to the ephemera of social structures, are conveyed through the filter of languages, images and natural logics (Grize, 1993; Vignaux, 1991). And through them one can at least be assured, thanks to the work not only of historians and anthropologists but also of social psychologists, that they aim at constituting mentalities or beliefs influencing behaviours.

There is the banality of the phenomenon when it is seen and observed as a describable effect, and its complexity when it is a question of flowing upstream towards what makes the 'semantic kernel' of some generalized conception in the social body and structures it at some moment to the point of motivating histories, actions, events. It is why once again the concept is only evocative: one must draw from the considerable mass of indices of a social situation and its temporality, and these indices take the form of linguistic traces, archives and, above all, 'packets' of discourse, an attentive examination of which should allow some light to be thrown on what they repeat – on the one hand on what they repeat permanently – the problem of semantic reduction – and on the other, what motivates and grounds them – the problem of those 'ideas' which in some way have the status of axioms or organizing principles at a given historical moment for some type of object or situation.

Nevertheless, if the concept of representation crosses so many domains of knowledge, from history to anthropology by way of linguistics, it is always and everywhere a question of understanding the forms of the practices of knowledge and of practical knowledge which cement our social lives as ordinary existences. And above all, this concept allows us access to those total social phenomena which Marcel Mauss spoke about, phenomena in which the practices of knowledge and of practical knowledge play an essential role, since this knowledge is inscribed in the experiences or events sustained by individuals and shared in society. Practical knowledge again because it always constitutes in some way a popular understanding (*folk knowledge, folk psychology*) which constantly reformulates the discourse of the elite, of the experts, of those in possession of a knowledge described as wisdom or science (Moscovici and Hewstone, 1983, 1984).

First, is it a question of the 'contents of thought' which might be given by the social, and which it would be enough to collect? Surely not: every social representation is constituted as a process in which one can locate an origin, but one which is always unfinished to the extent that other facts or discourses will come to nourish or corrupt it. It is at the same time important to specify how these processes develop socially and how they are organized cognitively in terms of arrangements of significations and of work on the references. Reflection on the ways of approaching the facts of language and image is primary here.

Secondly, these processes are the work of subjects acting through their representations of reality and constantly reworking their own representations. One is always in a situation of analysing representations of representations! This implies methodologically understanding how subjects, in the way that each of us does, come to operate at the same time to define themselves and to act in the social: 'What collective representations express is the way in which the group thinks of itself in its relationships with the objects which affect it' (Durkheim, [1895]/1982, p. 40). In this way every social representation performs different types of functions, some cognitive – *anchoring* meanings, *stabilizing* or *destabilizing* the situations evoked – others properly social, namely maintaining or creating *identities* and *collective equilibria*. This operates through the means of constant work, taking the form of shared judgements or reasoning. That is to say that this time, methodologically and conjointly with the linguistic tools previously evoked, rhetorical – modes of expression – and logical – natural forms of reasoning – approaches impose themselves on the evidence.

To summarize, from the epistemological point of view, what is in question here is the analysis of all those modes of thought which everyday life sustains and which are historically maintained over more or less *longues durées*; modes of thought applied to directly socialized 'objects', but which, cognitively and discursively, collectivities are continuously driven to reconstruct in the relations of meaning applied to reality and to themselves. From this comes the imperative of furnishing the critical means of treating these phenomena of socio-discursive cohesion and of analysing the principles of coherence which structure them in an internal–external relationship (cognitive schemes, attitudes and positionings, cultural models and norms).

From this point of view it is evident that cognition organizes the social in so far as this governs it, and that the symbolic constantly modulates our human adventures, under this higher form which is language. There are no social representations without language, just as without them there is no society. The place of the linguistic in the analysis of social representations cannot, therefore, be avoided: words are not the direct translation of ideas, just as discourses are never the immediate reflections of social positions.

SOCIAL REPRESENTATIONS, COGNITION AND DISCOURSE

Over the course of the last ten years we have seen the elaboration of an analysis of cognitive structures which allows us to deepen the theory of social representations. If we summarize the work that has contributed to this development, we can distinguish two hypotheses which have stimulated fruitful research programmes which justify closer attention than they have been given so far. First, there is the hypothesis of the central kernel (Abric, Flament, Guimelli) according to which every social representation is composed of cognitive elements or stable schemes around which are ordered other cognitive elements or peripheral schemes. The hypothesis is that the stable elements exercise a pre-eminence over the meaning of the peripheral elements, and that the former have a stronger resistance to the pressures of communication and change than the latter. One is tempted to say that the former express the permanence and uniformity of the social, while the latter express its variability and diversity. Beyond the experimental interest of this hypothesis, we should not neglect to mention its relationship to the current conception in the philosophy of mind concerning the difference between core and marginal ideas. Secondly, there is the notion of the organizing principle suggested by the Genevan researchers (Doise, Mugny) who have sought to account for the generativity of social representations. Without going into detail, we can say that we are concerned with ideas, maxims or images which in one way or another are virtual or implicit. They both are expressed through explicit ideas or images and order them by giving them a meaning they had not previously had; or they introduce a coherence among them by securing the meaning which is common to them through a work of selection. In other words, the organizing principle at the same time reduces the ambiguity or polysemy inherent in ideas or images and makes them relevant in any given social context. From many points of view, there is a profound analogy between these two hypotheses, which touch on the problems of how representations change and of their generativity respectively, to the extent that change and generativity concern the same fundamental phenomenon, that is to say, the question of the formation and evolution of social representations in the course of history, whether this is a short or long history, to use an expression of Fernand Braudel. But we must give some account of it. For various reasons, largely to do with dominant orientations in social psychology, there has been a tendency to leave in the shadow one of the essential references of the theory of social representations. We mean their reference to communication, to language, in short, to the discursive aspect of knowledge elaborated in common. It is true that social psychology has only had a marginal interest in this aspect, and that nearly all of the research on social cognition has not taken it into account. But, since its inception, the theory of social representations has rightly insisted on the deep link between cognition and communication, between mental operations and linguistic operations, between information and signification. Only on this condition has it been able to explain at one and the same time, in a non-reductive way, both the formation and evolution of practical knowledge and of what is called popular knowledge, as well as their social function. To this end, it seemed necessary to propose a concept which took account of the importance of the hypotheses we have been discussing, as well as giving concrete form to the link between cognition and communication, between mental and linguistic operations. At least it was from this perspective that the concept of *themata* was proposed (Moscovici, 1993) with the aim of responding to the demands of structural analysis, on which it was quite correct to have insisted. Actually, it is not only a question of responding to these demands, but also of enriching the possibilities of analysis by means of the openings which this concept allowed towards the history of knowledge, anthropology and semantics. These possibilities, it must be emphasized, are of course of a theoretical order, but also methodological. In order to introduce the concept in the clearest way and to make it familiar one should begin with certain questions with which we are already familiar in the study of social representations.

If one accepts, then, that social representations, in so far as they are particular forms (systems of prescriptions, inhibitions, tolerances or prejudices), participate each time in the global vision a society establishes for itself, then we need to know how to deal with the manner of these relations between general visions and particular representations, the latter being inscribed in the former or supposed to clarify them. And this is the paradox in the study of social representations: how to pass from the microsociological to the macrosociological? What theory can guarantee any concordance between these two levels? What conceptual tools will assure a legitimate generalization from facts observed in a specific situation? What property identified locally might be an example of the collective? What facts registered quantitatively will suffice to define a qualitative property attributable to a collective?

The problem is, in the first place, of a cognitive order, and rests on the following question: is every identifiable psychological property dependent on social interaction or on some human mechanism supposedly common to the 'species' and prior to all interaction? In response to this precise point, the history of science shows clearly that every restructuration of our representations and knowledge depends on the interactions of the moment – on the event as it occurs – though we need to make progress in our knowledge of our 'common mechanism' – what our intelligence is and what forms it can take, in order to make more explicit those which cognitively intervene in our processes of social interaction.

And this is where the problem of the congruence of representations occurs, in the sense of those which are translated or not and of how they are interpreted: our ideas, our representations are always filtered through the discourse of others, the experiences which we live, the collectives to which we belong. It is also the problem of those 'frameworks' or '*scripts*' which a certain cognitivist literature leaves us. There are few (Schank and Abelson, 1977), as if the human mind and memory functioned in terms of classified 'cases', and it is enough to summon up those contents in order to read them. Everyone knows that a description gives no information about the constitutive processes of the facts of which it gives an account. A simple hammer is describable not only in terms of its structuration or its purpose; this is why there are different types of hammer – for joiners or decorators, etc. – and each of them bears a long memory of gesture and function which has given them form.

The question becomes, then, the following: where do those ideas come from around which representations are constituted, or which even engender them? What is it in society which goes to 'make sense' and sustain the emergence and production of discourse? And, in consequence, how is it that certain representations – among all of those produced by each discourse – can come to be qualified as social, and on what basis precisely?

If we return to the earlier example of the hammer, it is clear that alongside a certain scientific representation (there must be a certain mass moved by a force directed towards pushing an object such as a nail or a peg), there is – and this is also important – a popular knowledge which is precise, functional and analogical (e.g. a claw hammer with two branching teeth which also allows nails to be removed), and which operates in the appropriation of the tool, its diffusion and transformations. We can go further: to illustrate his theory of the frameworks of experience and of the mental, Schank used the example of the Burger King restaurant, where the produce, orders, payments and gestures can be described exhaustively and defined in terms of organized action schemas (*frames*). But one can also show how the Burger King can be a place of improvisation on the basis of this restrained figure, and become not just a restaurant but also a meeting-place, a space for children to play, for chance encounters and imagery (like that of the *cowboy* associated with Marlboro cigarettes, in which the tobacco becomes emblematic of a virility associated with wide open spaces). 'Stereotypes' (in the ordinary sense of frozen images or opinions), therefore, are never as one believes them to be. And representations are never limited to a simple record of their contents, without talking of the strange idea which makes us conceive of memory as an enormous set of pigeon-holes for pre-cognized or pre-ordered situations from which it would suffice to draw as circumstances allow.

In fact, if human cognition presumes learning and memory one could not understand the extraordinary adaptability of our species (as witnessed by phylogenesis) if one did not also admit that the exercise and development of this cognition is actually founded on permanent processes of adaptability, in the form of elaborations of knowledge, and organized in terms of processes oriented towards common *themes*, taken as the origin of that to which it is devoted each time, like accepted knowledge or even like primary ideas. It is these primary ideas which come to instruct and motivate social regimes of discourse, which means that each time we must adopt common ideas or at least come to terms with them.

THEMES AND VARIATIONS

In any case we are at the beginning of our research, and, according to the Baconian percept, it would be dangerous to try and present as an established result something which for the moment is only a horizon. What we present here, *instantaneously*, is still a matter for debate and adjustments to points of view and to concepts which exist among us. Obviously, the concept we are proposing has a recent past of which, as is often the case, we suspect neither its breadth nor its ramifications. An exploration of this past is not without interest, since it not only allows us to situate the concept more clearly, but, above all, to grasp the theoretical roles it plays in the many domains which directly concern us. There is no need to traverse history to justify unsuspected convergences, nor to do so exhaustively to establish a pedigree after the event. It suffices to highlight certain reflections and intuitions, to look for their interaction from the point of view which concerns us in order to clarify a conceptual region which one can say remains bathed in a half-light. A physicist once remarked that such notions are the most fruitful. No doubt this is so, but on condition that the zones of clarity and obscurity are made explicit. Until then one must expect difficulties in understanding and a refreshing uncertainty as to their value.

However that may be, it must be agreed that reflections on 'themes' or 'themata' have not yet found a scientific niche nor penetrated scientific discourses. That they are concerned with something real and important is certainly recognized. Otherwise they would not have been evoked for such a long time. In the meantime they remain episodically used and situated at the intersection of many intellectual fields. Perhaps the context of social representations may produce the crystallization which would allow the scientific expression of what they designate intensively.

First in relation to sociology and anthropology, themes or thematic analyses express a regularity of style, a selective repetition of contents which have been created by society and remain preserved by society. They refer to possibilities of action and experience in common which can become conscious and integrated into past actions and experiences. In sum, the notion of theme indicates that the effective availability of meaning always goes beyond what may have been actualized by individuals or realized by institutions. When all is said and done, themes which traverse discourses or social practices cannot be simply 'deleted', as they say in the jargon of computers, but uniquely put into parenthesis, displaced from one moment to another in different ways, but they are always preserved as constant sources of new meanings or combinations of meanings if the need arises.

We should emphasize here that the notion of need appeared in the reflections which Schütz devoted to common sense. These reflections are of considerable interest to us in so far as the theory of social representations was elaborated in relation to ordinary and popular forms of knowledge. In his notes for his last courses at the New School for Social Research, he was concerned with the question of relevance. What is it that makes one part of our stock of knowledge relevant and focuses our attention? What is it that our consciousness experiences as being familiar and which concerns us in a given moment when we are assailed by so many experiences simultaneously? The *theme* in its conception appears as the form or kernel, the centre of the field of consciousness of which experience and non-thematic knowledge constitute the foundation:

> From among all these virtual realms of reality, or finite provinces of meaning, we wish to focus on that of working acts in the outer world. . . . Attention is thus restricted to the general problem of theme and horizon pertaining to that state of full-awakeness characteristic of this realm. But this focusing and restricting is itself an illustration of our topic: this particular realm of reality, this province among all other provinces, is declared to be paramount reality and made so to speak, thematic in the research of these philosophers (namely,

Bergson and James) – a move which renders all the other provinces surrounding this thematic kernel merely horizontal (and most unclarified as well). But the structurization into theme and horizon is basic to the mind, and to explain that kind of structure by confusing what is founded on with its founding principle is a true *petitio principii* indeed. (Schütz, 1970, pp. 7–8)

It is difficult to comment on an unfinished text, but one can see that thematic structuration coincides in some way with a work of objectification. And this is because, in making something thematic, relevant to their consciousness, individuals transform it at the same time into an object for themselves, or more precisely, into an object belonging to a reality chosen among all the possible or earlier realities. It is at least in this way that one should understand the reference to James and Bergson.

Let us consider the following example: when we walk in the street we act in relation to a great number of 'objects', cars, noise, café signs, the crowd, etc. To the extent that our attention or perception moves from one thing to another each is objectified by us in turn. But one cannot say that each object which holds our attention or is perceived by us is thereby objectified. Only those which are the 'centre', so to speak, of our field of consciousness become the theme of our representation and are objectified in the strict sense of the term. In sum, we experience many 'regions of reality' connected to a common representation. But only one among them acquires the status of a socially dominant reality, while the others appear to have a derived reality *in relation* to the dominant reality. All of this presupposes that the relation between the corresponding theme and the others can be relevant and shared simultaneously. Or to finish what we want to say, there can be a familiar framework in which all that exists or happens will have a non-problematic character. As soon as the framework is disturbed by an unexpected element, an event or some knowledge which does not bear the mark of the familiar, of the non-problematic, a thematic change is indispensable. As Schütz observed:

Something which was supposed to be familiar and therefore unproblematic proves to be unfamiliar. It thus has to be investigated and ascertained as to its nature; it becomes problematic and thus has to be made into a theme and not left in the indifference of the concomitant horizontal background. It is sufficiently relevant to be imposed as a new problem, as a new theme, and even supersede the previous theme of his thinking which, then according to circumstances, one man will 'let out his grip' entirely or at least set aside temporarily. (Schütz, 1970, pp. 25–6)

It is not necessary to insist further. Through these observations we wanted to underline, on the one hand, just how far the exploration of everyday consciousness and 'natural' understanding suggests the notion of theme, which designates the movement of structuration of a field of ordinary, common knowledge and available meanings (we shall see in a moment what it refers to in relation to scientific knowledge!). And on the other hand, we have sought to underline the kinship with some fundamental hypotheses in the study of social representations and the sociological and anthropological implications of this idea.

Next, by a sort of inverse movement, the study of linguistic phenomena requires more and more the study of common knowledge and hence of its representations. Clearly the analysis of social representations returns at the same time, namely to deal with the same phenomena in so far as they are phenomena of exchange between discourses or of convergence among discourses. At least we know, thanks to the work of linguists, that there exists in language a fundamental process which is that of *thematization*. In every utterance, for example, 'The Greens are a social movement,' there is a lexical focalization in the form of the orientation of the utterance towards a particular word – substantive or verb – which makes the 'kernel meaning', at the very least, a reference ('the Greens') to the sense of the utterance. And with the activity of reiteration or rewriting in discourse there is also progressively the construction of keys for the semantic reading which are imposed on the reader or listener. In a fundamental work Chomsky (1982) in some way allowed for the postulation of a level of thematic structure which orients the semantic fields, and controls or binds the grammatical functions of words. In abandoning a system of rules of transformation, he proposes a system of principles which recognizes the existence of thematic 'roles' which determine the association between verb and substantives in the formation of an utterance. For example, the verb 'to convince' has the property of determining a thematic role to its object and complement in the sentence: 'The Greens have been convinced to abandon their earlier position.' Here there is an important idea for the elaboration of a representation, since the principal function of thematic roles is to associate the argument of a verb to the meaning of the verb in a semantic field. This always implicates the content of the verb and an interpretation of the verb itself in a given context. Elsewhere the idea of thematic relations among words expresses the possibility of a 'primary' vocabulary comprising the semantic parts of discourse (events, place, agent, etc.) which remain constant and determine syntactic combinations: 'Thematic relations are grounded in the elements that constitute our mental representations of events. I take for granted that there is a correspondence between our mental representation of events and the meaning of sentences used to express them' (Culicover, 1988).

Without doubt there is a controversy over whether thematic relations are more semantic or syntactic in character, but no one contests that they have a structuring conceptual aspect in discourse. However that may be, it nevertheless seems possible to clarify the nature of social representations through these ideas, since social representations carry a thematic structure whose lexical and syntactic effects are incontestable. In this respect, Talmy (1985) demonstrates the existence of a thema which he calls *force dynamics*, and which expresses the way in which social or physical entities interact in relation to a force. He analyses their way of 'causing' something, expressed by the verbs 'to prevent, to help, to leave', which affect the semantic interpretation of similar utterances. But he also shows at the same time that this thema affects the usage of mental grammatical categories (duty, obligation, etc.). One can imagine that starting from these syntactic and semantic properties, and following Talmy's path, one could describe an underlying thema and the social and mental representations of which it would be the kernel.

Clearly these ideas are still provisional and arguable (Carrier Duncan, 1985; Jackendorf, 1991). Meanwhile we should consider that the processes of thematization aim in every discourse at the stabilization of meanings in the form of thema–property (adjectives) relations, inducing images of situations or ways of being of things and the world. They are processes, in sum, which constantly associate our common knowledge with our discursive knowledge and the construct of our ways of cognitive and cultural anchoring. Thus, in a concrete way our representations, our beliefs, our prejudices are sustained by a particular social representation. This works through establishing relations internal to discourse, hence linguistic relations, but necessarily acting externally through playing on references between, on the one hand, those which are oriented towards a new semantic reading of things (those which are thematized or not, and those which are spoken about) and, on the other, through the choice made each time of a particular given origin to these *routes* of saying and meaning. Some linguists seem to be persuaded that there are only a limited number of themes which have a universal value, and which regulate linguistic constructions which at first sight seem very distant from one another (Jackendorf, 1991).

THE ROLE OF THEMATA IN SCIENTIFIC REPRESENTATIONS OF THE WORLD

Finally we should pay particular attention to the idea we are discussing within the domain of scientific knowledge. The importance of this idea has been understood since people first wondered about the origin of the course of speaking and meaning, or of understanding or explaining. In the case of the discourse of ordinary knowledge, as with scientific knowledge, it is a question of asking what plays the role of the *primary idea* in the formation of families of representations in the given domain which give a 'typical' form to the objects and situations related to this idea within these domains. It is understood each time they repass the discursive deployments with the aim of illustrating them and of recalling them, and above all of reorganizing them as a function of a group, a history, a project for action.

Without doubt, what appears to us to be and what we believe is constitutive of the 'essence' of things, which Aristotle already expressed clearly:

> All teaching and all learning of an intellectual kind proceed from pre-existent knowledge. This will be clear if we study all the cases: the mathematical sciences are acquired in this way, and so is each of the other arts. Similarly with arguments, both deductive and inductive: they effect their teaching through what we already know, the former assuming items which we are presumed to grasp, the latter proving something universal by way of the fact that the particular cases are plain.... There are two ways in which we must already have knowledge: of some things we must already believe that they are, of others we must grasp what the items spoken about are (and of some things both). E.g. of the fact that everything is either asserted or denied truly, we must believe that it is the case; of the triangle, that it means this; and of the unit both (both what it means and that it is). (Aristotle, trans. Jonathan Barres, 1994, p. 1)

Again without doubt, and in the same way, we necessarily have intuitions about the general laws organizing our mental constructions. As Albert Einstein remarked, it is a question of the relation between the intuition of these general laws which form the basis for mental constructions and physics: 'To these elementary laws there leads no logical path, only intuition supported by being sympathetically in touch with experience (*Einfühlung in die Erfahrung*)... there is no logical bridge from perceptions to the basic principles of theory' (Einstein, quoted in Holton, 1988, p. 395).

In a similar way Peter Medawar remarks:

> Scientific reasoning is an exploratory dialogue that can always be resolved into two voices or two episodes of thought, imaginative and critical, which alternate and interact.... The process by which we come to formulate a hypothesis is not illogical but non-logical, that is, outside logic. But once we have formed an opinion we can expose it to criticism, usually by experimentation. (1982, pp. 101–2)

But, again without doubt, this is the case for all scientific processes, even ordinary reasoning: 'The E (experiences: *Erlebnisse*) are given to us. A are the axioms from which we draw consequences. Psychologically, the A rest upon the E. There exists, however, no logical path from the E to the A, but only an intuitive (psychological) connection which is always "subject to revocation" (*auf Widerruf*)' (A. Einstein, letter to M. Solovine, 7 May 1952, quoted in Holton, 1978, p. 96; a more extended discussion of this point can be found in Holton, 1998).

We necessarily therefore have an intuition of these 'primary ideas' – at least, because they effectively govern a number of discursive developments – and we can guess that they certainly underlie most of our collective representations, summarizing in these 'archetypes', 'common ideas', culture, histories, societies. Can we follow Holton and call them themata? Holton in fact demonstrates that they play a role as much through their blockages as through their openings, which punctuate the developments of modern science, through 'revolutions' in the representations.

According to Holton, 'themata' would also correspond to the kind of 'first deeply rooted conceptions, informing science as much as the perception we have of it': 'primitive ideas' have as much of the characteristic of original strata of cognition as of archetypal images of the world, its structure and genesis.

A first example is Copernicus, who achieved significant progress in mathematical astronomy. Looking closely at the work which made him famous (*De Revolutionibus*) one can see a deep reason, which is his vision of nature as the temple of God, and that because of this it is by studying nature that men will be able to distinguish the design of the creator. The book was placed on the Vatican Index precisely because of this proposition, which was understood as a kind of challenge to God. But the idea remained as the foundation of modern science, in the sense that henceforth it had the vocation of systematizing the real.

At that time two principal themata saw the light of day, as Holton emphasizes, those of *simplicity* and *necessity*. The correctness of every scientific system would be assured, from the moment that there is mutual adjustment, in a quasi-aesthetic way, between data and theory, but also of necessity adjusting each detail to a more general plan. Thus Copernicus explained that the heliocentric scheme he had discovered for the planetary system had the peculiarity that:

> not only do all their [the planets'] phenomena follow from that, but also this correlation binds together so closely the order and magnitudes of all the planets and of their spheres or orbital circles, and the heavens themselves, that nothing can be shifted in any part of them without disrupting the remaining parts and the universe as a whole. (Copernicus, *De Revolutionibus*, quoted in Holton, 1988, p. 322)

In this respect one cannot but think, as Holton does, of Einstein, who wrote to his assistant Ernst Strauss: 'What I'm really interested in is whether God could have made the world in a different way; that is whether the necessity of logical simplicity leaves any freedom at all' (Einstein, quoted in Holton, 1978, p. xii).

But to grasp themata it will not be enough to relate some types of commentaries made by scientists about the motivations for their work. One:

1 Must know how to grasp the scientific content of an event (E), both in the terms of its own epoch and in the terms which will henceforth be our own;
2 But establish the trajectory through time of a certain state of common scientific knowledge ('public' science), which means 'tracing the World

Line of the Universe of an idea, a line on which the previously cited element (E) is merely a point' (Holton, 1988, p. 21);

3 Consequently, it is important to identify the 'instant of birth' in some context of discovery;

4 The event (E) now 'begins to be understood in terms of the intersection of
two trajectories, two World Lines, one for public science and one for private
science' (Holton, 1988, p. 22).

There would also be, through the texts and representations which they
underlie and adjust, three levels in the emergence and implementation of
themata:

- That of the *concept* or the *thematic component of a concept*, for example, in
  science, the appearance of the concepts of symmetry or continuity;
- That of the *methodological thema*: this would be, again in science, the
  formulation of terms of invariance, extremes, or of impossibilities, applied
  to laws;
- Lastly that of *thematic proposition* or thematic hypothesis, that is to say, of
  globalizing utterances, such as the hypothesis of Newton about the immobil-
  ity of the centre of the universe.

Research on themata assumes therefore:

1 At the level of semantic and cultural analysis of discourses and texts a
thematic exploration (what is it that makes a common theme at any given
moment of consensus or of the break in a scientific consensus?);

2 At the level of cognitive and logical analysis a specification of types of
dialectical relations, which would be established between propositions and
between concepts in this confrontational relation, between public (official)
science and common knowledge or common sense.

An exemplary case is that of the thema of the *atom*, not only a concept but
also an image whose age we know reaches back into antiquity. Democritus or
Epicurus meant by this term a constitutive element at the basis of all matter,
an indivisible and homogeneous element. And although the search for a unique
'particle' which would constitute all bodies through combination has today
more and more reached its limits, the idea remains as pregnant today as it
did two thousand years ago. This is because it is strongly associated with a
number of methodological *themata*, which make sense at the level evoked
earlier of the 'harmony' between data and theory, and, above all, between
images and modalities of the scientific 'presentation' of things.

The thema of the atom does not necessarily refer to an object in the literal
or physical sense, such as the elementary discrete entities (discontinuities):
gamma particles, mesons or protons. It could just as well be a question of an
abstract type of element, but one which would be derived from entities with a

formal character: theoretical entities such as 'forces' (electromagnetic interactions) or composed of different terms, for example, a central term and a
certain number of correction terms. Methodologically, then, the thema of
atomism, that is to say of *decomposability*, finds itself confronted with the
thema of continuity, and one sees the recurrent emergence in science of
antithetical couples, such as those of evolution and involution, invariance and
variation, reductionism and holism, since what occurs here, at the level of
representations, is really persistence from the lighter to the heavier of this
ancient scheme with its reciprocal interactions, and there the need for an
'underlying identity' founding hierarchical classifications. Making order out
of chaos in modern physics assumes these four categories of methodological
thema; gravitation, electromagnetic interaction, and strong and weak interactions. One could think again here of the resurrection in the middle of the
twentieth century of the old antithesis between the full and the empty in
relation to the debates about 'molecular reality'.

Thus an article by the physicist S. Weinberg (1974) takes the form of a
'charter', both philosophical and programmatic, for this era when, according to him, it is a question of finding a common basis to the four types of
interactions ('forces') which together give a complete account of physical
phenomena:

1 Gravitational interaction which sustains all the particles,
2 Electromagnetic force which accounts for those phenomena where charged
   particles occur, as well as the interaction between light and matter,
3 The 'strong' nuclear force which occurs between members of the family of
   elementary particles called hadrons (mesons and baryons), and
4 The 'weak interaction' postulated to describe the interactions, of extremely
   brief range, of certain elementary particles (such as the diffusion of a neutrino by a neutron, and the radioactive disintegration of a neutron yielding a
   proton, an electron and an antineutrino). This is what Weinberg writes at
   the beginning of his article:

One of man's enduring hopes has been to find a few simple general laws that
would explain why nature, with all its seeming complexity and variety, is the
way it is. At the present moment the closest we can come to a unified view of
nature is a description in terms of elementary particles and their mutual interactions. All ordinary matter is composed of just those elementary particles that
happen to possess both mass and (relative) stability: the electron, the proton
and the neutron. To these must be added the particles of zero mass: the photon
or quantum of electromagnetic radiation, the neutrino, which plays an essential
role in certain kinds of radioactivity, and the graviton, or quantum of gravitational radiation.   (Weinberg, 1974, p. 56)

It is interesting to note here such expressions as 'general laws of a *simple*
form' and '*unitary* vision of nature' stemming from 'elementary particles and

their reciprocal interactions'. There is an echo here of Democritus' 'all is atoms and void.' And this property of elementarity helps to orient the whole chain of explanation, which goes from particles called elementary and arrives at constructed, antithetical entities (kernels, atoms or familiar 'matter', all 'composed' of elementary particles). Throughout Weinberg's article one can see this dominant conception of groups, families and higher-order families organizing the particles among them in an almost 'zoological' way. This is the methodological thema of *continuum*, but also with an echo of that other thema, the *life-cycle*, 'imported into the sciences from the world of human encounters' (Holton, 1978, p. 17):

> The technical report of, say, the analysis of a bubble chamber photograph is cast largely in terms of a life-cycle story. It is a story of evolution and devolution, of birth, adventures and death. Particles enter on the scene, encounter others, and produce a first generation of particles that subsequently decay, giving rise to a second generation and perhaps a third generation. They are characterized by relatively short or relatively long lives, by membership in families or species. (Holton, 1978, p. 17)

What this signifies is that a certain number of themata extend from one end to the other of the epochs of revolutions in knowledge, with the thematic oppositions which they generate, or which are associated with them, all within that interpenetration we evoked earlier between public science and common representations of knowledge and the world. Once more, it is not a question here of archetypes in the Jungian sense of the term, but rather of 'primary ideas' helping to recast the representation of domains of knowledge and the work on these domains. The notion of 'work', at once both cognitive and discursive, is important here because it is really in the incessant reformulations and rewritings implied in this historical work of representations that those themata emerge which become *reference points* in the sense of 'focal semantic points' for understanding the stabilization or destabilization of ideas or concepts.

The example of the work of Kepler, again analysed by Holton, is particularly demonstrative of the progression of such processes. Kepler remained anchored in an epoch in which animism, alchemy, astrology, numerology and sorcery continued to be questions discussed seriously. He recounts the stages of his progression in detail, and thus helps us to understand the multiple confrontations which accompanied the beginning of the seventeenth century, the dawn of modern science.

His first step is to unify the representation of the world inherited from antiquity by appealing to the concept of a universal physical *force* as based on a unitary figure – the sun ruling the earth from its centre – and a unitary principle: the immanent omnipresence of mathematical harmonies. He could not provide a mechanical explanation for the movement of the planets, but he did come to tie together two conceptions of the world: the ancient – that of an immutable cosmos – and the modern, dedicated to the play of dynamic and mathematical laws. And it is almost incidentally that he brought together the indications which Newton later used to establish definitively our modern conceptions.

Kepler is in effect the first to seek a physical law based on terrestrial mechanics to grasp the universe as a whole. Even though Copernicus still insisted on maintaining a distinction between celestial phenomena and those which belonged only to the Earth, Kepler rejected it. From the work of his youth, *Mysterium cosmographicum* (1596), one and the same geometrical procedure serves to establish the necessary nature of the observed arrangement of all the planets. The Earth is given the same value as the other planets!

A little later, working in 1605 on his *Astronomia nova*, he set out his programme:

> My aim in this is to show that the celestial machine is to be likened not to a divine organism but rather to a clockwork . . . in so far as nearly all the manifold movements are carried out by means of a single, quite simple magnetic force, as in the case of a clockwork all motions (are caused) by a simple weight. Moreover I show how this physical conception is to be presented through calculation and geometry. (quoted in Holton, 1988, p. 56)

Here then the celestial machine is considered as changed by a unique terrestrial force, to the image of a clock, a prophetic intention translated by the subtitle: *Physica Cœlestis*. To do this, Kepler first discerned that the cause of forces which make themselves felt between two bodies is not in their relative position, nor in the geometrical configurations in which they enter (as did Aristotle, Ptolemy and Copernicus), but in the mechanical interactions established between these material objects. Moreover, he already had a presentiment of a universal gravity: 'Gravitation consists in the mutual bodily striving among related bodies toward union or connection; of this order is also the magnetic force' (quoted in Holton, 1988, p. 57).

In the same way he stated what might be a precursor of the principle of the conservation of the quantity of movement: 'If the earth were not round, a heavy body would be driven not everywhere straight toward the middle of the earth, but toward different points from different places' (quoted in Holton, 1988, p. 57).

But he remained a prisoner of the Aristotelian conception of the principle of inertia, identifying inertia as a tendency to return to rest: 'Outside the field of force of another related body, every bodily substance, insofar as it is corporeal, by nature tends to remain at the same place at which it finds itself' (quoted in Holton, 1988, p. 58). And this axiom prevented him from actually formulating the concepts of mass and force; because of these concepts, the celestial machine of the world envisaged by Kepler is doomed to failure. He would have needed to foresee distinct forces to ensure the displacement of planets along the tangent to the trajectory, and to take account of the radial component of the movement. Further, he assumed the hypothesis that the force from the sun, which maintains the tangential movement of the planets, decreases as the inverse ratio of the distance. The image is suggestive, but it does not lead Kepler to the law of forces of the inverse square ratio of the distance, simply because he considers the spreading of light in *a single plane*, composed of the plane of the planetary orbits. In this way he makes the reduction in luminous intensity depend on the linear increase of the circumference, as one moves to more distant orbits!

Kepler's physics is therefore a pre-Newtonian physics: force is proportional not to acceleration but to speed. This was sufficient for him to explain his observation that the speed of a planet along its elliptical orbit decreased in a linear ratio, as its distance from the sun increased; from this came his second law, which founded a beginning of physical interpretation on the basis of many erroneous postulates.

Having, in effect, the conviction of the existence of a universal force stemming from magnetism, he represented the sun as a spherical magnet, one pole of which would be at its centre, and the other at its surface, so that a planet, itself magnetized as a bar magnet of constant orientation, would find itself sometimes attracted and sometimes repelled by the sun along its elliptical orbit. This explained the radial component in the movement of the planets: the movement following the tangent would result in a force or angular moment which he could prove by hypothesis, the planet swept along its path by the lines of magnetic force emanating from the sun as it rotated on its own axis. This representation is already remarkable, but it remained incomplete: Kepler did not succeed in showing: 'how this physical conception is to be presented through calculation and geometry' (quoted in Holton, 1988, pp. 59–60).

But in fact the block is only apparent because of Kepler's attempt to establish a mechanical model of the universe and a new philosophical interpretation of 'reality'. He wanted 'to provide a philosophy or physics of celestial phenomena in place of the theology or metaphysics of Aristotle' (letter to Johann Brengger, 4 October 1607; quoted in Holton, 1988, p. 60). His contemporaries saw only absurdity in this. They were tempted to see in Kepler the champion of a mechanical type of natural philosophy; the term 'mechanical' implies here that the real world would be the world of objects and their mechanical interactions in the Aristotelian sense.

However, from the failure of the programme announced in *Astronomia nova*, another aspect of Kepler can be affirmed, which can be better understood if, with Holton, we admit that the terms 'reality' and 'physical' here bear meanings which agree:

I call my hypotheses physical for two reasons . . . My aim is to assume only
those things of which I do not doubt they are real and consequently physical,
where one must refer to the nature of the heavens, not the elements. When I
dismiss the perfect eccentric and the epicycle, I do so because they are purely
geometric assumptions for which a corresponding body in the heavens does not
exist. The second reason for calling my hypotheses physical is this . . . I prove
that the irregularity of the motion [of planets] corresponds to the nature of
the planetary sphere; i.e., is physical.   (Kepler's notes on a letter from Mästlin,
21 September 1616; quoted in Holton, 1988, p. 62)

Everything for Kepler rests on the *nature* of the heavens and the *nature* of
bodies. And for him this derives from supporting two criteria of reality:

1   The real world, in the physical sense, determines the nature of things, and
    the world of ordinary phenomena of mechanical principles; this is the pos-
    sibility of formulating a generalized and coherent dynamics, which Newton
    later realized.
2   The real world, in the physical sense, is the world of harmonies of math-
    ematical expression, which man is able to detect from the chaos of the
    contingent. One must therefore do one's utmost to discover these 'math-
    ematical harmonies' of nature.

Thus when Kepler observed, following the first observations of the movement of sunspots, that the period of the sun's rotation was actually completely different from what he had postulated in his physical system, he was
not at all disturbed. He was not, as Newton later was, totally committed to a
mechanical interpretation of heavenly phenomena. His criterion was that of
the harmonious regularity of the descriptive laws of science. The 'Law of
Equal Areas' is a good example. For Tycho and Copernicus, the harmonious
regularity of the movement of the planets was recognizable in the uniformity
of the circular movements of which they were composed. But Kepler ended
up identifying the orbits of the planets as ellipses, a non-uniform form of
movement. The figure is irregular, and the speed is different at each point.
And carrying this double complication harbours a harmonious regularity: 'the
fact that a constant area is swept out in equal intervals by a line from the
focus of the ellipse, where the sun is, to the planet on the ellipse' (Holton,
1988, p. 63).

For Kepler this law is harmonious for three reasons:

1   It agrees with experience (he had to endure the sacrifice of his first ideas in
    order to respond to the imperatives of quantitative experience).
2   It appeals to an invariance, even if it is no longer a question of angular
    velocity but of areal velocity.

Recall that Copernicus's world system and Kepler's first system (*Mysterium
cosmographicum*) postulated ensembles of stationary concentric spheres.

Galileo never came to accept Kepler's ellipses, and remained to the end a
disciple of Copernicus, who had declared that 'the mind shudders' from the
supposition of a non-circular and non-uniform heavenly movement. Kepler's
postulate of elliptical orbits therefore marked the end of ancient simplicity.
The second and third laws instituted the law of physical invariance as a
principle of order in a situation of flux.

3 This law is also harmonious in the sense that the fixed point of reference of
   the Law of Equal Areas, the 'centre' of movement of the planets, is the
   centre of the sun itself, even though the Copernican scheme situated the sun
   as slightly recessed from the centre of planetary orbits. Through this discovery Kepler constituted a truly heliocentric planetary system, conforming
   to his instinctive demand for a material object at its 'centre' from which
   must follow the physical factors governing the movement of the system.
   This heliocentric system is also theocentric.

For Kepler the image is exciting: the planetary system becomes a figure in
a centripetal universe, controlled through and by the sun in its multiple roles:
'as the *mathematical* centre in the description of celestial motions; as the
central *physical* agency for assuring continued motion; and above all as the
metaphysical centre, the temple of the Deity' (Holton, 1988, p. 65). Three
inseparable roles equally correspond to the arguments having the status of
archetypes:

1 The heliocentric system allows a remarkable simple representation of planetary movements.
2 Each planet is necessarily subject to an invariable and eternal driving force
   on its own orbit.
3 There must be provision for what is common to all the orbits, namely their
   common centre, and this eternal source must itself be invariable and eternal.
4 These are the exclusive attributes of the single Divinity (Holton, 1988,
   p. 65).

Kepler then accumulated deductions and analogies in support of his thesis.
But the most resounding argument was the comparison of the sphere of the
world to the Trinity: the sun, being at the centre of the sphere, and consequently antecedent to its two other attributes – surface and volume – is
related to God the Father, a permanent analogy for Kepler, and an image
which obsessed him from beginning to end. In that ascendant traced by the
solar figure one can actually find a very ancient thema: that of the identification of 'light' with the source of all existence and the affirmation that space
and light are only a thema of Neoplatonic influence: as the references to
Proclus (fifth century AD) testify. In the Middle Ages the 'place' attributed to
God was either the whole world or the space beyond the last celestial sphere.
Kepler presents a new alternative: in the framework of a heliocentric system

God could be reintegrated in the solar system, enthroned in the object which serves as the stationary common reference, and which coincides with the source of light and the origin of the physical forces assuring the cohesion of the system. As Holton wisely says: 'Kepler's physics of the heavens is helio-centric in its kinematics, but theocentric in its dynamics' (1988, p. 66) – dynamics because the harmonies, originating in the properties of the Divinity, substitute for the physical laws originating in the concept of specific quantitat-ive forces. Kepler's harmonies, therefore, are quantitative, even though for the Ancients these laws were either qualitative or of a simple form; and this is where there is the point of rupture resulting in the modern mathematical conception of science. Although for the Ancients quantitative results only served to clarify a specific model, for Kepler it is in the empirical results themselves that the celestial construction is revealed. This postulate, that the harmonies are immanent in the quantitative properties of nature, actually returns to the very origins of natural philosophy: it is the assimilation of quantity in so far as it is an attribute of the Divinity; and this capacity for man to per-ceive the harmonies becomes a proof of the connection between his spirit and God (cf. *Harmonice mundi*, IV, 1).

The sensation of harmony appeared since there is an equivalence between the order of perceptions and the corresponding innate archetypes (*archetypus*). The archetype even becomes part of the spirit of God, since it is an imprint in the soul of man, since God created him, since the soul carries: 'Not an image of the true pattern [paradigma], but the true pattern itself . . . Thus finally the harmony itself becomes entirely soul, nay even God' (quoted in Holton, 1988, p. 69).

The study of nature is changed into the study of divine understanding, which is therefore accessible to us through the intermediary of mathematical language: God speaks in mathematical laws!

One finds here the image of the God of Pythagoras, incarnate in a directly observable nature and in the mathematical harmonies of the solar system: a God, writes Kepler: 'whom in the contemplation of the universe I can grasp, as it were, with my very hands' (letter to Baron Strahlendorf, 23 October 1613; quoted in Holton, 1988, p. 70).

Here is an absolute conceptual harmony which operates through three fundamental themata, at the origin therefore of three cosmological models: *the universe as physical machine, the universe as mathematical harmony*, and *the universe as theological order, governed from its centre*.

THEMATA AND SOCIAL REPRESENTATIONS

To sum up, at the heart of social representations, as at the heart of scientific revolutions, there are themata which endure as 'concept images' or which are the object of controversies before they are put into question. What are they? What forms do they take? 'Concept images'? 'Primary conceptions' profoundly anchored in collective memory? 'Primitive notions'? Certainly something of all of these. All our discourses, our beliefs, our representations come after many other discourses and many other representations elaborated before us and derive from them. They are a matter of words, but also of mental images, beliefs or 'preconceptions'. Lacking the capacity to completely master the origin of conceptions in the *longue durée*, the analysis of social representations can do no better than attempt, on the one hand, to identify what, at a certain 'axiomatic' level in texts and opinions, comes to operate as 'first principles', 'compelling ideas' or 'images', and on the other to strive towards showing the empirical and methodological 'consistency' of these 'concepts' or 'primary notions' in their regular application at the level of everyday or scholarly argumentation. That is to say that linguistics, as much as mental imagery, intervenes in these processes of social thinking; or again, that from this point of view the boundaries between 'scholarly' and 'common' discourse are never fixed, and that there is a continual passage between one and the other. How does this take shape? At least we shall attempt here to specify, from the top down, a configuration as much cognitive as applied.

Conceptual themata can, then, be considered as 'source ideas' ('the universe is a physical machine'; 'it therefore obeys mathematical laws'; 'the sun is at the centre as God and light') which bring about the generation of new axiomatics in the evolution of our representations of the world. They take the form of 'notions', that is to say, of 'potential places' of meaning as generators of conceptions, they are 'virtual' because these 'places' can only be characterized through discourse, through justifications and arguments which 'nurture' them in the form of productions of meanings.

> Example 1: 'The atom is the smallest of all things, that is to say it is the simplest, the most concentrated and the most universal; for there must be an "ultimate" kernel.'

This implies that these 'themata notions' have as complements a certain number of *methodological themata* taking the form of 'laws' applicable in given domains in the form of 'interpretive keys' for these domains: interpretive keys in the sense of statutes of the properties and modes of combination and inter-relation attributed to the objects of these domains, defining therefore the *interiors* (the contents of these domains in relation to the *exteriors* – what they are not or do not include).

> Example 2: 'The atom is the element which enters into the composition of all complex things (matter or living beings).'

In that way both the 'nature' and the range of social representations come to be grounded. Concretely, this cognitive work comes to operate through a double symbolic articulation:

1   In the definition of *boundaries* establishing these interior/exterior relations by indexation (referential anchoring) in relation to already existing or known domains (what they are responsible for/what they are not responsible for; what belongs to them/what does not belong to them);
2   By reciprocal legitimation of these reconstructions of representations through the argumentative 'presentation' of objects authenticating these domains (objectification of contents), objects themselves legitimated *modulo* the properties attributed to them each time, as typical if not exclusive.

Example 3: 'Every living being, all matter are constituted each time of specific atoms. There are atoms for the living and atoms for minerals.'

The whole socio-cognitive play of representation comes to rest then on the types of these properties attributed each time to the objects of a domain with the aim of exemplifying them. And considering the relations between 'interiors' and 'exteriors', that is to say, contrasting between social domains and hence between the contents which characterize them, one is clearly in the presence of local systems of opposition constructed through discourse; the properties assigned to objects in some way play the role of applicable functions for the setting of relations between elements of domains. These functions applied to objects (qualities, specifications and determinations of existence assigned to elements of a domain) are, one could say, *topocognitive functions*: they aim to specify the exemplary character of objects by completely positioning them in relation to other objects, and thereby establishing the legitimation of the domains of contexts supporting each representation:

Example 4: 'Every living being is made of atoms. One should therefore find atoms (cells) which differentiate the living from the "non-living" (corpuscles).'

At this level all methodological relations between objects or properties of objects go to work in the form of tributary 'rules' as much from the ordinary memory of 'things' (what they 'are' in relation to other 'things') as of 'maxims of beliefs' (what these 'things' bring with them and what they lead to or produce), which translate the endurance of a semiosis common to every human collectivity. These 'rules' then take the form of statements rethematizing the relation to the 'law' in question.

Example 5: 'The atom is different in a stone than in a living being, but some laws of construction of the stone are also found in the living being ("bricks of life").'

Figure 4.1 summarizes these developments in a configurational scheme. This means, to return to the question of social representations, that they are always derived from 'pseudo-conceptual' kernel elements: archetypes of ordinary reasoning or 'preconceptions' established over the *longue durée*, that is to say, tributaries of rhetorical histories and social beliefs having the status of *generic images*. In fact it is a question of *topoi*, that is, the 'places' of common sense where they find the source of developments and the means of legitimizing themselves, since these 'places' are anchored in the perceptible (shared and popular cognition) and in ritualized experience (culture and its rites, that is, its operative stakes in representation). This generally takes the form of notions anchored in *systems of oppositions* (i.e. terms which are contrasted in order to be related) relative to the body, to being, to action in society and the world more generally; every language bears witness to this.

Thus in French, as in many other languages, there is the opposition of **man/woman**, which allows some conceptual themata to be derived (**man = force; woman = grace**), which, over the *longue durée*, go to shape our behaviour, our conduct and, above all, our images, but which also come to operate as 'semantic kernels' generating and organizing discursive regimes, cognitive and cultural positionings, in other words, classes of argumentation (**'feminism'** versus **'male chauvinism'**, **'the woman at home'** versus **'the woman at work'**, etc.). Thus, comparing discourses bearing socio-ethical conflicts, we can find again those *topics* comparable to the properties assigned to the 'other' and legitimating opposition.

Every social representation returns therefore to the reiterated expression in discourses of these exchanges of locally or more universally negotiated *theses* or themata. The 'revolution of ideas', even, as we have seen, in science, demands arguments which have the power to overturn an idea or a dominant image. In the same way, there must be the 'good of histories' to make a 'history'. Consequently, what is important in the analyses of these discourses, which intuitively each time one collects as representatives of movements of opinion or social positions, is really to bring to light the negotiations at work here, linguistically, on the frontier between the 'negotiable' and the 'not negotiable', between what functions as stable belief or as developing social cognition. Concretely, this is to identify, on the one hand, what gives itself 'literally', and on the other, what arises from constructive debate and shows adaptive processes, indices of social and cultural changes. Thus at the grand opening of an American film about dinosaurs one could see the sudden reappearance of a clear-cut opposition between 'Darwinian believers' and those (religious 'fundamentalists') who do not accept any existence on earth prior to what the Bible says about the creation of man. This opposition again rests on the conflict between two types of thematization:

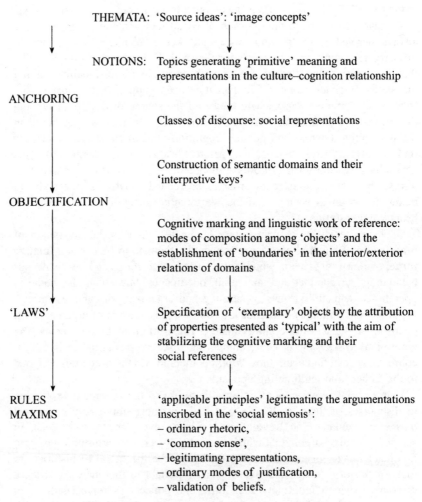

Figure 4.1. The generative function of themata

1 Man is the receptacle of God and cannot therefore have been preceded by a
   world seen as 'bestial';
2 God exists only in the progressive and evolutionary design of a world
   which is constructed and not in 'Creation'. This is a type of demarcation
   regularly found at this frontier between 'serious' (scientific) discourse and
   'non-serious' (i.e. contemptible) discourse, but which still constrains all
   social discourse to take its place in a certain relation to a 'police of the
   conflict of ideas'.

Consequently, one must admit that jointly with these perceptual or neuro-sensory 'invariants' which organize our basic cognitive mechanisms, there are also our ordinary cognitions, and that in the *longue durée* these are imprinted with postulates anchored in beliefs, and it is this 'imprint' one sees emerging in our discourse in the form of the dynamics of recurrent openings or closures – 'openings' and 'closures' since all these beliefs operate and become apparent through 'couplets' integrating 'opposites' in a flash. And it is this 'synthesis of opposites' which, as in language, grounds the integration of each perceptible thema in one or more notions.

So, for instance, the belief in the notion of 'liberty' assumes the representation of a particular couplet of reciprocities integrated in a *notional scheme*: 'the capacity to act without constraint versus constraints bearing down on one'. This reciprocity inherent in every notion allows in its turn the *commutations* of properties and determinations derived from the notion: 'liberty = well-being' versus 'malaise': 'liberty = licence' versus 'liberty = responsibility', etc.

It is these commutations which, with the flow of discourse, favour *permutations* in representations and the norms associated with them, in the form of:

1 'Blockages' or 'unblockings' in the axiomatic status (themata) of notions and their normative expressions (in French employment law the right to strike is primary, in German law it is the 'collective interest' which is primary and thus the necessity of preliminary negotiation);

2 The semantic and operational shifts which follow in the values or the traits which carry the anchoring of values (e.g. with food, fish which used to be part of the religious practice of 'lean Friday' has now become emblematic of a healthy diet and *cuisine légère*).

The consequence of such operative processes becomes evident in the play of negotiations about the status of objects and their contexts of 'existence', which are inherent in every discursive representation. It will be important here to distinguish in the analysis between those operating cognitively through expression in language itself, and those identifying artefacts of communication (types of situations, the presence or absence of the other, etc.).

In the first case this will be evident as much through the lexical thematization as through the semantic orientation of the syntactic arrangement of the expression:

Example: 'The *feminine woman* wears tights of brand X,' i.e.:
(a) '*At the centre of the class of women is the type of the "most feminine"*';
(b) '*She is recognized by what she wears; if you wish to identify her you should look first at the brand of her tights.*'

In the second case, at the 'communicational' level (i.e. *I–Other relations*), it will be a question of differentiating clearly the types of discursive and argumentative processes which lead on the one hand to focusing on the 'objects pretexts' or 'examples' (*exempla* or commonplaces), and on the other, to the positioning of the discursive representation in a referential context running from the *proximal* (dialogue, conversations, face-to-face exchanges) to the *distal* (the written or recorded discourse of the media or institutions). Thus we shall often be in the presence of 'packets of communications' expressing as much the social reiterations of representations as the evolution of images or notions in society. We need to know, then, taking account of this 'epidemiological' aspect of representations, though without thereby prejudging whether they all radiate from a central 'source', to know how to mark off the content of one domain from another, the convergences running back uphill a certain way, having more the status of *a schema of notional oppositions* than a stable source idea.

'Themata' never reveal themselves clearly; not even part of them is definitively attainable, so much are they intricately interwoven with a certain collective memory inscribed in language, and so much are they composites, like the representations they sustain, at once both cognitive (invariants anchored in our neurosensory apparatus and our schemes of action) and cultural (consensual universals of themes objectified by the temporalities and histories of the *longue durée*).

Let us take the example of food and the representations it carries or which are associated with it. The systems of oppositions which can be distinguished here are usually compromises between the biological and the social, between preoccupations about health or survival (images of the body and the self in relation to others) and memories or culinary cultures which found and position groups in relation to each other. And in this triplet 'food/body, health/cuisine, taste' one regularly sees the reappearance of such themata as the 'traditional', the 'natural' and the 'sophisticated', anchored in the corresponding 'image notions' – 'land', 'health or beauty', 'distinction' – where one can easily see the semantic domains they generate so abundantly among our contemporaries. And different types of 'laws' (medical, patrimonial, etc.) will be applicable according to each of these themata, from the 'rules' of consumption which are derived from them to the multiplicity of images and meanings this produces. From this point of view, the interesting thing is to measure how alimentary representations, indices of new categorizations of the social, are constantly recomposed, how boundaries in socio-historical presentations are overturned, and finally, how some representations have a direct impact on changes in practice: *active schematizations of common sense*, but also keys for understanding what in the analysis of each of our representations is given as *the conditions for the establishment of a 'common truth'*. Every social representation can only be analysed in terms of an *iconic and*

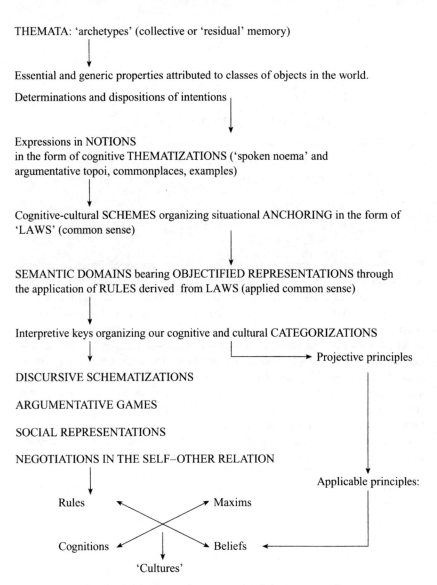

THEMATA: 'archetypes' (collective or 'residual' memory)

Essential and generic properties attributed to classes of objects in the world.

Determinations and dispositions of intentions

Expressions in NOTIONS
in the form of cognitive THEMATIZATIONS ('spoken noema' and argumentative topoi, commonplaces, examples)

Cognitive-cultural SCHEMES organizing situational ANCHORING in the form of 'LAWS' (common sense)

SEMANTIC DOMAINS bearing OBJECTIFIED REPRESENTATIONS through the application of RULES derived from LAWS (applied common sense)

Interpretive keys organizing our cognitive and cultural CATEGORIZATIONS

Projective principles

DISCURSIVE SCHEMATIZATIONS

ARGUMENTATIVE GAMES

SOCIAL REPRESENTATIONS

NEGOTIATIONS IN THE SELF–OTHER RELATION

Applicable principles:

Rules   Maxims

Cognitions   Beliefs

'Cultures'

Figure 4.2. From themata to social representations

linguistic trajectory, running up towards a source (the 'source ideas') and at the same time seeking to regulate downwards in the form of semantic domains and easily transmitted *argued schemas*. We have tried to recapitulate this operative architecture in figure 4.2.

5

The Dreyfus Affair, Proust, and Social Psychology*

It is unquestionable: some will judge the title of this paper frivolous, others will deem it risky, but everyone will find it uncanny. If you wonder what makes it uncanny, you will soon realize it is because the familiar words 'social psychology' are used in an association which is far from familiar. It would be enough to replace them with either 'history' or 'psychoanalysis' to do away with the uncanny and render the association banal. Now, and this may seem disconcerting, I have been indulging for some time in neither an analysis nor a criticism but *Gedankenexperiments* about fictitious characters and groups inhabiting the world of literature. Why is this? It is a fact that some French novelists, such as Michel Butor (1960), or historians, namely Georges Duby (1961) and Jacques Le Goff (1974), contend that social psychology is absolutely necessary if one wants to understand fiction and history in their depths. And they do not hesitate to avail themselves of it in their work. An American historian, James Redfield, has just declared that, in order to interpret the *Iliad*, it would be good to know Homer's social psychology: no doubt an arduous task. And the English historian M. I. Finley, discussing the change of attitudes towards the ancient world, reproaches most of his colleagues with neglecting the part played by social psychology: 'Most historians,' he writes, 'shy from psychological explanations of such change, partly from an understandable fear of the moralizing rhetoric that flows in their wake, partly from ignorance or distrust of social psychology, but largely because of hardened professional traditions' (Finley, 1983, p. 120). They are not the only ones and, I will add, through no fault of theirs.

For, and this is another fact, social psychologists do not share these interests. More exactly, they are reluctant to devote their time and skills to such

* The ideas in this paper were first presented in a conference at the general seminar of the New School for Social Research.

pursuits. But you need not be afraid. I do not intend to criticize my colleagues, whose motivations I understand perfectly well, all the more as most of them, living in the United States, are lucky in having a large scientific community and a wide audience, so they run fewer risks of being attracted or contaminated by the preoccupations of neighbouring disciplines. In Europe, as you are aware, the boundaries are less sharp and the pressure to answer the same general questions all the stronger. In any case, one is intrigued by the possibility of expanding one's quest to the areas of, say, literature or art, history or culture, just as it intrigues sociologists, anthropologists, and, of course, psychoanalysts. Yet one thing is certain. There are few chances that the findings of one science can create a great stir or have many effects if it turns its back on what happens in those areas. By not taking part in their mental life, it does not communicate with other sciences and remains a minor discipline.

Let us go back to our *Gedankenexperiments*. They can have three distinct purposes. First, to bring into play existing psychosocial theories instead of the *ad hoc* theories contrived by literary critics, historians, or sociologists to explain the human relations, feelings, or behaviour described in novels or plays. One can study the dynamics of imaginary groups exactly as if they were real groups. Second, every short story, novel or play contains a protocol of observations made by the author about a class of people, important social events, the frame of mind of a period. And each of these protocols includes, I feel, a psychological and social theory which has not been made explicit. Thus it provides us with a starting-point which helps us bring it out – as I could convince myself recently concerning the psychology of leadership and masses in Balzac's *Country Doctor*.

We are helped in this task by the writer himself when he states some fragments of his theory. For instance, in *War and Peace*, Tolstoy includes a real essay about the role of masses and great men committed to a common action.[1] And he opposes his theory to those of the thinkers of his time. Please notice that I am not saying that we are to consider an artist's theory in the same manner as a scientist's theory. They are obviously not of the same kind. The scientist's theory is a *form* which arrays the facts in as general an order as possible. The artist's theory is a *content*, the very stuff of which he makes up his characters and situations so as to dispose them in a peculiar order that makes us say: 'This is Stendhal's or Balzac's world, Dickens's or Hemingway's.' You can, however, rationally reconstruct, as we say, the artist's theory, and by doing this discover a prospect, problems, and solutions which had not been thought of before by scientists. They had not been thought of, indeed, because the writer allows himself to bring his ideas to their utmost consequences and to include in his fiction what we exclude from our theories, namely death. People die in novels and plays; they do not die in scientific theories, and that makes a difference.

Third, there is the case I call mixed of a theory having its origin in science and being subsequently changed in and by a work of art, for instance, mass psychology. In a first period we can find descriptions and explanations of the behaviour and mental life of crowds before the science has been constituted. There are in Balzac's, Flaubert's, Maupassant's or Tolstoy's works, to mention only those I know, extraordinarily elaborate reflections on these phenomena (cf. Moscovici, 1983). Then, once the science has been built, we notice that the theory of mass psychology has filtered into the novels written by the greatest German writers from Mann to Musil (cf. Moscovici, 1985). Some of them, and not minor ones, both write essays about this theory and take it as the fabric of their novels. It is enough to mention the names of Canetti and Broch (Moscovici, 1984). The latter worked out a complete original conception of mass psychology, as he was convinced of the political and historical necessity of that psychology: 'To lift up these irrational moments,' he writes,

> from the sphere of mere instinct, to make them rationally seizable and thereby put them in the service of human progress, such will be the new political task of science. The new political truths will have their foundations in the psychological. Mankind is about to leave the economic period of its development and enter into its psychological period.   (Broch, 1979, p. 42)

There can be no doubt about that: these words have lost nothing of their force and actuality. But the conception of mass psychology worked out by Broch has not remained confined in his essays. We find it again, so to speak, transfigured in his novels, namely, *The Death of Virgil*, which is numbered among the masterpieces of contemporary German literature. So that Hannah Arendt was justified when she wrote about it: 'Behind the novel on which he was working, and which he regarded as wholly superfluous . . . stood the torso of the *Mass Psychology*' (Arendt, 1970, pp. 115–16). I am fully convinced that social psychologists would find in such essays and the novels taking their inspiration from them many a seminal idea that could be tested. But, beyond this possibility, an analysis is absolutely necessary to make us understand one of the capital phenomena of contemporary history. I am alluding to what Thomas Mann called the popularization of the irrational (Mann, 1977). In the first half of this century we witnessed, starting from science and then penetrating into literature, the diffusion of a psychology of masses and leaders. This vision of the human psyche has had consequences in politics and culture which are so tangible (Berlin, 1981; Cassirer, 1946).

Truth to tell, these three purposes are not as distinct as I present them for the sake of analysis, and one cannot expect to attain them separately. Everything depends on the question one puts to oneself about the literary work and the extent to which one thinks it corresponds to a particular social or historical reality. I nevertheless hope I have justified the introduction of the words 'social psychology' into my title and made you forget the incongruous character they had at first sight.

WHY THE DREYFUS AFFAIR AND WHY PROUST?

Now let us see why the Dreyfus affair and why Proust. Great thunderstorms, great discharges of human energy, great breaks of tension in society remain opaque to contemporaries and are seen in their true light only after a time. But their riddle never seems to receive any unquestionable solution. This is what makes their fascination, which can last a long time. The Dreyfus affair was such a great thunderstorm, one of those breaks of tension whose riddle keeps fascinating us nearly a century after it happened. I will sum up the Dreyfus case briefly. Because of a resemblance between two handwritings, Captain Dreyfus, a career officer, was charged with selling confidential military information to the Germans. After a summary trial he was sentenced to degradation and transported to French Guiana in 1894. In 1896 another French officer was accused of being the real culprit yet was acquitted. This was the beginning of the Dreyfus affair. In his *Souvenirs*, Léon Blum gives us an idea of it when he writes: 'The affair was a human crisis, not as far-reaching and as protracted but as violent as the French Revolution or the Great War' (Blum, 1982, p. 35). It convulsed the political landscape in France, consecrated the new social relationships in the Third Republic, and brought out the new figure of modern nationalism and anti-Semitism. The thing is so obvious and so well known that I do not see that I could add to what is common knowledge.

Many books have been written to disentangle truth and falsehood and reconstruct Dreyfus's trial. Others have tried to describe and analyse the condition of French society at the time of the affair, a society in which there raged one of the fiercest ideological and political battles of the previous century. But, for aught I know, none of them is devoted to an analysis of the Dreyfusard *movement*, initiated by a minority, a handful of courageous and upright men. That this is an 'ideal-typical' movement of contemporary society, Gramsci was among the few people to grasp: 'There are other modern historical-political movements of the Dreyfus type to be found, which are certainly not revolutions, but which are not entirely reactionary either . . . in so far as they indicate that there were effective forces latent in the old society which the old leaders did not know how to exploit' (Gramsci, 1971, p. 223). Not much is done to understand the nature of such movements. And we possess few historical or sociological studies about the minorities which launch them. Now, for one who is concerned as I am about their social psychology (Moscovici, 1976), it is difficult to imagine a more enlightening case than the Dreyfus affair and a more exemplary active minority than the one which first raised the issue, then led it to success. Another thing not to be neglected, far from it, is that so many documents are available about it.

This is not all. The works about the Dreyfus affair in which these documents are collected and analysed are concerned with the great political and ideological battles and the major events of the trial. In keeping with a certain tradition, they do not touch upon the backlash of those battles and events on collective life, on the various tangible relations that were established or loosened between the groups and the people on that occasion. I mean especially the relations established or loosened with the Dreyfusard minority and the anti-Dreyfusard majority. An illustration of this kind of study was given by the French historian Le Roy Ladurie (1980) in his book on heresy hunting in the south-west of France, where he showed how important those tangible relations are to a right understanding of social and historical phenomena. With the available documents one could by the same method reconstruct the collective life during the Dreyfus affair. One could, I say, if this had not been done to a great extent by a few writers. In the first rank of them we have to put Marcel Proust, who did it with supreme art and unequalled depth. As a matter of fact, he did it twice, first in *Jean Santeuil*, several chapters of which constitute a protocol of observations similar to those I alluded to, both on the trial and on the reactions it brought about, then more conspicuously in *Remembrance of Things Past*, in which this protocol is recreated by a wider and, if I may say, more theoretical reflection. No doubt it is a fiction, but a fiction *cum fundamento in re*. It keeps close to historical reality for, it has been noted, Proust appears 'as the greatest historian of the mores of the Third Republic we have had up to now' (Delhorbe, 1932, p. 87).

A Dreyfusard and a Jew, so doubly a member of the minority in question, Proust wanted to recapture the psychic and social life of the people carried along with him by the event – an event of which he was, from the very start, both a witness and actor. We know that he was among the first writers (Charle, 1977) – marginal writers, in truth (Reberioux, 1976, 1980) – who claimed the reconsideration of Captain Dreyfus's trial and tried to get others to join them. His correspondence shows how deeply he was concerned by the affair and its consequences, and also by the crude, intolerable aspects of men and society in general it revealed. Be that as it may, his novel is both a minute protocol and a store of theories which are to make us grasp the relations and actions of his characters under those dramatic circumstances. If ever he puts himself as the narrator in his tale, at once the glimpses take on the character of historical truth and reality. People often say wrongly: 'It is truer than life.' With Proust these words are fully justified. Reading the parts of *Remembrance of Things Past* devoted to the affair, I have understood why Léon Blum could count them among the masterpieces of Dreyfusard literature, side by side with *J'accuse* by Zola, *M. Bergeret à Paris* by Anatole France, and Jules Renard's *Journal*, as well as *Preuves* by Jean Jaurès. He expresses, just as they do, a passion which is entire and a conviction devoid of any complacency.

Every reader of Proust is acquainted with such names as Albertine and Charlus, knows that there is a Swann's way and a Guermantes way. What about the Dreyfus affair? The reader has an impression that it is mentioned just in passing as an episode superadded to so many plots and events. Now I contend that this impression is not quite accurate. First, let us consider that the affair is approached in the middle of the novel, one is tempted to say at its core. This is indicated by Proust himself in a letter to Madame Strauss, a friend of long standing, who followed its publication from her bed of sickness. After all, did she not know the models of the characters in his novel, which was somewhat the story of her life? Here is what he wrote to her in 1920:

> What bothers me about this Guermantes way is that it looks so anti-Dreyfusard, by chance, because of the characters who appear in it. It is true that the next volume is so Dreyfusard that it will be a compensation, because the prince and princesse de Guermantes are Dreyfusards, and so is Swann, whereas the duc and duchesse are not.

I am not going to comment on this most strange account of a writer about the characters he created. Yes, it is indeed in *The Guermantes Way* and *Cities of the Plain* that the affair is most often mentioned, colouring the characters and their relationships. It belongs to the plot, so to speak.[2] In order to get a footing and have access to the core of the Proustian world, we have first to discover its driving force. Now this force, the gravity peculiar to the Proustian universe, which attracts and repels the characters to and from one another, is neither money nor power nor even social rank as in Balzac's or Zola's universes: it is social recognition. Balzac's *Father Goriot* ends on these words: 'As the first act of the challenge he was sending to society, Rastignac went to have dinner at Madame de Nucingen's.' This is a sentence Marcel Proust could never have written. Not that his characters do not care about dining out – on the contrary. But this act, with all the bourgeois consecration it brings, has quite another significance for them. Power, money, rank have no absolute worth in their eyes. They are valued only inasmuch as they allow them to be recognized by the people they aspire to consort with and who consecrate them as such. What is the use of being a renowned scientist, a gifted artist, or a man at the head of the state if one is not elected to an academy, received in certain salons, or invited to a party given by a glamorous host or hostess? This phenomenon is particularly evidenced in the higher spheres of society, yet no social class is exempt from it – the novel shows it among both bourgeois and servants.

Proust supposes a will to recognition which is as strong as Nietzsche's will to power. To be socially consecrated, everyone is capable of heroism, abnegation, or baseness. It is not a façade but a deep-lying trend, a quest. The quest is all the more hazardous and recognition slow in coming as the groups from which one expects it keep changing all the time. Despite appearances, Balzac's and Zola's universes are stable or aspiring to stability after the upheavals of the French Revolution and Empire or the perturbations of the nineteenth century; Proust's world is a changing world. Social groups and orders keep on being insensibly made and unmade. Cataclysms are at work in the depths. Rather than the accidents of history, they conjure up the upheavals of cosmology, when the only link between before and after is the permanence of a name: Swann, Guermantes or Charlus. Thus recognition is never definitely acquired, secure. At every moment one has to struggle to acquire it again. Yet as Max Weber wrote: 'Recognition is duty.' This means that the person in search of it has to acquire every necessary physical and psychic endowment and fulfil the requirements set by society. The question put to individuals and engraved in the minds of those who engage in this constant search has been ironically worded by Proust in a Shakespearian mood: 'The question is not, as for Hamlet, to be or not to be, but to belong or not to belong [*en être ou ne pas en être*]' (G 231).[3] This striking question, which he formulates in the particular context of homosexuality, crops up again and again under various disguises in the novel. It makes us feel in a few words the dilemma with which one is faced in one's life with and among other people, since, as he writes: 'They are all butter and honey to the people who belong, and have no words bad enough for those who don't' (G 231).[4]

It is impossible to convey more clearly and succinctly our way of behaving in society. To answer this question (which is of crucial importance to social psychology, as you are aware), Proust has introduced into his novel a theory of the human flow. As in a pack of cards, people are shuffled and separated, drawn apart and brought together, so that majorities and minorities or deviants (in this case Dreyfusards, Jews and homosexuals) are created. That he has sketched a theory of this flow Proust knows and says several times. And one is entitled to see it as the very fabric of his novel. But his view of art forbids him to spell it out as a Tolstoy or a Zola would have done: 'A work in which there are theories is like an object with the price-tag still sticking to it,' he aptly writes in *Time Regained* (882). The best way of defining it would be to say that it is a theory of the phenomenon of social recombination of the individuals in this flow. It allows them to qualify for a certain social milieu, so as to belong, *en être*. Like genetic recombination, from which I have borrowed the denomination, it associates in the individual some traits which were not originally recognized, according as he is carried along in society with the majority or pushed aside with the minority. So he becomes different from what he was. In this way groups change their components, even though they sometimes include the same people. One thing is important to remember: the flow is continuous and never congeals into stable ranks, differences, or relations.[5] 'We must bear in mind,' Proust observes, 'that the opinions which we hold of one another, our relations with friends and kinsfolk are in no sense permanent, save in appearance, but are as eternally fluid as the sea itself' (G 370).

Even the identity of an individual is not given once for all, since it depends on the perception other people have of him: 'We are not,' the writer notes, 'a materially constituted whole, identical for everyone, which each of us can examine like a list of specifications or a testament; our social personality is a creation of other people's thought' (*Swann's Way* 23). Here is the banal example of such a recombination. When Swann decides to leave the majority, to draw apart from his anti-Dreyfusard milieu and nearer to the minority, in short, to become a Dreyfusard, we witness his mental as well as physical metamorphosis. He undergoes it with relief and gratitude, with some resignation too. In the process there mingle with his gentlemanly attitudes, his polite way of speaking and behaving, some long-forgotten and even never-experienced features and gestures from his Jewish past, until he is changed into another person in his own and in other people's eyes. We will revert to this point later.

I have spoken of a theory of social recombination inspired by the observations one can make about the relations between majority and minority during the Dreyfus affair. Let me now state its principles. The first is that, whenever we deal with a dissenting minority, society passes against it and its members a verdict before any trial. So they are never supposed to be innocent, nor can they justify or defend themselves. In *M. Bergeret à Paris*, by Anatole France, Mazure, one of the characters, clearly states this principle: 'I am a patriot and a republican. Whether Dreyfus is innocent or guilty, I don't know. I don't care, it's no business of mine. He may be innocent. But Dreyfusists are certainly guilty.' Why is this? Why are the members of a minority never presumed to be innocent but always guilty? Simply because they have taken a dissenting stance, here Dreyfusism, which immediately associates them with a crime against society. And such a crime admits no excuse:[6] 'We pardon the crimes of individuals,' Proust writes, 'but not their participation in a collective crime' (G 204). Once we admit this principle, we understand why Proust's characters, like those of Kafka for that matter, take their guilt upon themselves when they are accused. And nowhere in *Remembrance of Things Past* did I see a single passage in which a Saint-Loup, a Bloch, or a Swann explains to his accuser why he has become a Dreyfusard.

The second principle entails a strict, I should even say a classical opposition, between public sociability and private sociability. In the former, people are the symbols of a family, class, nation, or else finance, etc. In their every relation, what they seem to be is more important than what they are. 'But of course you have to judge by appearances only,' Proust had already written in *Jean Santeuil*. Individuals are not independent beings who shape their own destinies and face a society whose values they are free to accept or reject. Inseparable from their milieu – from Swann's way or the Guermantes way – they are fashioned by rules and norms with regard to which they define themselves. If they happen to be prey to indecision or have to make a choice – we will see in a moment the psychological importance of this – it is the repertoire of rules and norms which dictates their decisions and guides their choices. In private sociability, on the other hand, the individuals are characterized by their skill to embody or master the symbols, their ability to transgress the rules and norms with the complicity of others. So they are vulnerable to passion and suffering, form preferential ties of friendship, fall sick and even commit the indecency of dying. Thus the individual appears as a succession of particular states whose unity exists only in and through memory. To put the matter in a nutshell, I could say that public sociability belongs to the dimension of space and private sociability to the dimension of time. The opposition obviously entails that one can be a Dreyfusard or an anti-Dreyfusard in the public sphere only. In the private sphere, such an opposition is quite meaningless.

We are now approaching the real object of our inquiry, which tends to show how these two principles fashion the recombination of individuals and groups in society. Let it be said at once that the movement has a cyclical character. Society recombines its members through cycles which are analogous to business cycles. Each cycle begins and ends with a great event: the Dreyfus case or the Great War, where Proust is concerned. We will now follow the steps by which Dreyfusards are forced down towards the minority position while anti-Dreyfusards are concentrated and pushed towards a majority position. One thing is remarkable: the first cycle described by Proust is not one of exclusion. Captain Dreyfus's supporters are not driven from the inside to the outside, nor openly submitted to pressures towards conforming again. It is a cycle of what I will call displacement, which brings the members of the dissenting minority from the public universe to the private universe of sociability. Hence, as members of the dissenting minority, they do not become outsiders but, on the contrary, insiders. Proust gives us a clue to this in a few words about the duchesse's opinion regarding Swann, once he has turned into a Dreyfusard: 'She was running no risk of having to talk publicly with "poor Charles," whom she preferred to cherish privately' (C 63). Thus Dreyfusards continue to subsist in the interstices of social life without existing fully there, at one and the same time visible and invisible. They are exactly like the displaced persons after the Second World War. Everything happens as if a tacit convention implied that, if the minority individual was to leave the group altogether, every hope of joining it again at a later time would be lost for ever and he would vanish out of sight. Like nature, society must be careful enough to keep every existing possibility for further unheard-of combinations in the future. If it excluded some individuals, it would not be itself and could not survive that loss. We can also think of a cook who does not throw away food remnants but saves them for further use.

You will certainly ask: what does the displacement imply? It entails a loss of social recognition with all its detrimental consequences for those who were so assiduous in their search for it. Well you can imagine that the loss is not the same for all. It affects every individual or category in proportion to what they have to give up or what the group takes away from them. So we will now follow this displacement step by step. This will allow us to see the relation between an individual's staying with the minority and his loss of social recognition. We will also note the psychic consequences of the displacement in the collective life of the men and women in Proust's novel.

Let us consider first those who belong to and participate in the group, namely the aristocracy, such as Robert de Saint-Loup. A nobleman and a military officer, he is convinced of Dreyfus's innocence and makes no secret of his opinion. But as he belongs to a very old family, to *le monde*, his public stand is treated as a private opinion, almost a fad. He avoids mentioning it to his brother officers, with a single exception. And they surround him with silence so as to prevent any clash: 'When the conversation became general, they avoided any reference to Dreyfus for fear of offending Saint-Loup' (G 156). He nevertheless feels the impact of his opinion on his situation in his milieu. In a sense, people try to disregard and excuse it. So they attribute his Dreyfusard opinion to an indirect cause and not to his reflection and conviction. This is in accordance with a well-known sociopsychological mechanism. The cause could be Rachel, a Jewish actress who is his mistress: 'There's a damsel, a fly-by-night of the worst type; she has far more influence over him than his mother, and she happens to be a compatriot of Master Dreyfus. She has passed on her state of mind to Robert' (G 323). Another explanation for his opinion is his pretence of degrading himself by becoming friends with intellectuals. Yes, at that time Dreyfusards were debased by being termed intellectuals, the worst insult in an aristocrat's or even a bourgeois's mouth.

Both these reasons still do not justify his having become vulnerable to the dissenting cause: Robert is not the only noble officer with a Jewish mistress or friends who are writers. So another reason is sought and found in the etymology of his mother's name, herself a fierce anti-Dreyfusard. She is called Mme de Marsantes, which is expounded as *Mater semita*. The etymology rests on a mistranslation, for 'semita', Proust writes, 'means "path" and not "Semite"' (G 241). In truth, no one gives it much importance, and you feel that it is a mere language game which is also a society game. Yet the game allows people to 'displace' Robert, who is unquestionably one of them, and to push him out towards the periphery of the public sphere, thus depriving him of social recognition. At least access to the centre is made difficult for him. So he is prevented from being elected a member of the Jockey Club, as he should have been by rights, like his father before him. The duc de Guermantes points out the cause for this ostracism: 'What can you expect, my dear, it got 'em on the raw, those fellows; they're all over it . . . but damn it all, when one goes by the name of "Marquis de Saint-Loup", one isn't a Dreyfusard – what more can I say?' (G 253). Yes indeed, the bearer of such a name professing to be a Dreyfusard would be displaced at the core of good society.

Then we have got individuals who belong to the group but generally do not participate in it. The case is less clear than the former. Odette, Swann's wife, is such a one. She could belong, because she is French and has the required social rank. But people begrudge her participation because she has been a light woman, a *cocotte*, as the French say. And also because Swann is a Jew and, in addition, a Dreyfusard. Her own anti-Dreyfusard opinions could open many doors to her, if her husband did not stand in her way. So she is put 'between brackets', that is, dealt with in the public sphere as a private person would be dealt with. The rules in force apply to her according to particular circumstances and situations – I mean, arbitrarily. She is made to feel that she is never in the place in which she ought to be, as in a game of musical chairs, just as would be the case for a nobleman's common wife or mistress. Now people invite her, now they avoid her. In any case they signal her presence to others, leaving them free to choose how to behave with regard to her. Thus Mme de Villeparisis warns the duchesse de Guermantes, who never liked her, that Odette is coming to see her:

> 'Listen,' said Mme de Villeparisis to the duchesse de Guermantes, 'I am expecting a woman at any moment whom you don't wish to know. I thought I'd better warn you, to avoid any unpleasantness. But you needn't be afraid, I shall never have her here again, only I was obliged to let her come today. It's Swann's wife.'   (G 346)

The afternoon party at Mme de Villeparisis will be the occasion for the novelist to have the main characters in his book meet and to make, so to speak, a spectral analysis of them in the light of the Dreyfus affair. We are, in fact, approaching the last case that Proust floodlights with his full genius. It is the case of the Jews or semi-Jews who do not belong to the group but fully participate in it. They, a Bloch or a Swann, for instance, are forced out of the public sphere into the private one. They literally become displaced persons. Of these characters Proust seems to say what Aristophanes said of Alcibiades in *The Frogs*: 'One loves him, one hates him, one cannot do without him.' So the duc and duchesse de Guermantes could not do without Swann. To support this view, I will mention a historical fact. The majority of Jews did not side with Captain Dreyfus. They accepted the sentence brought against him by the military court as just and final. This does not deter people from dealing with a Bloch or a Swann as *both* a Dreyfusard and a Jew. Only consider the situation: displacing Jews and semi-Jews, what a problem! We know it from a real conversation which took place between Mme Aubernon and other ladies in her social class. When asked: 'What do you do with your Jews?' she answered: 'I keep them.' Her reply is, however, mentioned by historians as an example and an exception.

In fact the displacement poses a number of sociopsychological problems, and I am not quite sure that science has solved or even tackled them satisfactorily. Indeed, ever since Jews were received everywhere and even got social recognition, like Swann, they have been assimilated. They have acquired the manners, the physical appearance, the proper names, in short they have learned to 'be like other people' (Berlin, 1981, p. 258). People have forgotten what they looked like before. The Jews themselves forgot it after concealing their origins and obeying the prevailing rules for such a long time. If you cannot make them out at first sight, then the similarity of Jews and not-Jews becomes puzzling in the context of the Dreyfus affair. (It is the same with the similarity between homosexuals and heterosexuals, and Proust reverts to it several times.) How can you discern that a person who *is* like you nevertheless does not *seem* to be like you? How can you detect a Jew under the guise of a Dreyfusard? Elaborating on Proust, we notice that the similarity poses a double problem: that of perception and that of recognition.

The first is the problem put to Mme de Villeparisis, who has to detect the presence of a Jew in her salon so as to control his movements. If only she could make him out! Little if anything in the face or garb of such or such an individual allows her to suppose that he is the one. She does not know or she does not remember what the distinctive features are. She only knows that there must be such features: the curve of a nose, or, even more elusive, the tone of a voice. To sum up her dilemma: how can you decide that the similar is not the similar? As concerns Jews as well as homosexuals, the similar is the bearer of a *signe qui fait signe* that only initiates can detect. In this case, Proust writes,

> the members themselves, who intend not to know one another, recognize one another immediately, by natural or conventional, involuntary or deliberate signs which indicate one of his congeners to the beggar in the street in the great nobleman whose carriage door he is shutting, to the father in the suitor for his daughter. (G 23)

As soon as the individual is perceived as the bearer of such a sign, in the midst of all that contradicts it, the initiate knows that he is 'one of them', *qu'il en est*. Yet the sign is invisible to non-initiates (Deleuze, 1970). Then, this is Proust's question: how do we perceive the imperceptible, how do we identify the non-identifiable, when we are Mme de Villeparisis and not a Jew like Swann, the duchesse de Guermantes and not a homosexual like Baron de Charlus? It seems to me that research on social perception has not put the question in such subtle terms, nor has it proposed a satisfactory answer. In any case, here is Proust's solution.

You can easily grasp his theory if you take into account the fact that for him as for his cousin-in-law, the philosopher Henri Bergson, perception and memory differ in nature, not in degree. Perception is individualistic, memory highly collective. With the immediate data of our senses we mingle a thousand details from our experience of the past which is most often shared with other people. To perceive is, in short, for the individual an opportunity to remember. In his early work, *Jean Santeuil*, the novelist had written: 'We can find everything in our memory; it is a kind of chemist's shop, of chemistry laboratory, where chance makes us lay hands now on a calming drug, now on a dangerous poison' (632). Remembering not only occurs before every perception, it also lays its foundation and can alone complete its meaning. To put the matter in simpler words, I could say that, in the case at hand, it is the memory which has been inherited and materialized in culture, art or language that allows us to perceive in living people the distinctive features of their ancestors, real or supposed. Unreal images are conjured up in the mind of the 'seeker after hidden faces', as Virginia Woolf once wrote, and change into real perceptions. But I had better let Proust speak. The occasion is still Mme de Villeparisis's *matinée*, at which Bloch is a guest:

> When we speak of racial persistence, we do not accurately convey the impression we receive from Jews, Greeks, Persians, all those peoples whom it is better to leave with their differences. We know from classical paintings the faces of the ancient Greeks, we have seen Assyrians on the walls of a palace at Susa. And so we feel, on encountering in a Paris drawing-room Orientals belonging to one or the other group, that we are in the presence of creatures whom the forces of necromancy must have called to life. We knew hitherto only a superficial image; behold, it has gained depth, it extends into three dimensions, it moves. (G 258)

Collective memory is a store of human prototypes, and we have it in our power to materialize them. In her 'remembrance of museums past', Mme de Villeparisis, like her guests, will seek and find Bloch's 'distinguishing features'. And Proust goes on:

> I felt that if I had in the light of Mme de Villeparisis' drawing-room taken photographs of Bloch, they would have furnished of Israel the same image – so disturbing because it does not appear to emanate from humanity, so deceiving because all the same it is so strangely like humanity – which we find in spirit photographs. (G 259)

The core of every social perception is to be found here: a man can perceive another man with the help of something he does not really perceive. A factor of illusion, if not of hallucination, is always blended in it.

Once they are detected in this way, Jews lose their anonymity, their sameness, their freedom of motion in the 'world' and can be discarded. At Mme de Villeparisis's, Bloch can move freely for some time and talk about the Dreyfus affair now passionately, now awkwardly, with a number of people. Until the culmination of the scene, when everyone has found out about him and he gets a rough answer: 'You must not ask me, sir, to discuss the Dreyfus case with you; it is a subject which, on principle, I never mention except to Japhetics' (G 359). Upon hearing these words, Bloch, who had thought of himself as above suspicion, feels that he has been, properly speaking, unmasked, and he is heard to mutter: 'But how on earth did you know? Who told you?' as though he had been the son of a convict. A little later, when he nears his hostess to take leave of her, she tries to find a means of notifying him that he must not come as often as before. 'And quite naturally,' Proust writes, 'she found in her worldly repertory the scene by which a great lady turns someone out of doors' (G 360), that is, by shamming sleep. With Proust, you realize, every word counts. If we have to extricate ourselves from an embarrassing public relationship, we must not let ourselves be carried away by our moods. We look up the code for a conventional method and apply it ruthlessly. Once he is 'found out', Bloch can easily be 'displaced'.

I have said that similarity, being like other people, creates a second problem. We usually construe discrimination against an ethnic or social minority as a response to its being different, not 'like us', or foreign. But think for a moment of what has happened in France. Owing to the fact that Jews, after their emancipation, have mixed with the French and become like them, the smallest deviation in those Jews is perceived as bigger than it is. And their slightest divergence in opinion elicits an exaggerated response. You see more distinctly something disturbing in a person who is close to you and you feel more vulnerable to it. This is either because he expresses a possibility that you have in you, or because he prefigures something that is liable to happen to you. We notice this in the attitude most of us have towards sick or handicapped people. On the contrary, deviations attract less notice, and divergences are not so sharply felt when the person is someone really different, a perfect stranger. From this argument we draw with Proust the conclusion that Jews would *not* have suffered so much from the Dreyfus affair or would not have been socially displaced if they had remained foreigners.

The following episode is a case in point. Baron de Charlus, a homosexual, inquires of the narrator (Proust) about Bloch. Hearing his name, he says: 'It is not a bad idea to include among your friends an occasional foreigner.' The narrator replies that he is a Frenchman. 'Ah,' Charlus said, 'I took him to be a Jew.' Which makes Proust believe the baron is anti-Dreyfusard. On the contrary, he protests against the accusation of crime against his fatherland of which the captain is a victim:

'In any case, the crime is non-existent, your friend's [Bloch's] compatriot would
have committed a crime if he had betrayed Judea, but what has he to do with
France? . . . Your Dreyfus might rather be convicted of breaking the laws of
hospitality.'   (G 395)

I was saying that, if they could have been regarded as foreigners, the Jews
would not have been displaced towards the private sphere because of their
Dreyfusard opinions. This is explicitly stated by Proust in another passage
relating to Swann.

Talking of Dreyfusards, I said, it appears, Prince Von is one. – Ah, I am glad
you reminded me of him, exclaimed M. de Guermantes. I was forgetting that he
had asked me to dine with him on Monday. But whether he is a Dreyfusard
or not is entirely immaterial, since he is a foreigner. I don't give two straws for
his opinion. With a Frenchman, it is another matter. It is true that Swann is
a Jew.   (G 108–9)

This dialogue shows clearly that Proust realizes that the anti-Semitism which
appeared during the Dreyfus affair is a new variety. It stems from the assimilation of Jews, from their living inside French society, not outside as was the
case in the past. This we knew already, but here we see it incorporated into a
more lively and detailed tableau of what happened at that time of deep change
and raging storm, a tableau which has lost nothing of its actuality.

I want to add something before going further. As could be expected, this
coming and going changes the feelings of people and the make-up of their
social milieu. Yet its effects are not identical on the displacing majority and
the displaced minority. And they are not in accordance with the predictions of
our sociopsychological theories where such phenomena come into play. Strange
as it may appear, it is the minority which seems to have won something and
the majority which feels the loser. No doubt, people experience some satisfaction from gathering together among themselves without any intruders, all
being of the same nation and the same opinion. Yet 'displacing' from the
'world' someone like Swann, who used to be recognized as belonging to it,
implies some sacrifice. The link with him has to be severed and everything it
means discarded. The group is cut off from its minority, as from a person
after a lifetime of working together. This feeling of amputation is crystallized in the ingratitude which traduces both disillusion and disenchantment,
self-dissatisfaction and regret. Proust very finely analyses the facets of this
ingratitude coloured by nostalgia. I will be content to quote M. de Guermantes's
reaction as concerns Swann. His wife confesses that she 'did feel a sincere
affection for Charles!' And he adds: 'There, you see, I don't have to make
her say it. And after that, he carries his ingratitude to the point of being a
Dreyfusard!' (G 108).

On the other hand, as the minority is sure of having the good cause on its side – what Proust calls a 'burning opinion' – it regains some sort of autonomy. Swann, for instance, feels as if his blood has started running again in veins dried up from long disuse. He is relieved from the effort he has made all through his life *pour en être*, the effort of resembling the people in his milieu and being recognized as one of them. I incline to say that the displacement he undergoes towards the minority gives him a feeling of recovery. It is like being one's old self again, once the strain which weighed upon one's life has been relieved. In the writer's words: 'Like a weary animal that is goaded on, he cried out against the persecutions and was returning to the spiritual fold of his fathers' (G 374). Whether it makes him happy or not, at least he learns to bear and cherish this feeling of recovery which allows him to be reconciled to the other group, the one that populates his memory. So he too, like other members of the minority, gets disassimilated. (By the way, today in Europe we can observe an analogous trend to disassimilation among Jews and other ethnic minorities. This phenomenon deserves to be researched just as the opposite has been.) There occurs in him a recombination of his moral and physical characteristics: 'This new loss of caste would have been better described as a recasting' (G 375). Everything happens for Swann as if the past which had unrolled step by step suddenly came back to him at once and turned him into another person. I will quote Proust again to conclude this point:

> Besides, in recent days, race made perhaps the physical type which is characteristic of it appear more strongly marked in him, at the same time as the feeling of moral solidarity with other Jews, a solidarity which Swann seemed to have forgotten all through his life and that, grafted upon one another, deadly illness, the Dreyfus case and anti-Semitic propaganda had re-awakened.   (C 42)

Turning Nationalism and Anti-Semitism to Good Use

I could go on for a long time about this point, for Proust's novel deals with it in depth. I will, however, stop to examine for a moment the second cycle his novel describes. It is the cycle of insertion into the public sphere, *le monde*, of the individuals who previously stood outside or were confined to the private sphere. (The word is of course a biological metaphor describing a mutation in which one or several new bases are inserted between the existing ones on a chain of nucleic acid of the genetic code.) Their insertion goes hand in hand with an increase in social recognition. And of course the Dreyfus affair is the opportunity for such an increase, a gain that had been impossible before. Proust's analysis of this second cycle is less protracted here. He will deal with it in more detail for the period of the First World War. Be that as it may, we see clearly that the possibility of recognition is brought about by a deep change in society. With the Dreyfus affair, a new criterion is added, giving one the right to belong and participate, to be received in *le monde*: I mean nationalism and anti-Semitism.[7] To put the matter in a nutshell: if you are French you can contend that you 'belong', *vous en êtes*. Simply by becoming anti-Dreyfusard or professing to be an anti-Semite, you can see the doors which were closed to you so far open wide before you. If being an anti-Dreyfusard equals being a Frenchman or Frenchwoman, then people gather together in the majority. They thereby gain a social qualification which had hitherto been refused to a number of them, because they were just French. Thus Odette, Swann's wife, avails herself of the opportunities when her husband is away to sport her nationalism, which allows her to establish relations with aristocratic ladies.

But by those who, in a way, hold fast to the ancient criteria for social recognition, this insertion is resented as an intrusion. Proust makes the duchesse de Guermantes utter these terrible sentences:

> 'But on the other hand I do think it perfectly intolerable that just because they're supposed to hold "sound" views and don't deal with Jewish tradesmen, or have "Down with the Jews" printed on their sunshades, we should have a swarm of Durands and Dubois and so forth, women we should never have known but for this business, forced down our throats by Marie-Aynard or Victurnienne. I went to see Marie-Aynard a couple of days ago. It used to be so nice there. Nowadays one finds all the people one has spent one's life trying to avoid, on the pretext that they're against Dreyfus.' (G 325)

M. de Charlus chimes in with this opinion when he complains of the mixed company he meets at his cousins':

> 'All this Dreyfus business,' went on the Baron, still clasping me by the arm, 'has only one drawback. It destroys society . . . by the influx of Mr. and Mrs. Camels and Camelries and Camelyards, astonishing creatures whom I find even in the houses of my own cousins, because they belong to the Patrie Française, or the Anti-Jewish, or some such league, as if a political opinion entitled one to any social qualification.' (G 398)

Later Proust will affirm that yes, on the contrary, it does give you a right to it. The picture which is most often offered to our contemplation and represents social recombination is that of a cycle of displacement and a cycle of insertion, of people departing being replaced by people arriving. The latter are going up at the same time as the former are going down, like the passengers on the double escalators in the underground. In the process the social recognition that is lost by the displaced ones is gained by the newcomers. Everyone's social personality undergoes a change. But success itself brings about a disappointment of sorts. For the circles to which we aspire and the people we are longing to meet are always more glamorous than those in which we move, with whom we consort. Everything happens as if, by lifting us up to them, they would be lowered and degraded to a common denominator. In Proust's words: 'That Mme de Guermantes should have been like the other women had first been a disappointment for me; it was almost, by reaction, and with the help of so many good wines, a wonder' (G 637).

SWANN AND THE MOURNING SHOE

I am conscious of overstating the case a little. But if what I have just said is clear, you can see the resulting paradox. On one hand, the more that some are inserted into the public sphere of the majority and restricted to it, the more that others, let us say a Bloch or a Swann, are displaced from it. On the other hand, their relations with anti-Dreyfusards such as the duc and duchesse de Guermantes are concentrated in the private sphere and take on an intimate character. No doubt, all the time a feeling of insufficient coincidence between public and private relationships is retained. But the cycles of recombination I have just described sharpen the permanent conflict between the two. How is this conflict solved? What accounts for the psychology of its solution? To answer both these questions, we have to turn to social psychology and not to literature. It will help us instil sense into the famous finale of *The Guermantes Way*.

Let us view again, with the eyes of memory, the finest scene. Swann, knowing the affection of the duchesse de Guermantes for him, calls on her one evening. As she is dressing for a *diner de gala*, she has her footman usher him to her husband. The duc is glad to see him again, yet at the same time apprehensive, for he surmises that Swann is not a guest at the dinner party. So he cautiously asks the narrator, who is present, not to mention it, for 'now, don't you see, the Dreyfus case has made things more serious' (G 370). While waiting for the duchesse, they talk of many things. Everything remains in the private sphere. At last she appears, 'tall and wonderful in a gown of red satin bordered with sequins'. As she sees Swann's admiration in his eyes, a connoisseur's, she deprecates her dress and complains that the rubies of her magnificent necklace are too big for her taste.

There begins between the four characters one of those meandering conversations about art, the genealogy of great families, etc. that Proust is a master of. The duchesse sparkles with wit and is charming with her 'petit Charles' without our knowing exactly whether she wants to give him solace for not being invited to the dinner party or to apologize for dedicating so little time to him. We are nearing the dénouement when, full of affection for each other, they go out at the hall door which will begin to separate them, she leaving for the *diner de gala*, he returning home. Just then he tells her with the calm attitude of a man conscious of his grave responsibilities, for whom every affectation would be out of place, that he is very ill and will soon be dead. This sudden intrusion of an element of private life into the course of public life creates in her a state of dissonance. This is an earlier, social version of Festinger's (1957) dissonance theory. The duchesse is greatly shaken. She cannot disbelieve what she knows is true. But she behaves as if it were not, so as not to have to change her plans. And the solution she finds is exactly the solution predicted by the theory. In Proust's beautiful prose:

> 'What's that you say?' cried the duchesse, stopping for a moment on her way to her carriage, and raising her fine eyes, their melancholy blue clouded by uncertainty. Placed for the first time in her life between two duties as incompatible as getting into her carriage to go out to dinner and showing pity for a man who was about to die, she could find nothing in the code of conventions that indicated the right line to follow, and, not knowing which to choose, felt it better to make a show of not believing that the latter alternative need be seriously considered, so as to follow the first which demanded of her at the moment less effort, and thought that the best way of settling the conflict would be to deny that any existed. 'You're joking,' she said to Swann.   (G 392)

This is a remarkable farewell message. Her answer, I must insist, expresses a first dissonance which is due to the conflict created by the irruption of the private sphere within a public one, when no pre-established rule for avoiding or solving it is available. In other words, the cause of the dissonance, socially speaking, is not so much the existence of two opposite cognitions as the lack of a convention in the duchesse's repertoire. Her answer slashes the conflict, revealing, however, another conflict behind the first, pointing in the opposite direction: the intrusion of the public obligation to dine out into the duchesse's private obligation to stay at home and talk with Swann. This second dissonance, of which she is not aware, is solved by an *acte manqué*, breaking a norm of decorum. This great lady, who is so careful about etiquette, so fastidious about wearing the right clothes, is seen to lift her red skirt to get into the carriage. But the foot she exposes is encased in a black shoe, so as to express the impossibility of going to a party. When he sees this shoe, the duc, who is always so exquisitely polite and old France, cries out in a terrible voice: 'Oriane, what have you been thinking of, you wretch? You've kept on your black shoes! With a red dress! Go upstairs quick and put on red shoes, or rather,' he said to the footman, 'tell the lady's maid to bring down a pair of red shoes' (G 394). Though annoyed that Swann can hear, she has to comply.

   The two dissonances express the psychic tension between private sociability and public sociability created in this case by the Dreyfus affair. The first dissonance is provisionally solved by the person. Nevertheless the duc's insisting that his wife change her shoes shows that only the conventional rule imposed by the social milieu can put an end to the conflict. The chapter ends with everybody being appeased, Swann and the narrator going to their homes and the Guermantes to their *diner de gala*. Once more the rule which, according to Proust, has to prevail in social life, prevails: 'No dissonance; before everlasting silence, chord of dominant!' (G 689). As you can see, two socio-psychological theories, one of literary origin, the other of scientific origin, seem to hinge on each other so as to reveal a certain order underlying one of the most important plots in the novel.[8]

A PRINCELY CONVERSION

It remains that the opposition between Dreyfusards and anti-Dreyfusards ended with the victory of the former over the latter. Once again, in history, an energetic minority got the better of a majority. Now Marcel Proust, who put himself so many questions, did not fail to put the following one: how does a minority position change into a majority position? Or, in more concrete words, how could anti-Dreyfusards who were so hostile in the beginning be converted to Captain Dreyfus's cause? The writer reverts several times to the question of influence in society. One of his analyses is of particular interest to me, since it throws light on some ideas about innovation I have developed in the course of my research and is in accordance with them. Proust defines the minority as active and the majority as reactive. During the Dreyfus case 'there came into conflict,' he writes, 'on one side a timid apostolate, and on the other a righteous indignation.' Besides, in such a period of tension and controversy, everyone must form an opinion, adopt a position. The pressure thus exerted on the individuals results in their drawing together and adopting similar opinions. The reason he gives for this is ingenious: 'There are far fewer ideas than men, therefore all men with similar ideas are alike' (G 138).

Let us now try and follow, in *Cities of the Plain*, one of the scenes that ranks for Léon Blum among the masterpieces of the Dreyfusard soul. Here is the Prince de Guermantes obliged to have an opinion about the affair which divides France. Things being what they are, he cannot but be anti-Dreyfusard, like all the people in his milieu with whom he gathers. But one night he has Swann come to him and gives him a strange account, a confession. I will cut it up so as to briefly reconstruct Proust's theory. Convinced, like all his kinsfolk, of Dreyfus's guilt, the prince begins to waver when he gets acquainted with some contradictory facts put forward by Dreyfusards. This is the first phase, which I call the revelation phase; it takes place when the minority puts forward an idea which is new or prohibited, in the case at hand, the idea of Dreyfus's possible innocence and of the army being implicated in forgery. Though troubled, the prince resists, refuses to listen to Dreyfusard arguments or to read Dreyfusard papers. In this way he thinks he can remain invulnerable to all the dangers such knowledge would bring to him.

There now follows a second phase, that of incubation, in the course of which, despite his resistance, insidious doubt amplifies without his knowing it and the rejected ideas thread their way into his mind, the more so as the Dreyfusard minority hammers on them insistently or, if you like, consistently. The prince tells no one about it, not even his wife, who was born in Bavaria: 'I did not feel that I could talk about it to the princesse. Heaven knows that she has become just as French as myself' (C 150). He is soon overwhelmed by what has turned into an internal conflict which is so serious that he cannot reveal it to anyone. Nevertheless he now reads the Dreyfusard press, but rather, so he thinks, to comfort himself in his own anti-Dreyfusard opinion than the other way round. In this way, however, the prince is eventually convinced of Captain Dreyfus's innocence: 'After that,' he says to Swann, 'without letting the princesse see me, I began to read the *Siècle* and the *Aurore* every day; soon I had no doubt left, it kept me awake all night' (C 151). Thus, where he had been looking for an antidote, it is poison he has found. His sleepless nights testify how intense the conflict has become.

He has now entered into the third phase, that of conversion. He goes through it all by himself, changing his opinion by intense psychic work. Yet he still stands on his guard, even with his wife, as if he feared being assimilated to the spurned minority. Like the subjects in our experiments, the prince has privately changed his viewpoint and kept it publicly. This silent, imperceptible tension is gnawing at him all the time, like a secret betrayal of one's kinsfolk. The Prince de Guermantes feels that he has to make amends for a misdeed he has committed as a Frenchman and a Christian. How could he do it, if not by confessing his conversion publicly to his relatives and to those he formerly rejected because they did not think in the same way as he? But this will never do.

Therefore, as a good Christian, he opens his conscience to his confessor, Abbé Poiré, and asks him to say a mass for Captain Dreyfus. The priest answers that he cannot comply with his request because another person has already made the same. The prince is surprised when he hears it is someone in his milieu and says: 'Indeed! There are Dreyfusists among us, are there? You intrigue me: I should like to unbosom myself to this rare bird, if I know him. – You do know him. – His name? – The Princesse de Guermantes' (C 154). So it is his own wife. Let us note, by the way, a lexical change Proust calls attention to, and a significant one at that. Former anti-Dreyfusards, when converted to the cause, change their name and become not Dreyfusards but Dreyfusists. The distinction means that they are converted, not to the minority like a Saint-Loup or a Swann, but to the minority position and to its movement of opinion.

I have speculated elsewhere (Moscovici, 1981) that conversion is accompanied in the phenomenon of change by what sociologists call pluralistic ignorance. One day, all of a sudden, people discover that they believe or feel the same things. Yet what seems so sudden is prepared by a hidden, internal, even secret process. You can see here that husband and wife were converted separately and in the same way, by reading the same papers, only hiding the fact from each other. The princesse had her maid buy them for her and was nearly caught by her husband reading the *Aurore*. If the Prince de Guermantes gives Swann an account of his change of mind which is a confession, this is to re-establish the link with him and solemnly consecrate what his confession to Abbé Poiré could not have achieved alone: his conversion to the minority. Here is a last quotation:

> 'My dear Swann, from that moment I thought of the pleasure that I should give you when I told you how closely akin my views upon this matter were to yours; forgive me for not having done so sooner. If you bear in mind that I never said a word to the princesse, it will not surprise you to be told that thinking the same as yourself must at that time have kept me farther apart from you than thinking differently.' (C 154)

Let me add that Proust's analysis of the princely conversion is grounded upon a real case. The comte and comtesse de Greffulhe were secretly converted to Captain Dreyfus's cause. The comtesse even wrote to the German Kaiser to know from him what was the truth of the affair. His answer was a magnificent crown of flowers.

Conclusion

It is a pleasure to follow Proust's genius all along his exploration of 'social astronomy' (Cocking, 1982), in which, as in the Latin adage, there is nothing for parade, everything for conscience. I do not know whether I have succeeded in giving you a true account, however partial of course, of the subtlety he puts in it. He conveys the meaning of the relations between men and women during one of the most powerful events of the modern era, an event which never ceased to be for him both puzzling and shocking. This is clear from a letter relating to the Dreyfus case that he wrote in June 1906 to Mme Strauss:

> I find that one is deeply shaken when reading those things again and thinking that this could happen in France a few years ago and not among the Apaches. There is an appalling contrast between on one hand those people's culture, distinction, intelligence and even the brightness of their uniforms and, on the other hand, their moral infamy.

Today, nearly a hundred years after the affair, the feeling still persists for Proust's reader, even though we have got more or less used to such things.

Indeed, which of us has not engaged in similar reflections relating to what happened in Germany or elsewhere[9] while deathly gloom rose and threatened to destroy civilization?

In any case, such are the *Gedankenexperiments* I wanted to present to you. I intended to show the various shapes dissenting minorities can assume under particular circumstances. And also to exemplify up to what point, with what precision, social psychology allows us a new reading of literature.

Notes

1 In *War and Peace*, Tolstoy opposes Napoleon and Kutuzov, the two types of leaders I defined in *The Age of the Crowd* (Moscovici, 1985) as totemic and mosaic.

2 Of course literary critics did not fail to mention the Dreyfus affair when examining Proust. After reading a number of them, I am inclined to believe that they have grasped the influence of the affair over his life better than over his work. From their writings you sometimes get the feeling that this considerable event happened close to him without touching him as a man, a half-Jew, and an artist. Those who do mention it are reluctant to insist too must and timidly examine his ideas about it. See Delhorbe (1932); R. L. Kopp (1971); J. M. Cocking (1982).

3 M. Proust, *Remembrance of Things Past*, translated by C. K. Scott-Moncrieff (London: Chatto & Windus, 1925). Quotations are taken from this edition, mainly from *The Guermantes Way* (indicated by the letter G in the parenthetical page citations) and *Cities of the Plain* (indicated by the letter C).

4 No wonder that the quest for social recognition assumed such importance for Proust, since it is the quest of every minority (see Moscovici, 1976). Himself a member of three minorities as a Jew, a homosexual, and a Dreyfusard, he experienced and watched social relations from this triple point of view.

5 In fact the theory of social recombination of individuals and groups in quest of recognition that I am stating here is more general than the theories of social stratification or differentiation. It presupposes a constant movement and mobility in society, whereas those theories consider society as a kind of mould or system in which individuals and groups are merely situated in relation to one another.

6 The refusal to pardon a collective crime has its probable origin in the theory of conspiracy. The individual real or supposed adhering to a gang of criminals lays to his charge all the crimes committed by his accomplices whether he has taken a share in them or not.

7 'French public opinion in the last two years of the nineteenth century was widely and intensely involved in the Dreyfus affair, an issue which crystallized many claims of anti-Semites regarding Jewish treason and conspiracy and lent such claims credence and an aura of respectability by attaching them to the cause of the Army and the Nation' (Wilson, 1976, p. 227).

8 You can hardly understand this beautiful finale if you are content to say, as one historian of literature does, that 'the most impressive scene of social hypocrisy is that of the red shoes' (Kopp, 1971, p. 45).

9   The Dreyfus affair was, so to speak, the dress rehearsal and setting in place of the political and ideological forces that were to burst out with such violence in the twentieth century. From this point of view, especially as concerns anti-Semitism and its consequences, Proust was extraordinarily clear-sighted. In his work we can read clear-cut sentences about Jews and non-Jews. But nowhere do we find the naïveté of the man of order and reason such as Durkheim, who believed in assimilation as the natural outcome of the affair: 'The faults of Jews are compensated by unquestionable qualities, and, if there are better races, there are worse ones. Besides, Jews are losing their ethnical characteristics very quickly. Another two generations and it would be a thing done' (E. Durkheim, 1975, p. 253). Unfortunately we know how the thing turned out after two generations.

6

Social Consciousness and its History

When I was a young researcher, Piaget, more than any other contemporary scientist, articulated a proper conception of research in psychology. I read *The Child's Conception of the World* (1926/1929) a little later than I should have done as I was already nearly 30. However, after I had read it I was in a state of a shock. I had a great opportunity. Thanks to that reading and to others of Piaget's writings, my thinking liberated itself from innumerable constraining notions with respect both to the methods of research and to the significant questions that our science addressed.

It is one of the paradoxes of psychology that the study of cognition in adults is concerned above all with attention, perception, basic learning and memory, hence with elementary processes to which the same simplified and non-linguistic techniques are applied as to the study of rats, pigeons and rabbits. In contrast, the study of the mental life of children provides a basis for a rich and detailed observation and tries to grasp anthropologically and philosophically such central issues as explanations, classifications, morality, spontaneous and scientific representations, language, that is, the higher mental functions, beginning with their content in the real context. It was tempting to regard Piaget's early work as an exploration of our culture through children's discourse, and the material he collected as expressing its folklore, common sense and knowledge, all of that in the thinking of a single child. This brought me to consider, in a new light, what could become of social psychology as a major scientific discipline: a type of knowledge of an anthropology of our culture, just as anthropology is often the social psychology of other, so-called 'primitive', cultures. When, in the late 1960s, Piaget invited me to Geneva to organize the first teaching of social psychology there, it meant for me a recognition of the efforts which I had pursued since my first reading of his work which changed the manner of thinking of a student who had started his studies too late, having been kept from them by the war.

By contrast, I only became acquainted with Vygotsky more recently. It was during the years of my teaching in New York that the ideas concerning culture, thinking and language, which were discussed in numerous books and articles, entered into my mental landscape. In many respects, he was a fashionable author. I started reading his work and found it invigorating, stimulating and unconventional. Above all I was curious to know who, in the 1920s, could write as if in the 1980s, and who did not believe he could distinguish the social from the Marxist. I was captivated by the power of his style, an unfailing impression which I retained the more I penetrated his intellectual horizon.

Whoever is well informed about the rather irregular careers of the lives of Piaget and Vygotsky knows that they were both, in their education, outsiders to psychology. Moreover, neither was, and perhaps still is not, a prophet in his respective country. It was America which conferred upon them that status and, just as one can speak of a 'king-maker', it was Jerome Bruner who was the prophet-maker. I did not stop, though, to reflect on the inevitable question: why celebrate Piaget and Vygotsky together?

At first sight they may seem to be an incongruous pair. I would like to assert, on reflection, that Piaget and Vygotsky had more things in common than the majority of great psychologists of the twentieth century. For a start, they shared the conviction that there was one serious problem for psychology: the problem of modernity. What was at stake here was to give an account of the evolution not so much from animal to human, as from the mental life of the so-called 'primitives' to the mental life of the so-called 'civilized'; from pre-rational and collective thought to individual and scientific thought. Briefly, the problem was to understand how humans become rational beings, how they master their own behaviour, and how they emancipate themselves from dependence on the environment and on tradition. Their work in its entirety, of which the psychology of the child is no more than one chapter, is a response to a fundamental question which occupied all the great thinkers of that epoch. Their work is in danger of becoming a Rorschach blot, and we can have as many Piagets and Vygotskys as we want if our understanding of their work is not anchored in its historical context. For it would be only a small exaggeration to say that the prolific literature which exists today on the subjects of their concern is reticent about exploring that historical background.

Speaking of Vygotsky – but one could say the same thing of Piaget – Van der Veer and Valsiner (1991) observe that 'with the burgeoning of "neo-Vygotskian" fashions in contemporary psychology, the historical focus of Vygotsky and his ideas has receded into the background' (p. 1).

This reticence, to my mind, results from a common tendency to search for the source of a theory within psychology itself. As if, in our science, one did not borrow or find inspiration in ideas and principles from other sciences, just as Maxwell's physics borrowed statistical hypotheses from the social mathematics that was fashionable at the time.

Curiously, even societal theories seem to have a psychological origin, as one reads in Wertsch's brilliant *Vygotsky and the Social Formation of Mind* (1985): 'Much that Vygotsky had to say about the social origins of human consciousness is not necessarily grounded in the ideas of Marx or of any other social theorist' (p. 60).

Of course, if every psychologist invented his or her own social theory, it would have the same scientific value as if every geneticist or astronomer invented his or her own chemical or physical theory. However, if one reminds oneself that Piaget and Vygotsky were two highly creative minds with a broadly based culture, one is led to observe that their ideas germinated within a wide spectrum of philosophical and scientific fields. Further, it is interesting that both of them base their theories in the same theoretical perspective, the influence of which was so pervasive on their generation. They inherited this theoretical perspective from sociology and anthropology and made ample use of it in establishing the foundations of child psychology. The lifelong inspiration which Piaget and Vygotsky acquired from these sources explains that enduring proximity, if not always similarity, which has kept their respective works 'on speaking terms' with each other, even if they never met. But this is another, though not all that different, story.

THE ROOTS OF PIAGET'S AND VYGOTSKY'S SOCIAL VISION

When the train took more than three hours to cover the distance between Paris and Geneva, one could read on all the level crossings: 'Attention, one train can hide another one.' At present, when we are interested in identifying the conceptual origins of particular ideas, we may warn: 'Attention, one centenary can hide another one.' Thus the centenary of Piaget and Vygotsky may hide the centenary which we celebrated in 1996/7, of the idea of collective representation which plays an essential role in their work and without which that work would be incomprehensible. Indeed it requires an effort of the imagination to see how one could seriously link culture and psychology without paying attention to this idea. Nor could one speak about the theories of Piaget and Vygotsky as if that idea had never been formulated. The idea of collective or social representation made possible the marriage of anthropology and psychology within a developmental framework. Let us consider the reasons for that marriage.

For a start, this idea introduces what the great American sociologist Talcott Parsons called a cultural conception of society in modern thought. Durkheim, who was the author of this conception, breaks with easy analogies between living organisms and human society; and with those between biological evolution and social history, which one could call the ideological by-products of vulgar Darwinism. He proceeds to a criticism of psychological and anthropological theories which explain ethnic and cultural peculiarities by race, instinct, heredity, in short, by the sociobiology of that time. For him, the natural environment of human beings is society. Society appears to be a system of relations generating collectively shared beliefs, norms, languages and rituals which hold people together. Just like any institution, knowledge and beliefs are in existence before, during and after the lives of single individuals. This is why all these forms of representations are stable, constraining and constitutive of society. That is to say, they have a reality which, however symbolic and mental, is just as real, if not more real, than a physical reality. 'Concepts,' Durkheim (1955/1983) writes, 'which are collective in origin (as all concepts really are) take on in our eyes, even when their object is not a real one, such a strength that it appears to be real. This is why concepts acquire the vividness and force of action of sensations' (pp. 101–2).

Collective or social representations are the force of society which communicates and transforms itself. Durkheim's view about the thinking and reality of a social representation embedded in its history is most clearly expressed in his *Pragmatism and Sociology* (1955/1983): 'Everything in man,' he declares, 'has been made by mankind in the course of time. Consequently, if truth is human, it too is a human product. Sociology applies the same conception to reason. All that constitutes reason, its principles and categories, has been made in the course of history' (p. 67). The consequence of this is that collective or social representations cannot be explained by facts less complex than those which govern social interaction. In other words, they cannot be explained by the facts of individual psychology or by some elementary processes.

This is a view which I find wholly plausible, though I suppose that not everyone does, and it makes the following sense of Durkheim's claim: all social representations, including myths and religion, irrespective of which culture they belong to, are rational. To paraphrase Hegel, one could say that, for Durkheim, everything which is social is rational and everything which is rational is social. In other words, mythical or religious representations, for example, of other people living in different societies, are not fallacious or irrational, as Frazer (1922), for example, believed. In his brilliant book *Reason and Culture*, Gellner (1992) presents the unique character of the theory in these terms:

> This theory is meant to explain why all men are rational: why all men think in severely circumscribed, shared and demanding concepts, rather than in terms of privately assembled and perhaps wildly diverging associations. This is what Durkheim means by rationality. . . . This theory, however, does not differentiate between one system of shared compulsions and another. It explains them all,

and does not on its own commend any one of them above the others. Like the rain which falls gently on the just and the unjust, it applies to all human cultures, favouring none.   (pp. 41–2)

What the attribution of biases, fallacies and illusions does is to disguise this shared compulsion of a community, and favours one mode of knowing *vis-à-vis* another. In this connection we may note that Horton (1993) has discussed the relevance of this work of Durkheim and Lévy-Bruhl for the present day and assessed its influence: 'even today,' he writes, 'many of the ideas that dominate the field derive from their work' (p. 63).

In any case, it has to be acknowledged that in the 1920s the idea of collective or social representation appeared in sociology, spread into anthropology, fertilized linguistics (e.g. Saussure), and entered into philosophy and epistemology, where, to mention but a few names, Cornford, Koyré and Fleck come to mind. In psychology, one can recall Ribot, Dumas, Wallon, Janet, Blondel and others.

When Piaget and Vygotsky undertook their first researches, the idea of collective or social representation was already in the air everywhere in Europe. One could say that Piaget was initiated into this idea and stimulated by the example of another great Genevan, Saussure. Piaget was so much associated in his reasoning with this way of thinking that his contemporary, the Russian psychologist Rubinstein, a connoisseur of the great currents of the time, specifically noted it. In a chapter in which he speaks about others in the West who shared the idea of collective representation, he pointed out: 'The same considerations relate, in principle, to the conception of the development of the child, elaborated by Piaget in his early works, as he has shown, under the direct influence of the "social psychology" of Blondel and Lévy-Bruhl' (Rubinstein, 1959, p. 328). As far as Vygotsky is concerned, he was 'converted' to the same idea after a serious intellectual crisis, as Kozulin (1990) relates, or, as I believe, under the influence of Janet and Piaget. However much I read what is written on Piaget and Vygotsky, I cannot but be astonished how little reference one can find to this scientific and historically essential relation.

REMEMBERING LÉVY-BRUHL

History, even that of schools of thought, is not a long quiet river. Durkheim's thoughtful conception of collective representations implies a continuity of concepts and of forms of thought from archaic religions to modern sciences. It recoiled from what elsewhere (Moscovici, 1998) I call a paradox of the rationality of social representations. In fact, all representations are rational, even if, to paraphrase Orwell, some appear more rational than others.

Representations of the civilized may appear to be more rational than those of the alleged primitives, scientific representations may appear more rational than religious ones, and so on. Such a suggestion, however, becomes deadlocked if one seriously adopts the position that the concept of collective representation is instituted by one culture only.

Lévy-Bruhl put his finger on this paradox. He tried to show that if social representations are rational in the eyes of members of one culture, they need not be so, either in the same sense or according to the same logic, in the eyes of another culture. Lévy-Bruhl's lifelong project was twofold: first, to explain the mentality of so-called 'primitive' cultures by social causes instead of by individual causes, as Frazer (1922) had done; and, second, to demystify Western thought as privileged in comparison with other forms of thought. Lévy-Bruhl was not a Durkheimian, and in contrast, he had worked towards a more rigorous grasp of collective representations which he then turned into a genuinely autonomous concept with respect to a particular theory of society and of history. As a consequence, he elaborated one of the most surprising and radical visions of mentality. According to him, it is impossible to convert superior forms of thought, chosen by one culture, into universal laws of the human mind. The concept of choice has a social nature from which it follows that one of these forms could be legitimized as a normal prototype at the expense of all the others. Today it is difficult to imagine the scandal which Lévy-Bruhl's vision provoked. The idea that humankind shares a psychic unity was the rock on which psychologists and anthropologists founded their churches. Just like Einsteinian relativity at that same time, the hypothesis of Lévy-Bruhl undermined the Kantian idea that the categories of the human mind are the same at all times and in all cultures. Lévy-Bruhl added an inscrutable, if not to say tragic, element in his concept of the social representation. He effected a change in what we think we are like, rational of course, but in deficient ways, depending on the culture to which we belong. There is a mental tension in every culture, including our own, because, he says, cognitive homogeneity is never achieved. Astonishingly enough, it is anthropologists and psychologists who of all people have been the slowest to recognize this tension. Lévy-Bruhl's hypothesis, which he elaborated in numerous books, spread widely in different spheres of artistic and philosophical life, from Musil to Fontane, from Husserl to Bergson, from Jung to Koyré or Fleck. 'Taking for granted,' Evans-Pritchard (1964) wrote with reference to Lévy-Bruhl,

> that the beliefs, myths, and in general, the ideas, of primitive peoples are a reflection of their social structures, and therefore differ from one kind of society to another, he devoted himself to showing how they form systems, the logical principles of which is what he called the law of mystical participation. (p. 53)

We have here a thinker whose work provided a common background for both Piaget and Vygotsky. Of course, they both also benefited from Darwin, Freud, Baldwin, Kofka, Bakhtin, Saussure, Janet, and many others. The hypothesis and the approach of Lévy-Bruhl was the catalyst for the initial theories of Piaget and Vygotsky. It was through their effort to explain, in psychological terms, the concepts of the French anthropologist that a new psychology emerged. Generally, everyone knows or should know this fact and should acknowledge its historical consequences. As a matter of fact, however, its recognition is usually avoided because of the understandable academic tendency of our contemporaries to blunt the teeth of highly provocative ideas and to abandon outmoded and harsh words: pre-logical mentality, primitivism, mystic participation and others like these. In any case, we do not need these words.

The prestige of a work is undoubtedly linked to the number of opponents it succeeds in mobilizing against itself. One can say the same about the quality of readers that the work attracts and whose reasoning it influences. On these grounds the prestige of Lévy-Bruhl is well justified as his work continues to be both admired and disputed. He was a remarkable thinker and writer who analysed the texts of traditional cultures with the same conceptual rigour which he brought to the analysis of the texts of Pascal or Descartes as a historian of philosophy. This talent was recognized by Husserl when he wrote to Lévy-Bruhl, saying that collective representations appeared to him as the world of culture inhabited by people.

Due to the polemical debates to which his ideas gave rise, certain remarkable specialists fail even to refer to his work. And I find it difficult to understand what other acknowledged specialists mean when they state that Vygotsky drew, above all, his ethnographic material from Lévy-Bruhl's work (Van der Veer and Valsiner, 1991, p. 209). It would be like saying that Weber drew from Marx's *Capital* the historical material of capitalist society and not the powerful ideas about its economic processes and the origin of surplus value. Luria (1979) in his memoirs did not make that mistake. Neither did Piaget, who always referred to the 'memorable' or 'essential' work of Lévy-Bruhl (e.g. 1951/1995, p. 147). Even as late as 1951, in his essay on explanations in sociology, Piaget defended Lévy-Bruhl against his opponents when he wrote: 'It appears that the notion of participation victoriously resisted its critics' (Piaget, 1951/995, p. 88).

However, those who have read Lévy-Bruhl's work know that he conceived it around a unique theme: how is logic formed in the human mind? Certainly, he claimed, through pre-logical ways which, originally, must have been countless. However, if innumerable cultures which reason differently from our own have disappeared, this should not mean that we privilege our own culture by adopting it as a model. The sole result of this would be to ratify, as the norm, the hierarchy of forms of knowledge and cultures. In this sense

Lévy-Bruhl is, as we would say today, non-Eurocentric. What the human sciences owe to him above all is a methodological rule which can be defined as follows: what is absurd in our eyes is not necessarily so in the eyes of others. Let us make an experiment, and if his conjecture is verified, this rule will necessarily become intelligible and clear so far as the facts permit.

We are here, I think, at the nub of the matter. Thus, faithful to this rule, Lévy-Bruhl examined collective representations in all their aspects to see if he could bring out their coherence, by following their particular concrete texture in all their twists and turns and by trying to justify their hold over people's lives. The clarity of Lévy-Bruhl, which I consider superb, has proved consistent from his initial assertions, right up to the final queries, in which he called into question his lifetime's work. Anyone who reads his *Notebooks* will be shaken by his scientific honesty and by the fugitive emotions of the man.

In the following paragraphs I shall summarize three themes which he developed with respect to the nature of representations in pre-modern or so-called 'primitive' cultures.

The first theme: these collective representations are impervious to experience. This may be because one considers them to be hallowed by authority or tradition and thus protected from information that would falsify them. It may also be that the members of the group never confront the experience directly, but only by means of shared categories and sentiments. In one sense, these representations are like paradigms, that is, they are incommensurable. In addition, according to Finis (1994), the notion of the incommensurability between paradigms was an outgrowth of Lévy-Bruhl's idea concerning the impermeability of experience.

The second theme: all people are sensitive to contradiction, and yet this claim is not true for all representations which they share. This is particularly true of pre-modern civilizations in which the law of participation takes precedence over the elimination of contradiction. By sticking to this law, individuals judge as identical objects which to them are either familiar or similar.

Finally, the third theme could be expressed as a semantic efficiency, alluding to the famous symbolic efficiency. In some ways, language, for Lévy-Bruhl, is a form of social representation, even a system based on social representations. And, in so-called 'primitive' cultures, its ultimate finality should be to reproduce, as closely as possible, images of objects and of persons, every situation or every change of situation. This is why, according to him, cultures have a particularly rich lexicon, flexible, mobile, almost fluid terms, always ready to be moulded according to changing images.

In recalling this historical evidence, I do not pretend to any originality except, very modestly, to place Lévy-Bruhl and Vygotsky in their context. They initiated a set of interconnected ideas and assumptions concerning the nature of the higher mental functions which for a while were laid aside because they lacked formal rigour, and because psychology became disconnected from culture. Culture was even referred to as a single outcome of this historical process. The autonomy of the individual was widely considered to be the natural outcome of this long history. This process was assumed to be a unique, progressive movement of human culture. Now, as the word 'culture' begins to be used in the plural, suggesting a number of distinctive, local and equally meaningful ways of life, assumptions regarding the shared nature of representations and their psychological distinctiveness can emerge once again in a new guise.

The Child, a Novice in Modern Culture

It is now time to ask ourselves: what kind of child, at least at the beginning, did Piaget and Vygotsky assume in developing their psychology? In fact,and this strikes us at a first glance, it appears that they both turned the child into a wholly cultural and social figure. However, if you want to know this child, and the basis on which Piaget and Vygotsky observed and constructed him or her, search for him or her not only in the schools of Geneva or Kharbin, but also in the books of Lévy-Bruhl! On examination, it seems that the adults of pre-modern cultures are reinvented as children, as novices of our pre-adult culture. In the end one has to face the following fact, never mind the inductive reasoning: what Piaget and Vygotsky were searching for at the time, when studying children, were clues rather than proofs. These were clues relating to this so-called 'primitive' mentality and not any other. And once they found these clues, they gave them a psychological formulation.

For this reason, I insist that the three themes in the work of Lévy-Bruhl which I have mentioned above are also the themes of the theories of Piaget and of Vygotsky. I think it necessary to suggest, though not to nail down, their intellectual affiliation. Perhaps I should say, one can show how they made the child the royal road to the understanding of mental life within a culture and a society. Piaget and Vygotsky follow a common road not because they are both interested in children, but because they construct and reinvent children using similar materials. I would like, first of all, to bring out those features that are common to Piaget and Vygotsky. This will enable me, later, to emphasize more easily the major reason for their divergences.

Is it not surprising and highly significant that Piaget and Vygotsky both established the law of participation, which was so much discussed at that time, as the backbone of childlike mentality? In doing so, they take the side of Lévy-Bruhl and buttress his conception of higher mental functions. How could we fail to note that for both of them the natural development of thought proceeds towards scientific thinking and towards non-contradiction? Piaget defined pre-logical and pre-operational thought, and Vygotsky defined thought in complexes, as the necessary stages of this development. In this respect, the law of participation is no longer a particular law of a specific culture, but a universal law of thought which everybody finds in the child's development. The theoretical connection between an anthropological experience and a psychological analysis is thereby achieved.

Piaget begins, moreover, by enlarging the range of participations and he considers that they appear at the time that the child begins to differentiate between the self and the world. Thus both the assumption of magical powers by the child and the endowment of things in the world with consciousness and life emerge simultaneously with this range of participations. Piaget explains participations by ontological egocentrism, which manifests itself in a confusion between a sign and a thing, between what is objective and what is subjective. Whether the child makes a conjecture concerning his magical powers when he says that he forces the sun or the moon to follow him, or attributes consciousness to material things, this is a participation at work. It is, Piaget believes, equivalent to an intuitive or a pre-operational thinking at the second stage of child development.

There is a certain Victorian style in how we deal with thinkers and their ideas. The 1920s were anything but Victorian. The intermingling of surrealism, futurism, anthropology and psychology was a reality, and I think that this influenced thinkers like Vygotsky, and fashioned his attraction for magical thought and so-called 'primitive' cultures. He was fascinated by the phenomena of totemic identification, which, he believed, were equally to be found in children's minds. If a member of a clan says he is a red parrot, this claim may seem strange when considered in terms of its physical validity, but is quite understandable in terms of participation, just like saluting the flag or identifying different members of the same family by name. The term 'complex' was coined by Vygotsky to account for such modes of thinking in the child of 4 or 5 years. At this age children are supposed to be able to arrange and to select objects on the basis of some concrete attribute – an attribute which adults may judge to be irrelevant – and which, anyway, will change many times in the course of the child's classifications of objects. Thinking in complexes, just like naming, means that an individual object is simultaneously itself, with its own features, and something belonging to a network of all other objects with which it has some attributes in common. There is an evident relationship between Vygotsky's notion of 'the complex' and Wittgenstein's notion of 'family resemblance'.

Be that as it may, thinking in complexes has a feature in common with the representations of alleged primitives, namely an insensitivity to contradiction. Vygotsky was convinced that his analysis explains the psychological formulation of the law of participation. In short, the thinking of the so-called 'primitives' is not so much pre-logical as it is pre-conceptual.

Piaget and Vygotsky adopted different strategies of analysis than did Lévy-Bruhl. Piaget came to believe, however, that all the characteristics of pre-logical mentality are transferred into the concepts of the psychology of the child. I shall mention here only one of the considerable range of such characteristics, namely egocentrism. This concept evidently owes much to Bleuler and to Freud. In addition, and this has not previously been noted, it owes much to Durkheim, for whom egocentrism was associated with anomie and alienation. According to Piaget, Durkheim's writings provide evidence for the idea that the child is alienated in gerontocratic society. The fact remains that egocentrism is situated mid-way between autistic and socialized thought, with the child being unable to grasp the point of view of the other. It is precisely because the child is centred on herself, just as the primitive individual is centred on his group, that she has only a partial and short-term grasp of reality, which does not, however, affect the general tendency of her reasoning. If one accepts that gerontocratic society, which, as Piaget underlined, affects the child's judgement, one might as well say that the child is over-sociocentric. In these circumstances where a person is entirely subordinated to his family, church, or community, he is unable to think of himself without thinking, at the same time, of his family, church or community. This applies equally to children and adults. This condition provides the model for Piaget's whole conception of participation. Whether it is a matter of egocentrism or, on the contrary, sociocentrism, the child's representations, like those of a 'primitive man', would be impervious to experience, and hence, also, to contradiction. 'Impermeability to experience and insensitivity to contradictions,' wrote Rubinstein (1959), 'similarly characterize the thought of the child in the works of Piaget as well as the thought of a "primitive" man in Lévy-Bruhl. Here, just as there, "participation" replaces the logical principles of identity and of contradiction' (pp. 328–9).

This passage involves a theme which also pervades the work of Vygotsky. According to him, the thought and the language of the child are subordinated to the language and thinking of society. The child acquires the greater part of her ideas and vocabulary through the socializing institutions of society. She thus does not master reality since she lacks access to the experience she would need to obtain because she lives in a world restricted by that of adults. For her, it will be liberating when, in accord with language, she starts to interiorize these representations.

THE DIVERGENCE BETWEEN PIAGET AND VYGOTSKY

It is impossible to understand the psychology of the child without understanding the ideas and findings of Piaget and Vygotsky. This, in turn, necessitates that we understand the findings of Durkheim and Lévy-Bruhl and how these findings differ in regard to the evolution of collective representations. It is precisely because the theories of Piaget and of Vygotsky are at the same level and have many points in common that the major source of their divergence, which does not belong to the same order of facts, becomes transparently clear. Indeed, Parsons remarked that the idea of social or collective representation was no more than outlined by Durkheim. Even so, there was, from the beginning, a fundamental opposition between Durkheim and Lévy-Bruhl. This was due not so much to the differences concerning the nature of representations as to those concerning their differing conceptions of evolution. Consequently, the two scholars provided different solutions to the problem of modernity which was outlined at the beginning of this paper. According to Durkheim, thinking of a 'primitive' religious representation and a 'modern' scientific one are two steps in a single historical process, the latter developing from the former. According to Lévy-Bruhl, 'primitive' and 'modern' representations are antithetical, the evolution from the former to the latter being the substitution of one pattern of thinking and feeling by its contrary. This is, of course, a very crude distinction which I shall clarify below.

I argue that this opposition between Durkheim and Lévy-Bruhl is reflected in the thought of Piaget and of Vygotsky. In brief, I suggest that Piaget follows Durkheim and Vygotsky follows Lévy-Bruhl. I would not like, though, to reduce the differences between Piaget and Vygotsky to this difference alone, because there are also other ideas, whether foolish or wise, with respect to which they differ. The belief that development is continuous, as Durkheim maintained, or discontinuous, as Lévy-Bruhl thought, is the crucial entry point to the theoretical singularity of each of these two great psychologists.

In a sense, the ideas of Piaget continue Durkheim's rationalism. This is a type of rationalism which reverses the classic formula from thought to action, and makes action or ritual the principal agent endowing people with stable and shared representations without which they would be neither human nor social. Starting from action, Piaget conceived of a new and sophisticated mechanism – accommodation and assimilation – to account for evolution from one state of equilibrium to another by a novel rearrangement of pre-existing elements. He perceived an uninterrupted continuity from child to adult. In 1965 he asserted that this, consequently, restores continuity more than Lévy-Bruhl could assume between so-called 'primitive' representations and our own. The very meaning of this evolution towards reversibility and towards scientific concepts corresponds to the Durkheimian conception according to which the more that individuals become autonomous, the more representations become differentiated and open to criticism. What previously was considered to be an intuition and a symbol will become lodged into concepts. In the process of decentration, sociocentric representations, as Piaget calls them, become transformed into scientific representations.

It is necessary to comment briefly on the historical-cultural theory of Vygotsky. Nowadays, words like 'culture' and 'history' evoke positive feelings and are widely popular. However, the meanings of these words are obscure in their origin. It is tautological to assert that the central idea of Vygotsky and of Lévy-Bruhl is that people living in different epochs and in different cultures have different mental functions or different representations. Who could imagine that a theory is needed to explain that the world is different at different times and places and that such a suggestion would have subversive implications? Let us take, in a literal sense, the writings of Vygotsky and Luria (Luria and Vygotsky, 1992). In Vygotsky's view, the origin of higher mental functions has to be sought not in the depths of the mind or in nervous tissues, but in social history, outside the individual organism. This, of course, entails a fundamental shift in every area of psychology. We recall that this was more or less the basic assumption made by Durkheim and his school.

Lévy-Bruhl, however, introduces the daring and scarcely credible hypothesis that the historical development of knowledge and of representations is the result of a series of qualitative transformations and of discontinuities not only of content but in cognitive structures.

> Lévy-Bruhl was the first to point out the qualitative feature of primitive thought and the first to treat logical processes as products of historical development. He had a great influence on psychologists in the 1920s who tried to go beyond simplistic notions about the mind and to understand human consciousness as a product of sociocultural development.   (Luria, 1976, p. 7)

The historical appreciation is neat and precise. Lévy-Bruhl abandoned the sterile path of the evolutionary psychology of his time and offered a new vision of social consciousness. At the same time he proposed a new hypothesis of historical development and a practical way of making it evident. Although he did not use the word 'revolution', it is, nevertheless, the qualitative jumps of representational revolutions that have a lot in common with the paradigm switches of Kuhn (1962). Such considerations led Vygotsky and Luria to believe that Lévy-Bruhl's conjecture deserved to be probed. The Bolshevik revolution constituted a natural experiment which actually allowed them to test it. 'The period,' Luria wrote about the years 1931–2, 'provided a unique opportunity to observe how decisively all these reforms effected not only a broadening of outlook but also radical changes in the structure of cognitive processes' (Luria, 1976, p. iv). One cannot better summarize both the task which they set out to achieve, and the hypothetical-deductive approach which makes this historical-cultural theory original. This is why I was surprised that such fine scholars as Van der Veer and Valsiner (1991) could write that 'Vygotsky and Luria felt the need [by planning this research] to witness these cognitive similarities and differences' (p. 242).

It appears from Luria's writings that he and Vygotsky felt the need to test a bold conjecture of Lévy-Bruhl and it was with this goal in mind that the expedition was organized. In his fine book of memoirs, Luria (1979) narrates their first encounter with Durkheim and his view of society as comprising social representations and norms shaping the mental life of individuals. Afterwards, he was acquainted with the ideas of Janet, who, under the influence of this French sociologist, deepened the understanding of the relation between social and intellectual activities in the development of the child. Finally, he writes about Lévy-Bruhl, who, in a way, had justified the natural experiment they wanted to perform in Uzbekistan. Luria was convinced they had proved that the revolutionary changes in society brought about fundamental changes in people's representations and in their mental processes. And so their socio-historical theory is dangerously correct, I should say. One can recall how Rubinstein in 1934 implicitly criticized Vygotsky for choosing the discontinuity hypothesis of Lévy-Bruhl rather than the continuity hypothesis of Marx: 'What is decisive here,' he writes,

> can be detected in a contrast between Marx and Lévy-Bruhl. The latter held for a not just quantitative but qualitative transformation of the psyche in the process of social-historical development – changes not only in content but also in forms and structures. . . . There is a *caesura* between the early cognitive and the intellectual. Continuity here becomes impossible. This basically false and politically reactionary stress on differences shows the outcome of ideological mysticism. (Rubinstein, 1934/1987, pp. 119–20)

But in choosing Lévy-Bruhl's discontinuity hypothesis, Vygotsky is rejecting at the same time Durkheim's continuity hypothesis. It was Durkheim's belief that as individuals become, in the process of evolution, less subordinated to the collectivity and become more capable of perceiving physical reality directly, and of reacting to their own thoughts, modern scientific representations replace the early non-scientific ones. Contrary to Durkheim, Lévy-Bruhl was convinced that scientific thought does not entirely replace pre-scientific thought, the law of non-contradiction does not eliminate the law of participation. In that sense Lévy-Bruhl's point of view is the key to the problem of historical-cultural theory. One understands why, according to this theory, scientific concepts or representations are eventually transformed into common-sense representations rather than being entirely eliminated by them.

We recall those seminal studies of the development of children's thinking from the level of complexes to that of rational concepts. They are unfinished in a sense, and they leave us awaiting continuation. I would have been unable to appreciate their significance without historical and theoretical comments provided by Professor Brushlinsky of the Moscow Institute of Psychology at the Russian Academy of Sciences. These studies and those which followed them, and this is rarely mentioned, are concerned with the 'diffusion' of knowledge, so to speak – more exactly, with the diffusion, after the Soviet revolution, of Marxist concepts into the everyday thinking of children. Clearly, the spontaneous or common-sense concepts and the scientific ones have two distinct, and possibly opposed, origins: first, at school or in the party; and, second, in the family environment. In the process of communication from the teacher to the pupil these representations clash and reciprocally transform each other. The spontaneous representations facilitate the assimilation of the scientific ones, and the scientific ones enrich spontaneous ones so that they become more abstract. Or, as Vygotsky put it, the former move upwards and the latter downwards, becoming more concrete. Thus Vygotsky and his students, just as Lévy-Bruhl before them, suggested that one cannot eradicate pre-scientific thought. On the contrary, they suggest that common sense is a necessary mediator of assimilation, whether cultural or scientific. To include these studies amongst the forerunners of our studies based on the theory of social representations and to include them as a part of social psychology would not be ungrounded. Is there more to them than meets the eye? Let us remind ourselves that these studies were debated during the period that was concerned with the question of a socialist pedagogy. According to Lenin, social consciousness is created outside the individual's mind by the party and it enters people's and especially the workers' minds by removing their spontaneous, non-revolutionary ideas and beliefs, and non-Marxist concepts. Rubinstein in his article mentions in what sense this is relevant to psychology: 'The Leninist problem of the spontaneous and conscious (cf. *What is to be done?*) falls, of course, outside psychology, but the transition from one to the other is a profound psychic change' (Rubinstein, 1934/1987, p. 123). Thus the studies of Vygotsky and of his colleagues can be also seen as testing, in exciting but dangerous times, Lenin's dogma of social consciousness, which had been strongly criticized by his social democratic opponents. Probably more than anything else, this endeavour must have aroused criticism and suspicions towards the great Russian psychologist.

Our epoch is not theirs. However, from what I have just said, one can imagine the root of the difference between Piaget and Vygotsky concerning the solution to the problem of modernity. For the former, that problem was concerned with the capacity to think scientifically and to decentre from society in order to cooperate or act rationally. For the latter, the solution to the problem of modernity was to create a social consciousness based on a scientific vision, no doubt a Marxist vision, of the world and society. This difference was not unique to the two great psychologists. It corresponded to the two currents which divided Europe in the march of modern history.

CONCLUDING REMARKS

Fleck wrote in 1936: 'The embryo of the modern theory of cognition is found in the studies of the school of Durkheim and Lévy-Bruhl on the sociology of thinking and on the thinking of primitive people' (Fleck, 1936/1986, p. 80). It is this embryo that Piaget and Vygotsky have enlarged in their developmental psychology and that was elaborated in social psychology in the theory of social representations. I have also tried to remind you that the idea of social representations is fundamental, not only in the past but also in the future, for a vigorous cultural psychology. It is, so to speak, at the core of its genetic code.

Before finishing, it is necessary to emphasize that the essential point is elsewhere than in comparing the two theories of the two thinkers. They lived at the same time, but not in the same history. Vygotsky worked right in the eye of the storm and in one of the greatest tragedies of our time. And although Piaget was perhaps more sensitive than one might think to the ebb and flow of democracy in Europe, he had, more or less, an opportunity to observe it from Geneva, just as Kant observed the French Revolution from the other side of the Rhine. The work of Piaget is a monument, that of Vygotsky a magnificent torso, but a torso nevertheless, a bit like one of Leonardo da Vinci's, who wrote so much, who started works without completing them. The great temptation is to oppose Piaget and Vygotsky as controlled reason over passion, a managed life versus a disorganized existence, a normal career against rebellion, the classical versus the romantic.

In short, we face what Nietzsche called an Apollonian spirit, totally balanced, regular, continuous, expressing the unity of psychic life, and a Dionysian spirit of rupture, irregularity, conflict and the duality of psychic forces and of unforeseen novelties. History invites us there, when we compare Wundt and Fechner, Freud and Janet, Lewin and Skinner, Baldwin and Tolman, to speak only about the dead. This contrast of scientific vision, however, would be very rough without gaining insight into the origins of their parallel histories and inquiring whether or not they represent a more permanent intellectual opposition dating from the birth of psychology. I beg you to read all this with tolerance: as an aspiration to make the history of psychology more interesting both as a science of humanity and as a humane science.

Acknowledgement

This paper was originally prepared for a public lecture at the Second Conference on Socio-Cultural Studies in Geneva, September 1996, as a part of the centenary celebration of the birth of Jean Piaget and of Lev Vygotsky.

7

Ideas and their Development: A Dialogue between Serge Moscovici and Ivana Marková

IM Your theory of social representations is nearly forty years old, yet today, various social psychological activities surrounding this field seem to flourish more than ever; much research into social representations is being carried out, not only all over Europe, but also on other continents. There is a European Ph.D. programme on social representations and communication which organizes an annual summer school for young researchers; there is an association and a network on social representations which publishes a journal and has organized a series of international conferences. At the same time the theory has its critics; some of them argue that the theory is too loose; others, that it is too cognitive; that it is not clear how the concept of social representation differs from other concepts, say, from attitudes, social cognition, beliefs, stereotypes, etc; still others would like to marry the theory either to discourse analysis or to social constructivism(s) and constructionism – or to both of them at the same time.

The theory of social representations, however, is only one area of your research interests. Other areas in which you have been a leading figure for a long time include minority influence and innovation, ecological psychology and crowd psychology. Your studies in these areas have been translated into a dozen languages.

Readers of French are also familiar with your work in the history and philosophy of science, human invention and technology, the psychology of resistance and dissidence, and most recently with your magnificent autobiographical study, *Chronique des années égarées* (*Chronicle of Stray Years*, Moscovici, 1997). Although based permanently in Paris, you have worked at a number of American universities, you have been invited to lecture all over the world and have received a number of honorary doctorates at various European universities.

Before we start talking about these issues, I would like to repeat here something which Willem Doise said at a summer school on social representations in Lisbon in 1997, when he was talking about his early career with you in the 1960s in Paris. This is not a direct quotation, I am paraphrasing what Willem said:

> women worked in the laboratory on social representations (Claudine Herzlich and Denise Jodelet) and that was not accessible to the men; men worked in the laboratory on minority and majority influence (Willem Doise, Michel Plon); this was a hard laboratory science and I would have liked to work on social representations; and Serge on top of that wrote books about the history and philosophy of science, technology and innovation.

SM   Of course, I am delighted, but also surprised, that the theory of social representations has been here for a long time and that new generations of researchers are interested in it, develop it and make conceptual and methodological progress. I am pleased to see that new currents have emerged in the theory and that much diversity is expressed through the researchers' personalities – as one says in French 'il faut de tout pour faire un monde.' I am not against orthodoxies, but they never resist the test of time.

My first response will sound disrespectful. I am often called upon to justify the concept of social representation and to explain how it differs from other concepts such as attitudes, social cognition, and so on. I would like to remind you that the idea of collective or social representation is older than all these notions and that it is part of the 'genetic code' of all the human sciences. It is necessary to distinguish an idea from its conceptual expression in specific scientific areas. For example, one has to distinguish the idea of atomism as a discontinuous view of matter from the concept of the particle, say, in quantum mechanics, or the idea of the molecule from the concept of the gene in molecular biology, etc. Likewise, the idea of collective or social representation has been the source of extremely fruitful concepts in anthropology, linguistics (e.g. *la langue*), history (e.g. mentality), child psychology and social psychology. But as we shall see, social psychology has a more general task concerning this idea. Indeed, from this point of view one might expect the reverse, that these diverse notions should be defined with regard to the basic idea of social representations. In fact, the majority of 'requests' I receive are not criticisms or preludes to a dialogue but demands for credentials. Moreover, I do not know what is meant by 'cognitive', because today the word cognitive has a very general meaning and it applies to any kind of information processing. Social representations are of course related to symbolic thought and any form of mental life which presupposes language. Finally, is the concept of social representations 'too loose'? How loose is 'loose'? If one compares it with formal, mathematical concepts, then this is certainly true. If one means that it is too complex, that is equally true. However, this is an option I took at the beginning of my research and one you will also find in my theory of influence. Can one assume that social-psychological phenomena are simpler than linguistic or economic phenomena? Or should social-psychological theories be simpler than other theories? Should they be reduced to simple propositions, as they often are? I discussed this question many times with Leon Festinger when we were colleagues at the New School in New York and he was involved in anthropological and historical research. These discussions were nourished by concrete questions during our trips to prehistoric sites where we met specialists in palaeontology, anthropology, and so on. And we came to the conclusion that in social psychology, theories have to be 'richer' than they usually are, so as to adequately describe and possibly explain specific phenomena. Moreover, having discussed some remarks of Francis Crick in his memoirs, we both agreed that the model of these theories could not be the hypothetico-deductive model of physics, but the more inductive and descriptive model of biology, both in terms of evidence and of the relationships between theories and phenomena.

I am touched by Willem's interesting remarks. Allow me to add something. I have always avoided proselytism. You are now acquainted with my cultural background. There was a quasi-religious respect for knowledge and learning. In that culture one thinks that if an idea is right, then it will make its way through in spite of any outside resistance. To impose it authoritatively is to devaluate its genuine content. I did not want Willem to think that I used my authority in this matter. Later on I was very happy to see that he was inspired by the theory and has contributed to it in an original way.

1 THE ORIGIN OF IDEAS ON SOCIAL REPRESENTATIONS

IM   Clearly, your ideas on social representations form an integral part of your work as a whole as I have just outlined it. Thus, this dialogue will give us an opportunity to discuss your ideas on social representations in the context of your life-long passion for the quest of the origin of ideas, the history of human knowledge and technology, the manufacture of myths, and the transformation of ideas into common sense. In addition, I hope we can talk about the interdependence of social representations and language – an issue that you yourself brought into the focus of social representational research from the very beginning but which, in my view, has been largely ignored or misunderstood.

SM   If we talk about the origins of my ideas on social representation, then I would say that the theory of social representations is a fruit of my age of innocence. When I say 'age of innocence' I mean that I started working in this direction when I was still a political refugee in Paris. I was a student at the Sorbonne and had no idea about my professional future, if any. At that time, there was little social psychology in France or in Europe, generally speaking. I did not have any contact with American or English colleagues. I read on my own and, in addition, I took some very interesting courses by Professor Lagache on Kurt Lewin. So I freely imagined what social psychology could look like, but I had no idea of what it really was until much later. This is why I say that the theory of social representations is a fruit of my age of innocence. It does not mean that I was in a state of intellectual innocence because, as I wrote in my autobiography, I had already written some essays and published with my Romanian friends an avant-garde review in Bucharest, among other things.

There is one point I would like to make about that period. There was a problem that my generation widely debated: the problem of science. It was after all the problem of modernity. We were all interested in understanding in what ways science had an impact on historical change, on our thinking or our social prospects. We were much less interested in how science affects our culture, everybody's ideas in ordinary life, or how these ideas could become a part of people's beliefs and so on. All young people who were attracted by Marxism, communism and socialism were preoccupied by the question of science, technology and such matters.

IM   So, what did Marxists think about the effect of science on ordinary people? Did you accept the Marxist position?

SM   No, I did not. Let me explain. War was a hell for me. In hell one learns a lot about oneself and humankind in general. You become more lucid and face the hard issues of life and death. In my opinion the richest and most profound part of Dante's *Divine Comedy* is the *Inferno*. So already during the war I started wondering about the impact of science on people's culture, how it alters their minds and behaviour, why it becomes part of a system of beliefs, etc. Your see, they are the kind of questions that Gramsci asked himself during his prison years. At that time there were two clear-cut positions about the problem. First the Marxist position with which I became familiar because, as a young man in Romania, at the beginning of the war, I enlisted in the Communist party. The Marxists – or, more precisely, Lenin! – were mistrustful of the spontaneous knowledge and thinking of the masses. They were convinced that spontaneous knowledge had to be stripped of its ideological, religious and folk irrationalities and replaced by a scientific view of man, history and nature, that is, by the Marxist and materialistic view. Marxists did not believe that the diffusion of scientific knowledge could improve common knowledge or thinking. The former had to eradicate the latter. You know the formula: social consciousness comes from the outside.

The other position was a more general one, we might call it the position of enlightenment. To put it briefly, scientific knowledge and thinking dispel the ignorance, prejudices or mistakes of non-scientific knowledge by means of communication and education. So, in a way, its goal was to transform all men into scientists, to make them think rationally.

At the same time, paradoxically, everyone regarded the diffusion of scientific knowledge in the public, popular science – *vulgarisation* is the French word for it – as a devaluation or a deformation or both of scientific knowledge. In other words, when science spreads in the social area, it turns into something impure and degraded, supposedly because people are incapable of assimilating it as scientists do. You see, there was a convergence between the Marxist and non-Marxist points of view: common knowledge is infectious, deficient and wrong. So, after the war, I reacted in a way against this point of view and tried to rehabilitate common knowledge which is grounded in our ordinary experience, everyday language and daily practices. But deep down I reacted against the underlying idea which had preoccupied me at a given moment, that is, the idea that 'le peuple ne pense pas', people are not capable of thinking rationally, only intellectuals are. I grew up at a time when fascism reigned, so one could say that, on the contrary, it is the intellectuals who are not capable of thinking rationally, since in the middle of the twentieth century they have produced such irrational theories as racism and nazism. Believe me, the first anti-Semitic violence took place in colleges and universities, not in the streets, and it was legitimated not by ignorant priests or politicians, but by such learned people as Mircea Eliade, Emile Cioran and other philosophers.

Thus the problem for me became the following one: how is scientific knowledge transformed into common or spontaneous knowledge? In this process it acquires the qualities of a real creed. This problem was also related to an essay I wrote immediately after the war in which I criticized the Marxist duality of science and ideology as the roots of social consciousness. I suggested that a third component intervenes, that is, common sense. More precisely, what I had in mind was its relation to culture because, in this order of things, you have to take as active, real, only what enters into manners and practices, that is, into the life of common sense. So when I started my research in France I tried to understand and rehabilitate common thinking and common knowledge. Moreover I did not see it as something traditional or primitive, as mere folklore, but as something quite modern, originating partly in science, as the shape that this assumes when it becomes part and parcel of culture. I saw the transformation of scientific knowledge into common knowledge as a possible and exciting area of study.

IM   To explore common sense is a difficult task indeed. Did you have any idea how to do it?

SM Of course I didn't. I have always liked doing things, not just speculating about them theoretically. In the years 1948–9 there were two theories which were beginning to penetrate into French society: first, Marxism, shared and propagated by the largest Communist party in Europe; and second, psychoanalysis. I was excluded from choosing Marxism because I was a foreigner and a refugee from a Communist country; it was also a politically difficult issue. So what remained for me was psychoanalysis, which turned out to be a better choice in the long run, since it has penetrated more deeply into French society than Marxism. Moreover Daniel Lagache, who was my professor, was himself a psychoanalyst and he became interested in my ideas and encouraged me to start research in that area.

IM For me, this issue is particularly interesting because I could never understand how, in France, Marxism and psychoanalysis could go together. When I was a medical student in Communist Czechoslovakia, psychoanalysis was forbidden. In the textbook of psychiatry we had only one and a half lines, at the bottom of a page and in small letters, on Freud and on psychoanalysis described as a bourgeois pseudo-science. We were always made to believe that the next Communist revolution would be in France with the Communist party there being so strong – and this probably partly influenced my own decision to emigrate to the United Kingdom rather than to France. So for me it was always a question of how Marxism and psychoanalysis could coexist in France.

SM At that time, in the fifties, they were fighting each other. Or rather Marxists fought against psychoanalysis, which made my study all the more fascinating. As you know, in the second part of *La Psychanalyse, son image et son public* (Moscovici [1961]/1976), which is devoted to the study of communication, I analysed the propaganda against psychoanalysis in the Communist press. This was also the occasion to show that, when a new idea or scientific knowledge penetrates into the public sphere, the cultural life of a society, then you have a real *Kulturkampf*, cultural struggles, intellectual polemics and opposition between different modes of thinking. This was also the case for relativity, thermodynamics and Darwinism. There is a drama involved in the process of transformation of knowledge and the birth of a new social representation. This explains the clash between psychoanalysis and Marxism when the Communist party was on the rise. Sartre tried to find a compromise that, in my opinion, was not on the whole successful. After the student revolution in 1968, when an ideology was necessary to integrate and recuperate the students into the existing social framework, Althusser initiated a peaceful coexistence with Lacan, and Marxism with psychoanalysis. By that time, however, the Communist party was no longer a leading one and psychoanalytic ideas and language were already a great part of common knowledge and culture. The gurus of mass demonstrations from the place de la République to la Bastille had been replaced by the gurus of individual couches in cosy flats in the area extending from the Latin Quarter to Saint-Germain-des-Prés.

IM   It is a pity that *La Psychanalyse* has not as yet been translated into English. It is a classic book; there you define the elementary concepts and present the theoretical basis of social representations. In particular, it is the second part of *La Psychanalyse* that is not well known among psychologists working in the area of social representations. I consider it important for at least two reasons. First, it is here that you explored the relationship between social representations and language. And second, you examined the strategies that the Communist ideology, using propaganda, applied in the press in order to make it a part of the existing social reality. These two issues are interconnected in the second part of *La Psychanalyse* and therefore I want to speak about them in some detail.

In studying social representations of psychoanalysis in France you have shown how propaganda, focusing on some linguistic insights through the use of words, associating them with new meanings and with alternative socio-cognitive-affective categories, attempted to create new representations, new common knowledge. You described that process as consisting of three stages. The first stage was based on general evidence that psychoanalysis could be associated with various spheres of human activities, such as a science, a therapy, a particular doctrine or an ideology. Selecting ideology as an association with psychoanalysis, the word 'psychoanalysis' was given a particular new sense. For example, the Communist press described psychoanalysis as a symbol of an American lifestyle, of American decadent culture, or as a pseudo-science. We can say that the meaning of the word 'psychoanalysis' was particularized with the intention that this particular meaning would later acquire a new and a global significance. In order to achieve that, the word 'psycho-analysis' was subsequently never used on its own but always with an adjective or a group of words that re-emphasized the new connections. Thus the Communist press never used combinations of words such as 'psychoanalytic science', 'therapeutic psychoanalytic effectiveness', 'objectivity of psycho-analytic conceptions' and so on. Instead, it always used combinations such as: 'the myth of psychoanalysis', 'American psychoanalysis' or 'a bourgeois science'. The use of these constraints fixed the particular content as a general content. As you pointed out, the meaning of the new combination of words became a kind of a label or a title, like the title of a book or a film. In the final stage the rule of hierarchy determined the order in which particular significations were organized. For example, the word 'science' became part of some kind of an artificially created hierarchy with, say, the 'Soviet science' on top, followed by, say, 'the proletarian science', 'the materialist science' and so on.

Such a hierarchy would be ranked much higher than, say, 'the rationalist science', 'the American science', 'the bourgeois science' etc. In this way propaganda, through the effects of selection of associations between categories, through the rule of constraint, reduced the range of significations in order to eliminate the risks of relativization and of free interpretations of meanings by its audience or by interlocutors. The result of these operations was both the creation of a specific language and an elevation of a semantic barrier between words. It is the constitution of this specific language which accompanies the formation of a representation. Once this is achieved, words obtain their specific meanings and these in turn justify their use in propaganda. Repetition of elements formalizes and solidifies thinking, making it part of the individual's linguistic and cognitive make-up.

I found your study illuminating because it showed a direct relationship between thought and language. More specifically, in this case, it showed the relationship between the workings of ideology and the meanings of words with an ideology attempting to become a social representation, a part of culture.

But let us return to the origin of your ideas on social representations. You have explained that the first reason that brought you to the study of social representations was your conviction that common sense or common knowledge needed to be rehabilitated. It must not be treated as something irrational but as an important third factor between scientific knowledge and ideology. What was the second reason that brought you to study social representations during your age of innocence?

1.1 Social representations and attitudes

SM It is difficult to know how an idea is bred in one's mind. There is always a cross-fertilization of conjectures, interests and intentions, once you take hold of a good question. At that time I met Professor Jean Stoetzel, who was then the only professor of social psychology in France, in Bordeaux. He was also the director of the Institute for the Study of Public Opinion in Paris and the author of a classic book on the theory of opinions. I went to him because I had to learn survey methods and also because I was in need of money. I not only learned survey methods, especially scaling, but also some social psychology. As you know, until the Second World War social psychology was defined as the science of attitudes and public opinion. I read about them and came to the conclusion that such notions were too atomistic and superficial for my theoretical purpose. A social psychology of knowledge could not be built on such foundations; so much was clear. Help had to come from another source. At the same time I was fascinated by cybernetics for two reasons. It seemed to announce a new type of science, unifying different fields of knowledge and bringing together researchers from both the natural and the human sciences. Somehow it fitted my own idea of social psychology as a new science in itself. Moreover, it comprised an interesting blend of the mathematical theory of information with the 'socio-physical' theory of communication. I vividly remember a paper by Roman Jakobson on that topic by the time I had already begun my pilot study on the diffusion of psychoanalysis. Both information theory and communication theory brought me closer to the idea of representation. Although I had never followed a regular course of studies because I was excluded from the *lycée* in Romania for racial motives, I was always keen on mathematics and could understand it rather easily. Therefore I studied information theory and tried to apply it to the Guttman attitude scales, successfully, I think, at least in the eyes of Guttman himself.

Let me be a little more specific on this point. The originality of Guttman's scales lies in their dealing with the sampling of ideas, rather than the sampling of individuals. They suppose a universe of social items (objects, opinions, etc.), a small number of which is sampled in order to reveal, so to speak, the structure which holds them all together. This raises two questions. First: what is this universe socially and mentally? And secondly: what keeps the items of an attitude together and orders them on a scale, especially on a Guttman scale which represents a meaningful content and pattern?

My private answer was that the items were kept together and ordered by an underlying mental structure expressed by the redundancy of individual responses, a structure which they shared since, if they did not, there would not be a normal ordering of the items in the population. And the errors (or noise, as they are called in information theory) express the responses deviating from this normal mental structure. They are therefore purely individual mental patterns. The computations of information theory showed all this elegantly. This was fantastic because, at that time, I made the scales by hand, arranging subjects and ordering items. So I could see on the scalogram the items which were excluded and those which were kept as parts of this so-called mental structure. One could also *see* the contrast between the redundant and 'noisy' answers, between the social mental patterns and the individual ones. What I was measuring was somehow the degree of structuredness of this social mental structure. So at the beginning the social representation was a sort of visual idea which I then tried to understand, to give a meaning to it. In this context, to answer part of your question, attitudes appeared to me as a dimension of our shared representations.

Working on information theory and scaling, I had the privilege to be invited to a seminar organized by Claude Lévi-Strauss on these questions. In fact it was a unique seminar; among the participants were, if I remember exactly, Koyré, Lacan, Mandelbrot, Schützenberger and other researchers of high intellectual qualities. Of course I did not open my mouth but I kept my ears open. And one learns a good deal more when hearing people speak than when reading what they wrote. Be that as it may, in the course of this seminar and later, I attempted to learn more about communication theory. And I wondered how useful this theory is for a social psychology of knowledge. Several English authors, I do not remember which ones, said that communication is impossible when there are no preconceived possibilities or standardized or prefabricated representations. This was, however, the way the notion of representation entered into my vocabulary or my mind. In any case, I tried to formulate a theory of communications whose code was the normalized representation, and the attitude, knowledge or opinion items were the forms of messages. The only thing that embarrassed me in that theory was the fact that communication was conceived as a sort of exchange and reproduction of representations.

When I wonder today about what has crystallized this notion of representation in my mind, I think it was reading Merleau-Ponty. I also attended some of his courses when he taught child psychology at the Sorbonne. He wrote and perhaps talked a great deal about the primacy of perception. I thought that primacy of perception is justified in every non-social branch of psychology, or in a conception of common sense as pertaining to the senses, to sensorial knowledge, according to a great tradition of European philosophy. And indeed more recently many social psychologists have followed this tradition when using the term 'the social perceiver', which refers to people acquiring their common-sense knowledge on the basis of observation and experience. It seemed to me that we are concerned with symbols, social reality and knowledge, communicating about objects not as they are but as they ought to be, so what comes to the fore is a representation. In other words, I thought that a social psychology of knowledge implies *the primacy of representations*. This is what fixed this notion in my mind, how it was associated with certain ideas on the relationship between communication and knowledge, and the transformation of the content of knowledge. This content was given little importance, no more than today. But what can we say of thought or knowledge when we know nothing about its content? No more than we can say about language when we do not take meanings into account. Anyhow, I came to the conclusion that, just as one can consider a system of representations which forms scientific knowledge, one can also consider a system of representations which forms common-sense knowledge. As you know, I was brought up in Romania, a country where folk knowledge was predominant, indeed it was the only widespread kind of knowledge. Probably that 'feeling' played a part in my intellectual choices.

IM   It has been pointed out many times by critics of the traditional concept of attitude that the main problem is that the studies of attitudes were concerned with the individual expression of attitude rather than with an attitude as something that is socially or collectively shared. Would you agree with this diagnosis?

SM   I would not even say that. Social psychologists, in my opinion – and I think that I know the field well – wanted to study a kind of a substitute for behaviour, one could say a pre-behaviour, which would permit them to predict the behaviour. Most definitions of attitudes tell you that. There is also an underlying idea that if we can predict behaviour, we can also change it. To my mind, social psychologists studying attitudes are not really interested in people's knowledge and in their symbolic world. They are interested in how attitudes are structured and what we can find about structures by means of scales – actually, my first paper (Moscovici 1954), based on the use of Guttman's scale, was concerned with this issue.

IM   As you know, there has been a tremendous interest among social psychologists to pinpoint the difference between attitudes and social representations. In their acclaimed article, Jaspars and Fraser (1984) argued that while the most distinctive characteristic of social representations is that they are shared by many individuals, constituting their social reality, in contrast the concept of attitude has become individualised. A similar argument, further elaborated, has been put forward by Rob Farr. The basic idea of this argument is that while in the 1920s, in the work of Thomas and Znaniecki (1918–20) on the Polish peasant in America, the notion of attitudes was social and, therefore, very similar to the concept of social representations, subsequently attitudes were individualized in the sense that they were treated as an individual's response disposition.

It seems to me that what you have just said somehow changes the focus of the relationship between attitudes and social representations. In principle, presumably, you would not oppose the argument that attitudes were individualized. However, I understand you to be saying that to acquire an attitude towards an object means that you must have a representation, which is part of your cultural or folk knowledge as well as part of your cognition. Of course, one talks about cognition in a very broad sense, including images, emotions, passions, beliefs, and so on. Thus you bring into focus a basic ontological question concerning thought and an object. I understand that it is the answer to this ontological question that distinguishes traditional approaches to attitudes and the theory of social representations. While traditional approaches to the study of attitudes viewed an attitude and an object of attitude as two discrete entities, you view an attitude and a representation of the attitudinal object as being interdependent. Would you agree with such a formulation?

SM   I agree with it on the condition that we remind ourselves of a certain number of things. We are born into a large library in which we find all kinds of knowledge, of idioms, of norms and so on. None of us can theorize or talk about nature and reality – just as Adam, before he was thrown out of paradise, did not know anything about the difference between good and bad, true and false. If you like, our knowledge is an institution like other institutions. Our representations too are institutions we share and which exist before we are born into them; we form new representations from previous ones or against them. Attitudes do not express knowledge as such, but a relation of certainty and uncertainty, belief and disbelief, in relation to that knowledge. One also speaks about an attitude in relation to an object, a person, a group, and so on. However, concerning the social entities, these are the represented entities. The most salient of them are those representations that concern phenomena like money, markets, human rights, France, God, and so on. Thus I do not know how one can choose between the two notions, namely attitudes or social representations. I have arrived at your basic ontological concern. When one talks about the relation between thought and an object, an attitude (or cognition) and an object, one is concerned with a binary relation, with an opposition between subjectivity and objectivity. However, the metaphor of the library suggests a triadic relation between social representation, individual representation and the so-called object which is often the ontological expression of a social representation. Think of a credit card. You go and buy a suitcase, you hand your credit card to the sales assistant who puts it into the slot of a special apparatus which registers the sale. Apparently the transaction is between two persons, one of whom is on the side of the object. In truth there is a third partner, the bank, the institution that issued the card and establishes the balance between debit and credit. Likewise social representations always make this third partner intervene in the relationship to the other or the object. Frankly, I do not know why the concept of attitude is opposed to that of social representation, since it is one of its dimensions. Neither do I understand how one can replace one concept by the other when one proposes to study the genesis of common sense.

IM   I would like to give an example in order to elaborate on this issue. What you have said about the study of attitudes in social psychology applies in general also to the study of thinking, problem-solving, concepts and concept formation. These issues too have been based on the ontological assumption that the object of the study and the self are independent. This has had important epistemological consequences for theories of the formation of concepts, the solution of syllogisms and anagrams, the acquisition of word meanings and so on. My own criticism of such a position goes back nearly twenty years, but to make the point clear I shall refer to a more recent example in the area of health education with respect to AIDS. The campaign in the UK in the eighties ran under the title 'don't die of ignorance.' It was assumed in that campaign that the individual, in order to protect him- or herself from HIV/

AIDS, had to acquire an expert knowledge. What was totally ignored was that there was already folk knowledge in existence, that there were representations of HIV/AIDS which were part of culture and which therefore were already part of the individual's mind; that this folk knowledge and these representations were anchored in sin, sexually acquired diseases, dirt, and many other undersirable phenomena. These representations had a much stronger influence on people's activities than a neutral and objective knowledge about viruses, anti-viruses, infected needles and condoms given to them through health campaigns. The representations of HIV/AIDS were threatening to the self: doing something that might be a preventive action with respect to acquiring or passing on HIV could, at the same time, serve as a proof to others that the individual, in fact, might already have been infected. This, in turn, might lead to the rejection of that individual by others. In general, what those campaigns should have done was to take seriously the folk and social representational knowledge, their linguistic expression, and the individual's reasoning. Do you have a different view on this issue?

SM   No, I don't have a different view. When the epidemics of AIDS began among groups of homosexuals, I was in the United States. I remember that the social representation and language were elaborated around the denomination of 'gay cancer'. This permitted the groups in question to talk, to share their knowledge, to familiarize themselves with this 'strange' disease and to act collectively. The medical research was triggered by this folk knowledge and language. And the choice of a 'scientific' name involved negotiations between different groups. They chose a 'neutral' acronym without any reference to homosexuals, so as to avoid spreading existing prejudices. This acronym transformed itself into a proper name and became the symbol of a new social representation, developed in the course of communication which mixed scientific and popular knowledge. In the seminars I gave later at the New School, my students and I discovered that the elements of the new and the previous social representations overlapped.

1.2   Social representations and the social psychological theory of knowledge

IM   Therefore, if I understand you correctly, in order to develop a social psychology of knowledge, one needs to start with questions concerning folk knowledge and cultural knowledge of which social representations are part and through which they develop. One studies their genesis through conversation, propaganda, media and other language-based means of communication. Representations are embedded in the meanings of words and thus recycled and perpetuated through public discourse. And, of course, you mentioned earlier that culture plays an important role in the formation of social representations.

SM   When I talked to you about ideology and science, you remember that I located common sense as a third genre of knowledge, different from the other two. It cannot be reduced to ideology as some people wanted to do. This is why, when studying common sense, folk knowledge, we are studying something that links society or individuals to their culture, their language, their familiar world. It will perhaps make you laugh, yet for me that autonomy of common sense as a third genre of knowledge, so to speak the need for common sense, was proven in the Russian dissidents' fight for *glasnost*, for the right to express what everyone could see and know, for ordinary language, in short, for common sense in a society that proclaimed itself ideological and scientific. *Glasnost*, indeed, was one of the reforms which allowed civil society to come into existence with numerous groups and movements. Our dialogue is discontinuous, as every dialogue must be. In my age of innocence, I had one concern: every science has an 'object', a 'phenomenon', a 'stuff' that is proper to it and that it studies throughout its history. What about social psychology? I thought that common sense was the 'phenomenon' or 'stuff' of social psychology, just as myth is that of anthropology, dreams that of psychoanalysis, or the market the stuff of economics. And students understood what I meant when I told them that we have so many folk sciences, folk psychology, folk physics, folk medicine, folk magic and so on, all of which offer wonderful materials for a rich exploration of our culture, our ways of thinking and speaking, our modes of relating and behaving in groups. Nothing but the study of this kind of material can be the source of more general and complex theories which could explain the structure and genesis of our knowing and acting in common. They could be of interest for other human sciences too, such as sociology, economics or history. You see that what I had in mind was a social psychology of knowledge as the core of our science.

1.3   Scientific and common-sense knowledge

IM   You have said earlier that Marxists didn't think that the diffusion of scientific knowledge would increase the level of public knowledge and that, moreover, linking common sense to irrationality was a view shared by some other social scientists. In contrast, your aim was to rehabilitate common thinking and common knowledge and you assumed that common knowledge is something quite modern, something that comes from science.

I would like to make several associations. The first one concerns scientific knowledge and common sense. Some time ago you made a distinction between two universes: reified and consensual. Scientific knowledge belongs to the reified universe while common-sense knowledge belongs to the consensual universe. These two kinds of universe differ from one another in the sense that the former tries to establish explanations of the world that are impartial and independent of people while the latter thrives on negotiation and mutual acceptance. However, equally important, they differ with respect to the kind of thinking and methods of reasoning. The former proceeds systematically, from premise to conclusion, and it relies on what it considers to be pure facts. The method of the latter is not so systematic; it relies on collective memory, on consensus. Yet what should be emphasized is that both ways of thinking are based on reason. Common-sense thinking is reasonable, rational and sensible – to use the terms of Alfred Schütz. Even better, to quote from your recent paper, 'all representations are rational, even if, to paraphrase Orwell, some appear more rational than others' (Moscovici 1998, p. 416, see also chapter 6, p. 212). You yourself wanted to rehabilitate common sense because you were convinced that Marxists and others were wrong when they thought that common thinking is irrational.

However, I wanted to make this particular point here because, despite what you have repeatedly said, I think that the point concerning the rational nature of social representations is sometimes misunderstood even by the students of social representations. It is easy to take a short cut and to say that science is rational because it relies on reason and, because social representations rely on consensus, they are based on irrational thinking. In other words, it is easy to take 'reasoning' as having only one meaning. This is another reason why I think that it is important to emphasize the polyphasic nature of knowledge and of reasoning. Reasoning in common thinking and in common sense on the one hand, and in scientific thinking and scientific knowledge on the other, show this polyphasic nature.

In my view, the claim concerning the 'reasonable' nature of common sense is a major difference between the point of view of social representations and between, say, Lewis Wolpert's views in *The Unnatural Nature of Science* (1992) which Rob Farr discusses in his article on 'Common sense, science and social representations' (Farr 1993).

But let us continue with the question concerning science and common sense. In contrast to Marxists and to Wolpert, there are social scientists who take – or took – common sense knowledge more seriously and, in fact, they saw a direct path from common sense to science. You wrote about the path from science to common sense in your paper on 'The phenomenon of social representations (Moscovici 1984a; see chapter 1). You said there something like this: formerly, science was based on common sense and it made common sense less common. In contrast, today common sense is science made common. This is a provocative formulation and therefore we should stay with it for a moment. There are – or at least there were – social scientists who subscribed to the former part of the claim, that is, from common sense to science. Folk knowledge, cultural knowledge and common sense and their relationship to scientific knowledge have been studied quite extensively by anthropologists, sociologists and, to some extent, by social psychologists. One can think of people like Schütz, Heider, Gadamer, Garfinkel and Bartlett.

For example, Schütz, in his phenomenological writings, draws a distinction between common-sense and scientific knowledge. Referring to Whitehead, he points out that science has two aims: first, to produce a theory that agrees with experience and second, to explain the common-sense concepts of nature. Explanation consists in the preservation of these common-sense concepts in a scientific theory.

For Schütz, common-sense knowledge relies on the stock of knowledge that is socially derived and approved. It starts from a presupposition of the reciprocity of perspectives. In contrast, science starts from a corpus of evidence, from the rules of procedures, scientific methods, etc. Heider's position with respect to common sense I see as being very similar to that of Schütz. He too claims that common-sense knowledge must be taken seriously and that it is a basis of scientific knowledge. He refers to Whitehead for the same reason as Schütz does. For Schütz, common-sense and scientific thinking are two parallel ways of dealing with social reality. They both correspond to experience, in particular to physical observation. Schütz considers common sense as something – and you yourself already commented on this earlier – that is often assumed to come from senses, from sensorial knowledge. The road from common sense to science is, strictly speaking, rational. Schütz always referred to the rationality of action and basically, what he meant was a correspondence between sense perception, observation, etc. on the one hand, and reality on the other. Similarly, Whitehead referred to physics, to physical observation – as did Heider when he talked about common sense.

Thus both positions have their advocates, one viewing scientific knowledge as a continuation of common sense, and the other viewing common sense and scientific knowledge as totally separate and opposing one another. We should therefore clarify the similarities and differences between these two positions and your own. For me, this question is interesting not only for historical reasons but, above all, conceptually.

SM   To answer your comments on science and common sense, I would be obliged to write a whole book. You ask me to define myself with relation to other authors and other theories. Before doing this, I have to tell you what I am thinking myself, how certain ideas were born and came into place, since most of my work has been along solitary lines. I was not much concerned with knowing what other people thought, as I had enough trouble already to know what my own thoughts were. Therefore, to resume the thread of my life-story, it seemed to me that I had made a great step forward, that I knew what the field of social psychology was when I supposed that its 'stuff' was common sense. I experienced this step forward as an intellectual discovery and a practical inspiration, because there is something poetical about folk knowledge just as there is about dreams and myths.

At the same time as I worked enthusiastically on what was going to be the theory of social representations, I attended a seminar on the history and philosophy of science under the guidance of Professor Alexandre Koyré. As you know, the first time I went to the United States, it was not as a social psychologist but as a historian of science. I had a fellowship at the Institute for Advanced Studies in Princeton. I gave my first lectures in English at Yale and Harvard on topics related to the scientific revolution and met Thomas Kuhn who, in a way, had been a disciple of Koyré. Koyré was a superb master and his seminars about Galileo, Kepler, etc. were magnificent. In any case they allowed me to get a deeper insight into the notions of common sense, to see how and why common sense can be coherent, and have its own logic while differing from science.

From the historical viewpoint, Aristotelian physics is a physics of common sense. It was elaborated by systematizing some current ideas, and is grounded on sensorial qualities – the famous secondary qualities – of objects, on the direct observation of phenomena, and on a teleological explanation, on final causes. It is, however, neither incoherent nor illogical, nor is it a welter of errors as people thought before Duhem or Koyré showed the opposite. Galilean or Cartesian science is different, because it eliminates the sensorial properties of objects, introduces the experimental method in the study of phenomena, and therefore formalizes theoretical reasoning. At the same time it substitutes an explanation by efficient causes for the explanation by final causes. All of this is well known, yet must perhaps be recalled, because it was the reason why common sense appeared to me as a form of systematic, coherent knowledge. It also led me, on Claude Faucheux's recommendation, to read Kurt Lewin's wonderful article about the passage from Aristotelian to Galilean science which he wanted to undertake in social psychology. This is an article that every student ought to read even today. Be that as it may, it was during those seminars about the history of science that the specificity of common sense in relation to science took a more precise shape in my mind, at the same time as I became convinced of their respective value and coherence. I also want to insist on another difference that seems important to me. By contrast with scientific thought, which in the ideal can be understood independently from its content in a formal, mathematical-logical manner, spontaneous or everyday thought cannot be split up into two; the content inflects the reasoning, making it plausible, and but for it, the form would appear incomprehensible, nonsensical. In other words, the structure and dynamics of thought cannot be grasped when you start only from cognitive processes, since they cannot be divided from what is, so to speak, the substance of the actual knowledge. By working on the philosophy and history of science, I acquired a richer and a more 'realistic' view of what the life of knowledge is. Kepler is certainly the first to have stated the mathematical law of the motion of planets, but he also thought that these planets were moved by animated forces. Newtonian action at a distance is no doubt familiar and fundamental from the scientific viewpoint. Yet people have had some difficulty in accepting it – how can a body act where it is not? – since it always rests on a magical representation of force.

Let us go further. If there is a system of knowledge, one has to put the question: who is the knowing subject, how are we to imagine him in his current practice? For example, in recent social psychology he has been viewed as a lay scientist or a novice with regard to a sophisticated scientist or an expert. When I began my research in the fifties, I envisaged an opposition between the professional researcher and the dilettante, the scientist and the amateur philosopher, the former asking himself precise questions about phenomena, while the latter asks himself general questions even about particular phenomena. Instead of systematizing, the amateur files the items of knowledge and information he collects in his mental archives. So he draws heteroclite elements from science and invests them in a significant whole which has practical value for him. In common sense 'realistic' and materialistic elements from the immediate context predominate. It includes speculative, metaphysical interrogations, such as 'Where do we come from? What are we? Where are we going to? What is the origin of the universe or of man?' and so on. I chose Bouvard and Pécuchet, Gustave Flaubert's famous heroes, who are involved in a practical and theoretical jaunt through agriculture, history, chemistry, archaeology, medicine, as prototypes of the subject of common sense. Like every one of us, they move across fields of science, as travellers in time and knowledge, pigeon-holing notions and experiments, trying to reconstruct a global vision. They rebuild an ordinary world based on *idées reçues*, not on *idées fausses* inspired by scientific ideas. In his unfinished novel Flaubert gives us a view of popular science as the nineteenth century spread it, full of enthusiasm and boring clichés. James Joyce took some inspiration from it: in a sense Bloom is Bouvard and Pécuchet's heir in our century.

Last, I cautiously suggested the hypothesis of cognitive polyphasia. Basically I thought that, just as language is polysemous, so knowledge is polyphasic. This means in the first place that people are able in fact to use different modes of thinking and different representations according to the particular group they belong to, the context in which they are at the moment, etc. No further investigation is necessary in order to perceive that even professional scientists are not entirely engrossed in scientific thought. Many of them have a religious creed, some are racists, others consult their 'stars', have a fetish, damn their experimental apparatus when it refuses to work, which is not necessarily quite rational. And just as some studies have shown, when asked to explain some ordinary physical phenomena, they even make use of Aristotelian physics instead of the Galilean physics they learnt at school and which they trust. If these various, even conflicting forms of thought did not coexist in their minds, they would not be human minds, I suppose.

What matters now are not these sweeping observations but the twofold meaning of my hypothesis. First, individuals are not monophasic, capable of only one privileged manner of thinking, with other ways being accessory, pernicious, even useless survivals of earlier ones. Second, in our psychological theory, we suppose, as did Auguste Comte, that eventually one single form of thought, that is, science, will prevail and the rest will die out. Such is the law of progress and of rationalization. Now there is no reason why, in the future, only one form of 'true' thinking should predominate, *logos* being definitely substituted for *mythos*, since, in every known culture, several forms of thinking coexist. In short, cognitive polyphasia, the diversity of forms of thought, is the rule, not the exception. To be sure, you can observe partial and temporal hierarchies. Yet it would be a risky generalization, in which science ought not to indulge, to grant an exclusive privilege to such or such a genre of knowledge or form of thought which would be proclaimed the first and last. Starting from this hypothesis, we can put the genuine social-psychological questions of the transformations of the systems of knowledge, of the forms of thought or discourses within the social context. Hence we can understand how it is possible that, not only in different societies, but also within the same individuals, there coexist incompatible ways of thinking and representations. Of course, this is at present too general a hypothesis and also one which it is difficult to admit. And yet I do not think that one could question either its factual relevance or its social relevance in our post-modern time. At least for me it was a helpful intuition. Here again common sense appears as the privileged place in which such questions can be put and, as the case may be, answers could be obtained.

I apologize for speaking at such length, but otherwise I could hardly justify what is going to follow, the clarification of rationality you are expecting. You are putting me in a delicate position. The progress of the human sciences has divided them from philosophy and propelled researchers into the pigeon-holes of specialized disciplines. The more people advanced in their knowledge, the more they lost sight of the whole of phenomena and of themselves. In my youth, to say of a researcher that he was a philosopher or was interested in philosophy was almost to insult him. Now it is the other way around, a researcher has to be a philosopher, to call upon philosophy as an authority. Yet I think it would be naïve not to see that to penetrate into the world of philosophers requires some initiation and a particular discipline. Otherwise one risks being in one's turn a sort of Bouvard or Pécuchet wandering from one philosopher to another, gleaning here and there a key-word or metaphor without really grasping their deep meaning. This is why, when expressing some philosophical opinions, I only do so with the smile of one who entertains no illusions about what he knows or does not know.

This is to say that the way in which I conceive common sense comes mainly from such philosophers of science as Meyerson, Frank, Mach, Peirce, Duhem, Bachelard and others with whose work I became familiar when working in this field. I did not read Heider until I was at Princeton in 1962. I very much liked his book as a literary work rather than a book on social psychology – this shows how ignorant I was. Likewise, I did not read Schütz until I was a professor at the New School in the eighties. His view of common sense as a kind of direct and sensual knowledge *à la* Mach was not my view, though his approach was really subtle and rich. I gave several courses integrating his analysis of the life-world. Yet the spirit of phenomenology did not capture me. Of course I read Husserl's *Krisis* for nostalgic reasons. It was difficult for me to accept his idea that the roots of the crisis of modern times are to be found with Galileo and Descartes. Or that its solution lies in the rediscovery of the concrete world of life, the *Lebenswelt*, as he said. It is a fine, almost magic phrase, yet it does not suffice to indicate the place where people can find shelter from the forces of technology, politics or history, especially given that he wrote it in 1935, on the eve of the triumph of fascism.

Be that as it may, when reading Schütz I did not become a fanatic of such notions as taken-for-granted, typicality, etc. They presuppose an orderliness and predictability of human affairs, a solidity of the life-world in which I do not believe. Our intersubjective relations and personal decisions are rather unpredictable and improvised. As Napoleon said: 'One improvises and then one sees.' Life-worlds just as any other worlds are sequences of more or less regular events, surprises and routines in the midst of which people manage to live together. This is social magic. On the other hand, all that Schütz wrote on anonymity, on the distribution of knowledge, on themata, 'unfroze' many ideas which I had before. Consider, for example, anonymity. It is first a loss of name, meaning that what originally was an individual's possession has become a common possession. Many people talk about and use notions pertaining to Darwinian theory or psychoanalysis, without even knowing the names Darwinism or psychoanalysis, Darwin or Freud. Secondly, anonymity is itself a name. It categorizes a kind of person or knowledge in opposition to a particular person or knowledge which has a name. Common sense is categorized as an anonymous kind of knowledge in opposition to science or philosophy, which are considered non-anonymous. These are very important categories of our culture, since that which has a name is considered lasting, memorable, of great worth, whereas that which has no name is ephemeral, transient, perishable. There is no doubt that passion for the name is one of the strongest of all passions, on which there are admirable pages in Plato's *Symposium*.

Returning to phenomenology – don't you find it too static? In any case, what I tried to elucidate at that time was the genesis of common sense, the transformation of forms of thought. While in my research on the history of science I studied with Koyré the transformation of Aristotelian common-sense physics into Galilean scientific mechanics, in my research on psycho-analysis I was concerned with the converse transformation. Whenever I talked about social representations later, I focused on their genesis, on representations in the making, not as something already made. I would even add that it is essential for us to study them in the making from the viewpoint of their history and development. It goes without saying that the comments of our consciousness and representations are elaborated during our communications. The 'passion for knowing', which Husserl wrote about, and the passion for communicating go hand in hand. This is why I wrote that 'we think with our mouths,' stressing the particular role of conversation in the genesis and sharing of our common representations.

I am aware that I owe you an answer about the rationality or irrationality of common sense. In fact one can ask this question in the wake of all the research on cognitive biases. What made psychologists take an interest in common sense was Heider's work, which opened up a field of research on the thought of laymen and people in ordinary life. In the introduction to his book Heider (1958) reminds the reader that he should not ask questions about the truth and falsity of common-sense notions. This has been overlooked, so that social psychologists began asking themselves, not how and why people think correctly in their familiar contexts, but how and why they think incorrectly. Thus in the eighties we experienced this remarkable though curious episode during which ordinary men were shown to make fundamental attribution errors, to be deficient data-gatherers, to overlook base-rate information, to have limited deductive reasoning skills, and so on. To all appearances this proved our irrationality in everyday life on the one hand, and on the other hand the uselessness of studying common sense, which disappeared from the horizon of research. By the same token, the reasons why behaviourists said that one should not be concerned with the mind were confirmed, as were the arguments of philosophers who asserted that common sense has to be banished from the study of thought, in short, that man has no mind, just a brain. I call this episode curious because it reproduces, except on the point of methods, Frazer's conception of primitive thought and primitives dubbed novices as intuitive and deficient scientists. By this I mean a revival of the individualistic psychology of English anthropologists, their downgrading of popular thinking and the thinking of other cultures. It was Lévy-Bruhl who showed the flaws of Tylor's and Frazer's conceptions and revealed the coherence and uniqueness of the so-called primitive mentality and common ways of thinking. If, as he argued, people are not deficient scientists, they are good mystics or everyday philosophers. It is on the soil of Lévy-Bruhl's work that the developmental psychology of Vygotsky and Piaget has grown. This is an exceptional episode because criticisms were few and seldom went to the root of the matter.

Now, are we really to consider a bias as a deviation of thought, an index of error, a lack of logic? The great linguist Emile Benveniste has pointed out that in the study of grammatical or lexical significations, you must avoid using polar notions of regularity or deviation in a strong sense. Those who do generally obliterate the hierarchic structure of language and bury it in the notion of deviation. A secondary element, however, is one thing, whereas a deviant element is quite another thing. Let us take, for example, the fundamental attribution error, whose main element nevertheless rests on the possibility of thinking that there must be a link between an effect and its cause. This error consists, as everybody knows, in attributing the cause of some behaviour or event to a person instead of attributing it to the situation. The layman commits this error while the expert avoids it, thereby supplying a correct answer. But where is the difference between the former and the latter? Does the layman ignore the category of causality? Is he incapable of causal reasoning, while the expert, knowing that category, is therefore capable of causal reasoning?

This is obviously not the case. Both are capable of making attributions, of giving causal explanations. So the only difference lies in the fact that one prefers personal explanations while the other prefers situational explanations for motives which have not been made clear. Therefore they do not apply the category of causality in the same way; and there is no more of an error in reasoning here than there is when you compare Ptolemaic astronomy with Copernican astronomy, since each of them is grounded on a distinct hypothesis about the motion of planets. Yet I do not want to insist on the obvious fact that the question of rationality cannot be reduced to a matter of process and logic without taking into account the content and finality of common thought. Nobody takes the conspiracy mentality as a summit of science or reason. But taking into account its amplitude, frequency and importance in social life, it would be ridiculous to explain it just as a bias or a default of logic, since it condenses a whole vision of man and the world. To enumerate its irrationalities is one thing, to understand what people do with it is quite a different matter. Much writing on the history of the arts shows the creative feats which painters have achieved because we are subject to perceptual illusions or what novelists have achieved because of our cognitive illusions. Only within the context of historical and cultural reality can the relations of reason and unreason be fully assessed and understood.

The hypothesis of cognitive polyphasia assumes that our tendency to employ diverse and even opposite ways of thinking – such as scientific and religious, metaphorical and logical, and so on – is a normal state of affairs in ordinary life and in communication. Consequently, the logical or cognitive unity of our mental life, which is taken for granted by most psychologists, is a desideratum, not a fact. We can assume that there are three elements – context, norms and goals – regulating the choice we make of one form of thinking in preference to another one. And perhaps we qualify it as rational. To begin with, it is obvious that some particular information can be identified and dealt with only within a context. For example, an event has not only one cause but an indefinite number of causes, which depend on the multiplicity of other events articulating this context and also on the representation we have of it. Think of Newton's famous apple. The fall of an apple, as a single fruit, may well have as its cause the weight, the maturation of the fruit, which depends on the sunshine reaching the orchard, the variety of apple, but also on atmospheric circumstances, a strong wind blowing on that day. Given his mechanical representation, Newton looks at the falling apple within a context from which he excludes the maturation of the fruit, the wind, etc. in the causal chain so as to retain only the direction of the movement and the weight of the fruit. Therefore the way we deal with any information and the rationality of our dealing with it is a question of context and representation prescribing what counts as a cause or as an effect.

Norms define what is considered rational thinking and knowledge in Western culture. Since the Greeks, the ruling norm has been the principle of non-contradiction which has become, as it were, a categorical imperative. It is both a juridical and a rhetorical imperative, telling you that you must not contradict yourself. By transgressing it, you qualify as irrational. Primitive thinking was defined in the nineteenth century on the basis of the supposition that it transgresses the principle of non-contradiction or the laws of association. Towards the middle of the last century another norm came into existence: the principle of probability. The transgression of this principle has since been considered as a sign of bias and irrationality, although Einstein himself doubted this, saying 'God does not play dice.'

The goals of cognitive activity can be manifold, ranging from a search for truth, persuasion and exerting power, to seduction and the enjoyment of life. Hence knowing takes on a different shape according to the specific aim it strives to achieve. It could be a scientific aim if one wants to verify or falsify a bold idea, or an ideological one when one tries to convince and exert power. It could also be a 'folk' aim, to enjoy thinking and talking, or to achieve spontaneously a given task. It is obvious that a person or a group cannot reach all these different and opposite aims through the same cognitive unity. Many comical effects arise when a person uses an inadequate form of thinking or talking. For example, a scientist trying to seduce someone by scientific reasoning and rhetoric is as ridiculous as Don Quixote addressing a peasant woman as if she were a lady. To penetrate the rationality of people's thinking or of common sense is no easy task. Think of the question of method. When studying scientific thought you analyse the production, theories and experiments of researchers, and their writings. Or you observe how they work in labs, and so on. No one has ever suggested that scientific knowledge should be studied by choosing a sample of Nobel laureates and asking them to solve a few problems involving syllogisms or statistical inferences, but this is what psychologists do when they study common-sense thinking and common knowledge. Instead, psychologists should study common-sense knowledge from its products embodied in texts, language, folklore or even literature. This is what Heider did. If you contrast his way of studying folk psychology with the way that came to predominate later in experimental social psychology using so-called novices, I hope you will grasp what I am trying to say. In my opinion, most of these experiments do not concern common-sense thinking. This does not mean that they are not interesting for the study of information-processing. If you project this on to an entire population which contains no more than 5 or 10 per cent of experts, then you can draw for yourself the conclusion about the social scope of such results.

Let us never forget that we acquired the imprint of common-sense knowledge in early childhood when we began to relate, communicate and speak. Most people talk quite correctly in their mother tongue, even if they did not have any schooling. Common-sense knowledge therefore cannot be so biased and wrong as has sometimes been assumed. It serves its purposes in daily life well, and has even enchanted and made life worthwhile for centuries, as it served me, during my childhood in the countryside in a folk culture, marvellous, poetic, despite the hardness and the poverty in most households. I think of a painting by Chagall, *Village et violoniste*; it may give you a picture of the small town in which I grew up.

IM   I think the point you have made about common sense and biases can be made not only about social psychology but also about the psychology of thinking in a more general sense. When I came to the UK in 1967, I was astonished to find out that psychologists there did not study thinking as a social process, as was the case in the Marxist psychology to which I was used in Czechoslovakia. I have in mind people like Rubinstein, Vygotsky, Leontiev and so on. Instead, thinking and problem-solving were investigated as information-processing and as a process in which the focus was on logical errors or biases. You presented people with syllogisms or logical tasks based on propositional calculus and you were interested in the question as to what kinds of mistake they would make. It was assumed that there was only one way of correctly encoding such logical tasks. As a result, the subject's 'errors' were attributed to the content of the task, subjects' motivation, mental set and various other factors. I wrote about this quite extensively in *Paradigms, Thought and Language* (Marková 1982). In fact, it was largely the reason why, rather than continuing in the UK as a cognitive psychologist – that was my 'label' in Czechoslovakia – I wanted to become a social psychologist, to study thinking and language from the social point of view.

Continuing with the same issue, I would like to ask you about your views of Bartlett, to whom you refer relatively often in your work. What role would you say he played in the development of your ideas on social representations?

SM   I liked the work of Frederick Bartlett, whom I met when I went to the International Congress of Psychology in Brussels in the fifties. He was very funnily dressed but a very nice gentleman, and I was on a panel on scaling with Louis Guttman, in which I gave a paper. Bartlett was a very reserved man, yet I had a pleasant conversation with him. He was more 'social' with respect to thinking than many social psychologists today. During our conversation he made a remark about Lévy-Bruhl, saying that it was wrong to compare the primitive man with Kant. Later I found out that he had already made this remark in the twenties in his book on primitive culture (cf. Bartlett, 1923, p. 284). But this comment impressed me because I thought that it was in line with my own scientific method. This encounter prompted me to read his book *Remembering* (Bartlett, 1932). At that time I was working on the theory of social representations. And his analysis of conventionalization helped me to grasp the process of objectification more clearly.

IM   This brings me to an even more fundamental issue which concerns ontological assumptions on the one hand and their epistemological elaboration on the other. I would like to claim that phenomenology, the theory of social representations, and some other social scientific approaches such as Bakhtinian dialogism, Vygotskian socio-cultural theory of mind, Valsiner's co-constructivism, Nelson's theory of cognitive development, the Prague School of structuralism, all share some basic ontological assumptions about reality. These assumptions include, for example, the interdependence of culture and the individual mind; their co-development; the interdependence between thought/thinking and language/speaking. Ontological assumptions are the basis of our reasoning and often they are implicit, non-verbalized – or even difficult to verbalize. However, they sharply distinguish these approaches from those that are based on discrete entities, isolated processes, information processing, cause–effect relations. In other words, these ontological assumptions specify the differences between the dialectic/dialogical paradigm on the one hand, and the Platonic/Cartesian paradigm on the other. Moreover, they also distinguish them from aproaches such as post-modernism and constructionism and, in particular, from the 'dark' forms of constructionism, to use Danziger's (1997) term.

1.4   Social representations, Piaget and Vygotsky

IM   What differentiates between the particular approaches in the dialectic/ dialogical paradigm is the epistemological elaboration of some basic issues, the focus they place on particular questions and the foregrounding of specific phenomena. Thus what I said earlier about the differences between the theory of social representations and phenomenology concerned their epistemological differences, while the underlying ontological assumptions presumably remained the same. One could do a similar analysis with respect to social representations and other approaches within the same paradigm. This brings me to another influence in the origin of your ideas of social representations, which is also discussed in your paper on Piaget and Vygotsky (cf. chapter 6). You make it quite clear that Piaget always played a significant role in your intellectual life. Could you say something about this?

SM   If I turn round to cast a glance at the path leading to the theory of social representations, it appears to me strangely short, yet more complex than I thought when our conversation began. I have told you how and why my work on Guttman's scale and my interest in cybernetics and communication fixed in my mind the notion of representation. Of course, at the time it was imprecise and merely intuitive. Then I concentrated for some time on the question of the 'stuff' of social psychology and the discovery that this 'stuff' is common sense. And I saw social psychology as a genetic or developmental science, as the genesis of common sense, of modern common sense, that is to say, I saw it as the transformation of scientific knowledge into common-sense knowledge. And this was related to all these epistemological issues we have been talking about. Then came the difficult question: what idea, what concept would be fruitful in order to study common sense? When I say I was looking for an idea or concept, I do not mean a notion which could be used just by sticking the label 'social' to it, as when one says social cognition, social attitude, social construction in opposition to individual cognition, individual attitude or individual construction. I mean an idea or concept which has a theoretical meaning based on a demonstration that knowledge or thinking is necessarily social, just as in physics you demonstrate that matter has to be necessarily atomic. For all I know, such concepts or ideas are very rare in our field. This is not without consequence for the value of theories.

Here comes Piaget. Not only did he write on child psychology, he also wrote a great deal on the history and epistemology of science, and even on the relations between logic and society. In reading Piaget, it occurred to me that he studied the common sense of children just as I was trying to study the common sense of adults. This was the first link. Then I discovered that his method of studying children by means of observations and focused interviews could serve me as well. That was the second link. Becoming involved in his work, I began to investigate his theoretical systems, the meaning of the concepts he used, his logic, if you like. And here I found representation once again, this time not just as a notion but as a theoretical idea. And that literally changed my way of thinking. As you know, in European culture, and when we study psychology, we grasp thinking with the help of two distinctions, the man/animal distinction, and the man/machine distinction. From that point on, I grasped thinking by a third distinction, the society/individual distinction, which became for me the basic one. So it came about that, having discovered it in Piaget, I wondered if the idea of social or collective representation could not be made the heart of the theory I sought. This kept me busy for two or three years.

Retrospectively, I found some merit in following Piaget's ideas at that particular time. I was not only a young researcher in an untested situation but also a stranger. However, when Piaget arrived in Paris in 1953–4 (which was when I was asking myself all these questions) as a successor to Merleau-Ponty's chair in child psychology, the least one can say is that he did not have many admirers. Merleau-Ponty did not say very nice things about his ideas and influential people such as Fraisse or Zazzo, who was a student of Wallon, had little sympathy for Piaget's ideas. Thus in a certain way he was isolated. Perhaps this was what incited me to read more of his work. In addition, he made a strong impression on me when I used to see him in the Café Balzar.

IM   But you had already referred to Durkheim in *La Psychanalyse*. Are you saying that was not very important for the theory of social representations?

SM   I will not say that Durkheim was not very important, but I read very little apart from his paper on individual and collective representations. At that time his work and that of his school were not so popular as they are today. Lévy-Bruhl was quite ostracized and still is. *La Pensée sauvage*, Lévi-Strauss's ([1962]/1966) book, was directed against him. So I started reading seriously the work of the fathers of those ideas, Durkheim and Lévy-Bruhl, in the eighties, when I wrote *The Invention of Society* and understood what they were after. After all, Piaget took his concepts and many theoretical views, for example, on symbolic thinking and moral judgement, from Durkheim. In a way, I took up Durkheim's and Lévy-Bruhl's heritage without being aware of it. It is like a stranger who arrives in a country, learns its language, adopts its customs and unconsciously absorbs its history, its traditional character – all of which he may become conscious of only much later. I am a Frenchman, *n'est-ce pas*? Piaget meant to me something else in addition. As I said before, in my age of innocence I did not have a concrete vision of what social psychology is or should be. At the beginning of my studies I worked as a research assistant in experimental psychology. And some researchers told me that social psychology was a branch of experimental psychology, which I did not believe and which did not fit my aspirations. I stopped working as a research assistant and found a job as a tutor in a family. This left me some time to think about what the alternative might be. And as I became somewhat familiar with Piaget's child psychology, I had the impression of discovering what social psychology might be. This meant: social psychology is not a science of isolated functions – motivation, perception – but a science of whole individuals or groups in the continuity of child psychology. It is a science of development, change, not of reactions to fixed environments. I do not know if I can find the right words to convey to you this vision which took hold of me over forty years ago. I am not sure that even today I have another one which I would like more.

1.5 Social representations and beliefs

IM You describe vividly in the *Chronique des années égarées* your first acquaintance with Pascal's *Pensées* when you were about 18 years old. You describe the beginnings of your interest in the ideas which have preoccupied you ever since then (Moscovici, 1997, p. 286). I was very interested in that passage in the *Chronique des années égarées*, not only because it is beautifully and poetically written but also because you express there deep social psychological insights which clearly link up with social representations. First, you spell out explicitly that reading the *Pensées* marked the origin of your interest in social psychology. In particular, reading Pascal's claim 'believing is important' and his argument underlying this claim made you realize that one cannot know or act or create without believing. As you say, it is belief which fires ideas and words. Basically, you distinguished between two main 'impulses', religious and artistic. The former separates human beings from gods, the latter involves them in work, matter, technology, medicine and in social practices. Yet, instead of opening itself to science, what modernity has achieved with the secularization of religion is to prepare an era of new myths. Nazism amalgamated religion, poetry, folklore into new myths and, moreover, they made sciences, such as biology and medicine, part of their new myths. I would like to quote here from the *Chronique des années égarées* (pp. 288–9):

> I believe that I remember one of my points of departure. Science is a modern form of the artistic 'impulse'. It is a kind of art if one thinks about the amazing inventiveness in mathematics and in physics, about the extraordinary nature of their ideas of the universe and their material discoveries. Another point of departure is that science was contaminated by religion. Instead of including human beings in nature, it claims their exclusion. This is one of its illusions, one of its dangers. To put it simply, instead of affirming itself as *an ars vivendi*, it allowed itself to be assimilated to an *ars moriendi*.

In this passage one can clearly see a link between your ideas in the history and philosophy of science expressed in *Essai sur l'histoire humaine de la nature* (Moscovici [1968]/1977) and your ideas on knowledge and faith as you developed them in *La Psychanalyse*.

SM   It is a topic that has always preoccupied me, yet I do not know how to talk about it as a social psychologist. Knowledge and belief are paired opposite concepts like reason and faith. They can have the same content and yet different qualities. Think of a very popular idea that is in a way the principle of modernity: *there is human progress*. In one context, it can be considered as a matter of knowledge. Great thinkers have attempted to verify or falsify it, to establish its domain of validity by saying, for example, that there is progress in science but not in morality, and so on. In another context, we can consider the idea that there is human progress to be a matter of belief. In this case it requires a commitment to modernity and a trust in human endeavour. It is a matter of striving for a better future. What has been called the religion of progress has been formed through such commitment and trust. If the idea that there is human progress refers in one case to knowledge and in another to belief, it cannot be negated in the same way in these two cases. In the former you have to provide evidence and arguments to negate it. In the second case you have to present an opposing image or belief, a belief in tradition, an image of some idyllic past, to which people are committed and which they trust when reflecting on their belief. In order to deny belief, it is necessary to oppose it by another image, but not arguments or observation. Proof for or against belief is secondary. Proof of the existence of God has probably converted very few Christians or Jews. In fact it is not difficult to be converted and believe; it is more difficult to stop believing, even if one has good reasons for doing so.

I am not going to outline a philosophy for you, or even a theory. From my youth – and you have read *why* in my autobiography – I have been concerned with the power of belief, among other things, because during the war I could see the terrifying power of nationalism and racism. Although they were presented as having been based on biological and ethnological knowledge, they appeared to be of the same nature as political or religious beliefs. I do not think that one can separate knowledge and belief for long. Even a philosopher such as Bertrand Russell acknowledged the mysterious nature and the centrality of belief in every aspect of mental life. What could I add to what he said: 'Believing seems the most mental thing we do, the most remote from what is done by mere matter. The whole of intellectual life consists of belief.' And William James! In his famous article, 'The Will to Believe', he argues that belief is essential to action. Any thing that is contained in our belief is an idea, and this in turn can be alive or dead. And whether it is alive or dead can be assessed by the readiness to act. For me racism and all that has always been a matter of mass belief, not of prejudice or stereotypes, etc. Those who have mobilized people to create this modern world, at least this is how I saw them, have put to themselves Plato's question: 'how can one give to philosophic ideas the power of mythical ideas, that is, how can one give to scientific ideas the power of religious ideas?' I have touched upon this interrogation in *The Age of the Crowd* (Moscovici, 1985) and mostly in *The*

Invention of Society (Moscovici [1988]/1993). There I wanted to show that, despite the tendency to rationalize and secularize, modern society is, like every society, a machine for making gods (which was the original French title of the book, *La Machine à faire des dieux*). And I contend that if, in the last analysis, the major explanations of social phenomena, Weber's and Durkheim's, for example, are psychosocial, this is because in fact they consider individuals alone or together as *homines credentes*, men of beliefs. There are many people who want to believe and cannot. They do not experience it as a triumph but as a tragedy. It is a pity that we look at the subjects coming into our laboratories as 'one-dimensional' individuals, as little golems with computers instead of minds, and we probably do the same outside the lab. We lose what makes the richness and torment of their lives, what really matters for them.

Let us go a little further. If it is true that common sense is a form of knowledge, at the same time it appears as containing numerous beliefs. How are we to recognize them? The mere fact that some propositions are taken for granted, and therefore are trusted, is an index. In addition they are mingled with values and attitudes which are not discussed, which it is even forbidden to discuss, so that the conclusions we draw from some information or ideas are, so to speak, given in advance. Thus we try to confirm them at any cost, which has been observed in anthropological or experimental studies. Through belief, the individual or group is not related as a subject to an object, an observer to a landscape; he is connected with his world as an actor to the character he embodies, man to his home, a person to his or her identity. Social representations that are seized in common sense are analogous to paradigms, which, contrary to scientific paradigms, are made up partly of beliefs based on trust and partly of elements of knowledge based on truth. In as much as they contain beliefs, validating them appears a long, uncertain process, since they can be neither confirmed nor disconfirmed. The origin of a social representation is not in pure reasoning or information, yet it is not often in blatant opposition to principles of reasoning or information. If it is fixated, as Peirce said, or rooted in culture, in language, then we absorb social representations, starting in infancy, together with other elements of our culture and with our mother tongue.

Far from merely recording data or systematizing facts, they are mental tools, operating on experience itself, shaping the context in which the phenomena are seized. Perhaps this also explains why different kinds of knowledge and representations can coexist together. Moreover, they do not eliminate older kinds of knowledge and representations, even if old and new kinds contradict one another. As Stéphane Laurent in France or McCloskey, Caramazzo and Green in the United States have observed, common-sense physics continues to be used even by individuals who know scientific physics quite well. For example, they may apply the medieval theory of motion in order to describe and explain the motion of a physical body. There is nothing surprising about the findings of those experiments, nor do they mean that our folk physics is based on irrationality. They confirm what we discussed in Koyré's seminars.

And then the linguist Leonard Talmy has remarked that this medieval theory of motion infuses our language too. When we say that the wind kept the ball rolling, we represent the ball as having an inner tendency towards rest. He might as well have noticed that the English, among whom Newton's theory was born, used to say that the sun never sets on their empire, which refers to the Ptolemaic theory. Linguists such as Talmy suppose, rightly in my opinion, that shared representations rule the meaning of language – not the other way about.

Of course you can find social representations which are more abstract, more impersonal, and others which are more concrete and personal. This is well known indeed, so that we can speak, for example, of hot and cold cognitions. But I think that, from the social viewpoint, what is at stake here is the degree of presence or the force of belief. Therefore we had better speak, as William James did, of the degree to which those social representations are alive or dead; people believe or do not believe in them at a given moment. Be that as it may, I doubt whether we really understand the mental life of individuals or groups if we overlook that cross-breeding of faith and knowledge, the mixture of what is considered true because we trust it and what we trust because we consider it true. The poverty of cognitivism is not that it ignores meaning; it skips beliefs.

1.6   Collective and social representations

IM   It is clear from your paper on Vygotsky and Piaget (cf. chapter 6, p. 208) that one can distinguish between two traditions of research with respect to the genesis of the concept of social representations. One comes from Durkheim and continues through Piaget. The other comes from Lévy-Bruhl and continues through Vygotsky. Although, as you pointed out, you took the term from Piaget and referred to Durkheim as early as in *La Psychanalyse*, I understand that in your own theoretical and empirical perspective it is allied with Lévy-Bruhl and Vygotsky. You point out that there is a fundamental difference between these two traditions and it concerns the dichotomy continuity/ discontinuity. In my view, it is so fundamental that it places these two traditions of social representations into quite different scientific paradigms in the Kuhnian sense. I shall try to explain.

In your (Moscovici, 1984) criticism of Durkheim you pointed out that he was true to the Kantian tradition and had a rather static conception of representations. Thus, although in Durkheim's theorizing there was concern with both society and the individual, it was the Kantian inability to master the concept of dialectical interdependence, or co-construction, that made Durkheim's representations so static. You point out in your 1998 paper that Piaget followed Durkheim's rationalism which, in fact, was Kantian rationalism. Piaget's concept of structure is no more than a rearranging of pre-existing elements within a bounded whole. This pre-dialectical concept of structure which one can find in Piaget, in French and perhaps in Danish structuralism, is sharply different from the structuralism of the Prague School, which is dialectical and dynamic. I would add that the notion of cognitive and linguistic universals fits the pre-dialectical perspective. So how does this perspective explain, in general terms, the notion of development? The concept of continuity implies that the child develops into an adult through stages, through a series of intermediate and mutually interconnected operations. These stages unfold in a similar manner, whether you study children in Geneva, Paris, New York or Moscow (Piaget [1970]/1972), which gives credence to universally valid operations.

The notion of discontinuity, however, is more than just an opposite of continuity. Continuity/discontinuity, to me, reflects ontological assumptions of dialectics/dialogism as I mentioned earlier: the interdependence of culture and the individual mind; their co-development; the interdependence between thought/thinking and language/speaking. We can find, I would say, some of these assumptions in Lévy-Bruhl and all of them in Vygotsky. One can talk about qualitative transformations of something only if one assumes an open structure, that is, a complementarity of structure with its relevant context. And this is what Luria and Vygotsky tried to investigate in Uzbekistan in the 1930s (see Luria, 1976, 1979). This is also compatible with what you say about Lévy-Bruhl: 'Just like Einsteinian relativity at that time, the hypothesis of Lévy-Bruhl destroyed the Kantian idea that the categories of the human mind are the same at all times and in all places' (see chapter 6, p. 213). Cognitive structure and culture mutually constitute each other.

People often ask: how is Moscovici's concept of social representation different from that of Durkheim? I hope, therefore, that an answer to this question is now clear. In studying social representations, one must study both the culture and the mind of the individual.

Unless the distinction between Durkheim/Piagetian and Lévy-Bruhl/Vygotskian concepts of social representation is understood, we may be celebrating a hundredth anniversary of the term 'collective or social representation', while hiding something much more fundamental: the paradigmatic differences between the two concepts of social or collective representations. Although you say in your paper on this issue that the difference between these two approaches is in the genesis of social representations but not in their nature, I would argue that, indeed, the difference in genesis leads to a difference in the nature of these social representations. This is in terms of the differences in their ontological basis.

Social psychologists often ask the question as to the difference between collective and social representations. For example, in his scholarly paper, Rob Farr (1998) is concerned with the historical issues surrounding the notions of 'collective representations' and 'social representations' and their usage. These historical issues are important and need to be known. Could you comment on this issue?

SM   Please do not expect me ever to be able to explain the difference between 'collective' and 'social'. I suppose that some differences do exist, but one has to look them up in a dictionary, because I do not find them in the work of any social thinker worth considering, including Durkheim. Most of the time the two words are used synonymously. I prefer, however, to use only 'social' because it refers to a clear notion, that of society, to an idea of differentiation, of networks of people and their interactions. In the nineteenth century the word 'collective' was more usual, suggesting the image of a heap of people, an aggregate of similar individuals forming a whole. Hence the term 'collective psychology', which was not very distinct from 'mass psychology'. I don't see the historical issue very clearly. But I can construct two scenarios. The first, the Mauss scenario, is linked to the Durkheimian school. Durkheim himself kept the social and the psychological together. After his death, Mauss insisted more on the specificity of the social, and took a very critical position towards Lévy-Bruhl, whom he considered to be insufficiently social because he was too psychological. The collective being was for him on this side of the barrier, as he was 'insensitive' to the singularity of social groups. The other scenario, the Moscovici scenario if you like, concerns the relations between society and culture. In *The Invention of Society* I have distinguished between 'lived societies' and 'conceived societies'. Briefly, I could say that in the former, cultures, traditions, rituals, symbolic creeds, etc. are the matrix of society. In the latter, it is the reverse, society is the matrix and shapes its culture. You can find a similar point of view in Raymond Williams's book *Culture*: 'The social character of cultural production, which is evident in all periods and forms, is now more directly active and inescapable than in all earlier developed societies' (Williams, 1989, p. 30). Dare I say that I do not really have much trust in either of these scenarios? I very much respect Farr's historical work. At one time or another, however, multiplying distinctions ceases to have the fecundity it is supposed to have. All through my work I have remained faithful to William of Occam's razor: one should not multiply concepts without necessity. One must not do with more what one can do with less.

2   THE THEORY OF SOCIAL REPRESENTATIONS AND THE THEORY OF SOCIAL CHANGE

IM   I would like to ask you about an issue that is of great interest to many social psychologists. Can you explain what the relationship is, if any, between the two major areas of your work: the theory of social representations and the theory of social change – or, as the latter is often called, the theory of minority influence? I think that, in general, social psychologists look at these two theories as independent areas of your work. Those who carry out research on social representations are not usually concerned with social influence processes. Moreover, these two areas are often taught by different lecturers in undergraduate courses of social psychology. Yet I see an important underlying conceptual unity between these two areas.

SM   In many ways the theory of social representations and the theory of innovation, as it should properly be called, belong to different domains of social psychology, answer different questions, and are related to distinct areas of my life experience. Not only did I myself belong to a discriminated minority, I also created a minority movement, as I recounted in my autobiography. Basically minorities are considered as existing at the social frontier or even outside it. The state of a minority is the state of a group which has been denied autonomy and responsibility, which is neither trusted nor recognized by other groups, either because it is dominated or because of its dissident, heretical position, etc. Such a group does not recognize itself in existing systems of power and belief, and it does not represent such a system for anyone. In order to provide a different system of beliefs, to obtain power or to become a model for others, such a group has to be capable of influencing others, changing their way of seeing and/or acting, until the point comes when it turns into a majority. Minorities are not the sole innovators, yet throughout history they have often been shown to be the main agents of innovation in art, science, politics, and so on. Therefore the theoretical and practical question concerning minorities is Gibbon's question: how was it possible for a handful of Christians to become a Church and achieve such an enormous and seemingly impossible change in Roman history? In other words: how do minorities manage to have an impact, how are they able to convert and recruit people and alter the social fabric? I have given an account of this theory elsewhere, and I am not going to restate it here. Yet the fact remains that it has always preoccupied me. You see, my first study in psychology was itself a study of innovation and social change (Moscovici, 1961).

By studying the penetration of psychoanalysis into French society, I also studied, in a sense, the penetration of the ideas of the minority which was disregarded in the scientific, political and religious milieux. It was even a foreign, non-French theory. What was not negligible, however, was the fact that at the same time as I pursued my field work on psychoanalysis, I carried out a community study on the psychological consequences of industrial change. As you know, at that time the Doctorat d'Etat in France consisted of two theses, a main thesis and a complementary thesis. The study of the social representation of psychoanalysis was my main thesis directed by Professor

Lagache, and my complementary thesis was this community study directed by Professor Stoetzel. In the fifties it was quite usual for a social psychologist, even in America, to pursue both pure and applied research.

IM   I didn't know that.

SM   At that time the main problem in France was the problem of industrial re-conversion, that is, changing old traditional industrial areas into modern ones. I created a research team which included six or seven psychologists, a sociologist and an economist devoted to this work, which continued for several years in mining and in textile areas. The results of this work were published in a series of books. My first research took place in a small region famous not only for its industry, that is, for making hats, but also for its socialist and trade unionist past. Like every social psychologist of that time, I started with attempts to detect the resistance to change and to defeat that resistance so that the region and its industry could be modernized. In that microcosm I discovered that resistance to change was not a problem. I also observed that if a change in a community takes place, it is because a minority or several minorities are capable of sustaining a conflict and negotiating the solution to that conflict in relation to the power they encounter and because they are able to carry the population along.

    At that time I was associated with Claude Faucheux, who knew Festinger and other English and American social psychologists working on group dynamics. He took an interest in my work, including my studies in the history of science, and made me read the literature on the dynamic of groups and on social influence. On the basis of this reading I came to the conclusion that social psychology was not much concerned with actions of minorities or with the change effected by a minority group. Its main concern was to discover how an individual or a deviant is changed by a group and how he becomes a group's 'normal' member. This is what Claude Faucheux and I called the conformity bias. In other words, social psychology was mainly concerned with conformity, and social influence was synonymous with social conformity. From that time on and in the course of the following years, that work took a more systematic turn, and in fact developed into a theory.

IM   I would like to point to one issue which, I think, differentiated your approach to the study of social influence from the very beginning. These traditional theories of influence based on unidirectional functional models are not social theories of knowledge – whether of lay or scientific knowledge or of common sense. Not only is the word 'knowledge' never mentioned there, but nor are conformity concerns in general, abstract typicalities such as norms, points of view, behaviour, general attitudes and so on. In contrast, the theory of social representations was concerned, from the very beginning, to identify the content of common-sense knowledge and to look for the ways it is expressed in language and communication. Equally, the theory of innovation, as you pointed out earlier, is concerned with the diffusion of scientific and of other kinds of institutionalized knowledge into common sense. In other words, both theories are concerned with the knowledge of majorities and of minorities. I wonder whether you would comment on the role of knowledge in the theory of influence.

2.1 Social influence and the circulation of knowledge

SM I cannot discuss here at length the phenomenon of the development and circulation of knowledge within a society. As far as I know, three models have been proposed and were widespread:

1 Diffusion by way of 'contagion', starting with Le Bon.
2 Propagating ideas by 'imitation'. To accept an opinion or information and making it one's own means to imitate, and to imitate is to repeat, to reproduce in oneself what has appeared in some other minds. Just as inferior individuals or groups imitate superior individuals or groups, the dominating ideas of our time which are reproduced are those of dominating groups, instruments enabling them to retain their power, and such ideas will be widespread.
3 The third mode is that of conformity. According to it, the rise and fall of ideas does not depend on their evidence or absurdity, but on the conformity and the degree of opposition they meet with, owing to their agreement or disagreement with the ideas adopted by the majority or authority. This model is no doubt true, yet remains innocuous like a tautology.

What these models seemingly lacked was tension, an exchange between the emitter and the receiver of knowledge. Diffusion is here reduced to an endless series of individual choices and acceptance of knowledge. As soon as you pass from an individualistic to a social vision of the circulation of knowledge and languages, you tend to see this process as one of communication in the course of which information is transmitted and transformed. Then the communication is oral, as is the case with common sense, its medium is *la parole*, (spoken) conversation. Here we have a fourth model, that of communication, which I have tried to elaborate.

One might suppose that in science and philosophy the stress is put on the features of the individual elaboration of knowledge; in common sense it is the reverse, for the stress is on the diffused features of a shared knowledge at a given time. Moreover, every scientific or philosophical theory tends to become first the common sense of a restricted group, of a minority, which is then distributed in connection with practical life, throughout the majority of a society, where it becomes common sense with a renewed content and a new way of thinking. In a letter he wrote to Necker in 1775, Diderot stated: 'Opinion, this mobile entity whose force for good or evil we all know is at its origin nothing but the effect of a small number of men who speak after thinking and continuously form in various points of society centres of instruction, from which errors and reasoned truths issue and gradually reach the last confines of the city where they are established as articles of faith.'

From these remarks, you can see how the model of the communication of knowledge is outlined. In the first place we have here a diffusion from the 'inventor', or generally speaking the minority of scientists, philosophers, etc. to the majority, a process in the course of which there occurs what we call the popularization of knowledge. This is the first transformation of a new, strange or esoteric idea by and in the social environment. Next, now circulating within the majority, the new, strange or esoteric idea interferes with existing ideas, becomes a focus of conversation, debate and the rest. The effect of these conversations and debates is to strengthen, intensify and carry into effect each idea or item of knowledge circulating in society, both old and new. Once the esoteric and strange ones have become stable and familiar, groups of folk specialists or believers are formed. Out of these communications, understandings and misunderstandings, out of numerous transformations and reshaping, something new is created in conversations and debates, that is, a new shared representation of common sense with its own style and content. The very content has sometimes changed beyond recognition, even if the name has been kept unaltered, for example, the name and notion of 'natural selection', which has been carried over from evolutionary biology to the evolution of psychological or social phenomena. But the initial individual or minority is not immune from pressures from the majority. This leads him to adjust himself to common sense, either by showing his reluctance to express his new ideas, or by proposing them so as not to go against religious ideas or political opinions, the prevailing mode of thinking of his fellow countrymen. One of the conclusions drawn from this model was that, contrary to a widespread conception, common sense is no less vulnerable to continuous change by social and communicative processes than any other kind of knowledge or belief. You have here a very simplified picture of what I have called a 'thinking society'.

Let us go one step further. As I said before, we generally separate communication, that is, the transmission of information, from influence, the aim of which is to get someone's consent. Yet a conflict still remains in the diffusion of knowledge, a conflict between new and old, between esoteric and exoteric ideas, which each party wants to win by strategies of persuasion. As Parsons said, in a communicator there is an 'intrinsic persuader'. And Berkeley observed long ago that this distinction is largely artificial because there is no communication without persuasive intention: 'The communicating of ideas marked by words is not the chief and only end of language, as is commonly supposed. There are other ends, as the raising of some passion, the exciting to, or deterring from an action, the putting the mind in some particular disposition.' In the communication model I have described, we distinguish two directions in which knowledge circulates and is transformed: first from science, philosophy, etc. towards common sense, and second, from common sense towards science and other kinds of knowledge. In the first case one can speak of innovation and in the second of conservation or conformity.

Thus the first move in the theory of influence was to distinguish between these two processes: innovation and conformity, which opened up a new field of phenomena to psychosocial exploration, which until then had only been interested in conformity. I could never understand why acknowledging these fundamental complementary processes met with so much opposition. Was it because of the autonomy of innovation? Was it because of the duality of the influence processes? Or was it felt necessary to re-establish the *status quo ante* by making innovation a particular case of conformity? Yet a similar duality exists in physics between the principle of entropy and the principle of conservation, in language between what Zipf called the forces of unification and the forces of diversity, in the philosophy of science between what Kuhn called revolutionary science and normal science, etc. Whatever the reason for this opposition, it resulted in retaining the older model which never acknowledged the two sources of influence: on one hand minority influence, which is conforming to a minority, on the other hand majority influence, which means conforming to the majority. Innovation with its original features and field of specific phenomena is kept out of social psychology. Perhaps people believe deep down that the 'social animal', to borrow Aronson's popular formula, is a conforming animal.

Let us forget that and return to our processes and especially to the notions of minority and majority. I would say that throughout different cultures one finds a couple of representational types which, in accordance with political language, have been labelled as majority and minority but which have a family resemblance associated in people's minds with orthodoxy and heresy, academism and avant-garde, normality and deviance, obedience and dissidence, autochthonous and foreigner, etc. Inside this dyad there is an invisible and ever present social representation of culture, of the very effective categories which are revived by being attributed to a role, a message, and so on. Obviously, one can symbolize them by numbers or by names. However, what matters are not numbers (what percentage of opinion or vote makes up a majority or minority?) or names, but the representational types which are active. I knew that I would be asked one day to explain by what empirical index I define a minority, yet it is difficult to enumerate all the scattered indices when dealing with these representations that are both typical and composite *à la* Galton.

IM   As you have stated, a minority cannot be defined independently of its social context. A minority, just as other societal concepts, for example, a social representation, a structure, a process, an individual, and so on, are all relational terms which can be defined only in relation to something else. This does not mean, of course, relativism, which is a different matter and which we cannot raise here.

SM   Innovation in minorities is not something I invented; it exists out there in social life, it is a cultural *thema* for groups in their representation of their origins – think of Socrates' trial, of Christ, Galileo or Giordano Bruno. The phenomenon is largely described in anthropology, economics, history, and so on. So what astonished me in this day and age was to be asked how I defined the minority. Minorities are defined according to historical situations and cultural models. And I sometimes wonder why people take them in a purely numerical sense. Long ago I gave the example of women, signifying clearly that to be a minority does not always mean to be less numerous. A majority can also be taken legally, culturally as minor. In French I coined the word *mineurité*, in English you might call it a *minor-ity*.

The theory of social representation I have sketched above asks and answers a question: '*What* is shared knowledge?' It restores to knowledge its character of a model idea as more or less standardized. Such representations serve people on one side as paradigms in communication, on the other side as a means of practical orientation. Be that as it may, the bases of a discourse on the nature of human knowledge suggested here, as you can see, have changed. In the first place, knowledge as I conceive it here is a process of struggle and persuasion in the course of human history, not the process of learning effected by the single person who is supposed to acquire knowledge from private information. This is a conception from theories of traditional knowledge that either neglect or make a world apart from ordinary knowledge and communication. This knowledge, just like other kinds of more exotic knowledge which one day or other are included in public discourse, raises another question: how is knowledge shared? How can a unique idea, one private vision, which can appear as the obsession of a single individual until the moment it becomes submerged in the mainstream of the development of human knowledge, make a passage to become a collective obsession? This happened in the case of Marxism, the theory of evolution, psychoanalysis and relativity theory. Nevertheless, this passage was not a miracle but only an example of how these minorities maintained a conflict with the opposition, how they viewed the hostility of 'men' and how they converted them 'to this new vision or idea' according to the dynamics which I explained, I hope, by the theory of innovation.

2.2   The interdependence of minority/majority

IM   I shall express my hypothesis about this opposition, which I view as a difficulty in comprehending the idea of thinking in complements. I shall start by quoting from your book on *Social Influence and Social Change* (Moscovici, 1976). You emphasized there that influence processes are based on two inter-related ideas. First, influence is exerted in two directions and is reciprocal: 'from the majority towards the minority, and from the minority towards the majority'. Secondly, and following from the first, 'each part of a group must be considered as emitting, and receiving influence simultaneously . . . every individual and sub-group . . . is both being acted upon and acting upon others at the same moment, whenever influence occurs.' Both these ideas, of reciprocity and simultaneity, created a conceptual difficulty for mainstream social psychology because they belong to a dialectical or – I would say – a dialogical way of thinking. A theory of interaction between entities was a difficult concept for mainstream social psychology at that time because its fundamental assumption was that of discrete entities which, for one reason or another, may enter into interaction. For you, in contrast, the starting-point was a dyad, that of majority/minority: one component is meaningless without the other component. They are mutually interdependent like figure-and-ground, because majority is defined in terms of minority and minority in terms of majority. As you say, this notion of reciprocity – or complementarity – has been used for a long time in physics. Bohr introduced this principle in his attempt to resolve the problem as to how to attribute contrary properties to objects, that is, the wave-like and particle-like properties. This internal relationship – a tension – within the dyad is an essential presupposition for social change. However, this concept was strange for traditional influence theories. Their starting-point was the two independent entities: majority and minority. So influence theories based on conformity started with a norm on the one hand and a deviant individual – or a deviant minority – on the other. The question for a social psychologist was how to bring them together: you bring them together by influencing the weaker entity: unidirectionally, by flow from majority to minority.

The second point I would like to make follows from the first one. If you have a model based on separate entities, then the idea of simultaneity of influence is impossible to conceive. This was also a problem in linguistics, based on oppositions as independent entities in the Saussurean tradition. Roman Jakobson (1987) was critical of the Saussurean thesis which ascribed the sounds of language linearity measurable in one direction only. As he pointed out, sounds were defined in terms of mere temporal sequentiality rather than simultaneity. Instead, Jakobson viewed the sounds of language in terms of interdependent oppositions. We are talking here about a conceptual difficulty which stems from two alternative paradigms: one based on the notion of discrete entities and the other based on interdependencies. Although conceptually, what you proposed in the theory of innovation has a long tradition, from Hegel through to, for example, Mead, Vygotsky, Baldwin and the linguists of the Prague School, in empirical social psychology it was a new conception and therefore difficult to comprehend.

SM There is an additional point. I asked myself: how can such a strange and disturbing theory as psychoanalysis, advocated by such a small group, alter common sense? Obviously, other people, for example, those working in the field of belief or science, have asked this question before me. You know that this was Heisenberg's question: 'We must ask how was a seemingly small group of physicists able to constrain the other to these changes in the structure of science and thought.' He considered that to be the main question in understanding scientific revolutions.

Well now, not to stray too far from your question, which is the relation between the theory of social representations and the theory of innovation, here is another point: the representations of groups constituting one type or the other no doubt have some importance in the communication of influence. This concerns types which are normally pictured as antagonistic or alternative. How can one account for the reluctance which people, especially in America, have had against this perturbing and disturbing aspect of minorities? America is a country of immigrants; there have been religious dissenters, nonconformists, independent thinkers. In reading Hawthorne's *Tanglewood Tales*, you can see that the American religious life has been fraught with heresy and fighting heresy, not to mention civil disobedience and so on. This background of the theory of innovation, of the meaning of minorities and majorities, did not ring a bell when I spoke about it there. Some time ago I made a literary analysis of *The Scarlet Letter* from the viewpoint of my theory, just as I did about Proust's *A la recherche du temps perdu*, or rather, of one limited aspect of that work (Moscovici, 1986; see also chapter 5).

2.3 Behavioural style

SM Now I come to a more precise point of convergence between the two theories. As you know, to the question as to what can help a minority to have influence, I answered that it is not its prestige, power or expertise, but its style of behaviour. It is the behavioural style which conveys to other people the actor's intention, influence, his degree of firmness of conviction, decisiveness, consistency, courage, etc. However, behavioural style, in order to have an effect, must be understood by the majority, who must share the same representation of that style as the minority in order to detect its same structure and give it the same meaning. It is like observing someone who is on stage, for example, a Chinese theatre, or performing through gestures. In order to enjoy the miming, people must share the representation of what these gestures and encounters mean, otherwise they would appear crazy or ridiculous. For instance, if I am consistent when expressing my ideas about the theory of social representations, there is some possibility that people will perceive the firmness of my intellectual commitment. This is precisely why dissidents like Havel, Sakharov, and others were quite effective in their opposition against the regime.

IM   Behavioural style brings us back to common-sense knowledge. Our representations of other people in terms of motives, intentions, goals and reasons are so ingrained in our social reality that we tend to perceive their actions directly as having a particular meaning – rather than interpreting them. Equally, we have a good picture of how we are perceived by others and therefore we can apply strategies enforcing particular perceptions. This is good social psychology on the part of minorities and it is an application of Hegel's principle of recognition.

SM   It is not only an application of Hegel's principle. In the book you talk about (Moscovici, 1976) I developed a theory, I dare to call it, of social recognition. I showed that this is what minorities are after. They really get access to existence for themselves and to the will of becoming a majority only by being recognized by other groups. I had talked with Henri Tajfel about these social minorities, making the hypothesis more precise by saying that the need for social recognition is at the heart of innovation, its motor, so to speak, just as the need for social comparison is at the heart of conformity. For the individual who is uncertain about his opinions or judgements will seek to reduce this uncertainty by referring to the majority's opinions and judgements. We ourselves have verified this hypothesis in a study with Geneviève Paicheler, which was published in the first book by Henri Tajfel on the difference between groups (Moscovici and Paicheler, 1978).

You see, I think that in social psychology there are two orientations in the study of relations between groups. One is Sherif's orientation concerning the relation between 'in' and 'out' groups, and the other is Lewin's orientation in *Resolving Social Conflicts* (1948), concerning the relations between majorities and minorities, or rather between one group which represents itself as being the majority and the other as being the minority, or vice versa. Depending on what one represents oneself as being, one seeks recognition or compares oneself with the other. But whichever way a group represents itself, it can only communicate or influence if it adopts a behavioural style. Behavioural styles are symbolic behaviours. In a behavioural style an action and a representation are associated, given meaning and communicative relevance.

This could be and has been questioned. Yet Professor Wendy Wood and her colleagues have shown in a brilliant meta-analysis of a great number of experiments that behavioural styles, particularly consistency, do indeed play the causal role that the theory ascribes to them.

I have spoken often enough of the tendency to cut theories, and even worse, phenomena, into thin slices. The same thing happened with the theory of innovation: minorities, conversion, attitude change, etc. were considered as independent slices of influence. Why this is done and with what consequences does not appear clearly, or appears all too clearly. It does not mean that the theory has not made notable progress. Fascinating empirical studies have been carried out and new ideas have been proposed. Yet, you see, I sometimes feel remote, even old-fashioned. For me experiments are part of the *ars inveniendi*, the art of discovery, rather than of the art of proof, and explanation is neither everything nor the main thing in science. What there is to be explained must first be carefully described. My pleasure when I am making experiments is to discover new or uncanny phenomena, for example, the research on the phenomena of group polarization with Mariza Zavalloni (Moscovici and Zavalloni, 1969), among others.

IM   So it is the behavioural style that directly connects the two theories, social representations and innovation theory. You have studied behavioural style and consistency not only in the laboratory but also among dissidents.

2.4   Dissidents as a minority

SM   Yes. Dissidents have chosen consistency because they knew what consistency represents for others and what compromise represents for others. So behavioural styles came from the study of social representations; underlying that we have social representations of intention, of behaviour, of rules of behaviour, etc. and you can say that it results in representation. If we don't have the same representation then behavioural style has no effect.

IM   Behavioural style is based on consistency and on repetition. Repetition is something that is very important in the development of representation. You discuss this point in *La Psychanalyse* as a way of showing how propaganda is trying to change representation. So one could see this role of behavioural style in two ways, first, as a shared representation, as an expression of goals, intentions, motives that are understood by others; and second, as a consistent and repetitive activity which gives strength to these goals, intentions and motives.

SM   I didn't think about that but it's true.

IM   I wonder whether at this stage you might say something about the study of dissidents, because your excellent essay on Solzhenitsyn and Tvardovsky is known only to French readers. You wrote it after the English edition of *Social Influence and Social Change* (1976) had been published and it is included in the French version of this book entitled *Psychologie des minorités actives* (Moscovici, 1979) which, in some ways, expresses more appropriately the main focus of the book.

SM   One thing I wanted to show in that study was that once you are in the position of a dissident, your way of thinking, your style of relationships or behaving totally changes. I could see to what extent the behavioural style is consistent, related to the psychological climate or the situation and the personalities involved. In the essay on Solzhenitsyn and Tvardovsky I wrote about two people who, at a time of a grand historical experiment, were strong and very prominent individuals, deeply conscious of what they were doing and what was happening socially and politically. They both had goals for which they fought. Their dramatic relationship revealed many aspects of the influence they exerted on each other and I found that illuminating. This was also an occasion to confirm the hypothesis about conflict and conversion. So in a way they gave me theoretical material. These two characters – and by a character I mean someone who does what he thinks and thinks what he does – express the relationship between the mental and the behavioural activity. Since I have written that essay I have worked on a third character and made notes on him: Sakharov. He is a very interesting character. He has written his memoirs and I started working on these. So you see I think that the analysis of literary texts based on dissidents is one way to progress in the study of minorities. Laboratory experiments could sometimes become no more than a series of little studies, one leading to another, one a refinement of the previous one and so on, all together a kind of a closed intellectual world.

IM   These literary analyses are imaginative and invaluable social-psychological studies. Yet it is your experiments on minorities that have influenced social psychologists. Psychologists can carry out relatively simple and tidy experimental studies and they can search for variables which Moscovici didn't take into account, confirm and disconfirm Moscovici on those variables; they can elaborate on these experiments, improve them, and so on. In other words, they can carry out 'normal science', to use Kuhn's term. I would say that, in fact, every American textbook speaks about your studies on minority influence.

SM   But not about innovation.

IM   Not about innovation. These experiments can be viewed as another face of the experiments in social change.

SM For me, studies inside or outside the laboratory have the same value.
Only heuristic considerations decide which kind is appropriate for which
phenomena. The creation of new ideas and new phenomena is what we are
looking for and even get paid for. Methods are only means toward an end. If
they become an end or a criterion of the selection of topics and ideas, then
they are just another form of professional censorship. So you can call me
a methodological opportunist and I will not feel insulted. Returning to dissidents, they have chosen in a consistent way and refuse any compromise because they know that, in other people's eyes, this represents a new
attitude and an expression of opposition, the sign indicating that they think
differently. Only the faithful Communist or the 'collaborator' compromised,
behaved in an inconsistent way in public trials, now opposing, now accepting
the attorney's accusations. This was no doubt, as Yakir says in his memoirs,
because of the physical and moral pressures of the police to which all dissidents were submitted. Be that as it may, if dissidents had not shared the
same representations of behavioural style with the majority of people and had
not had some idea about its effects, they would not have chosen it as a
strategy and would never have converted so many people who in their turn
influenced others.

Laboratory studies are interesting because they can provide a more detailed
analysis of specific phenomena. I learned rather late how to make experiments, though I had a notion of their function from my knowledge of the
history of science. I gathered that the main ingredient of an experiment is a
hypothesis, a hypothesis which makes you grasp the phenomena in a different
light. Usually experiments are not carried out mainly to validate a hypothesis
but to invent a new phenomenon. Concern is not with truth but with new
truth. Some time ago I sent an article to a journal and one of the reviewers
said that I did not make an effort to falsify my hypothesis. Many people think
that Karl Popper's dictum was 'Falsify ideas.' In my opinion, his dictum was:
'Falsify bold ideas.' And bold ideas are rare. For the others, the more usual
ones, to confirm or falsify them does not make any difference. And even with
bold ones, you have to be careful. They cannot be easily and readily submitted
to a rigorous experimental test; it would kill them. When molecular biology
was *in statu nascendi*, one of its pioneers, Delbruck, recommended the rule of
limited sloppiness in appreciating the results. I think this is a wise rule.

I remember discussing it with Leon Festinger, who also thought that when
we open a new field of research or deal with complex phenomena people and
journals have to show more flexibility than they usually do. I think that
Asch's review of dissonance theory, which ended with the judgement 'not
proven', was at the back of his mind. Anyhow I learned how to make experiments, because they offer an exciting possibility of exploring new phenomena, not because they are *the* scientific method. However, I always feel the
need to seek their meaning and validity in the social or historical context.

This is why I gathered some materials about the dissidents which were available in French and English. And the outcome was the paper on Solzhenitsyn and Tvardovsky, in which I stated the difference between a dissident minority and a deviant one, which are often confused.

IM Could you explain the difference between these two concepts?

SM A dissident is a person who has broken with an institution or a majority and proposes an alternative view, fights for it. A deviant is an individual or a sub-group who draws away from the institution or majority, yet continues to share its views and norms. Solzhenitsyn wanted to undermine Marxism and abolish the Soviet regime. Tvardovsky tried to criticize, to liberalize them in order to improve his society. Solzhenitsyn was exiled, and Tvardovsky 'only' deprived of his functions in the party and as the editor of *Novy Mir*. Of course, this kind of explanation and phenomenon cannot be tested in a laboratory. There is a huge gap between trying to change someone's mind about a pair of colours, on one hand, and to change a dissident's mind about his beliefs about Communism, on the other. Theory deals with this kind of gap better and gets enriched by it.

IM Well, you cannot study such questions in a laboratory because the work of dissidents is a long-winded process – and such processes are studied in terms of social representations. In laboratories you study different kinds of things.

SM They are different kinds of things but underlined by the same conceptual framework and related by the same theory.
There are, therefore, a few foot-bridges between the two theories and I hope that others will build more of them; for example, one can think of a process of the genesis of a new social movement. If a minority is to create a movement, change its position in society and become active, it has to propose an alternative social representation. Subsequently, it has to communicate, implement a strategy of persuasion so as to recruit new members and influence the way of thinking and acting of the majority. In *Social Influence and Social Change* (1976), I tried to build up a psychology of active minorities as a counterpart to the psychology of masses on which I later wrote another book, *The Age of the Crowd* (1985), as you know. Once taken out of what Norbert Elias called *academismus*, 'the projection of academic divisions and relative rivalries into the object of research of departments', social psychology is at bottom nothing but a marriage between the psychology of active minorities and the psychology of the masses. With these two psychologies, social alchemy manufactures all the rest: identities, groups, collective behaviours, stereotypes, discourse, and so on. You have to believe in your lucky star in order hastily to materialize your dreams, seek an answer to the questions

that have sprung up in the course of your life. I am not a particularly optim-
istic individual. Yet I tell myself that I must have believed in my lucky star
to go in search of those theories, to pursue them for such a long time, so as
to find an answer to what has haunted me for years, to make sense of my
experience. Did I succeed or did I not in other people's eyes? It is not up to
me to answer. Anyhow, they have helped to create a better understanding of
the world in which I have lived and the one in which we are living.

Finally I would like to tell you that the theory of influence exerted between
a minority and a majority was not born out of the current of research on
influence (Sherif, Asch, etc.), but out of research on group dynamics. As you
are aware, for twenty years at least the group has disappeared from social
psychology. To fill this vacuum of well-established, heuristic phenomena and
notions will be a hard task. However that may be, we have continued the
research on group dynamics of the Lewinian school in two directions. On the
one hand I would mention the studies on innovation and creativity, extending
our criticism of the way in which deviation and the action of minorities in a
group was conceived. On the other hand, I can name the research which led
to the discovery with Mariza Zavalloni of *group polarization* (Moscovici and
Zavalloni, 1969), something which not only brought me great happiness but
was also one of the phenomena which gave me most satisfaction on both
aesthetic and intellectual planes. Not only because it is strong and beautiful,
but also because it is at the heart of a theory of collective decisions (Moscovici
and Doise, 1994), the first sketch of which can be found in Lewin and Sherif.
The theory is about the change in preferences, the attitudes induced *in* and *by*
the group through the participation and normative involvement of its members. Given the coherence and fecundity of the theory, it has been possible to
formulate it in physico-mathematical terms (Moscovici and Galam, 1991),
which allows a new light to be shed on group dynamics, the genesis of
minorities and majorities, the relations between influence and power, and,
something remarkable, the evolution of groups. I like it very much because it
carries further the strong points of Lewin's research on change within the
group and Sherif's research on involvement and attitude change.

Now, as soon as we turn group polarization into an intra-individual phenomenon, not only has the theory lost its beauty, but moreover, the interest,
the centrality of the phenomenon is lost. At the time of its discovery we saw
in it one of the main contributions of European experimental social psychology. This was why the Bristol laboratory, thanks to Colin Fraser's important
studies, took part in it, just as, if I remember rightly, the lab founded by
Martin Irle in Mannheim did. Remember that, at that time, we were busy
consciously building up a social psychology in Europe. It may not be devoid
of interest for you to learn that in a meeting Henri Tajfel said: 'OK. We have
something like an interesting group dynamics. Now, like Sherif after Lewin
we also need something like an interesting inter-group dynamics.' I did not

know this relation, which he explained to me in detail. This was one of the motives for his involvement in what was going to become his life work and one of the most original theories in this area. And my lab tried to contribute to this work. It was quite exciting to build a scientific field in Europe from scratch, so to speak. Of course, this is history. But I regret it, and I fail to understand how it is possible to conceive a social psychology without society and without the group, I mean without interaction. Or how other people outside the area can believe in the worth of such a social psychology. This is not a matter of anti-individualism and all that. Simply, words still have their meaning and scientific fields their logic. For my own part I feel very sad about this shrinking, this loss of work which gave me so much joy and confidence in the chances of social psychology getting involved in highly significant problems.

2.5   The genetic model

IM   You have explained the relationship between the innovation theory and the theory of social representations in two basic ways. First, both theories are concerned with social change. Social representations are often concerned with macrosocial phenomena that are of a long-winded nature and such phenomena are difficult to study in the laboratory. It is minorities who carry out social change by introducing innovations. Second, there is a notion of behavioural style which is common to both theories.

However, I would argue that it is in the genetic model that you present a very new perspective in social psychology, and this is something which American textbooks avoid discussing. They talk about minority influence but never about the theoretical issue which underlies the genetic model.

To my mind, what is totally overlooked is that Part I of your book on minorities has the title 'Social influence from the functionalist point of view' and Part II 'Social influence from the genetic point of view'. As we spoke about it earlier, you present majority and minority influence processes not as two separate processes but as two facets of influence which are mutually interdependent. You clearly state there this essential difference between the functionalist and the genetic models (Moscovici, 1976, p. 6). For the former model, the social system and the environment are givens, for the latter they are products; for the former, the stress is on the dependence of the individuals on the group and their social reaction to it, while for the latter the stress is on the interdependence between the two; for the former, the individuals and group tend to adapt, while in the latter they grow. By growing is meant here, for example, the development of the capacity to create new ways of thinking, of redefining one's boundary, of modifying the environment and expanding the network of social relations, although I think that it is important to emphasize that 'growth' actually means 'co-growth', that is, the growth of both parties in the dyad individual/group or minority/majority.

SM   Of course I did not think that the genetic model is specifically related to influence or to social representations. It is an underlying conception of both the phenomena and, indeed, it expresses the purpose of science. For example, when I understood that common sense is the privileged area of social psychology, the first thing in which I took an interest, the first question I asked myself was to find out how common sense is generated, how it comes into existence and how it passes away, to use Aristotle's words. I shall state explicitly what I have said implicitly time and again: the concept of common sense is anchored in communication; and communication implies a creativity similar to that of language, *à la* Humboldt, or a transformation, the development from one level of knowledge to another one. In this way human practice gets access to questions that were formerly inaccessible.

I have tried to show that there is a functionalist model underlying the theories of knowledge and influence in social psychology, and I thought that it should be replaced by the genetic model; that is to say, by a model which considers society as a more or less structured network and which views relationships as in the making, not as already made. In this model, social influence is viewed as a reciprocal action or negotiation, not as a form of pressure exerted by the group or the individual to re-establish the equilibrium.

Of course, all this ought to be discussed at greater length and in more detail, which would require more time. There are relations between the model I have proposed, Giddens's idea of structuration or Vygotsky's model of development. I think that a number of critics of majority/minority reciprocity do not always grasp the issue at stake. They do not seem to be interested in my opinion, nor do they ask for a rejoinder. I often have the impression that some people think I cannot read or understand English. So they attribute opinions to me, or pass judgements over my head, as anthropologists do with articles over the heads of so-called primitives, trusting that they will not read what is written about them. Is it because I live in France? All things considered, they say what they want and are satisfied simply with agreeing with one another. I regret this state of affairs more for the intellectual climate of the field than for myself. What matters and what remains with us is what brings new ideas and new phenomena. And this is different from mere polemics, which is not always a happy time. I simply want to say that behind the objections of some and the irony of others, there lies the unmentioned but ever present functionalist model which corresponds to our spontaneous positivism, empiricism and a particular representation of society. This accounts for its extraordinary persistence, as well as that of the notions deriving from it in our discipline. It is a static, mechanistic model with a preference for automatic repetitive processes. I am attracted by dynamic phenomena, generative notions and the study of phenomena *in statu nascendi*. This, in a nutshell, is the spirit of the genetic model.

IM   Yes. I certainly agree with your diagnosis – in fact, some years ago I expressed, in a similar manner, the hidden nature of our 'Cartesian', by which I meant static, thinking. However, although the conception on which the genetic model is based has a general validity in sciences, including natural sciences, it is important to point out that you were the first to introduce it in empirical social psychology.

To me conceptually the genetic model also underlies the theory of social representations because there too we have the relationship between majority, whatever that is, and minority. This mutual interdependence, however, is difficult to capture in the laboratory because such a process is complex and long-term. One can examine only parts of that process and piece them together only later. For example, one can demonstrate in the laboratory the operation of behavioural style, but its formidable strength and consequences in the activities of a dissident and their effect on the totalitarian regime are not, surely, the subject-matter of a laboratory examination. If one wanted to study social influence in the laboratory one would probably have to do something else, one would also have to show how majorities and minorities achieve this social change.

SM   That is difficult to study in the laboratory.

IM   Precisely, and this is why I thought that the study of representations and influence are complementary in this way. I equally think that it's difficult to study representations in the laboratory. You gave some examples when you did it with Faucheux. I think that these examples, however, are of a different nature because you already know what the representation is.

3   SOCIAL REPRESENTATIONS, THE THEORY OF INNOVATION, LANGUAGE AND COMMUNICATION

IM   Parsons (1968) reminds us of Durkheim's emphasis on the symbolic nature of collective and social representations. For a system to be symbolic, it must be cultural and social, and language, Parsons points out, is the prototype here. Throughout our dialogue today the question of the relationship between social representations and language has kept recurring at various stages. Language and communication were part of your original definition of social representations as you gave it in *La Psychanalyse*. However, one can go even further back. You describe in the *Chronique des années égarées* your observations of conversations in Italy before you first came to France. At that time, you did not speak Italian and you commented on your observations as 'my Berlitz school for Italian' (Moscovici, 1997, p. 506). Rhythm of body movement, nuances in the tone of voice, interdependence between gestures and words and their effect on thought – all this seems to have led to the realization of 'the importance of conversation in my theory of social representations' (ibid., p. 506). The same theme, the importance of communication in the development of knowledge in human science is also emphasized in your *Essai sur l'histoire humaine de la nature* ([1968]/1977). Therefore our dialogue today would be incomplete without touching on the interdependence between language and social representations.

SM   Oh, I knew you were going to raise this issue. It was essential from the very beginning to establish the relationship between communication and social representations. One conditions the other because we cannot communicate unless we share certain representations, and a representation is shared and enters our social heritage when it becomes an object of interest and of communication. Without it, it would lead to atrophy and, in the end, it would disappear. Thus in *La Psychanalyse* I differentiated between three systems of communication – diffusion, propagation and propaganda – according to the source, the goal and the logic of messages. If I remember this well, these were the first articles I published in social psychology. Sure, this preceded the fashion for semiotics; it was before I discovered Bakhtin. Today I speak about communication genres. Conversation is the primary genre of communication in which, I suggested from the start, common-sense knowledge is formed. The other three, diffusion, propagation and propaganda, are secondary genres of communication and they are, unfortunately, much less studied. Following this idea, one has to regard forms of thought or knowledge as inseparable from language and from the genre of communication. Clearly this is the *background*, to use Searle's word, of a particular vision. One of the more general ideas about which I have never stopped thinking since the day I discovered Tarde is the comparative science of conversation in different cultures, according to the posture of bodies; the rules one has to respect, relations between sexes, and so on. And I imagined hypotheses based on the comparison of the modes of speaking and knowledge. Then I carried out two or three studies which enriched my initial hypothesis about the respective positions of the bodies – for example, back to back, etc. – and the syntactic features of the language spoken or of the ideas expressed. In Belgium, my colleague Bernard Rimé has developed this kind of study and I see that, more recently, Robert Kraus at Columbia University has got interested in the same phenomena. Despite Rommetveit's efforts and my own in Europe and those of Robert Kraus in the United States, language does not yet have a place in social psychology, as if people did not think with words and utterances but with 'bits' of information, whatever that means, as if they did not engage in dialogue and did not even have an internal monologue – actually internal monologue has been dubbed rumination. Introducing language into social psychology, studying men after and not before they had discovered this marvellous ability of speech, was a pleasant dream – and has remained so.

It is right to say that when people talk about *La Psychanalyse* they focus on representation and overlook the second part of the book, which deals with communication and language. As you say, I paid attention not only to changes in contents but also to changes in the way people talk about it. If we are interested in social thinking, we cannot just imagine people chewing information or chewing knowledge as if they were speechless or body-less. My hypothesis in *La Psychanalyse* was that there are different systems of communication and conversation at interpersonal levels, just as there is diffusion, propagation and propaganda at the 'mass' level; and that their 'rules' or logic shape these social representations in specific ways. Psychoanalysis was not just taken out of books and made public. There was a cultural fight, the Communists fighting against it, the Catholic Church subtly and consistently resisting it and constructing a rather different innocuous representation. It was only in the seventies that the situation changed with psychoanalysis becoming a quasi-civil religion. I showed how social practices became related, for example, the talking cure and confession, how these practices express their representations in language and how language itself changes at the same time. For me, communication is part of the study of representations because representations are generated in this process of communication and then, of course, expressed through language. I have always thought that conversation is something very basic to social psychology. This point of view was – and still is – sometimes ridiculed in the sense that conversation was thought to be something in itself, something hanging metaphysically on its own. It was in the context of the study of communication that I started thinking about cultural fights – what the Germans call *Kulturkampf* – something like 'a battle of ideas', and these take place in the field of communication in the formation of social representation. So a social representation is not a quiet thing consisting of an object and a science and the transformation of that object. Usually, there is kind of ideological battle, a battle of ideas, and such battles are important even in science. As Einstein said, the only difference between a science and a war is that in science you do not kill people; people do not die in the scientific battle of ideas. I think that what is very much lacking in social psychology today is concern with the strife of ideas.

IM So studying social representations of psychoanalysis was particularly relevant because the issue was important at the time, it was in the foreground, it was salient. It was, so to speak, in the language and communication of the time. When my colleagues and I started research, after the collapse of Communism in Central and Eastern Europe in 1990, into the social representations of democracy, I knew nothing about your analysis of language in *La Psychanalyse*. Yet, our questions were similar to yours: has Communist propaganda, during forty years in power, succeeded in changing social representations of democracy? Just as in your study of psychoanalysis, so the word 'democracy' was particularized, it was given specific ideological meanings which, however, obtained a global ideological significance, for example, 'bourgeois democracy', 'Soviet democracy', and so on. It was then that Ragnar Rommetveit brought to my attention the work of the philosopher Arne Naess on the semantic analysis of democracy. Naess carried out his research as part of the UNESCO study during the Cold War in 1950. The aim of this study was, through an understanding of word meanings used by the rival ideologies of the socialist East and the capitalist West, to decrease international tension. Naess observed that the Soviet politicians never used the term 'democracy' without an adjective, referring to either 'proletarian democracy' or 'capitalist democracy' and so on, with 'Soviet democracy' being at the top of all possible democracies. Thus they obviously used the same rules of propaganda that you described in *La Psychanalyse*.

3.1 Persuasion and propaganda

SM   You can consider the theory of innovation as a deepening of the theory of communication which captivated me at the time, and still captivates me. Unfortunately people take only a marginal interest in it. Many of the psychologists I know separate the phenomenon of communication from the phenomenon of influence. Even if I understand their reasons for doing so, I do not think these reasons are convincing. In many respects I consider the distinction between these two phenomena as artificial. Every message, every linguistic emission is based on a persuasive intention. Is not this idea inherent in the model of communication put forward by Grice? My theory is a theory of influence; but by the same token it is a theory of the communicative process that normally takes place between the partisans and the opponents of different points of view. This is how I applied it when I was a party to the creation of the ecological movement in Europe and some people accepted it as expressing the psychology of those who took part in the movement. I was lucky to propose theories on what is considered as the basic phenomenon in social psychology. Yet I think that we should make an effort to unify the concepts and phenomena, to put an end to subdivisions that have subsisted for thirty or forty years, and somehow use Occam's razor on such notions as attitude, normative and informational influences, prejudice and many others, even if I, just like others, have worked with them. These notions no longer seem to me to have heuristic value. This remark is not going to win me any friends, yet I am convinced that this is what we have to do.

IM   You pointed out that when we talk about influence and communication we have to distinguish the problem of persuasion from the genres of communication. I am not clear about this distinction.

SM   I shall try to explain. Communication is a social process and a social institution. Changing people's minds is just a part of it but it is not the goal of that process. You can say that prayer is a communication genre, it is very important, it is the cure of the soul. Prayer changes people's minds but it is not the real goal of this communication genre. Now persuasion is the part of the process which has to do with changing people; you have to have an idea of the structure of the culture, of the structure of the group which uses the continuous communication institution. We have communication institutions; a school is a communication institution. Depending on whether it succeeds or not it has a certain structure; at a certain time you can ask yourself does it succeed, does it change, and that is the persuasion problem.

IM   Would persuasion and propaganda be at the same level then?

SM   No, no. Propaganda is something that is in institutions; propaganda is not just 'I want to change people's minds,' it is something that an institution does continually and changing people's minds is a part of it. Propaganda attempts to maintain the structure of the institution, maintain the representation and maintain the social fabric. We communicate, society has to communicate continuously, whether well or not so well. So representations are related to this ongoing process of communication and changing opinions is a part of it. Briefly, propaganda and prayer are also rituals and their function is to maintain the institution, party, etc.

IM   I shall attempt to summarize what I understand. Propaganda does many things in society in order to maintain and strengthen existing social representations – and also to create new social representations. Earlier in this dialogue we were speaking about the attempt of the Communist press and of the Church to create new social representations of psychoanalysis. Among all these things that propaganda does it also changes people's minds. It is not its main goal – although it might be quite an important goal, as both you and I experienced when living in totalitarian regimes.
   In contrast, processes of influence operate largely through persuasive communication, the primary goal of which is to change people's minds. This process might involve some other changes, but these would not be strategically planned. At the beginning you were talking about science, ideology and common sense. So in some sense in Communism or in Marxism propaganda used both science and ideology for its purposes. In fact, in the Soviet bloc there was a profession of 'propagandist' whose task was to educate people in Marxism-Leninism.

SM   Yes, but it was the institution of the society, of the party. It was communication, as prayer is the communication of the Church. It was not done independently of that institution. So when you try to understand propaganda you have to look at all that, and not only at changing the minds of the people. Propaganda is an institution and we experience it, for example, in the media. The media make propaganda all the time. Concerning the social psychology of influence, here we are concerned only with the problem as to how this process of communication changes the minds of people. In the studies on minority influence I focused mainly on persuasion, how minorities influence.

   The study of communication which I did on psychoanalysis and propaganda was not the study of persuasion, it was the study of certain communication genres, of certain institutions. In contrast, in the studies on minorities I focused on another aspect of communication, on persuasion and influence.

3.2   Social representations and social construction

IM   You said earlier that you do not accept just talk for talk's sake as being a basis of social psychology, metaphysically hanging on its own. This brings me to the last point I would like to discuss with you, that is, the questions concerning the relationship between the theory of social representations and social construction. When I use the term 'social construction', I must be more specific: I mean what today is known as constructionism, related to some 'radical' forms of discourse analysis. I have recently heard arguments – and I think they are heard more and more often – that social representations and discourse analysis are similar for the following reasons: they are both concerned with language; both are constructivist; both are concerned with the critique of individualist and positivist science. In my view, these quoted similarities are too general to form the basis of any serious integrative attempts. I would like to remind you of what Kurt Danziger (1997) said recently about social constructionism, discourse analysis and post-modernism in his review essay, published in *Theory and Psychology*, of eleven books written on the subject of constructionism and similar subjects: 'the relativistic implications of treating all knowledge as locally constructed forbid the privilege of any agenda, whether it be that of authoritarian objectivism or that of emancipation.' He continues by saying that, in the end, it is not even clear why one should prefer social constructionism to traditional empiricism. Moreover, social constructionism started as a critique and it continues as a critique. In this sense it is parasitic on the theories it criticizes. As a result, it hardly develops a positively stated theory that would withstand criticism.

SM   I was amused in reading Danziger's (1997) review and seeing that of the two topics he singled out, one is concerned with collective remembering and the other with causality, the topics which have been grounded in the idea of representation by Halbwachs and by Fauconnet. A propos, do you know that Lévy-Bruhl was considered in France to be a social psychologist and so was Halbwachs?

I have several pictures of social constructionism. To begin, there is Richard Rorty's ironical stance and the attempt to 'unmask' some of the existing categories, such as beliefs about science, about schizophrenia, race and so on. But it is never clear what is unmasked, whether a shared representation, an idea or 'the thing', to take a term from Lacan. Unmasking is Mannheim's view, which was practised by the intellectuals of the left. Is it radical or does it pretend to be radical? Marx said somewhere that to be radical means to go to the roots, to be critical, and to transform your criticism into a political weapon. You have read my autobiographical story and you know that this is what I did. And later in life, my criticism concerning science, nature and women's inequality made me become one of the pioneers of political ecology, actively participating in demonstrations against nuclear plants or standing as a candidate for election. I believe that social representations imply a critical and not an ironical stance, which can lead to practical engagement. The theory of minority influence has been consciously applied by some of the 'green' movements.

Secondly, I see social constructionism as opposing positivism and promoting a technique, namely discourse analysis. Frankly, positivism is a stance which has been dead for a long time. Concerning discourse analysis, it is perfectly compatible with the theory of social representations. In fact, discourse analysis started next-door in my lab with the work of Pecheux and Henry. It was applied to the study of social representations by Pecheux himself. This is not astonishing, given that Ragnar Rommetveit and I were the first two social psychologists to advocate seriously the integration of language in social psychology. I even published the first book of readings on the social psychology of language in English. It is true, though, that I do not subscribe to the formula 'language *über alles*'. This I consider wrong and no serious thinker would ever endorse it, including Wittgenstein or Austin.

Thirdly, I did not encounter any convincing paper saying how we construct socially. Just by conversation and negotiation around the position on the power scale? And how can you construct something without having a shared representation, even a Utopia? In my experience and vision society is too big an animal, too forceful a one, to be reduced to interpersonal transactions and intersubjective negotiations. I wrote about this topic in my book *The Invention of Society*, so I will not repeat my arguments here.

Finally, I am very reluctant to accept that science is, to borrow a phrase from Hegel, 'the night in which all cats are grey', meaning that nothing is either true or false, that all theories and ideas have the same value or rather non-value. Curiously, one gets the impression that, if science has become an ideology,

Ideas and their Development

what was ideology has been substituted for knowledge or science. But this is not certain. Having no philosophical training, I would not like to pass a judgement on those who are supposed to know. Yet it is true that sometimes, when reading one of those books, I am struck by the trenchant character of their assertions. Then I suddenly remember that epistemology too can be a form of censorship which, in other climates, may have cost many a life. In ours, it only touches on intellectual ostracism. There is a sociological fact for you!

IM   You often refer to the researcher's creativity and to the importance of the discovery of new phenomena, which you see as being features of the theory of social representations. Could you say a few words about this?

SM   This is a matter of personal experience and choice. When I was young many people in France were writing articles and books about what was right or wrong, what was a critical or an apologetic science, what was good or bad social psychology, and so on. Although I had some ideas about this I rarely expressed them. I did not believe – and I still do not believe – that a good epistemology or a good ideology leads to creativity. For me, science and philosophy are forms of art. Like artists, researchers strive to create something, to coin new notions, to discover phenomena, to invent alternative theories or practices. Such creative practices are in themselves a criticism of existing theories and practices. One does not destroy what one replaces. This was the goal I set myself when I became a researcher: to discover, to invent, and to be critical by way of achieving something new. I think that you can change social science, social psychology, by creating a new theory, and that the creation of a new theory is in itself criticism. Moreover, I think that criticism without a real alternative theory has no teeth, it is something fictive. Here as elsewhere, it is true that 'men make history, but they do not know what history they make.'

IM   Why do you think people are trying to put constructionism and discourse analysis together with social representations?

SM   Do they? For the worshipper of the computer metaphor, all these trends represent holism, language, meaning, who knows. For others, it is just a good intention. But as the proverb says, 'The road to hell is paved with good intentions.' How could I know whether this could be achieved in a creative way? Social constructionism is at its best a metatheory. The theory of social representations, I would say, can be viewed in two perspectives. First, it is a theory conceived to respond to specific questions concerning beliefs and social bonds, and to discover new phenomena. Secondly, it is also the basis of a social psychology of knowledge. It is concerned with common-sense thinking and with language and communication. Parsons reminds us that language was a prototype integrating cultural and individual phenomena and that therefore it was part of the study of collective and social representations from the very beginning. Discourse analysis, so far, lacks a genuine theory of dialogue and language. The theory of social representations is concerned on the one hand with questions of social bonding and action and on the other hand with social knowledge, communication and language. In my opinion, discourse analysis is a part of it. After all, you know these questions better than I do, you have written about them.

4 THE EUROPEAN ASSOCIATION OF SOCIAL PSYCHOLOGY

IM We have spoken about your work as a social psychologist. However, you were also very influential in establishing the European Association of Social Psychology. Could you give some biographical details relating to that part of your work?

SM My age of innocence ended at the beginning of the sixties when I met other European and American social psychologists. It was actually John Lanzetta, an American social psychologist, who organized a meeting in Sorrento, then in Frascati, where I met with other colleagues. I suppose you are not interested to know how I was elected at Frascati into an *ad hoc* committee, then made the proposal to create a European association, as a kind of active minority, and became its first president. You are probably interested in more substantial choices. Let me put the thing in the following way. The Americans I met were thinking of us, European social psychologists, in terms of two tendencies. The first, let us call it the cloning tendency, was to use Europe as a field of comparative studies and generalization. So they wanted to train social psychologists in their image, sharing their ideas and methods, in short, to create a branch of American social psychology in Europe. The second tendency, let us call it the dissemination tendency, tried mainly to help us create laboratories, to associate with those who were, they supposed, creative social psychologists and let them do what they judged fruitful. For them, of course, the growth of European social psychology did not mean the growth of theories with only local validity; these theories were to expand in the context of research traditions and thinking that they knew were specific to this context. I would not like to name people, but Festinger was the advocate of the second tendency.

I remember meeting him, Schachter and Lanzetta in the Hôtel de la Ville in Rome and we discussed that. We agreed that you cannot hope to foster research in a young science which has hardly crystallized, even in America, just by imitation, just by importing ideas or methods. They were even more radical than I. Festinger said, we'll just help you to start, meaning you create your field and the association in your own way, and then we leave, institutionally speaking. At first I was reluctant, because I thought it was too good to be true, and also because of some previous experiences I would not like to mention. Events, however, have shown that I was wrong. I became a member of the Transnational Committee on Social Psychology whose president was Leon Festinger. This committee was very active in the building of the European Association and later in that of the Latin-American Association. I became the president when, for institutional reasons, the committee was transferred from the Social Science Research Council in New York to UNESCO in Paris. Throughout those years, although its membership altered, we remained an active, friendly group, and I think we did a reasonably good job.

There are many social psychologists who consider me as a European patriot. That is comic and reassuring, given my nomadic life. Of course I like Europe, its style of life, richness of culture, diversity of people and historical creativity. And Paris does not exist on any other continent and I love Paris. But the other side of the coin in Europe is its tragedies, cruelties and terrible wars, which are not creative destructions but destructions *tout court*. Our attitude in relation to other people depends on history and then on experience. For me the United States and the Americans are neither any country whatever nor any people whatever. It was not on a campus that I first met some Americans, it was in Vienna, Munich and also in the camps for displaced persons just after the Second World War. My feelings, my impressions relative to them date back to those experiences. Like many other Europeans, I owe them my life, my liberty, and this creates a link of the heart, an everlasting gratitude. It continued, since I understood a lot of things concerning research in general and social psychology in particular, thanks to my contacts and work with them. I would not have become the same man and I would not have worked in the same way if I had not been lucky enough to meet and bind myself in deep friendship with Americans such as Festinger, Deutsch, Lanzetta, Schachter, Kelley, Berkowitz, Zajonc and so many others who have stimulated, criticized me, but who also took seriously what I was doing, and even encouraged me to publish in English some research work *in statu nascendi*, as did Berkowitz when I talked to him about my work on language or innovation.

And then, in a way, I have had a parallel career in America, at the New School. No doubt we had certain intellectual and generational affinities and a *libido sciendi* going far beyond considerations of interest or career, which does not mean that we had the same vision of social psychology or of theoretical problems. I would not say, for example, that the theory of social representations in particular was their cup of tea. But I never heard anyone telling me that it is stupid, European, unscientific, or that I should not go on with it. I think we had genuine respect for one another. Look, I will tell you an anecdote. When Faucheux and I published our first paper on minority influence, it elicited both curiosity and scepticism. Now, during the summer vacations Lanzetta organized a kind of seminar in Dartmouth. And for three weeks every afternoon we discussed the ideas and experiments concering this form of influence. If I remember well, among the Americans there were, in addition to Lanzetta, Brehm, Kelley, Sarah and Chuck Kiesler, who allowed me to grasp more clearly the theoretical and empirical questions that could be put.

This is to explain how close the links between Europeans and Americans were and how much I wanted to work with them. After all, social psychology had only just crystallized into an autonomous discipline and we had a common goal. I repeat, there were differences indeed, but in retrospect some people exaggerate them, as they do not know the other side of the coin. Be that as it may, at least this is how I felt it: the Americans did not see Europe as an intellectual desert, and we did not look up to America as some sort of Mecca to which people have to make a pilgrimage to come back as qualified believers. This may be due to the fact that our American colleagues had been the students of European professors, and we were already too far advanced in our personal thinking, had undergone too difficult experiences to give up ideas, a style of research that we took to heart. We wanted to restore in Europe the kind of scientific life that the war had interrupted and make up for its losses in talent and ideas. Some Americans expected and wanted it too. In this sense alone I am a European patriot. Nietzsche said that when one culture imitates another, it imitates its superficial characters. This is also true as it concerns science. I was lucky to know America and the Americans in depth, without trying either to imitate or not to imitate them, simply to understand and learn by impregnation.

No doubt things have altered since and perhaps, as often happens, they did not turn out as I would have liked them to. I am not always happy about the way in which my research has been dealt with and appropriated over there. I do not think that Americans do a service to social psychology and to themselves in their way of considering the research that is done elsewhere, or when they impose a premature uniformity, a professional code, writing and initiation rules that detract much from intellectual life and hamper its creativity. No more than some European colleagues do a service to our discipline when they think that they will earn more professional respectability and scientific security by following the pattern of a 'normalized' science. I mean by that, doing what scientists do in the United States at a certain time and being approved by them. It simplifies life, yet it does so on condition that one underestimates the actual diversity of research currents, even in America. Just walk along Fifth Avenue in New York from New York University to Columbia, going by the New School and the Graduate Center, and you will see this diversity! At the same time, it is a fact of life, the Americanization of human sciences, in Manicas's words, is a reality and we cannot turn our heads away from it. Yet I am persuaded that, if not the present generation, another one will realize that there are different ways of facing this fact of history. And that it is dangerous as well as illusory, as I told our American colleagues of the American Society of Social Psychology in Ohio, to create a science for and in a single country, as it was dangerous and illusory to create a socialist society in a single country. In every scientific endeavour, and especially in human science, diversity is an asset and uniformity a loss.

I have always tried to encourage such a diversity, related to cultural and research traditions in the network of people working on social representations. And when someone asks me to tell him what is the 'true' way of doing it, my answer is that I am not the owner of the fruits of the theory. In this sense, I am a European patriot. I like the diversity of its research and epistemological styles, its tradition that an intellectual still speaks and writes in several languages, its respect for history and the work of past generations, and many things of this kind, which you also find in America if you take your time and look for the right people. It is true that, looking back, the idea of social representation is very much embedded in the European tradition of linking scientific areas, anthropology, sociology, history, linguistics, Piaget's and Vygotsky's and even social psychology. But let's not indulge in stereotypes.

Another biographical point is related to social representations. I remember presenting the theory for the first time at Sorrento, at the first meeting of European social psychologists organised by John Lanzetta. Hilda Himmelweit was chairing the session and my English was terrible. Nobody understood what I was saying but my talk was followed by a very lively discussion about what my colleagues really saw as a projective test. This is how the theory started to spread a little in France, then in Bologna and afterwards in London through Hilda, who became intrigued by it. Not that she understood the theory but because she was convinced that I was not entirely stupid, so she thought that there was probably something in what I was saying.

5   THE FUTURE OF SOCIAL PSYCHOLOGY

IM   Is there anything else you would like to add to complete this dialogue?

SM   In a way I am a chauvinist concerning social psychology because I believe that it is a discipline that really grasps the main historical and cultural phenomena, phenomena which are also politically sensitive. I would like to conclude this dialogue by saying a word about the last part of your earlier question which is a matter of an epistemological stance. Speaking in general terms, how does one combine and unify two disciplines or two scientific fields? Obviously this question is relevant to social psychology and even more so to the theory of social representations. To be sure, the idea of social psychology encompasses a very broad field of knowledge ranging from the framework of sociology to the framework of psychology. And thus, some believe that the theory of social representations, because of its origin, should be situated more in the former than in the latter framework. This, however, can lead to a reductionist epistemology as was the case when it was thought that the only way to approach phenomena of a complex nature is to situate them in different universes. Thus psychology was reduced to a social explanation, and sociology, in turn, was reduced to a psychological explication. There is yet another epistemology that does not attempt to 'reduce' but to search for a 'commonality' or a unity between the separate disciplines in the study of certain phenomena. The most famous case is that of electromagnetism. For decades there had been attempts to 'reduce', without success, mechanical models or mechanical phenomena to electrical models. Finally, the model of relativity unified both. Obviously I am not Einstein, and the theory of social representations is not the theory of relativity. However, this does not prevent me from considering social psychology as a discipline which seeks to discover unity and commonality among models of sociology and models of psychology concerning certain phenomena which neither one nor the other could take up alone, such as, for example, the communication of influence or the study of social networks. There is a built-in limit to the effectiveness of any reduction for the discovery of novelty, and certainly we could make more progress or advance better by pulling together the resources of two or three disciplinary fields, just as was the case with cybernetics.

In other words, the ideal condition is one in which we enlarge the scope of social psychology, not one in which we divide the loaf into two halves by considering two sub-specialities, a 'sociological psychology' and a 'psycho-sociology'. I did not respond, in the past, to claims that the theory of social representations is more a sociological form of social psychology than a psychological form of social psychology because I did not want to complicate an already complex debate. And yet, I do not want our theory to be evacuated from social psychology into sociology by a reductionist epistemology, which is so widely adopted. As prominent a thinker as Chomsky rejects the latter for reasons which deserve to be mentioned. In a recent book on *Language and Thought* (1993, p. 80) he observes that: 'The problem of science is not reductionism, it is unification, which is something quite different. There are different ways of looking at the world. They work to whatever extent they do, we would like to integrate them; but reduction is one way to integrate them. And in fact, through the course of modern science, that has rarely been true.' Seen in this light it is possible to suppose that social psychology will not mature until it starts to consider this problem of unification seriously. And to revert to where we started this dialogue, to the age of innocence, I think that the theory of social representations and communication touches on the main phenomena of the field of social psychology. Therefore I consider the theory of social representations to be a theory unifying the field of social psychology – the field which appeared, from a distance, in my age of innocence – and even to move towards solving its problem of unification. I am convinced, on conceptual grounds, that it is the only theory which today can unify our highly fragmented discipline, which has reduced the humanity of individuals and social groups to something abstract, stereotyped and minimal. Man today, Kundera said somewhere, finds himself in a true vortex of reductionism, and our discipline also contributes to it, as if a human being were not complex and full of contradictions, had no passions and beliefs, were not always in the tension between knowledge and belief in his personal life just as in social movements. But I do not want to make prophecies about the future of social psychology. I want to say simply that social psychology could occupy a significant place among other sciences and in society, and that it should leave the vortex of reductionism and take hold of the phenomena of thought and communication among people in their unity, this is to say, in their labyrinthine existence. Deep down, what I have always believed – and still believe – is that social psychology should strive to be a kind of anthropology of our culture. If this becomes true one day, then it will occupy its place as a major discipline which all our classics have anticipated and prophesied. And not to strive for such a place is not to have a hope.

References

NB. Where two dates are given for a text, the first indicates the date of the original publication, and the second that of a later edition or an English translation.

Ableson, R. P., Aronson, E., McGuire, W. J., Newcomb, T. M., Rosenburg, M. J. and Tannenbaum, P. H. (eds) (1968). *Theories of Cognitive Consistency*. Chicago: Rand McNally.

Abric, J.-C. (1976). *Jeux, conflits et représentations sociales*. Thèse de Doctorat ès Lettres. Université de Provence, Aix-en-Provence.

—— (1984). A theoretical and experimental approach to the study of social representations in a situation of interaction. In R. Farr and S. Moscovici (eds), *Social Representations*. Cambridge: Cambridge University Press, 169–83.

—— (1988). *Coopération, compétition et représentations sociales*. Cousset: Del Val.

Abric, J.-C., Faucheux, C., Moscovici, S. and Plon, M. (1967). Approche et évitement dans des jeux à motivation mixte. *Psychologie Française*, *12*, 277–86.

Ackermann, W. and Zygouris, R. (1974). Représentation et assimilation de la connaissance scientifique. *Bulletin de CERP*, *22* (1–2).

Alexander, L. N., Zucker, L. G. and Brody, C. L. (1970). Experimental expectations and autokinetic experiences: consistency theories and judgemental convergence. *Sociometry*, *28*, 108–22.

Allport, F. (1924). *Social Psychology*. Boston: Houghton Mifflin.

Anderson, H. N. (1968). A simple model for information integration. In R. P. Ableson, E. Aronson, W. J. McGuire, T. M. Newcomb, M. J. Rosenburg and P. H. Tannenbaum (eds), *Theories of Cognitive Consistency*. Chicago: Rand McNally.

Ansart, P. (1988). Le concept de représentation en sociologie. In L. Marbeau and F. Audigier (eds), *Seconde rencontre internationale sur la didactique de l'histoire et de la géographie*. Paris: I.N.R.P.

Arendt, H. (1970). *Men in Dark Times*. London: Jonathan Cape.

Aristotle (1994). *Posterior Analytics*, trans. Jonathan Barnes. Oxford: Clarendon Press.

Asch, S. (1952). *Social Psychology*. Englewood Cliffs, NJ: Prentice-Hall.

Back, K. W. (1964). La domaine de la psychologie sociale. *Bulletin du C.E.R.P.*, *13*, 21–33.

Barbichon, G. and Moscovici, S. (1965). Diffusion des connaissances scientifiques. *Social Science Information*, *4*, 7–22.

Bartlett, F. C. (1923). *Psychology and Primitive Culture*. Cambridge: Cambridge University Press.

—— (1932). *Remembering – A Study in Experimental and Social Psychology*. Cambridge: Cambridge University Press.

Bauer, M. and Gaskell, G. (1999). Towards a paradigm for research on social representations. *Journal for the Theory of Social Behaviour*, *29*, 163–86.

Bem, D. J. (1965). An experimental analysis of self-persuasion. *Journal of Experimental Social Psychology*, *1*, 199–218.

Berger, P. L. and Luckmann, T. (1966). *The Social Construction of Reality*. Garden City, NY: Doubleday.

Bergson, H. ([1932]/1935). *The Two Sources of Morality and Religion*, trans. R. Ashley Audra and Cloudesley Brereton. London: Macmillan.

Berlin, I. (1981). *Against the Current*. Oxford: Oxford University Press.

Billig, M. (1987). *Arguing and Thinking: A Rhetorical Approach to Social Psychology*. Cambridge: Cambridge University Press.

—— (1988). Social representation, objectification and anchoring: a rhetorical analysis. *Social Behaviour*, *3*, 1–16.

—— (1993). Studying the thinking society: social representations, rhetoric and attitudes. In G. Breakwell and D. Canter (eds), *Empirical Approaches to Social Representations*. Oxford: Oxford University Press, 39–62.

Blum, L. (1982). *Souvenirs sur l'affaire*. Paris: Gallimard.

Bower, T. (1977). *The Perceptual World of the Child*. London: Fontana.

Brehm, J. W. (1966). *A Theory of Psychological Reactance*. London: Academic Press.

Broch, H. (1979). *Massenwahntheorie*. Frankfurt: Suhrkamp.

Brown, R. (1965). *Social Psychology*. New York: Free Press.

Butor, M. (1960). *Répertoire*, vol. 1. Paris: Editions de Minuit.

Carrier Duncan, J. (1985). Linking of thematic roles in derivational word formation. *Linguistic Inquiry*, *16*, 1–34.

Carroll, J. S. and Paine, J. W. (1976). *Cognition and Social Behaviour*. Hillsdale, NJ: Lawrence Erlbaum.

Cassirer, E. (1946). *The Myth of the State*. New York: Doubleday.

Chapanis, N. P. and Chapanis, A. (1962). Cognitive dissonance: five years later. *Psychological Bulletin*, *61*, 1–22.

Charle, C. (1977). Champ littéraire et champ du pouvoir: Les écrivains et l'affaire Dreyfus. *Annales*, *32*, 240–64.

Chombart de Lauwe, M. J. (1971). *Un Monde autre: l'enfance, de ses représentations à son mythe*. Paris: Payot.

Chomsky, N. (1975). *Reflections on language*. New York: Pantheon.

—— (1982). *Some Concepts and Consequences of the Theory of Government and Binding*. Cambridge, MA: MIT Press.

—— (1993). *Language and Thought*. Wakefield: Moyer Bell.

Coch, L. and French, J. R. P. (1953). Overcoming resistance to change. In D. Cartwright and A. Zander (eds), *Group Dynamics: Research and Theory*. Evanston, IL: Tow Peterson, 336–50.

Cocking, J. M. (1982). *Proust*. Cambridge: Cambridge University Press.

Codol, J. P. (1974). On the system of representations in a group situation. *European Journal of Social Psychology*, *4*, 343–65.

Codol, J. P. and Flament, C. (1971). Représentation de structures sociales simples dans lesquelles le sujet est impliqué. *Cahiers de Psychologie*, *14*, 203–18.

Collins, B. E. and Guetzkow, H. (1964). *A Social Psychology of Group Processes for Decision Making*. New York: John Wiley.

Corbin, A. (1977). Le péril vénérien au début du siècle: prophylaxie sanitaire et prophylaxie morale. *Recherches*, *23*, 63–71.

Cornford, F. M. (1912). *From Religion to Philosophy*. London: E. Arnold.

Culicover, P. (1988). Autonomy, predication and thematic relations. *Syntax and Semantics*, *21*, 37–60.

Danziger, K. (1979). The positivist repudiation of Wundt. *Journal of the History of the Behavioural Sciences*, *15*, 205–30.

—— (1990). *Constructing the Subject*. Cambridge: Cambridge University Press.

—— (1997). The varieties of social construction. *Theory and Psychology*, *7*, 399–416.

Davy, G. (1931). *Sociologues d'hier et d'aujourd'hui*. Paris: Alcan.

Deaux, K. and Philogene, G. (eds) (2000). *Social Representations: Introductions and Explorations*. Oxford: Blackwell.

De Rosa, A. M. (1987). The social representations of mental illness in children and adults. In W. Doise and S. Moscovici (eds), *Current Issues in European Social Psychology*, vol. 2. Cambridge: Cambridge University Press, 47–138.

Delacampagne, C. (1983). *L'Invention du racisme*. Paris: Fayard.

Deleuze, G. (1970). *Proust et les signes*. Paris: Presses Universitaires de France.

Delhorbe, C. (1932). *L'affaire Dreyfus et les écrivains français*. Paris: Attinger.

Deutsch, Morton (1969). Organizational and conceptual barriers to social change. *Journal of Social Issues*, *25*, 5–18.

Deutsch, Morton and Krauss, R. M. (1965). *Theories in Social Psychology*. New York: Basic Books.

Deutscher, I. (1984). Choosing ancestors: some consequences of the selection from intellectual traditions. In R. Farr and S. Moscovici (eds), *Social Representations*. Cambridge: Cambridge University Press, 71–100.

Doise, W. (1969). Intergroup relations and polarization of individual and collective judgements. *Journal of Personality and Social Psychology*, *12*, 136–43.

—— (1992). L'ancrage dans les études sur les représentations sociales. *Bulletin de Psychologie*, *45*, 189–95.

—— (1993). Debating social representations. In G. Breakwell and D. Canter (eds), *Empirical Approaches to Social Representations*. Oxford: Oxford University Press, 157–70.

Doise, W. and Palmonari, A. (eds) (1990). *L'étude des représentations sociales*. Paris: Delachaux et Niestle.

Duby, G. (1961). Histoire des mentalités. In C. Sameran (ed.), *L'histoire et ses méthodes*. Paris: Gallimard.

Durkheim, E. (1895/1982). *The Rules of Sociological Method*, trans. W. D. Halls. London: Macmillan.

—— (1898/1974). Individual and collective representations. In E. Durkheim, *Sociology and Philosophy*. New York: Free Press, 1–34.

Durkheim, E. (1912/1995). *The Elementary Forms of the Religious Life*, trans. Karen Fields. New York: Free Press.

—— (1955/1983). *Pragmatism and Sociology*, trans. J. C. Whitehouse. Cambridge: Cambridge University Press.

—— (1975). *Textes*, vol. 2. Paris: Editions de Minuit.

Duveen, G. (1998). The psychosocial production of ideas: social representations and psychologic. *Culture and Psychology*, *4*, 455–72.

Duveen, G. and Lloyd, B. (eds) (1990). *Social Representations and Development of Knowledge*. Cambridge: Cambridge University Press.

Eiser, J. R. and Stroebe, W. (1972). *Categorization and Social Judgement*. London: Academic Press.

Ellison, R. (1965). *Invisible Man*. Harmondsworth: Penguin.

Emler, N. and Dickinson, J. (1985). Children's representations of economic inequalities. *British Journal of Developmental Psychology*, *3*, 191–8.

Evans-Pritchard, E. E. (1937). *Witchcraft, Oracles and Magic among the Azande*. Oxford: Oxford University Press.

—— (1964). *Social Anthropology and Other Essays*. New York: Free Press.

—— (1965). *Theories of Primitive Religion*. Oxford: Oxford Univesity Press.

Farr, R. M. (1977). Heider, Harré and Herzlich on health and illness: some observations on the structure of 'représentations collectives'. *European Journal of Social Psychology*, *7*, 491–504.

—— (1978). On the varieties of social psychology: an essay on the relations between psychology and other social sciences. *Social Science Information*, *17*, 503–25.

—— (1981). On the nature of human nature and the science of behaviour. In P. Heelas and A. Locke (eds), *Indigenous Psychologies: The Anthropology of the Self*. London: Academic Press.

—— (1984). Social representations: their role in the design and execution of laboratory experiments. In R. M. Farr and S. Moscovici (eds), *Social Representations*. Cambridge: Cambridge University Press, 125–47.

—— (1993). Common sense, science and social representations. *Public Understanding of Science*, *2*, 189–204.

—— (1996). *The Roots of Modern Social Psychology*. Oxford: Blackwell.

—— (1998). From collective to social representations: *Aller et Retour*. *Culture and Psychology*, *4*, 275–96.

Farr, R. M. and Moscovici, S. (eds) (1984). *Social Representations*. Cambridge: Cambridge University Press.

Faucheux, C. (1970). *Cross-cultural Research in Social Psychology*. Unpublished manuscript, Social Science Research Council.

Faucheux, C. and Moscovici, S. (1960). Etudes sur la créativité des groupes: tâche, structure des communications et réussite. *Bulletin du C.E.R.P.*, *9*, 11–22.

—— (1968). Self-esteem and exploitative behaviour in a game against chance and nature. *Journal of Personality and Social Psychology*, *8*, 83–8.

Festinger, L. (1957). *A Theory of Cognitive Dissonance*. Evanston, IL: Row Peterson.

Festinger, L. (1964). *Conflict, Decision and Dissonance*. Stanford, CA: Stanford University Press.

Finis, de V. G. (1994). La filosofia nello specchio della cultura, *Il Mondo*, *31*, 266–77.

Finley, M. (1983). *Politics in the Ancient World*. Cambridge: Cambridge University Press.

Fishbein, M. and Raven, B. (1962). The AB scales: an operational definition of belief and attitude. *Human Relations, 15*, 35–44.

Flament, C. (1965). *Réseaux de communications et structures de groupe.* Paris: Dunod.

—— (1989). Structure ct dynamique des représentations sociales. In D. Jodelet (ed.), *Les Représentations sociales.* Paris: Presses Universitaires de France, 204–19.

Fleck, L. ([1936]/1986). The problem of epistemology. In R. S. Cohen and T. Schnelle (eds), *Cognition and Fact: Materials on Ludwick Fleck.* Dordrecht: Reidel, 79–112.

Flick, U. (1998). Everyday knowledge in social psychology. In U. Flick (ed.), *The Psychology of the Social.* Cambridge: Cambridge University Press, 41–59.

Fodor, J. A. (1975). *The Language of Thought.* New York: Thomas Cromwell.

Foucault, M. (1983). *This is not a Pipe*, trans. James Harkness. Berkeley: University of California Press.

Fraser, C. and Gaskell, G. (eds) (1990). *The Social Psychological Study of Widespread Beliefs.* Oxford: Clarendon Press.

Fraser, C., Gouge, C. and Billig, M. (1971). Risky shifts, cautious shifts and group polarization. *European Journal of Social Psychology, 1*, 7–30.

Frazer, J. (1922). *The Golden Bough.* London: Macmillan.

Frege, G. (1977). The thought: a logical inquiry. In P. Strawson (ed.), *Philosophical Logic.* Oxford: Oxford University Press.

Freyd, J. J. (1983). Shareability: the social psychology of epistemology. *Cognitive Science, 7*, 191–210.

Gellner, E. (1992). *Reason and Culture: the historical role of rationality and rationalism.* Oxford and Cambridge, MA: Blackwell.

Giddens, A. (1985). *Durkheim.* London: Fontana Press.

Goldmann, L. (1976). *Cultural Creation.* St Louis, MO: Telos Press.

Gombrich, E. (1972). *Symbolic Images.* London: Phaidon.

Gorin, M. (1980). *A l'école du groupe: heurs et malheurs d'une innovation éducative.* Paris: Dunod.

Gramsci, A. (1971). *Selections from the Prison Notebooks*, trans. Quintin Hoare and Geoffrey Nowell Smith. London: Lawrence and Wishart.

Grize, J. B. (1993). Logique naturelle et représentations sociales. *Papers on Social Representations, 2*, 151–9.

Harré, R. (1984). Some reflections on the concept of 'social representation'. *Social Research, 51*, 927–38.

—— (1998). The epistemology of social representations. In U. Flick (ed.), *The Psychology of the Social.* Cambridge: Cambridge University Press, 129–37.

Heider, F. (1958). *The Psychology of Interpersonal Relations.* New York: Wiley.

Herzlich, C. (1973). *Health and Illness: A Social Psychological Analysis.* London: Academic Press.

Hewstone, M. and Jaspars, J. (1982). Intergroup relations and attribution processes. In H. Tajfel (ed.), *Social Identity and Intergroup Relations.* Cambridge: Cambridge University Press, 99–133.

Hocart, A. M. (1987). *Imagination and Proof.* Tucson: University of Arizona Press.

Holton, G. (1978). *The Scientific Imagination: Case Studies.* Cambridge: Cambridge University Press.

—— (1988). *Thematic Origins of Scientific Thought.* 2nd edn. Cambridge, MA: Harvard University Press.

Holton, G. (1998). *The Advancement of Science and its Burdens.* Cambridge, MA: Harvard University Press.

Horton, R. (1993). *Patterns of Thought in Africa and in the West.* Cambridge: Cambridge University Press.

Hovland, C. I., Janis, I. L. and Kelley, H. H. (1953). *Communication and Persuasion.* New Haven: Yale University Press.

Israel, J. and Tajfel, H. (eds) (1972). *The Context of Social Psychology.* London: Academic Press.

Jackendorf, R. (1991). *Semantic Structures.* Cambridge, MA: MIT Press.

Jahoda, G. (1970). A psychologist's perspective. In P. Mayer (ed.), *Socialisation: The Approach from Social Psychology.* London: Tavistock.

—— (1982). *Psychology and Anthropology.* London: Academic Press.

—— (1988). Critical notes and reflections on 'social representations'. *European Journal of Social Psychology, 18,* 195–209.

—— (1992). *Crossroads between Culture and Mind.* London: Harvester Wheatsheaf.

Jakobson, R. (1987). *Language in Literature.* Cambridge, MA: Harvard University Press.

James, W. (1890/1980). *The Principles of Psychology.* New York: Dover.

Jaspars, J. (1965). *On Social Perception.* Unpublished Ph.D. thesis, University of Leiden.

Jaspars, J. and Ackermann, E. (1966–7). The interdisciplinary character of social psychology: an illustration. *Sociologica Neerlandica, 4,* 62–79.

Jaspars, J. and Fraser, C. (1984). Attitudes and social representations. In R. M. Farr and S. Moscovici (eds), *Social Representations.* Cambridge: Cambridge University Press, 101–23.

Jodelet, D. (1984). The representation of the body and its transformations. In R. M. Farr and S. Moscovici (eds), *Social Representations.* Cambridge: Cambridge University Press, 211–38.

—— ([1989]/1991). *Madness and Social Representations,* trans. Tim Pownall, ed. Gerard Duveen. Hemel Hempstead: Harvester Wheatsheaf.

—— (1989). Représentations sociales: un domaine en expansion. In D. Jodelet (ed.), *Représentations sociales.* Paris: Presses Universitaires de France, 31–61.

—— (1991a). Soziale Repräsentationen psychischer Krankheit in einem ländlichen Milieu in Frankreich: Entstehung, Struktur, Funktionen. In U. Flick (ed.), *Alltagswissen über Gesundheit und Krankheit – Subjektive Theorien und soziale Repräsentationen.* Heidelberg: Asanger, 269–92.

—— (1991b). Représentation sociale. In *Grand Dictionnaire de la Psychologie.* Paris: Larousse.

Jodelet, D. and Milgram, S. (1977). Cartes mentales et images sociales de Paris. Mimeo, Laboratoire de Psychologie Sociale, Ecole des Hautes Etudes en Sciences Sociales, Paris.

Jovchelovitch, S. (1996). In defence of representations. *Journal for the Theory of Social Behaviour, 26,* 121–35.

Kaës, R. (1968). *Images de la culture chez les ouvriers français.* Paris: Editions Cujas.

—— (1976). *L'Appareil psychique groupal: constructions du groupe.* Paris: Dunod.

Kelley, H. H. and Thibaut, J. W. (1969). Group problem solving. In G. Lindzey and E. Aronson (eds), *The Handbook of Social Psychology,* 2nd edn, vol. IV. Reading, MA: Addison-Wesley, 1–101.

Kolakowski, L. (1978). *La Pologne: une société en dissidence*. Paris: Maspero.

Kopp, R. L. (1971). *Marcel Proust as a Social Critic*. Rutherford, NJ: Fairleigh Dickinson University Press.

Kozulin, A. (1990). *Vygotzky's Psychology*. Hemel Hempstead: Harvester Wheatsheaf.

Kuhn, T. (1962). *The Structure of Scientific Revolutions*. Chicago: University of Chicago Press.

Laudan, L. (1977). *Progress and its Problems*. Berkeley: University of California Press.

Le Goff, J. (1974). Les mentalités: une histoire ambigue. In J. Le Goff and P. Nora (eds), *Faire l'histoire*. Paris: Gallimard. English translation: Mentalities: A history of ambiguities, trans. David Denby. In J. Le Goff and P. Nora (eds) (1985), *Constructing the Past: Essays in Historical Methodology*. Cambridge: Cambridge University Press, 166–80.

Le Roy Ladurie, E. (1980). *Montaillou: Cathars and Catholics in a French Village 1294–1324*, trans. Barbara Bray. London: Penguin.

Lévi-Strauss, C. ([1962]/1966). *The Savage Mind*. London: Weidenfeld and Nicolson.

Lévy-Bruhl, L. ([1925]/1926). *How Natives Think*, trans. Lillian Clare. London: George Allen & Unwin.

Lewin, K. (1948). *Resolving Social Conflicts*. New York: Harper and Row.

Lloyd, G. E. R. (1990). *Demystifying Mentalities*. Cambridge: Cambridge University Press.

Luria, A. R. (1976). *Cognitive Development*, trans. Martin Lopez-Morillas and Lynn Solotaroff, ed. Michael Cole. Cambridge, MA: Harvard University Press.

—— (1979). *The Making of Mind*, ed. Michael and Sheila Cole. Cambridge, MA: Harvard University Press.

Luria, A. R. and Vygotsky, L. S. (1992). *Ape, Primitive Man, and Child: Essays in the History of Behavior*, trans. Evelyn Rossiter. New York and London: Harvester Wheatsheaf.

MacIver, R. M. (1942). *Social Causation*. New York: Ginn.

Mann, T. (1977). *Essays*, vol. 2. Frankfurt: Fischer.

Marková, I. (1982). *Paradigms, Language and Thought*. Chichester and New York: Wiley.

Marková, I. and Wilkie, P. (1987). Representations, concepts and social change: the phenomen of Aids. *Journal for the Theory of Social Behavior*, *17*, 389–401.

Markus, H. and Nurius, P. (1986). Possible selves. *American Psychologist*, *41*, 954–69.

Marx, G. T. and Wood, J. R. (1975). Strands of theory and research in collective behaviour. *Annual Review of Sociology*, *1*, 363–428.

McClelland, D. C., Atkinson, J. W., Clark, R. A. and Lowell, E. L. (1953). *The Achievement Motive*. New York: Appleton Century Crofts.

McDougall, W. (1920). *The Group Mind*. Cambridge: Cambridge University Press.

McGarth, J. and Altman, I. (1966). *Small Group Research: A Synthesis and Critique of the Field*. New York: Holt Rinehart and Winston.

Mead, G. H. (1934). *Mind, Self and Society*. Chicago: University of Chicago Press.

Medawar, P. (1982). Induction and intuition in scientific thought. In *Pluto's Republic*. Oxford: Oxford University Press.

Milgram, S. (1984). Cities as social representations. In R. M. Farr and S. Moscovici (eds), *Social Representations*. Cambridge: Cambridge University Press, 289–309.

Montmollin, G. de (1959). Réflexions sur l'étude et l'utilisation des petits groupes: I Le petit groupe: moyen et objet de connaissance. *Bulletin du C.E.R.P.*, *8*, 293–310.

—— (1960). Réflexions sur l'étude et l'utilisation des petits groupes: II Le petit groupe comme moyen d'action. *Bulletin du C.E.R.P.*, *9*, 109–22.

Moscovici, S. (1954). Analyse hierarchique. *Année Psychologique*, *54*, 83–110.

—— (1961). *Reconversion industrielle et changements sociaux. Un exemple: la Chapellerie dans l'Aude*. Paris: Colin.

—— ([1961]/1976). *La Psychanalyse, son image et son public*. Paris: Presses Universitaires de France.

—— (1967). Communication processes and the properties of language. In L. Berkowitz (ed.), *Advances in Experimental Social Psychology*, vol. 3. New York: Academic Press, 226–70.

—— (1968). *L'Expérience du Mouvement*. Paris: Herman.

—— ([1968]/1977). *Essai sur l'histoire humaine de la nature*. Paris Flammarion.

—— (1976). *Social Influence and Social Change*, trans. Carol Sherrard and Greta Heinz. London: Academic Press.

—— (1979). *Psychologie des minorités actives*. Paris: Presses Universitaires de France.

—— (1981). Bewusste und unbewusste Einflüsse in der Kommunikation. *Zeitschrift für Sozialpsychologie*, *12*, 93–103.

—— (1982). The coming era of social representations. In J. P. Codol and J. P. Leyens (eds), *Cognitive approaches to social behaviour*. The Hague: Nijhoff, 115–50.

—— (1983). Les foules avant la foule. *Stanford French Review*, *7*, 151–74.

—— (1984a). The phenomena of social representations. In R. M. Farr and S. Moscovici (eds), *Social Representations*. Cambridge: Cambridge University Press, 3–69.

—— (1984b). The myth of the lonely paradigm: A rejoinder. *Social Research*, *51*, 939–67.

—— (1985). *The Age of the Crowd: A Historical Treatise on Mass Psychology*. Cambridge: Cambridge University Press.

—— ([1985]/1987). Social Collectivities. In *Essays in Honour of Elias Canetti*, trans. Michael Hulse. London: André Deutsch.

—— (1988). Notes towards a description of social representation. *European Journal of Social Psychology*, *18*, 211–50.

—— (1990a). Social psychology and developmental psychology: extending the conversation. In G. Duveen and B. Lloyd (eds), *Social Representations and the Development of Knowledge*. Cambridge: Cambridge University Press, 164–85.

—— (1990b). The generalized self and mass society. In H. T. Himmelweit and G. Gaskell (eds), *Societal Psychology*. London: Sage, 66–91.

—— ([1988]/1993). *The Invention of Society*, trans. W. D. Halls. Cambridge: Polity Press.

—— (1993a). The return of the unconscious. *Social Research*, *60*, 39–93.

—— (1993b). Introductory Address. *Papers on Social Representations*, *2*, 160–70.

—— (1997). *Chronique des années égarées*. Paris: Editions Stock.

—— (1998). Social consciousness and its history. *Culture and Psychology*, *4*, 411–29.

Moscovici, S. and Doise, W. (1994). *Conflict and Consensus*, trans. W. D. Halls. London: Sage.

Moscovici, S. and Faucheux, C. (1972). Social influence, conformity bias and the study of active minorities. In L. Berkowitz (ed.), *Advances in Experimental Social Psychology*, vol. 6. New York: Academic Press, 150–202.

Moscovici, S. and Galam, S. (1991). Toward a theory of collective phenomena. I. Consensus and attitude change in groups. *European Journal of Social Psychology*, *21*, 49–74.

Moscovici, S. and Hewstone, M. (1984). De la science au sens commun. In S. Moscovici (ed.), *Psychologie Sociale*. Paris: Presses Universitaires de France, 539–66.

Moscovici, S. and Paicheler, G. (1978). Social comparison and social recognition: two complementary processes of identification. In H. Tajfel (ed.), *Differentiation Between Social Groups*. London: Academic Press.

Moscovici, S. and Plon, M. (1968). Choix et autonomie du sujet – la théorie de la réactance psychologique. *L'Année Psychologique*, *68*, 467–80.

Moscovici, S. and Zavalloni, M. (1969). The group as a polarizer of attitudes. *Journal of Personality and Social Psychology*, *12*, 125–35.

Moscovici, S., Lage, E. and Naffrechoux, M. (1969). Influence of a consistent minority on the responses of a majority in a colour perception task. *Sociometry*, *32*, 365–80.

Mugny, G. (1982). *The Power of Minorities*. London: Academic Press.

Mugny, G. and Carugati, F. (1985/1989). *Social Representations of Intelligence*. Cambridge: Cambridge University Press.

Mulder, M. (1959). Power and satisfaction in task-oriented groups. *Acta Psychologica*, *16*, 178–225.

Nelson, J. (1974). Towards a theory of infant understanding. *Bulletin of the British Psychological Society*, *27*, 251.

Nisbett, R. and Ross, L. (1980). *Human Inference: Strategies and Shortcomings of Social Judgement*. Englewood Cliffs, NJ: Prentice-Hall.

Oyserman, D. and Markus, H. (1998). Self as social representation. In U. Flick (ed.), *The Psychology of the Social*. Cambridge: Cambridge University Press, 107–25.

Palmonari, A. (1980). Le representazioni sociali. *Giornale Italiano di Psicologia*, *2*, 225–46.

Palmonari, A. and Ricci Bitti, P. E. (eds) (1978). *Aspetti cognitivi della socializzazione in età evolutiva*. Bologna: Il Mulino.

Parsons, T. (1968). Emile Durkheim. In D. Sills (ed.), *The International Encyclopedia of the Social Sciences*, vol. 4. New York: Free Press, 311–20.

Piaget, J. ([1926]/1929). *The Child's Conception of the World*, trans. Joan and Andrew Tomlinson. London: Routledge and Kegan Paul.

—— ([1970]/1972). *The Principles of Genetic Epistemology*, trans. Wolfe Mays. London: Routledge and Kegan Paul.

—— ([1965]/1995). *Sociological Studies*, ed. Leslie Smith. London: Routledge.

Plon, M. (1970). A propos d'une controverse sur les effets d'une menace en situation de négociation. *Bulletin de Psychologie*, *23*, 268–82.

Potter, J. and Edwards, D. (1999). Social representations and discursive psychology: From cognition to action. *Culture and Psychology*, *5*, 447–58.

Potter, J. and Litton, I. (1985). Some problems underlying the theory of social representations. *British Journal of Social Psychology*, *24*, 81–90.

Quaglino, G. P. (1979). *Relazioni tra gruppi e percezione sociale*. Studi di ricerche di psicologia. Turin.

Reberioux, M. (1976). Histoire, historiens, Dreyfusisme. *Revue historique*, *518*, 407–33.

—— (1980). Zola, Jaurès et France. *Cahiers naturalistes*, *54*, 266–81.

Ricoeur, P. (1981). *Hermeneutics and Human Sciences*. Cambridge: Cambridge University Press.

Rommetveit, R. (1972). Language, games, deep syntactic structures, and hermeneutic circles. In J. Israel and H. Tajfel (eds), *The Context of Social Psychology: A Critical Assessment*. London: Academic Press.

Roqueplo, P. (1974). *Le Partage du savoir*. Paris: Le Seuil.

Rosch, E. (1977). Human categorisation. In N. Warren (ed.), *Studies in Cross-Cultural Psychology*, vol. 1. London: Academic Press, 3–49.

Rossignol, C. and Flament, C. (1975). Décomposition de l'équilibre structurel: aspects de la représentation du groupe. *Année Psychologique*, *75*, 417–25.

Rossignol, C. and Houel, C. (1976). Analyse des composantes imaginaires de la représentation du groupe. *Cahiers de Psychologie*, *19*, 55–69.

Rotter, J. B. (1966). Generalized expectancies for internal versus external control of reinforcement. *Psychological Monographs*, *80*, 1.

Rubinstein, S. L. ([1934]/1987). Problems of psychology in the works of Karl Marx. *Studies in Soviet Thought*, *33*, 111–30. [Originally published in Sovetskaja psichotechnika, 1934, 7, no. 1.]

—— (1959). *Principi I puti razvitija psichologii*. Moscow: Izdavatelstvo Akademii nauk SSSR.

Schütz, A. (1970). *Reflections on the Problem of Relevance*. New Haven: Yale University Press.

Shaver, K. G. (1975). *An Introduction to Attribution Processes*. Cambridge, MA: Winthrop.

Sherif, C. W., Sherif, M. and Nebergall, R. E. (1965). *Attitude and Attitude Change: The Social Judgement-involvement Approach*. Philadelphia: W. B. Saunders.

Sherif, M. (1936). *The Psychology of Social Norms*. New York: Harper and Row.

Smedslund, J. (1998). Social representations and psychologic. *Culture and Psychology*, *4*, 435–54.

Sperber, D. (1990). The epidemiology of beliefs. In C. Fraser and G. Gaskell (eds), *The Social Psychological Study of Widespread Beliefs*. Oxford and New York: Oxford University Press, 25–44.

Stich, S. (1990). *The Fragmentation of Reason: Preface to a Pragmatic Theory of Cognitive Evaluation*. Cambridge, MA: MIT Press.

Tajfel, H. and Wilkes, A. L. (1964). Salience of attributes and commitment to extreme judgements in the perception of people. *British Journal of Social and Clinical Psychology*, *2*, 40–9.

Talmy, L. (1985). Force dynamics in language and thought. *Cognitive Science*, *12*, 49–100.

Tarde, G. (1910). *L'Opinion et la Foule*. Paris: Alcan.

Thibaut, J. W. and Kelley, H. H. (1959). *The Social Psychology of Groups*. New York: John Wiley.

Thomas, W. I. and Znaniecki, F. (1918–20). *The Polish Peasant in Europe and America*. 5 vols. Boston: Badger.

Thompson, J. B. (1995). *The Media and Modernity*. Cambridge: Polity Press.

Tversky, A. and Kahneman, D. (1974). Judgement under uncertainty: heuristics and biases. *Science*, *185*, 1124–31.

Van der Veer, R. and Valsiner, J. (1991). *Understanding Vygotsky: A Quest for Synthesis*. Cambridge, MA: Blackwell.

Vignaux, G. (1991). Catégorisations et schématisations: des arguments au discours. In D. Dubois (ed.), *Sémantique et Cognition*. Paris: Editions du CNRS.

Vygotsky, L. S. (1934/1986). *Thought and Language*, ed. Alex Kozulin. Cambridge, MA: MIT Press.

Vygotsky, L. S. (1978). *Mind in Society: The Development of Higher Psychological Processes*, ed. M. Cole, V. John-Steiner, S. Scribner and E. Souberman. Cambridge, MA: Harvard University Press.

Wallach, M. A., Kogan, N. and Bem, D. J. (1964). Definition of responsibility and level of risk taking in groups. *Journal of Abnormal and Social Psychology, 68,* 263–74.

Wason, P. C. and Johnson-Laird, P. N. (1972). *Psychology of Reasoning*. Cambridge, MA: Harvard University Press.

Weber, M. (1968). *Economy and Society*. New York: Bedminster Press.

Weinberg, S. (1974). Unified theory of Elementary-Particle Interaction. *Scientific American, 231,* 1, 50–9.

Wertsch, J. V. (1985). *Vygotzky and the Social Formation of Mind*. Cambridge, MA: Harvard University Press.

Williams, R. (1989). *Culture*. London: Fontana Press.

Wilson, S. (1976). Anti-semites and Jewish response in France during the Dreyfus Affair. *European Studies Review, 6,* 225–48.

Wittgenstein, L. (1953). *Philosophical Investigations*. Oxford: Blackwell.

Wolpert, L. (1992). *The Unnatural Nature of Science*. London: Faber and Faber.

Wyer, R. S. and Srull, T. K. (1984). *Handbook of Social Cognition*, vol. I. London: Erlbaum.

Zajonc, R. B. (1966). *Social Psychology: An Experimental Approach*. Belmont, CA: Wadsworth.

Zimbardo, P. G. (1969). *The Cognitive Control of Motivation*. Glenview, IL: Scott and Foresman.

Index

310 *Index*

Saint-Loup, Robert de (Proust) 193–4
Sakharov, Andrei 265, 267
Sartre, J.-P. 229
Saussure, Ferdinand de 212, 263
Schank, R. 161, 162
Schütz, A. 163–4, 238, 239, 243
science 9, 18, 41–2, 66, 90, 230–1
  art 185
  common sense 65, 144–5, 243
  communism 230–1
  culture 227–8
  familiarization 40–1
  ideology 82–3, 92, 144
  learning 52
  Marxism 227–8
  modernity 227
  paradigms 151
  philosophy 118–19
  popularization 68, 147, 148, 228
  positivism 142–3
  reasoning 167
  as social institution 83
  society 141–2
  see also folk science
scientific knowledge 41, 166–7, 228,
    237–48, 253
scientific representations 145, 166–71,
    219, 221
scientists, professional 241–2
Searle, John 274
semantic efficiency 215
sexuality 50, 146–7
Shaver, K. G. 60
Sherif, C. W. 94
Sherif, Muzafer 74, 97, 100, 106, 108,
    265, 270
Simard, J.-J. 61
Simmel, Georg 5
Simon, Herbert 74–5
small groups 79, 88, 91, 94
Smedslund, Jan 14
sociability 191–2
social acceptance 23, 120–1
social influence 16, 17, 118
  individuals 122
  innovation/conformity 260–1

knowledge 258, 259–62
minority/majority 256–9, 269–70,
    282
simultaneity 263
social movements 187–8, 269
social processes 10, 74
social psychology 4, 5–6, 16–17, 94,
    284–6
  attitude 234, 235–6
  autonomy 77n3
  behaviourism 4, 105, 115–16
  causality 60
  common sense 148–9, 240
  communication 111–12
  Durkheim 5, 27, 104
  Ego – Object 106–7
  European/American 3, 78–81, 84,
    185, 281–3
  Festinger 226
  genetic model 271–3
  innovation 7
  knowledge 2, 236–7, 272
  language 274
  minorities 267
  pre-knowledge 102
  proto-science 103–4
  pure/applied research 84, 117–18,
    257–8
  as science 91, 102
  scientific thought 19, 149
  social representations 3, 9–16, 30–2,
    146, 225
  sociology/psychology 75–6
  systematic 107–8, 109, 110
  taxonomic 106
  universal mechanisms 72, 73
social recognition
  Jews 195, 197
  minorities 265
  Proust 189–90, 192–3, 195–6, 206n4
social recombination 191, 201–2, 206n5
social representations 12, 31, 76,
    152–5, 224–31
  categories 129
  and collective representations 155n2,
    255–6
  collectivities 32–3, 124–37

Lightning Source UK Ltd.
Milton Keynes UK
UKOW032335050412

190229UK00002B/69/P